Elesha Miranda

A Poetics of Resistance

A Poetics of Resistance

Women Writing in El Salvador, South Africa, and the United States

---

Mary K. DeShazer

Ann Arbor

THE UNIVERSITY OF MICHIGAN PRESS

Copyright © by the University of Michigan 1994
All rights reserved
Published in the United States of America by
The University of Michigan Press
Manufactured in the United States of America
⊗ Printed on acid-free paper

1997 1996 1995 1994   4 3 2 1

A CIP catalogue record for this book is available from the British Library.

Library of Congress Cataloging-in-Publication Data

DeShazer, Mary K.
    A poetics of resistance : women writing in El Salvador, South
Africa, and the United States / Mary K. DeShazer.
        p.   cm.
    Includes bibliographical references and index.
    ISBN 0-472-09563-3 (alk. paper). — ISBN 0-472-06563-7 (pbk. :
alk. paper)
    1. Revolutionary poetry, Salvadoran—History and criticism.
2. Revolutionary poetry, South African—History and criticism.
3. Revolutionary poetry, American—History and criticism.
4. Salvadoran poetry—Women authors—History and criticism.
5. South African poetry (English)—Women authors—History and
criticism. 6. American poetry—Women authors—History and
criticism. 7. Poetry, Modern—20th century—History and criticism.
I. Title.
PN1083.R47D47   1994
809.1'9358—dc20   94-6207
                                                              CIP

For the women in struggle in El Salvador and South Africa

Contents

Acknowledgments

A book that examines contemporary poetry from three countries could not happen without the support of many individuals and institutions, and some of that support must, of course, be financial. For travel funds to El Salvador and South Africa, I am grateful to the Archie Fund and the RECREAC Fund of Wake Forest University and to the Pew Foundation for Research in International Studies. For time to envision this book, I thank the Kentucky Foundation for Women, which provided funding for my project at its inception in 1987. I am indebted to Wake Forest University for a Reynolds Research Leave for 1990–91. For library privileges and affiliate status while I was on leave, I owe thanks to the Center for the Study of Women in Society at the University of Oregon.

My research in El Salvador was greatly enabled by the talents and commitments of Serena Cosgrove, who served as translator of unpublished Salvadoran poems and became my friend as well as interpreter. For helping me give voice to what I witnessed in El Salvador during the summer of 1991, I must express gratitude to Sarah Barbour, who accompanied me on part of that journey; to Cathy Cornell and Paul Knitter, who generously offered me their insights into the Salvadoran situation and their contacts there; and to the leaders of CRISPAZ, Cristianos por la paz in El Salvador. I wish also to pay homage to the courage and creativity of the women I interviewed there: Blanca Mirna Benevides, Robyn Braverman, Serena Cosgrove, Michele Herrera, Dra. Matilde Elena López, Nora Méndez, Tania Molina, Celia Moran, Eva Ortíz, and the women of CEMUJER, IMU, and CONAMUS. And I would be remiss if I did not honor Claribel Alegría, whom I have never met but admire enormously, and Carolyn Forché, whom I had the pleasure of interviewing at the University of Cincinnati in 1985, for enhancing my understanding of the lives of Salvadoran people through their writing.

In South Africa during the summer of 1992 I was ably assisted by Ivor Jenkins and Robin Phillips of IDASA, the Institute for a Democratic Alternative in South Africa, and by Junaid Ahmed and other leaders of COSAW, the Congress of South African Writers. My work would have been impossible without the companionship and collaboration of Hannah Britton, who traveled with me as a research assistant and kept me sane and prompt. For shelter and a sense of home during our South Africa sojourn, Hannah and I would like to thank Peggy and Mike Twala and their lovely friends and family in Soweto; Ivor Jenkins and his family in Pretoria; Fatima Meer, Nise Malange, Ari Sitas, and Astrid von Kotze of Durban; and Abu and Hermoine Solomons and Geraldine Engelman of Cape Town. Thanks are also due to Fatima Meer for inviting me to participate in her seminar on "Women in South Africa" at the University of Oregon in 1990 and for her hospitality during my time in South Africa.

I am grateful to the many women writers who shared their work and insights with me during my visit to South Africa, among them Joan Baker, Lisa Combrinck, Ingrid de Kok, Menan du Plessis, Gertrude Fester, Baleka Kgositsile, Deela Khan, Ellen Kuzwayo, Nise Malange, Emma Mashinini, Beverly Mitchell, Boitumelo Mofokeng, Roshila Nair, Sobhna Poona, Portia Rankoane, Mavis Smallberg, Irene Stephanou and the women of the Progressive Arts Project, Mary Thibedi, Gladys Thomas, and Miriam Tlali. Advice and research assistance were generously provided by Sheena Duncan of Black Sash, Annie Gagiano of Stellenbosch University, Lynda Gilfillan of PROMAT-Mamelodi, Margaret Lenta and Cherryl Walker of the University of Natal, Shamim Meer of *Speak*, Sheila Meintjies of the University of the Witwatersrand, Pamela Ryan and Marianne de Jong of the University of South Africa, Micki Flockemann and Rhoda Kadalie of the University of the Western Cape, Barbara Schreiner, and Gillian Slovo. For offering me a viewpoint quite different from any other I heard while in South Africa, I wish to thank Lauretta Ngcobo. And for sharing their political perspectives and histories, I am grateful to Frene Ginwala of the African National Congress's Executive Committee, to Ellen Mothopeng of the Pan-Africanist Congress, and to the late Helen Joseph, who graciously received Hannah and me in her home when she was too ill to travel.

My work on El Salvador and South Africa was inspired by the writings of three distinguished U. S. women: Adrienne Rich, Barbara

Harlow, and the late Audre Lorde. I am indebted to them for their visions of a just society.

Many friends and colleagues have believed in this book from the beginning, and without their encouragement I might never have persevered. In particular I want to thank Anita Helle, who tells me that as long ago as our graduate school days I discussed with her my desire to write a book on women's political poetry; Lynda Hart, my frequent sounding board on matters of feminist theory; Catherine Keller, whose loving dialogues continue to inspire me; and Susan Carlson, who never wavered from her view that this project was valuable. Marilyn Farwell taught me much of what I know about women's poetry, and I remain grateful for that teaching. Monza Naff and Sharon Ellison sustained me over rough times during my sabbatical, and I owe much to their friendship. Sandra and Alan Bryant helped by visiting me in Oregon and bringing me home.

Gillian Overing was ever willing to read chapters and offer help, and her comments were always perceptive. I appreciate as well the support of other colleagues at Wake Forest University, especially Maya Angelou, Inzer Byers, Nancy Cotton, Kate Daniels, Andrew Ettin, Laura Ford, Dolly McPherson, Linda Nielsen, Elizabeth Phillips, Alton Pollard, Eva Rodtwitt, Bob Shorter, Sarah Watts, and Ulrike Wiethaus. McLeod Bryan shared with me his South African knowledge and connections, which proved invaluable; he and Edna Bryan also gave me tea and confidence. Irena Klepfisz kindly provided essential material on the Thula Baba collective. For instruction in Spanish, I am grateful to Ramiro Fernandez and Barbara Shulz; for assistance with translations from the Spanish, to Gary Ljungquist. For efficiently organizing the Office of Women's Studies and my workdays, I am grateful to Beatrice Dierks. And I appreciate the insights of my students, with whom I have enjoyed years of dialogue about women's poetry.

It has been my great delight to acquire a family while writing this book, and I thank my partner, Martin Jacobi, and my stepchildren, Sasha, Evan, and Andy, for the love and patience they have shown me. I also am grateful to my family of origin: my parents, Marian and Henry DeShazer; my sisters, Kathy DeShazer and Bettye Grogan; my brother Sam and his family—Vickie, Ryan, and Will DeShazer; and my aunt, Perdita Ashby. For offering me a home away from home, I want to thank Sarah Lu Bradley and Joan Essic.

I have been aided by a discerning and supportive editor at the University of Michigan Press, LeAnn Fields, and by the press's readers of this book in manuscript. I warmly thank all of you.

Grateful acknowledgment is made to the following authors for permission to publish previously unpublished material: Blanca Mirna Benevides for *"Mujer de nuevo acento"* and *"Reflexiones,"* copyright © 1991 by Blanca Mirna Benevides; Lisa Combrinck for "Concerning the Subject Matter of This Poetry," "The Journey," "On Reading Marechera's Mindblast," "To the Reader," and "When at Last We Love," copyright © 1992 by Lisa Combrinck; Ilsa Margarita Escobar for *"La Promesa,"* copyright © 1993 by Ilsa Margarita Escobar; Michele Herrera for *"Noviembre"* and *"Rompiendo el silencio,"* copyright © 1991 by Michele Herrera; Deela Khan for "Cocktail Party Effect" and "Love Song," copyright © 1992 by Deela Khan; the Estate of Amada Libertad for "XIV" and *"Dentro de la voz,"* copyright © 1993 by A. Mooxelly de Q; Matilde Elena López for *"Contra todo esperanza tu esperanza"* and *"Lloro en la oruga por las alas del mañana,"* copyright © 1991 by Matilde Elena López; Nora Méndez for "Ana María," *"Nuevas sensaciones,"* "Noviembre 1989," and *"Testimonios,"* copyright © 1991 by Nora Méndez; Boitumelo Mofokeng for "Domestic Workers' Plea," "Inside a Domestic Worker (in the 1950s)," "Inside a Domestic Worker (in the 1980s)," and "With My Baby on My Back," copyright © 1992 by Boitumelo Mofokeng; Tania Molina for *"Preferio morir,"* copyright © 1991 by Tania Molina; Celia Moran for *"A Emérita, Nina, Mercedes, y las muchas trabajadoras del sexo,"* *"Paralelo de amor,"* *"Soledad,"* and one untitled poem, copyright © 1991 by Celia Moran; Roshila Nair for "But Oneday Madam," copyright © 1992 by Roshila Nair; Eva Ortíz for *"En El Salvador,"* *"Entrega,"* and *"Eva,"* copyright © 1991 by Eva Ortíz. *"Escritura desatada"* [Writing Deconstructed] by Iris M. Zavala, trans. Myriam Díaz-Diocaretz, first appeared in *Knives and Angels: Women Writing in Latin America,* ed. Susan Bassnett. Copyright © 1990 by Zed Books.

Every effort has been made to trace the ownership of all copyrighted material in this book and to obtain permission for its use.

Introduction

Poetry is not the exclusive art by and for an élite. . . . The poet is part of the
world, and that world belongs in our vision.
                                    —Myriam Díaz-Diocaretz, *Knives and Angels*

Yo amo
. . . sus poetas muertos de hambre, transparentes,
que trabajan en puestos clandestinos

[I love . . . the lucid, threadbare poets/working on subversive tasks]

                                    —Martivón Galindo, *Ixok Amar Go*

. . . now we are mourning our sisters
lost to the false hush of sorrow
to hardness and hatchets and childbirth
and we are shouting
Rosa Parks and Fannie Lou Hamer
Assata Shakur and Yaa Asantewa
my mother and Winnie Mandela are singing
                                    —Audre Lorde, *Our Dead behind Us*

Contemporary women's poetry that is political, ideological, and gen-
dered—poetry that helps to define a women's poetics of resistance—
provides the focus for this book. The women from El Salvador, South
Africa, and the United States whose poems and theories are investi-
gated here contribute significantly to a growing oeuvre of resistance
literature emerging from many countries in the Third and First
worlds. Resistance poems, as U.S. scholar Barbara Harlow has ex-
plained, "actively engage in the historical process of struggle against
the cultural oppression of imperialism."[1] They refuse both elitism
and the guise of objectivity, opting instead for inclusivity and impas-
sioned engagement. They are works of witness and confrontation.
Salvadoran and South African women resistance poets document ex-
periences of war, poverty, loss, and exile—their own and those of
their families and communities—and reveal their determination to
continue the struggle against their oppressors whatever the toll. In

the words of Salvadoran poet Martivón Galindo, they are lucid, threadbare, and subversive. Many U.S. women poets express solidarity with resisters in these countries, especially other women, while examining as well their own and their government's complicity in supporting racist and classist institutions and practices at home and abroad. Moreover, as African-American poet Audre Lorde declares, they mourn the loss of these women to hardness and hatchets and childbirth, raising their protestant voices alongside their sisters': "my mother and Winnie Mandela are singing."

It is important that the term *resistance* be defined as an active quest for justice, and as a means of collectively empowering a particular group of activists, not merely as a reactive phenomenon created in response to power and its abuses. Revolutionary efforts are not locked into binary structures; as theorist Chandra Talpede Mohanty has argued, to define resistance solely as oppositional—for instance, as being powerless as opposed to possessing power—suggests that resisters are always victims and that struggles for a just society can be viewed only in terms of inverting the current paradigm.[2] South African writer Frank Meintjies concurs, asserting that the phrase "culture of resistance" has too often been used synonymously with words like *alternative* and *oppositional*, with the prefix *anti-*; for the 1990s this concept requires creative redefinition at the grassroots level.[3] I use the term *resistance* as an umbrella covering poetry that challenges oppressive governments, policies, and institutions but often goes beyond mere opposition. At its best, resistance poetry offers and supports various counterhegemonic models of social justice and racial/gender/class empowerment, and it engages in acts of political and aesthetic intervention in the service of one or more of these models. I am especially interested in poems that help readers explore, explicitly or implicitly, a question asked by Nigerian scholar Chikwenye Okonjo Ogunyemi: "How do we share equitably the world's wealth and concomitant power among the races and between the sexes?"[4]

Women's voices have been consistently underrepresented in previous analyses of Third World resistance poetry from Marxist/leftist or liberal perspectives. Barbara Harlow's otherwise excellent *Resistance Literature* mentions only one woman in its section on poetry; and in chapters on revolutionary poems from Nicaragua, Guatemala, and El Salvador, John Beverley and Marc Zimmerman's *Litera-*

ture and Politics in the Central American Revolutions analyzes men's writing extensively and pays only passing attention to what the authors call "the new women's poetry."[5] Similarly, critical assessments of black South African protest poetry by Nadine Gordimer, Ursula M. Barnett, Jacques Alvarez-Peyeyre, and Piniel Viriri Shava deal almost exclusively with work by men.[6] Yet examined collectively, women poets bring overtly gendered and sometimes feminist perspectives to the topic of resistance that distinguish their work from that of their male counterparts. Their explorations of sexual vulnerability during interrogation or invasion, their depictions of pregnancy and its attendant joys and fears in the context of combat or imprisonment, their portrayals of maternal grief at the loss of children and husbands, their expressions of solidarity with other women in struggle, and their celebratory recountings of defiant acts performed as women reveal a poetics of resistance that is distinctly female. Contemporary women writing from and about postcolonial, nationalistic, and/or anti-imperialistic struggle both reinforce and expand the revolutionary and creative agendas of men, and they do so despite centuries of socialization toward silence. Díaz-Diocaretz notes that being a woman writer in Latin America is "more than an intellectual task," since male-centered paradigms of women's inferiority have long been applied to women's cultural production, including poetry, and since internalized oppression has contributed as well to many women's perceptions of themselves as "passive receptors of patriarchally identified and oriented discourses."[7] Writing from a South African context, poet Ingrid de Kok agrees: "To speak as a woman is to enter a role even more intersected with questions of authority, audience, modes of productivity, than those who speak politically as committed men."[8] An analysis and evaluation of women's resistance poetry, and of resistant women as creative agents, is long overdue.

My scholarly approach in this book is feminist, although it is informed as well by Marxist perspectives: Frantz Fanon's analysis of the strengths and pitfalls of a nationalistic consciousness, Amilcar Cabral's connection of the struggles of Africans and African-Americans, Andre GunderFrank's articulation of the center-periphery debate viewed from a Latin American context, Immanuel Wallerstein's lessons from the 1980s on the ethics and viability of a "world culture."[9] Like all persuasive scholarly efforts, feminist scholarship is "not the mere production of knowledge about a certain subject. It is a directly political and discursive practice in that it is purposeful and ideological. It is best seen as a mode of intervention into particular hegemonic discourses."[10] As I see it, feminist intervention assumes that gender, race, class, ethnicity, and national identities are shifting, intersecting, multiply mediated axes from which one can, with validity, undertake literary and cultural analysis. Race and gender are especially tricky axes, since they are often seen as biologically grounded but, in actuality, are socially constructed. Furthermore, as South African theorist Zoë Wicomb argues, the construction of race through language—through the desire to find an Other to occupy the gaps in the sentence "At least I am not . . . "—may be viewed as "a precursor to the construction of nationhood. Race has the double-edged function of playing primary roles both in oppression and in the fostering of nationhood that aims to overthrow oppression." Although gender has traditionally played an oppressive role in El Salvador and South Africa, recent postrevolutionary and "postapartheid" discourse in each country suggests that gender is becoming another lynchpin on which to construct a concept of new national identity. National identity itself, moreover, is a socially envisioned concept "that comes into being at a particular historical juncture, a concept needed for survival."[11] As Wicomb notes, a goal of progressive—and I would add, of feminist—political discourse is to recognize that race, ethnicity, gender, class, and nation can best be seen in dialectical rather than hierarchical relationship with one another.

Why focus specifically on poets writing from El Salvador, South Africa, and the United States? Of all the Third World sites of conflict from which oppressed people were striving during the 1970s and 1980s for freedom and self-determination—Guatemala, Nicaragua, Argentina, Chile, the Philippines, Mozambique, Zimbabwe, Lebanon, and the West Bank come immediately to mind—El Salvador and South Africa have arguably been most devastated by systematic genocide. Both countries' governments have been directly responsible for the intimidation, dislocation, and murder of large percentages of their populations and in both countries, ordinary people's courageous resistance to efforts to eliminate them is well documented and inspiring. Certainly these are two countries in which U.S. involvement has been especially controversial and U.S. complicity blatant. In 1982 U.S. aid to El Salvador amounted to $264.2 million; by

1986 it had increased to $625.4 million, more than $1.5 million each day. By 1988 the United States had contributed more to the "centrist" government of El Salvador than that government had contributed to its own budget. The total amount of U.S. aid during the 1980s exceeded $4.5 billion. Meanwhile, during that same period over 75,000 Salvadorans died in politically related violence, much of it perpetrated by the army and its extralegal death squads. More than 7,500 people disappeared, and 1.5 million (of a total population of 5.2 million) became refugees.[12] In South Africa the landscape differed, but the picture was equally grim, as Nationalist president P. W. Botha continued his party's apartheid policies, including (since 1948) the practice of forcing Africans to relocate in "homelands" remote from their original or chosen residences and economically stagnant as well. The Reagan and, later, the Bush administrations in the United States offered Botha (and his successor, F. W. de Klerk) tacit approval through their policy of "constructive engagement," even though countless analysts documented the effectiveness of economic sanctions, and many U.S. corporations and citizens supported this strategy.[13] Thus, U.S. policy in the 1980s helped to uphold death squad activity in El Salvador and apartheid in South Africa, even as these administrations claimed to deplore them.

Radical women poets in the United States, defining themselves as warriors with words and combatants in a shared quest for justice, have written an impressive body of solidarity poetry honoring the struggles of Third World people; the two countries about which they have most often and most powerfully written are South Africa and El Salvador. African-American poets Audre Lorde, June Jordan, Ntozake Shange, Sonia Sanchez, and Alice Walker, among others, have lent their voices to the worldwide antiapartheid movement, decried the U.S. government's policy in South Africa as unethical and acknowledged simultaneously their own "struggles for accountability" as North American, middle-classed, educated citizens of the world's wealthiest nation.[14] U.S. writers involved in Central American activism—including Carolyn Forché, Jessica Hagedorn, and Grace Paley—have written empathically of campesinas whose children were missing or dead and of women and men who took up arms to protect themselves and their families during guindas, forced evacuations of Salvadoran villages during military raids. Although the literatures of many countries in turmoil could justifiably be in-

cluded under the rubric of a women's poetics of resistance, poems
by Salvadoran, South African, and U.S. women seem especially well
suited to comparative analysis, since these poets are already in dia-
logue with one another across cultures.

In chapter 1, then, I define resistance poetry as a vital discursive
means of political intervention for radical women writing from El
Salvador, South Africa, and the United States. I interrogate what
women's resistance poems *do* as well as what they *say*, how they
produce counterhegemonic knowledge and thereby contribute to
movements for social justice. Furthermore, I link Third World resis-
tance discourse, which has often omitted women and/or eschewed
feminism as a relevant area of inquiry, with U.S. feminist theory,
which would benefit from closer attention to cross-cultural perspec-
tives and to a poetics of resistance. As part of my interrogation, I
assess women poets' articulations of a diasporic consciousness, their
explorations of identity and difference as theoretical/political/poetic
constructs, and their assertions of gendered revolutionary subjectivi-
ties.

Chapters 2 and 3 focus on political poetry by Salvadoran women,
who articulate with passion their commitment to peace with justice.
In chapter 2 I analyze a wide range of poetry, much of it unpublished,
that chronicles the experiences of war, dislocation, and loss of
women living in El Salvador today. Relying primarily on interviews
with and materials gathered from women poets during my month in
El Salvador in June 1991, I assess poems of outrage and reconciliation
by poets ranging in age from thirteen to seventy. Many poems ex-
plore the intersection of motherhood, sexuality, and militancy; others
document women's struggles as combatants with the Faribundo
Martí National Liberation Front (FMLN) or as political prisoners. In
chapter 3 I offer three conceptualizations of exile derived from the
poetry of Salvadoran women living outside their country: exile as the
forced absence from one's native land, imprisonment and sexual tor-
ture as forms of women's exilic experience, and displacement and
dislocation of refugees as sources of exilic art. Salvadoran women
who write from exile in the United States, Europe, and Latin America
document their guilt, loss, and determination to return to their home-
land. Former rape and torture victims refuse to metaphorize their
experiences but recount their terrors in eloquent prose. Child poets
remember longingly the villages they left and describe the communal

projects they have undertaken in refugee camps along the Honduran border.

In chapters 4 and 5 I examine South African women's resistance poetry between 1972 and 1992, poetry committed to the eradication of apartheid and concerned with issues of race, class, and, in recent years, gender. Chapter 4 focuses on black women's protest poetry from 1972 to 1988, which intervenes politically by expressing rage toward the government and the machinery of apartheid, exposing and condemning economic injustice, and chronicling their experience of racist oppression. Poems by militant women fighting with Umkhonto we Sizwe, the African National Congress's (ANC's) guerrilla organization, and by women incarcerated for their antiapartheid work reveal their determination to survive and struggle for change. Poems by urban domestic workers recount the daily tolls of the apartheid system on economically exploited black women in the cities, while rural Zulu women's praise poems reveal the enduring cultural and aesthetic power of orature and thus invite us to redefine resistance and hegemony. Chapter 5 examines recent poems by South African women of all races in light of current debates about the nature and intersection of cultural production, women's empowerment, and political resistance in the context of a "postapartheid" society. Debates sparked in part by Albie Sachs's controversial 1989 essay, "Preparing Ourselves for Freedom," have foregrounded the role of lyricism and sexuality in politically committed art, discussions in which I participated during the month I spent in South Africa in June 1992.[15] At the same time, debates about the changing roles of women and the place of feminism within the ANC, the Women's National Coalition, the Congress of South African Writers (COSAW), and other political and cultural organizations, as well as in academia, are opening up additional political and artistic space for women poets.

Chapters 6 and 7 concentrate on U.S. women's poetry of solidarity and struggle. In chapter 6 I describe five poetic strategies that distinguish this poetry from resistance poetry by Salvadoran and South African women and analyze how these strategies produce meaning. I then analyze how African-American, Caucasian, and Latina women have expressed their solidarity with black South African women and how Salvadoran women and their resistance efforts have been addressed in poems by U.S. activist writers. I end by assessing *what* these poems resist and *how* they resist. In chapter 7 I pose several questions about poetics, identity politics, and resistance as articulated by U.S. feminist poets of color, who employ what I term a "warrior construct." In what ways have these women claimed warrior identities as part of their goal to eliminate oppression and to call for justice? How have they avoided essentializing (men as Evil Enemies, women as Just Warriors) and, instead, problematized the warrior construct, thereby increasing its rhetorical effectiveness? What distinctive vision of war and warring—of the rhetoric of violence and the violence of rhetoric—have U.S. women poets of color offered, and what can other feminists learn from them?[16] I go on to examine three ways women of color have used a warrior construct: by representing themselves as warrior poets, by writing as war correspondents, and/or by invoking warrior muses.

In the conclusion I assess how women's resistance poetry from these three countries produces alternative knowledge. I focus specifically on six poets who write "metacommentaries," poems about the role of poets and poetry as tools for political and social change. These self-reflexive poems open up questions of representation, ideology, and audience. As concerned readers, what do we learn, finally, from a women's poetics of resistance? I end by exploring possible answers to Audre Lorde's provocative question: "What do we want from each other / after we have told our stories?"[17]

Chapter 1

"We Make Freedom": Historicizing Contemporary Women's Resistance Poetry

> Poetry, as part of the cultural institutions and historical existence of a people, is itself an arena of struggle.
>
> —Barbara Harlow, *Resistance Literature*

> Habemos la revolución cuando escribimos un poema.
>
> [We make revolution when we write a poem.]
>
> —Rosario Murillo, *En las espléndidas ciudades*

In her study of the concept of resistance in emerging world literatures, Barbara Harlow claims that this term was first used by the Palestinian writer and critic Ghassan Kanafani in 1966 to describe contemporary literature of protest by his people, literature written under cultural siege. "Resistance literature," Harlow argues, "calls attention to itself, and to literature in general, as a political and politicized activity. The literature of resistance sees itself further as immediately and directly involved in a struggle against ascendant or dominant forms of ideological and cultural production."[1] Practitioners of this writing across cultures view armed or nonviolent struggle and literary-historical reclamations as equally important areas of cultural terrain; theirs is a literature of overt commitment quite distinct from the Western ideal of art as detached, objective, "universal." Typically polemical, resistance literature addresses thematically the sociopolitical context from which it emerges and rigorously chronicles the writer's experience of colonialism, revolution, solidarity, dislocation, and/or exile. Furthermore, it challenges traditional generic and formal categories by breaking down conventional literary divisions and hierarchies (between fiction and the memoir, e.g., or lyric poetry and the polemic) and offering alternative patterns of periodization (e.g., colonial, cosmopolitan, and nationalistic as categories to replace the Eurocentric ones of classical, romantic, and modern). Many, though not all, resistance writers are located within the various political movements for change occurring in Africa, Latin America, Asia, and the Middle East. "The theory of resistance," Harlow claims, lies "in its politics."[2]

Resistance is also an important concept in U.S. feminist theory and literature, particularly that articulated by women of color, who recognize, because of their positions on the margins of institutional structures, that radical systemic transformation is necessary if social inequities are ever to be removed.[3] Chicana theorist Chela Sandoval posits that women of color are "survivors in a dynamic which places them as the final 'other' in a complex of power moves"; their goal in challenging the system extends beyond self-interest toward a shared commitment to an alternative world view that nurtures new citizen-subjects.[4] Such visions frequently lead to collective resistance to the apparatus of the state, a resistance manifested not in a militant revolutionary context but, rather, in sustained, daily acts of courage and rebellion: convincing Aid to Dependent Children workers not to discontinue their coverage, educating students in elite white colleges to the fact that women of color can be professors as well as custodians, demonstrating in front of courthouses or gathering in churches to express solidarity with black South Africans and to protest the U.S. government's economic policies there. In *Black Feminist Thought* Patricia Hill Collins delineates several traits that characterize what she calls a black women's epistemology, drawn from feminist, womanist, and Afrocentric standpoints: an emphasis on personal accountability, the belief that concrete experience is a source of wisdom and knowledge, a commitment to dialogue as a tool for exploring differences, and an ethic of empathy.[5] This blend of caring and confrontation can be seen in the theoretical analyses and writing produced by feminists of color in the United States during the past two decades. These qualities also inform much of the resistance literature and theory emerging from countries in Africa, Latin America, Asia, and the Middle East.

One of my goals in this chapter is to link resistance discourse from El Salvador and South Africa, which sometimes has marginalized women and/or eschewed feminism as a relevant area of inquiry, with U.S. feminist theory, much of which has been informed by cross-cultural perspectives but nonetheless could benefit, in my view, from closer attention to a multivocal women's poetics of resistance. A second and equally important goal is to provide an overview of the themes and strategies of contemporary women's resistance poetry, foregrounding not only what these poems *say* but also what they *do*. I want to investigate how women's poetry of struggle produces knowledge and makes political interventions, thus opening up questions of ideology. *How* does resistance poetry resist, and *what* does it resist? How does it address and link issues of gender, race, class, nationalism, colonialism, and postcolonialism? For whom are these women's poems written, and what are the ideological and discursive implications of attempts to reach multiple audiences as diverse as Salvadoran campesinos, South African cultural workers, and U.S. and European academics?

Radical writers in both the Third and First worlds see literature as a crucial aspect of what Antonio Gramsci has called "counter-hegemonic ideological production," part of a revolutionary reclamation of the terms of knowledge.[6] Writing and publishing, especially in the oppressor's language, constitute an "essential weapon for wrenching power from the white man's hand," asserts South African novelist Ezekial Mphahlele.[7] Creating black literature in the cultural context of apartheid has been an urgent business, not a question of merely claiming equality but of claiming the right to one's own existence. Analyzing contemporary Latin American women's poetry, Myriam Díaz-Diocaretz outlines an equally complex project, as she describes a new discourse characterized by anti-authoritarian intertextuality, linguistic reclamation, and a radical "poetics of the social text." Challenging both the androcentrism of Hispanic cultures and the imperialistic tendencies of Eurocentric traditions, these Latin American women illustrate that "discursive practices are resistance, a resistance which is the source of writing."[8]

Women's discursive resistance takes myriad forms. For South African women protesting pass laws in the 1950s, it emerged as a militant slogan shouted at police and government officials attempting to break up their demonstrations:

You have touched a woman
You have struck a rock.

You have dislodged a boulder
You will be crushed.[9]

For Salvadoran women today, it comes as an articulation of cultural, class, and gender-based oppression: "El Salvador has always been a country in which art and literature, for most of us, has remained out of reach. This marginality imposed by a hostile system has affected artists and writers, and especially our women."[10] For Latina women living in the United States, Maria Lugones claims, resistant discourse may occur as code switching, writing alternately in Spanish and English, a form of language-play that reveals the writer's multidimensionality and challenges readers who privilege English: "To play in this way is then an act of resistance as well as an act of self-affirmation."[11] Discursive resistance also involves breaking silence. Assessing the importance of *This Bridge Called My Back* (1981), the first anthology devoted to writing by radical U.S. women of color, Chicana theorist Norma Alarcon posits that "*Bridge* leads us to understand that the silence and silencing of people begins with the dominating enforcement of linguistic conventions, the resistance to relational dialogues, as well as the disenablement of peoples by outlawing their forms of speech."[12] Many U.S. and Third World women writers share the realization that their cultural, literary, and linguistic traditions have been catastrophically disrupted by racism, sexism, militarism, and/or colonialism; they likewise share a strong commitment to radical reclamation and change.

The revolutionary role of language and discourse is well articulated in this poem by Puerto Rican poet Iris M. Zavala, *"Escritura desatada"* [Writing Deconstructed]:

Sentado entre tú
y yo
el lenguaje;
un lenguaje
el único abecedario espacial
(rebelde)
arma
hermandad
fusil

lucha
libertad

[Sitting between you / and me / is language: / one language / the
sole spatial alphabet / (in revolt) / weapon / brotherhood / rifle /
struggle / freedom].[13]

Díaz-Diocaretz argues convincingly that Zavala's poetics of resistance
challenges imposed representations of colonized peoples and asserts
her own agency as human/female revolutionary subject. By interact-
ing textually with the language of authority, furthermore, Zavala
simultaneously critiques a rhetoric of violence and asserts for her own
militant purposes a violent rhetoric.[14] In so doing, she claims central
political and rhetorical space for the once marginalized. Her audience
is both intimate (addressed to *tú*, a *compañero/a*) and communal (ad-
dressed to all comrades in struggle). "*Escritura desatada*" offers a po-
lemical challenge to accepted doctrines and creeds, redefining lan-
guage as a tool of collectivity. Words can bind instead of separate us,
Zavala implies; language in revolt can be a weapon *for* community
and freedom, no longer merely a weapon to be used against women,
peasants, the dispossessed.

Poetry is a genre frequently chosen by both Third and First world
resistance writers. As a "fugitive means of expression," it offers the
practical advantage of being easier to copy, distribute, memorize, and
chant or perform publicly than either fiction or memoirs.[15] Further-
more, in emerging societies, resistance poetry transmits history as it
simultaneously advocates revolutionary change. This poetry pre-
serves and redefines cultural images for particular historical mo-
ments, Barbara Harlow argues, in contrast to narratives, which ana-
lyze the past in order to interpret the present and envision alternative
futures.[16] Speaking of South Africa, in particular, Jacques Alvarez-
Peyeyre claims that poets of commitment write to make others think,
to clarify their own thinking, to exorcise nightmares, to reveal re-
pressed truths to the world—briefly, graphically, imagistically. They
may define themselves as poets by profession, or they may write as
ordinary people struggling for self-determination, choosing words
as weapons to inform, accuse, warn and exhort. As slain Black Con-
sciousness leader Steve Biko noted, such poems can also be acts of

self- and collective affirmation: "We have felt and observed in the past, the existence of a great vacuum in our literary and newspaper world. So many things are said so often to us, about us and for us *but very seldom by us.*"[17]

Resistance poets from all three areas of the world that I want to foreground—El Salvador, South Africa, and the United States—have taken up the question "Why poetry?": Why, that is, might this genre be an especially effective, multifaceted form of political protest? In *A People's Voice: Black South African Writing in the Twentieth Century* (1989), Piniel Viriri Shava describes resistance poetry as political and proletariat, concerned primarily with issues of color and class and committed to revolutionary transformation. South African resistance poetry is most often characterized by anger and introspection; it expresses rage at the government's repressive measures and at the poet's own internalized oppression, pain at the rampant poverty and systemic violence experienced by black people, frustration at the endless waiting that accompanies any process of change. Despite the declamatory nature of such expression, however, this poetry may paradoxically serve as an indirect form of political protest when compared to direct action, which almost surely brings imprisonment or banishment, or even autobiographical testimonials, in which the use of a persona offers no possible shield. Nadine Gordimer has speculated that, due to heavy governmental brutality and censorship in South Africa, "black writers have had to look for survival away from the explicit if not to the cryptic then to the implicit, and in their case they have turned instinctively to poetry."[18] For poets writing in Zulu, Sotho, Xhosa, and other indigenous languages, moreover, resistance to the status quo includes a challenge to the hegemony of English and Afrikaans, the oppressors' languages; their poems are acts of cultural re-vision, radical openings of "mouths sewn up in silence."[19]

Certainly, enormous risks accompany such literary opposition to official history. Writing of South African poets who have been murdered or committed suicide, both black and white, David Evans portrays with ugly vividness the toll poetic protest can take:

> The poets of our time are born in a mess of blood
> and those who don't die in a mess of blood
> may drown or jump or, the horror ingested,
> choke after the last lonely supper in a mess of spew.[20]

Still, resistance poetry can provide comfort in struggle; it helps people in rebellion discover their spirit, and it contributes significantly to both their sense of collective consciousness and their production of alternative knowledge and histories.

Becoming known as a poet in any country controlled by a repressive political regime means risking governmental reprisal, as it has meant in South Africa. Despite the risks, in many Central American nations, poetry is considered the foremost genre of the people—dialogical, inclusive, and visionary. This is true whether the country has forged a tentative peace or continues to be at war. Adrienne Rich recounts that, when she was preparing to visit Nicaragua for the first time in the 1980s, a woman told her, "You'll love Nicaragua: everyone there is a poet." Perplexed at first by this remark, Rich came to understand the validity and complexities of the woman's comment and to be struck painfully by the difference between this attitude and that prevalent in the United States, where political poetry is rarely taken seriously.[21] As Patricia Murray notes, few places in the world valued artistic creativity as highly as Nicaragua did under the Sandinistas during the 1980s: "The belief that a poet is necessary to society, and the dignity and strength such necessity carries with it, is unique to Nicaraguan society, as is the relationship between poetry and ordinary human activity. Poetry *is* regarded as an ordinary human activity, written in local workshops and on the battlefield as well as in private."[22]

Although Murray's assertion describes accurately the role of poetry in Nicaragua, evidence from El Salvador suggests that this attitude is not unique to its neighbor. The anonymous editor of the Salvadoran section of *Ixok Amar Go: Central American Women's Poetry for Peace* (1987) claims that more and more ordinary people, and especially women, are writing poems "on scraps of paper from supermarkets, in prisons and refugee camps."[23] While she realizes that women poets will never thrive until there is a lasting peace, she nonetheless recognizes that during tumultuous times poems have strengthened both combatants and noncombatants, revealing and enhancing their ability to persevere with dignity and, many times, with humor. Poems are often larger than life, many Salvadoran poets agree, even as they insist on their immediacy and historicity. With slain Salvadoran poet Roque Dalton, they would declare, "Poetry / Forgive me for having helped you understand / you're not made of words alone."[24]

Contemporary U.S. poets also have explored the complexities of poetry as a genre of resistance. Carolyn Forché went to El Salvador in the late 1970s after translating a volume of poetry by exiled Salvadoran Claribel Alegría. Politically unaffiliated at that time, Forché was moved by this experience to delineate a poetics of passionate witness and confrontation: "All language . . . is political; vision is always ideologically charged; perceptions are shaped *a priori* by our assumptions and sensibility formed by consciousness at once social, historical, and esthetic. There is no such thing as non-political poetry." The problem for writers steeped in postromantic Western aesthetic traditions is that their inherited poetic insists on certain subjects, styles, and forms as appropriate and others as didactic, crude, unpoetic. Sensitivity to nature, to the plight of the isolated individual, and to the intricacies of metaphor have typically characterized and reproduced a self-reflexive, inwardly oriented poetry and poetics that have dominated Eurocentric literary canons for centuries. Resistance poetry challenges this dominance, Forché asserts, and thereby creates political and aesthetic dilemmas for its practitioners and, by implication, its readers—dilemmas such as "the problem of metaphor which moved Neruda to write: 'the blood of the children / flowed out onto the streets / like . . . like the blood of the children.' "[25] Forché has determined to write poems of documentation that refuse to prettify all that she has witnessed. With the Salvadoran editor of *Ixok Amar Go*, she believes that poetry today "cannot afford to be enamored with the moon."[26]

Adrienne Rich addresses related concerns in "Poetry III," the final poem of a trilogy exploring the guilt and wonder she feels as a politically conscious person turning her attention to the writing of verse. Is poetry ever enough? she queries.

> Even if we knew the children were all asleep
> and healthy   the ledgers balanced   the water running
> clear in the pipes
>   and all the prisoners free
>
> . . . .
> would we give ourselves
> more calmly over   feel less criminal joy
> when the thing comes   as it does come

clarifying grammar
and the fixed and mutable stars—?

That Rich feels unable to resolve this dilemma is evident in her strat-
egy of writing the entire poem as a question. Elsewhere in it she
contrasts images of poetry as self-indulgent ("these lax, indolent
lines") with those of poetry as an essential ritual, not a luxury ("these
litanies," "this . . . honest work"). Poetry is *"not a key / nor a peacock
feather / not a kite nor a telephone,"* Rich asserts; that is, it does not
unlock mysteries or offer decadent beauty or float away toward
heaven or send practical messages. Poetry is *"the kitchen sink   the
grinding-stone,"* part of the basic survival work done frequently by
women across cultures and through the ages. Poetry *does* provide
necessary cultural sustenance, Rich finally implies, even if poets do
not always know how to teach us to live.[27]

If poetry is distinctive as a genre of resistance literature, so
women's poetry distinguishes itself from that of men poets and is
thus deserving of independent investigation. Despite its otherwise
excellent insights, Barbara Harlow's study mentions only one woman
in its chapter on Third World poetry of resistance, the Mozambican
"poetess" Noemia de Sousa, even though women's protest poetry is
prominent in many countries in Africa, Asia, and Latin America.
Critical works by Alvarez-Peyeyie and Shava on black literature from
South Africa likewise examine only men poets. Díaz-Diocaretz as-
serts that women have been absent or misrepresented in most analy-
ses of Latin American cultural production, even though they have
consistently "taken on insurgent and revolutionary avant-garde proj-
ects in solidarity with the social destinies of each country and of Latin
America" as a whole, and she further claims that anthologies and
critical studies edited by men have systematically excluded women
poets.[28] Whether because of sexism or myopia, women's contribu-
tions to Third World poetry of protest have not been adequately
examined.

For U.S. feminist theorists and readers, however, it is crucial to
consider on what bases Third World women poets form a constitu-
ency: What circumstances and commonalities contribute to the valid-
ity of studying as a group women poets from disparate cultures?
Chandra Talpede Mohanty claims that, while Third World women

constitute no unitary group, since ideological differences mediate against any notion of "natural" bonds among them, they nonetheless represent a political constituency linked by a shared context of struggle. They might therefore be described as an "imagined community" engaged in interrelated, oppositional forms of resistance and potentially connected by mutually sustained and sustaining coalitions.[29] It is important for First World feminists to recognize that Third World women may eschew or counter Western definitions of feminism, even though they have long been involved in antisexist, anti-imperialistic work. And it is equally important that Third World women not be seen as a negatively defined social category—that is, solely as women confronting and documenting problems of illiteracy, underdevelopment, etc., rather than as women offering positive insights, experiences, and wisdoms through their literature and theories.

That women's active participation and literary voices have been crucial to revolutionary struggle in both El Salvador and South Africa has been well documented by many of the women themselves and by scholars and activists from these countries and the United States. Ana Guadelupe Martínez, a writer and a former commandante with the FMLN in El Salvador, claims that women's presence in her country's revolution has affected profoundly the character of this struggle. Campesinos have urged their wives and daughters to join the effort, using Martínez's leadership role and that of other FMLN women as both incentives and examples. Campesinas whose husbands or fathers were resistant to women in nontraditional roles have collaborated on strategies designed to diminish these social and ideological barriers between women and men. Martínez believes that women's revolutionary writing is important to U.S. women as well as to other Salvadorans, since it challenges distorted pictures of her country's political situation and draws parallels between women's lives everywhere. Like mothers in North America, she explains, she suffers when she must leave her young daughter with child care and go off to fight: "It's like any middle-class North American professional woman who goes to work in the morning and comes back at night when her children are already asleep, and who only has time to kiss them in the morning when she gets them ready for school."[30] By linking militancy and motherhood in ways unfamiliar to First World readers, Martínez intervenes politically to construct alternative knowledge about women's daily experience.

Moreover, testimonies by the Comadres, the Salvadoran Mothers of the Disappeared, and other similar organizations have been used by human rights committees worldwide to challenge U.S. and other countries' support of the right-wing Salvadoran government. Most of these testimonies are written in prose, but a few Comadres have documented their struggle in poems. As exiled poet Claribel Alegría further notes, powerful poetry has been produced by her country's dispossessed, the majority of whom are women and children writing from urban shantytowns or border refugee camps after having seen their homes and loved ones destroyed by military raids on their villages. Revolutionary poems by women as well as men have been broadcast throughout such provinces as Chaletenango and San Vicente on the FMLN's clandestine radio station, Radio Farabundo Martí. And as Alegría's own work illustrates, a significant body of poetry has emerged from Salvadoran women in exile, poets who offer a geographically distant yet emotionally attached communal vision alternating between despair and hope. These women bear witness to "the poem we all are writing, with tears, with fingernails and coal."[31]

In the preface to her anthology of Latin American women's poetry, *Woman Who Has Sprouted Wings* (1988), Joanna Bankier claims that simply to imagine what being a woman and a poet in Latin America means is extremely difficult, and, given the size and diversity of the continent as well as the significant social and aesthetic obstacles in Hispanic cultures to women's finding voice, her assertion has resonance. Numerous feminist theorists of Hispanic women's literature have noted that stereotypes of women as virgins (Mary, Guadelupe) and whores (La Malinche, Coatlicue) abound in cultural legends and in literature by men, stereotypes too often presented as facts; accompanying these portrayals is a mandate to silence, a taboo against women's assertion or defiance.[32] To come forth as individual and collective speaking subjects, as "gendered voices," constitutes a courageous act of linguistic reclamation and "reterritorialization," Díaz-Diocaretz argues, especially when women's resistance poetry challenges notions of women as passive receivers of patriarchal discourses and asserts instead their own "strategic discursive consciousness."[33]

Women in South Africa have also led the way in political rebellion against the state, beginning with Indian women at the end of the

nineteenth century, who marched in Durban and Johannesburg pro-
testing the government's decision to outlaw traditionally performed
marriages; this first act of passive resistance provided a model for
Mahatma Gandhi, who lived in South Africa for twenty-one years.
In 1913 and again in the 1950s a coalition of African, Indian, and
Caucasian women, the latter organized under the umbrella of the
Federation of South African Women, demonstrated effectively
against the government's efforts to institute pass laws for African
women similar to those long in effect for men. In the 1960s African
women organized a successful boycott of government-sponsored
beer halls, which developed after the government outlawed home
brewing, a traditional source of revenue for African women and of
recreation and community for women and men. And during the
1970s and 1980s women spearheaded protests against rising rents
and transportation costs, organized to support the educational de-
mands of African children challenging their inferior schooling in
Soweto and other townships, and participated in and sometimes led
union strikes demanding livable wages and better working condi-
tions. In 1990 the Women's League of the African National Congress
was initiated, to "unite all women, black and white, young and old
at a political level, so that we can participate in actively building a
future South Africa that is free of sexism and oppression, especially
of women."[34] African women such as Lillian Ngoyi, Albertina Sisulu,
and Winnie Mandela; Indian women such as Fatima Meer and Ela
Ramgobin; and Caucasian women such as Helen Joseph, Ruth First,
and Helen Suzman have led the effort to end apartheid and bring
self-determination to all African peoples.[35]

Many of these women have written scholarly works, memoirs,
or autobiographies and have spoken eloquently in interviews and at
rallies about their commitments to and actions on behalf of resistance;
none of them, however, are known as poets. But other South African
women have written poems of confrontation and collective vision:
Barbara Masekela, head of the ANC's Cultural Affairs Division;
Baleka Kgositsile, executive secretary of the ANC Women's League;
Gcina Mhlope, an actress at the Market Theatre of Johannesburg as
well as a writer of short stories, plays, and poems; and Zindzi Man-
dela, youngest daughter of Winnie and Nelson Mandela and an anti-
apartheid activist in her own right, to name only a few. Although
these women have occasionally been represented in anthologies of

South African writing edited by men, their work remains less widely known than that of their male counterparts. A recent anthology of a century of women's poetry in South Africa goes some distance toward righting this wrong, but, despite its strengths, black women poets are underrepresented in the collection. Furthermore, critical studies of South African poetry typically have not examined either black or white women's work.[36] Like black male poets, black women address issues of race and class in their poetry, but they also foreground concerns related to their gender. Masekela describes the agony of exile and her accompanying loss of identity when she encounters in a U.S. city window "my scarred face alien mask / shaded and rouged," an imposter wearing the trappings of Western female camouflage. Kgositsile compares the battle of labor in childbirth with her efforts to challenge a fascist government in "For My Unborn Child." Mhlope identifies painfully with "mothers

> Who give birth in squatter camps
> Under plastic shelters
> At the mercy of cold angry winds."

Zindzi Mandela writes at age thirteen "Where were you mama?" a poignant lament at the absence of her own mother, imprisoned frequently during those years for her political activities, that raises difficult questions about the effect of apartheid on the mother-daughter bond.[37] Like their Latin American counterparts, South African women poets address some topics as poets, some as *women* poets. Explorations by militant women of sexual vulnerability when captured or imprisoned; depictions of pregnancy and its attendant joys or fears; expressions of pain and rage at the loss of mothers, children, or spouses; and empathy with other women's triumphs or despair are themes whose treatment contributes overtly gendered perspectives to resistance poetry.

U.S. feminist theorists and literary critics concerned with challenging sexism, racism, classism, and heterosexism as interrelated forms of oppression have begun in the last decade to delineate an imperative of inclusivity. That is, they have recognized increasingly the need to hear and heed firsthand accounts of the effects of cultural chauvinism, colonialism, militarism, and imperialism on Third World women and children as part of any broad-based feminist analysis.

Women's resistance movements worldwide have inspired and guided U.S. feminists, just as women from countries other than the United States have learned from the successes and failures of Western feminisms. In *Passionate Politics* (1987) Charlotte Bunch cites numerous examples of international feminist conferences and collaborations as proof that global feminism exists, but she recognizes also that it is crucial for U.S. feminists to realize more fully the limitations of their own perspectives as they attempt to "bring the global home." In Bettina Aptheker's words, they must learn to "pivot the center."[38] Adrienne Rich has recounted the amazement she felt when she first learned about women's mass marches in South Africa in 1913, 1956, and 1959; and she wonders why white Western feminist thinkers have failed to recognize the theoretical implications behind the leadership and strategies of powerful African women, a question answerable only in terms of racist and chauvinistic ideologies.[39] More skeptically, Gayatri Chakravorty Spivak asks, "What is the constituency of an international feminism?" arguing convincingly that too often U.S. feminists have emphasized England, France, the former West Germany, Italy, and Latin America at the expense of less familiar countries.[40] Latin American women from fourteen countries meeting in Mexico in 1986 called for the development of a broad, pluralistic women's movement that would recognize that for them gender issues are linked inextricably to political and socioeconomic concerns and are not necessarily primary; their 1989 *encuentro* likewise emphasized that for them feminism is a way of understanding reality, not any one specific set of demands.[41] Similarly, ANC women interviewed in Britain in 1985 explained that feminism has a negative connotation for many South African women because of its association with bourgeois Western ideology. "The organisation is very seriously committed to the emancipation of women but cannot see that as a separate struggle from our overall liberation struggle," representatives claimed, a viewpoint echoed in much of the language contained in the recently formed ANC Women's League's statement of purpose.[42]

For U.S. feminists concerned with the problem of inclusivity and with the acknowledgment of difference, understanding what Salvadoran and South African women's resistance poetry says and does would contribute significantly to the development of a more pluralistic movement and a more pluralistic feminist theory. Women's writing from these countries raises new feminist questions, epistemological and discursive as well as sociohistorical, and thereby helps all women reconceptualize community and struggle. U.S. women, white women in particular, might explore Salvadoran and South African women's poetry as part of their commitment to what Maria Lugones calls "world-travelling," the adoption by those women comfortably located in the "mainstream" (as white, North American, middle-class, heterosexual, etc.) of strategies long familiar to those outside it: namely, the ability to create various "homes" across racial and cultural boundaries, truly to *see* one another's worlds.[43] Likewise, Salvadoran and South African women can learn from poetry by U.S. women written in solidarity with their struggles, poems by Audre Lorde, June Jordan, and Jessica Hagedorn, among many.[44] Saying both "I am like you" and "I am different," posits Trinh Minh-ha, is a way for women across cultures to challenge polarized forms of thought, to "unsettle every definition of otherness arrived at."[45] Women's resistance poetry helps with this unsettling. From the fragments of divided identities, interrupted histories, and disrupted cultures, a significant new literary corpus has been born. "The resistance poems are an important part of such a corpus, part of the Third World's challenge to the propagation of Western literary conventions negotiated within and between the academies of the U.S. and Europe."[46] Whatever their specific positionalities, feminists can only benefit from studying women's contributions to this corpus and re-visioning any theoretical articulations accordingly.

World-Traveling: Diasporic Consciousness and Resistance Poetry

> Afraid is a country with no exit visas
> a wire of ants walking the horizon
> embroiders our passports at birth.
>
> —Audre Lorde, "Diaspora"

> We write to contradict a history
> that says we are a dead
> a conquered people.
>
> — Janice Gould, "We Exist"

The belief that marginalized people—whether black South Africans, Salvadoran campesinos, African Americans, or Native Americans—

have been successfully silenced pervades the racist and chauvinistic thinking and writing of many European Americans, even those otherwise liberal or politically well intended.[47] Much women's resistance poetry today seeks to challenge this phenomenon by chronicling the effects of various contemporary diasporas on oppressed people, dispersals motivated by poverty or war and often orchestrated by repressive governmental regimes and policies. Four poems by radical U.S. women of color will serve to illustrate the powerful connotations of diaspora as historical reality and poetic metaphor.

Black feminist poet Audre Lorde's "Diaspora" opens with paradoxical images of entrapment and forced movement. The poem situates itself in a country that people are not allowed to leave yet must leave, its borders rigorously guarded by soldiers poised on the horizon like "a wire of ants." Lest readers assume this country can only be located in the Third World, Lorde quickly positions us in *either* Johannesburg or rural Alabama or on the Texas-Mexico border. In all these places, Lorde posits,

> a dark girl flees the cattle prods
> skin hanging from her shredded nails
> escapes into my nightmare.

Obsessed with this vision, the empathic poet is charged with bearing witness to the girl's escape from further torture and capture. As readers, we too accompany her on her journey as she wakes "half an hour before the Shatila dawn / . . . in the well of a borrowed Volkswagen" or boards "a rickety midnight sleeper out of White River Junction / Washington bound" or "gulps carbon monoxide in a false-bottomed truck / fording the Braceras Grande." Lorde's dark girl is desperate, but she is not without resources. In her last lines the poet's tone is ominous, warning: such women are armed. The dark girl crossing the Braceras Grande illegally is a sister to the woman fording an up-country river in South Africa or the U.S. South, "grenades held dry in a calabash / leaving."[48] These women are determined to survive, through countermilitancy if need be, and the poet is determined to document their resistance in poems of political and discursive intervention.

Gale Jackson's "On Nites like These" also addresses the subject of dark women and diaspora, revealing this poet's identification with displaced peoples in her country and elsewhere. Her own ethnicity is foregrounded through certain stylistic and structural elements, such as exclusive use of the lower case, the colloquial spelling of *nite*, and her reliance on "black English" phrases like "we be so separate":

> on nites this cold i think of palestine
> of modern diaspora
> of thin dark women and children
> hushed with an urgency
> only those who have lived
> by the gun will understand
> and on nites this cold i worry
> for all the wanderers who just go
> when they say home
> in a shopping bag or two

Like Lorde, Jackson draws parallels between homelessness in the United States and dislocation elsewhere; like Lorde, she feels compelled, as a poet of color, to chronicle what she sees. She worries about the fate of New York cabbies who don't speak English, of desperate kids who steal old ladies' purses, of pretty young women followed home on nights so cold; she aches and fears for people drifting on the late-night streets in New York or Cape Town, "separate   torn." As she watches her lover undress, the poet's vision becomes more serene and she imagines a peaceful future:

> when all is still on nites like this
> i think of freedom the future palestine
> south africa how nothing really dies i think
> of twilight and the language of the city
> and i think of you undressing unafraid.

Her lover's body and her utopian fantasies fuel her dreams of justice.[49]

"Ghazal at Full Moon" by African-American poet June Jordan links the genocide of American Indians with the dispersals of indigenous Indian peoples worldwide. Like Lorde and Jackson, Jordan aches as she contemplates her topic while gazing at "an obsolete coin and the obsolete head of an obsolete / Indian." As Jackson repeated the phrase "on nites like these" to emphasize the ongoing nature of the problem of diaspora, so Jordan repeats *obsolete* and *Indian* in an ironic revelation of the evils of forced dislocation and cultural arrogance:

> I thought, "Indians pray. Indians dance. But, mostly, Indians
>   do not live.
> In the U.S.A., we said, "The only good Indian is a dead Indian."
>
> Dumb like Christopher Columbus I could not factor out the
>   obvious
> denominator: Guatemala/Wisconsin/Jamaica/Colorado: Indian.
>
> Nicaragua and Brazil, Arizona, Illinois, North Dakota and New
>   Mexico:
> The Indigenous: The shining and the shadow of the eye is
>   Indian.

The poet goes on to reveal that, indeed, the majority of the world's indigenous people are Indian, and almost all "one billion-fifty-six, five-hundred-and-thirty-seven-thousand" of them are among the suffering poor. As a resistance poet, Jordan places her anger at injustice just beneath the surface of her words:

> I am following an irresistible a tenuous and livid profile:
>   Indian.
> I find a surging latticework inside the merciless detritis of
>   diaspora
> We go from death to death who see any difference here from
>   Indian.

Here Jordan emphasizes the connections among all people of color, indeed among all people of conscience regardless of color; she also envisions the rage of oppressed people preparing to rise up. The poet sees herself as a diasporic ally of these Indians. As long as she lives and can speak, the poet implies, indigenous people will not be forgotten.

> The voice desiring your tongue transmits from the light of the
>   clouds as it can.

Indian Indian Indian   Indian Indian Indian Indian.[50]

"We Exist," by Native American Janice Gould, takes as its point of departure a letter the poet receives from a friend, asserting that "Indians must be / the loneliest people on Earth." A history of losses compels contemporary Native Americans to rewrite themselves into history, but at times their words seem

> like a shout in a blizzard.
> We shout
> to prove we exist.

Drawn inexorably back into her most painful cultural and familial legacies, Gould depicts the dying Sioux at Wounded Knee, mouths frozen silent, vengeful soldiers dumping their bodies into ditches as unmarked graves. From the suffering of masses, she shifts to one woman's internalized pain, a daughter lying silently on her bed in a fetal position, mourning the loss of her mother:

> My mother is not here.
> They mined her
>   for her grief,
> they followed each vein,
> invading every space,
> removing, they said, the last
> vestige of pain.

The Anglo doctors who treated her dying mother took away the mother's identity but not her suffering, Gould suggests; her daughter has inherited her mother's soul sickness. But illness of the spirit will not silence this speaker. Despite her pain, she persists in acts of poetic and cultural reclamation, counteracting the colonizers' version of history by affirming her diasporic existence.[51]

The Greek term *diaspora*, meaning "dispersal," differs slightly from its Hebrew counterpart *galut*, which signifies "exile."[52] African-American and Native American resistance poets use the term in both senses, as they explore the historical and cultural exigencies experienced by dispersed peoples as well as the personal and psychological tolls exacted by exile. To understand more fully First and Third world women's poetry of resistance, it is necessary to explore further their diasporic consciousnesses, which I see as having both negative, painful dimensions and positive, strengthening ones. First, a diasporic consciousness suggests an awareness of a perpetual state of transition, what Gloria Anzaldúa has called "living in the borderlands." That territory where two or more cultures "edge each other," borderlands represent both literal and psychic sites of awareness. As members of a mixed breed, diasporic inhabitants of borderlands experience cultural and emotional alienation; as women writers who are multicultural, bi- or trilingual, cultured yet cultureless, they suffer from *nepantilism*, an Aztec word Anzaldúa uses to describe the feeling of being torn between ways. Such feelings often result in a multivocal identity and poetics:

> Because I, a *mestiza*,
> continually walk out of one culture
> and into another,
> because I am in all cultures at the same time,
> *alma entre dos mundos, tres, cuatro,*
> *me zumba la cabeza con lo contradictorio.*
> *Estoy norteada por todas las voces que me hablan*
> *simultáneamente.*[53]

Furthermore, diasporic consciousnesses are revealed in written accounts of homelessness or forced dislocation and their attendant memories and traumas. "Our people have been put on the run," claims the author of the Salvadoran introduction in *Ixok Amar Go*, speaking of the results of the decade-long civil war there. Such politically motivated dispersals are often accompanied by shock, fear, and psychic restlessness. *"Me sacaron de mi país* [They sent me out of my country]," claims Salvadoran poet-in-exile Reyna Hernández; the lights of Stockholm bedazzle, but they feel neither familiar nor safe. *"Lloré mi derrota! / Cuántos fantasmas!* [Defeated, I wept. / So many ghosts!][54] In refugee camps along the Honduras–El Salvador border, living conditions make such dislocation even more desperate. In San Jose de la Montana Refuge, refugee and former nursing student Adriana Rodriguez writes, two thousand people lived without toilets or water; in addition to illness and overcrowding, each person there had

witnessed or experienced torture and other atrocities that they were
later compelled to remember, sometimes in graphic poems.[55] As Jean
Franco has pointed out, the Salvadoran government's war against its
people has resulted in the destruction of "felicitous spaces" once
found in the institutions and edifices of family, church, and village,
formerly powerful sources of refuge and shelter for ordinary campesi-
nos.[56] For refugee women who take pen to paper, a configuration of
the memory of these felicitous spaces, an exilic awareness, and the
desire to resist characterizes any poetic undertaking. Often the result
is an articulation of helplessness or hopelessness that is, paradoxi-
cally, discursively powerful. For Claribel Alegría, for example, any
memory of her country brings with it the knowledge of the thousands
of dead whom she wishes to commemorate:

> Mis muertos acechando
> en cada esquina
> las rejas inocentes
> de un balcón
> el reflejo borroso
> de mis muertos
>
> [My dead wait / at every corner, / the innocent grillwork of
> balconies / the filmed mirror
> of my dead].

It brings as well the guilt of the survivor, artistic and psychological
baggage with which she strives to come to terms.

> Hice también un pacto
> con los niños pobres de mi tierra
> que tampoco he cumplido.
>
> [I also made a pact / with the poor children of my country / which
> I haven't fulfilled.][57]

A similar consciousness of the painful effects of diaspora can be
found in African women's poems about their forced removals to ban-
tustans, those remote government-designated "homelands" in which
black people in South Africa were assigned to live under apartheid,

and in poems about their efforts to make homes for themselves and
their families in such (dis)locations. The shantytowns and squatters'
camps in the townships outside of Johannesburg and other major
cities, areas of resistance subject to constant police harassment, also
provide politicized subject matter for diasporic art. "Home is where
sorrow is born," writes Zindzi Mandela, "the living grave / the bur-
ial," if one is black. Or, in a poem probably about her residence with
her mother in the Afrikaaner stronghold of Brandfort in the Orange
Free State, to which Winnie Mandela was banished for several years
while Zindzi was a teenager:

> I remember
> a home so far away
> there is no bridge
> to take me there
> but a wet world
> of obstacles.[58]

The loss of home and childhood, one result of modern diasporas, is
a subject frequently articulated by poets scarcely more than children
themselves.

A diasporic consciousness is not only a socioeconomic and politi-
cal reality for many artists but also an aspect of their creative and
personal struggle. In his *First Diasporic Manifesto* Jewish painter R. B.
Kitaj describes himself as "a guest in the house of art," impatient
with his polite British hosts and fully aware of himself as outsider,
whether overtly despised or benignly tolerated. Diasporic art is often
perceived as a problem, he further asserts, and, indeed, "diasporist
painting is problemic. Its very paint stirs up these questions and
problems from a new painterly vantage, where each stroke is a be-
nerved Diasporist signature."[59] This notion of a "benerved diasporic
signature" also applies to much resistance poetry by women, for
whom questions of exile and dispersal have complex linguistic and
literary considerations. Words such as *home* and *exile* often embody
various tensions, located between rootedness and restlessness.[60]
Diasporic poets use such words to claim ideological space located
both outside discourses of oppression and, to the extent that they
must claim the oppressor's language as their own, on the periphery

of such discourses. Many women poets therefore situate themselves in exile and at home as they write.

In "The Space Between," for example, U.S.-Latina poet Ana Luisa Ortíz de Montellano explores the question of where the bilingual woman poet belongs. She concludes that, in choosing to write in Spanish, she lives and creates as a wayward child struggling "in the middle of the stream":

> Me fugué del español runaway child
> La mano larga de sus sílabas me envuelve
> como chicle de masear cuyas hebras rosadas
> se vuelven a pegar a la suela del zapato.

> "I'm a runaway child
>   left Spanish behind."
> The long grasp of its syllables holds me
> like chewing gum on a shoe.

Ortíz de Montellano reveals her diasporic consciousness through images of being pulled and battered as she treads rushing water; "cada pez, cada rama, cada corcholata / deja su traza de helecho [Each fish, each branch, each bottle cap / leaves a crabbed pattern.] The strange marks of the Spanish language strain her eyes yet are unsettlingly familiar. "They are my own 'King's English,' / the one I long denied. [Es mi propio inglés, / el que tan largo rechacé.]" The poet's bifurcated vision is revealed in the fact that the first half of her poem is written in Spanish, the second in English. Each language provides her with a different maternal mirror; the giggling children whom she imagines peering into this glass must

> set their palms against
> those of the mother who turns
> into another.

> [ponen las palmas contra las de ella, / la madre que se desmadeja.][61]

Her diasporic awareness is palimpsestic; layer upon layer must be pulled back so that new aspects of her identity and creativity can be explored.

Ortíz de Montellano has claimed that "my mixed heritage makes me an exile wherever I live yet gives me a wide range of creative and cultural options."[62] Many women poets and feminist theorists believe that a diasporic consciousness can be strengthening, contributing to what Gloria Anzaldúa calls a "tolerance for ambiguity" that can challenge dualistic thought patterns and make significant political interventions.[63] The other side of feeling homeless, after all, is feeling at home everywhere. Women of color have had to learn to world travel out of necessity, Maria Lugones posits, yet, when chosen rather than forced, such mobility between languages, cultures, and homes combats arrogance and thus contributes to cross-racial loving.[64] In *Charting the Journey* (1988), an anthology of writings by black and Third World women, Claudette Williams similarly describes the difficult yet potentially positive effects of diasporic experience on African women living in Great Britain: "It often goes unacknowledged that the Black diaspora has survived, resisted and developed in exploitative hostile environments which threaten physical and psychological destruction. It has been our history and past struggles which have offered us the rejuvenating substance of struggle, to carry our fight forwards."[65]

The empowerment that can result from surviving diasporas has been documented by many Salvadoran women writers involved in repopulation efforts as part of that country's National Coordinating Committee for Repopulation (CNR). Formed in 1986, CNR was active in moving campesinos, once forced from their villages to surrounding mountains or to refugee camps during military raids, back to their own communities. Mireya Lucero, a community organizer in Chaletenango province, reveals the strength that comes when women officers of *directivos*, civilian structures of local popular power, take matters into their own hands and decide, despite the risks, to return home and to document that return. "We are no longer a community on the run," explains Lucero. "Now we're a legitimate civilian population. The government can no longer attack us with impunity or force us to flee to the mountains. Our right to exist as a stable community has gained national and international recognition." Such subversive strategies as becoming a sister city with places in the United States and Europe and articulating in prose her community's history have contributed to her feelings of triumph.[66] "*Es difícil cantarte / del exilio*" [It is difficult to sing you / from exile], Claribel Alegría claims in "Not Yet," a poem about her Salvadoran home:

Es difícil cantarte
cuando una bota gruesa
de clavos extranjeros
te desgarra la piel
y te desangra

[difficult to sing you
when a heavy boot
with foreign hobnails
tears your bleeding flesh].[67]

Yet for every poem of diasporic lament, a Salvadoran woman writes affirmatively of the process of resettling and rebuilding her country: "*Porque queremos construir / un tiempo nuestro* [Because we want to create / a time that is ours], writes activist Mirna Martínez, "*hoy hemos salido a caminar / por todas las heridas de la patria* [today we have started to hike / through all the bombed areas of our country"]—stockpiling the mountains and valleys with hope, refusing silence and despair, building a collective future.[68]

The diasporic treasure searched out and articulated by Salvadoran and South African women writers and U.S. poets of color is rich and multifaceted. As Gloria Anzaldúa has shown, the brownskinned woman has survived three hundred years of silence and servitude only to reemerge whole through acts of resistance, whether political or creative. "The spirit of the fire spurs her to fight for her own skin and a piece of the ground to stand on," she claims. "Living in a state of psychic unrest, in a Borderland, is what makes poets write and artists create."[69] To write from a diasporic consciousness is to chronicle an uneasy world and yet to assert a complex agency and relationality, both artistic and political. To read these chronicles also constitutes an act of intervention, since the meaning of resistance texts lies not in their mere existence but in how they are comprehended.

Like You / Not Like You: Identity, Difference, and
Resistance Poetry

> We believe that the most profound and potentially the most radical politics come
> directly out of our own identity, as opposed to working to end somebody else's
> oppression.
> —The Combahee River Collective, "A Black Feminist Statement"

> Knowledge is made possible and is justified by irreducible difference, not iden-
> tity.
> —Gayatri Chakravorty Spivak, *In Other Worlds*

Identity and *difference* represent key terms of discussion and debate
in contemporary U.S. feminist theory, terms with important implica-
tions for the study of resistance poetry by Third World and radical
U.S. women.[70] Identity as a political construct was first articulated
in U.S. feminist theory by the Combahee River Collective, a group
of black lesbian socialist-feminists from the Boston area, in 1977. Ar-
guing for an emerging identity politics based on the belief that, as
black women, they must concentrate on their own liberation, the
collective challenged both the women's and civil rights movements
for neglecting the sociopolitical needs of black women. Expanding
the feminist concept of the personal as political, the collective's brand
of identity politics linked racial, sexual, heterosexual, and class privi-
lege as overlapping forms of oppression, which they intended to use
their identity to challenge.

Chicana philosopher Linda Alcoff has expanded on the collec-
tive's definition of identity politics, clarifying that it constitutes not a
search for or reliance on some essential core selfhood (e.g., black
womanhood) but represents, instead, a political point of departure,
a reason and force for action. Identity is composed of fluid, contex-
tual, and multiple positionalities, Alcoff posits, and, as such, repre-
sents not a form of essentialism but an impetus for social and sys-
temic change.[71] Teresa de Lauretis argues similarly that identity can
be a form of disidentification, of self-displacement, and is thus con-
ceptually crucial to a feminist movement that is "concurrently social
and subjective, internal and external, indeed political and per-
sonal."[72] Identity politics as a theoretical and activist construct has
been most thoroughly interrogated by Diana Fuss, who in *Essentially
Speaking* (1989) initially defines it narrowly as the tendency to base

one's activism on self-definition (as gay, Jewish, black, female) but goes on to acknowledge its political usefulness and multiple meanings. Questions of sameness and difference lie at the root of traditional metaphysical explorations of problems of identity, she claims; for feminist theorists, the task is to dissect and perhaps deconstruct identity, not necessarily to disavow it. Still, both identity and politics can be elusive and troubling constructs.

> Is politics based on identity, or is identity based on politics? Is identity a natural, political, historical, psychical, or linguistic construct? What implications does the deconstruction of "identity" have for those who espouse an identity politics? Can feminist, gay, or lesbian subjects afford to dispense with the notion of unified, stable identities or must we begin to base our politics on something other than identity? What, in other words, is the politics of "identity politics"?[73]

Identity thus construed has multiple, contradictory, destabilizing meanings. Identity politics, when viewed contextually and actively interrogated, can perhaps be used strategically by feminists to build coalitions and effect social transformation.

Several Third World feminist theorists, however, have critiqued the concept of identity as dualistic and culturally chauvinistic and have advocated instead a politics of difference. Claiming triple identities represents a triple bind for women poets of color, argues Trinh Minh-ha; although they may prefer to be "neither black/red/yellow nor woman but poet or writer," women of color today cannot afford to identify confidently with this profession without linking it to their "color-woman condition." Which identity takes priority, she asks, "Writer of color? Woman writer? Or woman of color? . . . Where does she place her loyalties?" Such questions resonate personally and politically, but they also suggest a problem with the concept of identity that Trinh has labeled elsewhere as dualistic. In "identity," as traditionally defined, as an essential core to be sought, "the other is almost unavoidably either opposed to the self or submitted to the self's dominance. It is always condemned to remain in its shadow while attempting at being its equal. Identity, thus understood, supposes that a clear dividing line can be made between I and not-I, he and she; between depth and surface, or vertical and horizontal identity;

between us here and them over there." Such polarizing levels of consciousness are troubling to her as a Third World feminist living and working in the United States, and she offers as an alternative construct difference, "a tool of creativity to question multiple forces of repression and dominance."[74] Feminists cannot hope to challenge oppressions based on dualism if we ourselves think dualistically. If identity is a potentially conflictual construct, difference may be seen as a construct that refuses to endorse segregation, thereby undercutting oppositional thought. Perhaps identity and difference can best be perceived not as competitive concepts but as interlocking questions. Writing about Indian women's narratives of resistance, Gayatri Spivak concurs with Trinh that difference must be constantly kept in mind in any literary-political analysis. Asserting the need to distinguish, for example, between "the subaltern as gendered subject" and "the subaltern as class subject," Spivak claims that knowledge of a subject's position(s) depends not on interrogating identity but on interrogating difference.[75]

Examining three resistance poems by Third World women who wrestle, implicitly or explicitly, with the interrelated constructs of identity and difference will help to clarify why this issue in U.S. feminist theory bears significantly upon this body of poetry. Chilean poet-in-exile Marjorie Agosin's "Disappeared Woman I" gives voice to one of countless Latin American women missing as a result of being seized, imprisoned, or murdered by forces from political oppressive regimes. Agosin begins with a statement of identity that could be considered an essentialist assertion of core self were it not for the extenuating historical context from which this woman's cry emerges.

> I am the disappeared woman,
> in a country grown dark,
> silenced by the
> wrathful cubbyholes
> of those with no memory.

She is not *a* disappeared woman but *the* disappeared woman, a quintessential figure whose identity seems to be absolute. What appears to be a poem about a fixed identity, however, shifts quickly to a study in difference, as the disappeared woman, really a chorus of communal voices, asks a piercing series of rhetorical questions designed to call to action an unnamed audience, probably women from the First World:

> You still don't see me?
> You still don't hear me
> in those peregrinations
> through the dense smoke
> of terror?

The barrier to insight and recognition, of course, is difference—that construct that, in Spivak's terms, paradoxically makes alternative knowledges possible. Agosin's speaker goes on to ask the "you" repeatedly to step outside themselves, undercutting any dichotomous consciousness and affirming cross-cultural connection:

> Look at me,
> . . . sing me
> . . . call me
> to give me back
> name,
> sounds,
> a covering of skin
> by naming me.

To do less than name her, the woman asserts, is to conspire with the forces who captured her; to name her is to intervene politically and discursively, to catalyze her ability to name herself. In Trinh Minh-ha's terms, acknowledging interdependence across differences represents a way of claiming both "I am like you" and "I am different."

The interlocking nature of identity and difference is powerfully illustrated in Agosin's last stanza, in which the disappeared woman becomes almost mythic, seeking resurrection:

> Don't conspire with
> oblivion,
> tear down the silence.
> I want to be
> the appeared woman

> from among the labyrinths
> come back, return
> name myself.
> Call my name.[76]

Audre Lorde has claimed that much of Western European history has urged us to view difference in oppositional terms: dominant/subordinate, good/bad, up/down, superior/inferior. Instead of acquiescing to this hierarchical indoctrination, she argues, feminists must learn to relate as equals across difference and to use difference creatively to challenge oppressive structures.[77] Communicating as equals across cultures and acknowledging the interdependence of self and other are issues that lie at the heart of Agosin's poem, I would argue. Disappeared women can reappear through collective feminist voices and actions.

In "San Salvador 1983" Jacinta Escudos probes her own conflicted identity, which is interwoven with the plight of her war-torn city, anthropomorphized in the poem as a human lover. Like Agosin's disappeared woman, Escudos's speaker at first appears to define herself in static terms—in stanza 1, as an individual woman destined to eternal thralldom. But in the course of the poem, as her erotic, creative, and political energies emerge and converge, the speaker's identity becomes increasingly contingent, contextual. In de Lauretis's terms, Escudos explores personal and national identity as a form of disidentification and self-displacement:

> This is how I see myself,
> forever running through the streets with the ghosts
> of my San Salvador,
> although nostalgia
> takes over so easily
> because the city will never be the same
> when we get to know her again.

As the city's identity is fluid and shifting, so must the speaker's be; she cannot simply haunt the city streets, one-dimensionally, with old ghosts. Instead, she must struggle to maintain her eroticism and compassion in the face of rampant violence and destruction.

> Being subversive will be
> having the willpower to kiss someone
> with all the tenderness of the world.

The resistance poet's primary acts of subversion, Escudos implies, are naming and caressing her city under siege.

"San Salvador 1983" is punctuated by heady commands, capitalized for emphasis and dramatic effect, orders that the speaker hurls at her city lover. "DON'T LET THE BULLETS MESS UP YOUR SOUL, MY LOVE." "LET THEM BURY ME NAKED / WHEN PEACE COMES, MY LOVE." Interspersed with these impassioned cries are the speaker's quieter assertions of her own artistic identity, an identity shifting from a static, independent state to a fluid, communal state:

> This is how I see myself,
> far away being born and reborn
> with the mouth full of old poets,
> unknown but truly mine.

Her city lies so deeply in sleep, the poet continues, that the kisses of a thousand princes will not wake her nor the noises of a thousand market women. Like the speaker, San Salvador must be reborn. Despite her desire to awaken her city, Escudos lacks that magical power; she is but one individual among those who populate the many funeral processions occurring in the streets. Furthermore, she is nameless:

> I,
> so anonymous
> my name is never mentioned
> (because mentioning names can be prohibited).

Like Agosin's woman, Escudos's speaker virtually disappears in the streets of San Salvador. The assertion of her own anonymity sets off the poet's rage, however, and with it the collective rage of others who join her necrophilic homage to this phantom city, "my San Salvador, / MAGGOT OF A CITY, BUT I DO LOVE YOU." The remainder of the poem is a restive tribute to this city that the poet considers at once home and not-home.[78] Escudos's poem produces alternative knowledge by foregrounding the chaotic, transitional identities of her city and herself. Furthermore, she intervenes politically by condemning implicitly the instruments of oppression that contribute to their mutual turmoil.

The socioeconomic and political aspects of resistance writing, identity, and consciousness are addressed overtly in a poem by black activist Dora Tamana, written and probably chanted aloud in South Africa on Women's Day, 1981. The fact that the poem is entitled "Dora Tamana" suggests that it be read as a self-portrait of the poet as resister as well as a call to collective action.

> You who have no work, speak.
> You who have no homes, speak.
> You who have no schools, speak.
> You who have to run like chickens from the vulture, speak.
> Let us share our problems so that we can solve them together.
> We must free ourselves.

Change, the poet goes on to assert, is the mutual responsibility of women and men working together. Despite the poem's autobiographical title, any sense of Dora Tamana's individual identity is eclipsed here by the focus on communal identities, the multiple, hybrid realities of antiapartheid identity politics. This politics is based on a shared body of knowledge and a shared commitment to action, an ideology in which the poet expects her audience to have a stake:

> There are no creches and nursery schools for our children.
> There are no homes for the aged.
> There is no-one to care for the sick.
> Women must unite to fight for these rights.

Dora Tamana's poem is really a revolutionary edict, direct and clear, the voice of a grandmother instructing her heirs: "I opened the road for you. / You must go forward."[79] Her audience (younger women comrades) differs from Agosin's (First World women) and Escudos's (the traumatized victims of Salvadoran military oppression). More explicitly than the other two poets, Tamana uses a poetic discourse of shared identity to articulate a political agenda of empowerment.

For both feminist theorists and resistance poets, interrogating identity and confronting difference means acknowledging the interdependency of Third and First World peoples. As Trinh Minh-ha cautions, however, interdependency must not "be reduced to a mere question of mutual enslavement"; it suggests instead the need for "creating a ground that belongs to no one, not even to the creator. Otherness becomes empowerment, critical difference when it is not given but recreated."[80] Such reconceptualizations, practical as well as theoretical, challenge dualistic divisions between insider and outsider, self and other, political and artistic struggle. This interdependent way of approaching identity and difference is nicely summarized by Adrienne Rich in "Blood, Bread, and Poetry": "I write in full knowledge that the majority of the world's illiterates are women, that I live in a technologically advanced country where 40 per cent of the people can barely read and 20 per cent are functionally illiterate. I believe that these facts are directly connected to the fragmentations I suffer in myself, that we are all in this together."[81] Literate and illiterate women are both alike and unalike, their disparate lives linked as part of the continuum on which identity and difference fall. Women's poetry of resistance offers one vital format for investigating this continuum.

Denaturalizing the I: Revolutionary Subjectivities in Resistance Poetry

> What U.S. Third World feminists are calling for is a new subjectivity, a political revision that denies any *one* perspective as the only answer, but instead posits a shifting tactical and strategic subjectivity that has the capacity to re-center depending upon the forms of oppression to be confronted.
> —Chela Sandoval, "Feminism and Racism"

> Questions of subjectivity are always multiply mediated through the axes of race, class/caste, sexuality, and gender.
> —Chandra Talpede Mohanty, *Third World Women and the Politics of Feminism*

Questions of subjectivity are crucial to understanding the consciousnesses, discourses, and imagery of women resistance poets, who function simultaneously as both speakers and the "spoken," as chroniclers and sites of protest.[82] Indeed, the assertion of what we might call a revolutionary subjectivity constitutes an act of strategic resistance for many of these poets. As Trinh Minh-ha explains, "the domain of subjectivity understood as sentimental, personal, and individual horizon as opposed to objective, universal, societal, limitless horizon is often attributed to both women, the other of man, and natives, the Other of the West." Despite the prevalence of such stereotypes and their accompanying rhetoric and ideologies, feminist and resistance poets today are reconceptualizing subjectivity not as mere self-absorption, a narrow scrutiny of the subject as unilateral agent, but as a crucial aspect of a vision both singular and communal. In Mohanty's words, subjectivity re-envisioned is a "multiply mediated" construct that challenges liberal humanist notions of agency as individual. Or, as Trinh posits, this alternative subjectivity is more than self-indulgence, however justified such a focus might be. Instead, it refuses to "naturalize the I" and, by contextualizing it, uncovers "the myth of essential core."[83] Finally, the concept of revolutionary subjectivity may provide a bridge between theories of identity and theories of difference.

A poem by Lety, a political educator during the 1980s in one of El Salvador's FMLN-governed zones of control, reveals the power of revolutionary subjectivity as a strategy for both individual and communal voicings. The poem's occasion is its author's thirty-fifth birthday, celebrated while in combat. *"No es fácil vivir 35 años, /cuando la muerte se pone tan barata* [It's not easy to live 35 years / when death has become so cheap], Lety proclaims.

Afuera, el oreja que te acecha
busca tus señales: edad, color de piel,
estatura, relaciones familiares.
Adentro, en el frente,
un instante de combate,
una infortunada bomba,
un roquet,
pueden esperarte detrás de los minutos.

[Outside, the informer on your trail / assembles your data: age, color of skin, / height, family relations. /Here at the front / an instant of combat / a hard-luck bomb / a rocket / may await you any minute.]

Unpredictability dominates Lety's existence, and at first glance the distinctions she makes between insider and outsider, between self and other, seem clear and absolute. But Lety goes on to challenge such subject-object distinctions, to portray her own agency and voice as multiply mediated.

A veces, no es fácil
vivir sorteando las tormentas
interiores,
separados de los afectos
armonizando el interés de todos
con los pobres intereses de individuo

[Sometimes it's not easy / to pick your way through inner storms / separated from your affections / harmonizing the interests of all / with petty individual interests]

Despite these difficulties, at other times the universe seems to Lety a potent force that celebrates unity *through* difference, that demolishes borders.[84] Challenging boundaries and blending disparate voices are crucial aspects of this poet's revolutionary subjectivity. Agency for her is multifaceted and often contradictory, sometimes easy but usually difficult, as she attempts to develop and document both personal awareness and group solidarity.

Poems like Lety's invent new ideological and discursive space from which to encode resistance; they speak from *within* rather than *for* or *about* contexts of armed struggle. From such contexts, they challenge First World audiences to redefine both poetic and revolutionary agency. Gayatri Spivak claims that many U.S. readers have difficulty understanding or accepting the notion of a public, collective voice; what she calls "the particularity of the 'I' slot" must therefore be reconceptualized when Third World women's literary voices are being examined, given their communal orientations.[85] Even in exile, resistant women use their poems to explore identity as contingent and collective, to position themselves as speaking subjects defined relationally rather than autonomously. An example is South African poet Barbara Masekela's "Christmas 1976," a poem that, though set in the United States during her exile there, positions Masekela within an African revolutionary context. The poet belongs "there" in Johannesburg, even as she finds herself residing "here" in New York. On this day in South Africa, an appalling sacrifice is exacted, as

> young blood spurts on
> Fanatic celebrants
> Dressed in camouflage.

Eventually the bloodshed will not be confined to black townships, she warns:

> These rivers of blood
> Could flood over the high walls
> Not too soon
> Into the manicured gardens.

The phrase "not too soon" is deliberately ambiguous; it could mean not a moment too soon or not in the near future. The odds are stacked against the bleeding youths, however, and in this poem Masekela mourns their loss.

She goes on to juxtapose starkly the plenty of Christmas on Fifth Avenue with the funereal rituals for children in Soweto following the 1976 uprisings. Like Claribel Alegría, she conceptualizes the dead as her own. In the window of F. A. O. Schwarz,

> That doll . . .
> tagged five-hundred dollars
> Smiles   mocks
> My seven hundred children dead.

The poet reveals the importance of memory as a revolutionary tool, especially for the exile, for whom co-optation and forgetfulness are imminent dangers.

> Snow
> White silence
> The quiet rain of foreign parts

> Cannot powder sunshine memories
> Shall not wind a shroud
> Round my South Africa yearnings.[86]

U.S. feminist theorist Catharine MacKinnon has argued for the necessity of considering the connections between subjectivity and subjection, a consideration Masekela's poem invites.[87] For the revolutionary speaking subject, as the agent of resistance poetry, the historical realities and exigencies of subjection (here, subjection by race) dominate her subjective consciousness. Her country's children may be wrapped in shrouds, but a violent and racist government will never cover over her memories of or yearnings for home.

For many Latin American women resistance poets, Myriam Díaz-Diocaretz claims, the project of attaining revolutionary subjectivity occurs through a questioning of language and form, a subversion of official discourses and conventional notions of the self as a discrete entity. Frequently, they offer polemics against colonialism as well as critiques of the traditional position of women. Thus, their poetic "metamessages" constitute "fragments of social pragmatic action" that can be conceptualized as feminist. Indeed, "the very fact that the female speaking subject is addressing a given theme may indicate that the woman writer is *reterritorializing* discursive practices for herself." For many, Díaz-Diocaretz continues, "the resistance takes place within a social context that has already construed subject positions for the human agent. The site of that resistance is to be glimpsed in the interstices of those positions, through polemical intertextual bindings with authoritative language."[88]

A poem that illustrates well this rebellion against predefined subject positions, as well as a polemical, feminist challenge to a representative of white male authority, is U.S.-Latina poet Lorna Dee Cervantes's "Poem For The Young White Man Who Asked Me How I, An Intelligent, Well-Read Person, Could Believe In The War Between Races." Cervantes's choice of such a lengthy, discursive title, along with her capitalization of every word in it, reveals the passion with which she offers her response, an assertion and justification of her own radical subjectivity. To the young man's seemingly innocent question, Cervantes at first replies with an apparent naïveté of her own:

In my land there are no distinctions.
The barbed wire politics of oppression
have been torn down long ago. The only reminder
of past battles, lost or won, is a slight
rutting in the fertile field.

But such placid descriptions are profoundly misleading, the poet
goes on to imply; that slight rutting conceals major ruptures. That
oppression no longer exists in the United States must surely join the
ranks of other cultural myths, such as the belief held by many that
there is "no hunger, no / complicated famine or greed."

In stanza 3 Cervantes proclaims ironically that, although she is
not a revolutionary—she doesn't even like political poems—she does
believe in revolution. Not to acknowledge that a war between races
exists would be to deny her own reality, to be falsely conscious.

I believe in revolution
because everywhere the crosses are burning,
sharp-shooting goose-steppers round every corner,
there are snipers in the schools . . .
(I know you don't believe this.
You think this is nothing
but faddish exaggeration. But they
are not shooting at you.)

Like many other resistance poets, Cervantes challenges her reader
through the rhetorical device of direct address, here offered as a
disarming parenthetical. From this point on, however, the poem's
tone becomes increasingly polemical, the poet's voice terse:

I'm marked by the color of my skin.
The bullets are discrete and designed to kill slowly.
They are aiming at my children.
These are facts.

Cervantes is clearly angry, at both the racist oppression she docu-
ments and the tunnel vision of her interlocutor. Her wounds are
psychological as well as sociopolitical: inside she confronts a mind

that stumbles, a psyche that constantly feels inadequate; outside, "there is a real enemy / who hates me." As a poet who

> yearns to dance on rooftops,
> to whisper delicate lines about joy
> and the blessings of human understanding,

Cervantes regrets the harsh, racist reality under which she, a U.S. woman of color, must live and create. Yet she has no choice but to be resistant and vigilant:

> Every day I am deluged with reminders
> that this is not
> my land
>
> and this is my land
>
> I do not believe in the war between races
>
> but in this country
> there is war.[89]

Cervantes's diasporic consciousness is evident in her assertion of her legal alien, borderland status; this is and is not her country. Her revolutionary subjectivity can be seen in her resistance to the inaccurate social context that the young white man wishes to establish: a context in which people of all races are treated equally and fairly, in which oppression and racism are phenomena of an unfortunate past, in which a Hispanic woman poet is simply a creative agent devoid of race, gender, or class. Cervantes radically refuses these lies and thereby, in Díaz-Diocaretz's terms, "reterritorializes discursive practices for herself."[90]

In summary, I believe that women's resistance poetry produces meaning in at least eight key ways. First, it defines itself as political and politicized. As a crucial part of worldwide struggles for change, it offers angry challenges to dominant hegemonies, poignant laments for the dead or disappeared, and fierce calls to revolutionary action. Second, it foregrounds what Harlow has called "the catastrophic disruption of Third World people's cultural and literary traditions,"

thereby reclaiming history and rewriting cultures from the perspec-
tives of the colonized or the once-colonized.[91] Third, it reveals the
poet's awareness of the larger cultural context from which she writes;
it refers frequently to struggles for self-determination in countries
other than the poet's own and often evinces a diasporic conscious-
ness. Fourth, this poetry is committed to exposing graphically the
horrors of war, dislocation, and exile; to chronicling the daily events
of revolution as part of an interventionist strategy that Nicaraguan
poet Ernesto Cardenal terms *exteriorismo*. Reappropriating the terms
of knowledge, furthermore, women's resistance poetry presents itself
as an alternative educational tool. Much of it emphasizes the impor-
tance of literacy movements, some of it is written by the newly liter-
ate, and all of it exposes illiteracy as a vicious effect of a politics of
repression. At the same time, educated peoples are not privileged
audiences for this work—in both South Africa and El Salvador, work-
ers' poetry is performed on factory premises—and women's oral tra-
ditions are often honored. Sixth, since the production of alternative
knowledge requires interrogation of identity and difference, this po-
etry also examines self-consciously women poets' interdependence
in acts of political resistance and discursive reterritorialization—their
articulation of their experiences as women. Seventh, women's resis-
tance poetry presents a range of revolutionary subjectivities. Since
much of it is overtly gendered, many of its claims are implicitly or
explicitly feminist (although the poet may not use this term), thus
challenging androcentric assumptions. Finally, women's resistance
poetry is visionary: neither utopian nor dystopian, but forward look-
ing, imaginative, committed to peace with justice.

  Women resistance poets in both the Third and First worlds are
dismembering poetic identity in favor of a radical, alternative subjec-
tivity, a counterhegemonic creative agency that rejects self-other du-
alisms and reconstructs ties of solidarity among women across cul-
tures. Feminists from both the Third and First worlds are insisting
on new ways of occupying theorizing space and thereby challenging
dominant cultural readings of their lives and discourse. Re-visioning
feminist theory from multicultural, revolutionary perspectives is a
form of border crossing, a boundary blurring that seems to me essen-
tial if feminists are to pay more than lip service to honoring differ-
ence. Re-visioning resistance poetry from feminist perspectives is

equally crucial to an understanding of the complex relationality that exists between women at war, and not with one another or themselves.

Chapter 2

"We Cannot Consent to Being Complicitous": Political Poetry by Salvadoran Women

Poetry is not a luxury. It is a vital necessity of our existence. It forms the quality of light within which we predicate our hopes and dreams toward survival and change, first made into language, then into idea, then into more tangible action.
—Audre Lorde, *Sister Outsider*

Nuestra poesía no puede darse el lujo de enamorarse de la luna cuando tenemos hoyancanes debidos a los bombardeos aestados por una de las más grandes y poderosas naciones del planeta. Nuestra poesía puede permitirse la reminiscencia de un durmiente lago o un volcán, pero, no podemos consentirnos el ser apañadores, el hacerle el juego a los peligros que conllevan las conciencias dormidas.

[Our poetry cannot afford to be enamored with the moon when we have bombcraters in our own land dropped by one of the biggest and most powerful nations of the planet. Our poetry can take the luxury of reminiscing about a sleepy lake or volcano, but we cannot consent to being complicitous to the dangerous game that proliferates sleepy consciousness.]
—An anonymous Salvadoran woman poet, in *Ixok Amar Go*

For Audre Lorde, a black lesbian-feminist U.S. poet, poetry empowers women to speak, to distill personal experiences in light of their political contexts, to undertake pervasive life scrutiny. Such intimate creative investigation requires not only individual dreams and visions; it guides its practitioners toward rigorous analytical thought and, subsequently, toward collective sociopolitical transformation. As "the skeleton architecture of our lives," Lorde claims, poetry "lays the foundation for a future of change, a bridge across our fears of what has never been before."[1] In so doing it challenges those institutions and practices defined by profit motive and linear power and points toward alternative ways of thinking and living, toward radical resistance.

The anonymous woman who wrote, at enormous risk, the El Salvador introduction to *Ixok Amar Go* (1987), a bilingual collection of

Central American women's poetry for peace, shares many of
Lorde's insights. Her description of Salvadoran women's poetry as
not "enamored with the moon" challenges the post-Romantic aes-
thetic concept so prevalent in the West that defines poetry as best
when somehow "pure," transcendent, untainted by the poet's in-
volvement in politics. This anonymous poet counters that aesthetic
explicitly. With Lorde, she insists that poetry is no luxury but,
instead, provides essential, rigorous witness: to a consistently under-
reported war waged against the Salvadoran people by the Salva-
doran and U.S. governments, to the insistent voices of oppressed
campesinos who refuse to be silenced, to the beauty and dignity of
those voices.

Between 1979 and 1991 the United States gave over $4.5 billion
in military aid to the government of El Salvador. Meanwhile, more
than 75,000 Salvadorans died in the twelve-year civil war, most of
them killed by right-wing death squads connected to the military.
More than 7,000 disappeared, and 1.5 million were or are refugees.
In a nation of just over five million people, more than two million
live in extreme poverty, unable to meet their basic nutritional
needs. Seventy percent of Salvadoran households are headed by
women, and 57 percent of children born there die before their fifth
birthday. Sixty percent of the population is illiterate, and in some
areas up to 90 percent of the women are. Women prisoners of war
and victims of dislocation have been subject to rape and other
forms of sexual torture at the hands of the military.[2] The Sal-
vadoran woman writing in *Ixok Amar Go* claims that the war and the
daily struggle for survival have had a greater impact on women
than on men, since women bear most of the responsibility for
feeding and protecting children and often do so at their own
expense. If her assertion is accurate, then it stands to reason that
women poets might have greater obstacles than men to overcome—
external and internal—in finding their voices. Yet hundreds of
Salvadoran women have chosen to name themselves poets and to
write about a variety of subjects, from the revolutionary to the
intimate. "*Nuestra poesía va a expresar todos los sentimientos, desde el
ultraje hasta la reconciliación, porque sabemos que nuestras mujeres nunca
van a tener la oportunidad de escribir poesía a menos que haya paz.* [Our
poetry will express our total range of feelings: from outrage to

reconciliation. We know our women will never have the full opportunity to write poetry until there is peace.][3]

In the vital, stalwart poems anthologized in *Ixok Amar Go* and other collections, as well as in unpublished poems written by contemporary Salvadoran women, nostalgic reflections on sleepy volcanoes, while permissible, do not conceal the harsher truth of bombs regaling the countryside. These poems offer not lush images or metaphors so much as an urgent call to awaken from *las conciencias dormidas*, "sleepy consciousness," a lack of awareness this society-in-transformation simply cannot afford. *"Nuestra poesía habla: CADA HORA ES DECISIVA.* [Our poetry says: EVERY HOUR IS DECISIVE.]"[4] The anonymous Salvadoran writer's choice of the word *consciousness*, a term prevalent in contemporary U.S. feminist and cultural theory, links her claims to those of theorist Teresa de Lauretis, who argues that a nexus of language, subjectivity, and consciousness informs any effort to constitute the social or the speaking subject. As a term of feminist inquiry, de Lauretis notes, consciousness "is poised on the divide that joins and distinguishes the opposing terms in a series of conceptual sets central to contemporary theories of culture: subject and object, self and other, private and public, oppression and resistance, domination and agency, hegemony and marginality, sameness and difference . . . . "[5] Poetry by Salvadoran women is also poised on this divide; their efforts to find voice involve a reconceptualization of subjectivity and consciousness as fluid dimensions multiply organized across complex and shifting categories of nationality, class, gender, and historical circumstance. Living in the borderlands, to borrow Gloria Anzaldúa's phrase—writing inside their homeland but marginalized by its hostile system, working in zones of popular (FMLN) control but limited in their mobility and constantly endangered—Salvadoran women poets are attempting to redefine "elsewhere" as somewhere, marginality as centrality.[6]

Furthermore, their reconceptualizations are not only autonomous but also communal: *"No podemos ceder, una por una, esas conciencias puestas a dormir involuntariamente.* [We cannot relinquish one by one those whose consciousnesses have been put to sleep forever— involuntarily.]" In El Salvador, poet Eva Ortíz asserts, much of the population offers poems to the dead:

cada quien
pone a lavar bajo la lluvia
sus versos desvelados

[everyone / puts / their sleepless verses / out to wash in the rain];

cada quien
mantiene en un recodo de sí
una trinchera
una canción
un poema
esa flor invisible
que ofrecer

[everyone / keeps in a corner of themselves / a trench / a song /
a poem / that invisible flower, / to offer up].

Poetry is seen as universal and crucial: activist Mirna Martínez de-
scribes the ideal Salvadoran poem, one she hopes someday to write,
as "*el poema precisado / por las contradicciones de la historia* [an essential
poem / borne from historical contradictions]."[7] Salvadoran women's
resistance poetry moves not from language to idea to action, in ac-
cordance with Audre Lorde's paradigm for the creative process, but,
rather, from action and idea to language. Their poetic language of
protest, along with its compatriots thought and deed, undergirds a
cooperative resistance movement and contributes to the formation
of a collective women's revolutionary consciousness.

In this chapter, then, I will examine the poetry of women now
living in El Salvador and writing from that war-torn landscape: pub-
lished and unpublished poets, urban and rural women ranging in age
from thirteen to seventy, combatants with the guerrilla forces and
noncombatants who have written nonetheless fiercely of conflict.
Many of these women I interviewed during a trip to El Salvador in
June 1991, while peace negotiations were being held in Mexico be-
tween the ARENA government of Alfredo Cristiani and the FMLN,
but before the peace accords were signed (in January 1992); most of
this poetry was written during the 1980s and early 1990s. For pur-
poses of analysis, I have divided the poetry into four categories:
women's poetry of solidarity, written for sisters in struggle against

militarization, poverty, and oppression; women's poetry in arms, written in the trenches by female combatants with the FMLN; women's revolutionary poetry, written by noncombatants who evince a strong commitment to the grassroots movements for peace and justice in El Salvador; and women's poetry of desire, written to express female sexuality and a determination to achieve relational equality and/or bodily autonomy—poems that, in the Salvadoran context, constitute their own form of resistance.[8] I write this chapter committed to the belief that Salvadoran women's voices have not been widely heard by U.S. and European feminists, especially by those not fluent in Spanish, and that those of us involved in feminist movements must, as de Lauretis has argued, constantly rethink the relations between forms of oppression and modes of "doing theory," collapse the boundaries between margin and center, as we reaffirm our efforts to "bring the global home."[9]

1

Ana María compañera
cómo arde este silencio
Ana María pone a hervir ya la poesía
mientras va sembrado de handeras el coraje

[Ana María *compañera* / how the silence burns / Ana María puts the poetry on to boil / while her courage sows banners]
—Nora Méndez, "Ana María"

Corre por los montes
la lluvia deslizándose en el cuerpo
empapada la ropa
el frío atravesándole los huesos
devora distancias
llevando a cuestas el futuro de la patria.

[You run through the mountains / the rain sliding over your body / your uniform soaked / the cold seeping through to your bones / you devour distances / carrying the future of your country / on your back.]
—Blanca Mirna Benevides, *"Mujer de nuevo acento"*
[Woman with a New Accent]

Being a woman poet in Latin America is "more than an intellectual task," argues literary critic Myriam Díaz-Diocaretz.[10] She goes on to explain that, while there have always been a few isolated women

writing poetry, defining oneself as a poet and getting widely pub-
lished have been difficult for women in countries that are highly
militarized and male dominated. Identified by the dominant culture
not as producers of literary discourse but, rather, as "passive recep-
tors" of it, creative women in Latin America share a common experi-
ence of "collective cultural muteness." Despite this heritage, how-
ever, women all over the continent today are writing poems that are
surrealistic, lyric, erotic, revolutionary, and/or feminist. Their explo-
rations of political issues and of individual and collective identities
from the perspective of women reveal the nature of what Díaz-
Diocaretz calls their "strategic discursive consciousnesses."[11] For
many women, such explicitly gendered poetry is part of a larger
revolutionary awareness; for others, placing women in the subject
position is an end unto itself.

Salvadoran women's poetry of solidarity is best understood in
the context of Díaz-Diocaretz's theories. Many poets explore their
own shifting, contingent identities—as artists, lovers, exploited
workers, mothers of the disappeared, prisoners, guerrillas—in po-
ems that assert a strategic discursive consciousness of what it means
to be a woman in El Salvador today. Their poems reveal a sense of
mutuality and reciprocity with other women, a sense of collective self
constituted of nationality, class, and gender. In these poems Salva-
doran women use "social imagery" in ways that challenge traditional
authorities and hierarchies of authorship.[12] That is, they celebrate as
extraordinary ordinary women who rebel against the status quo, and
they identify strongly with such women. They are committed to
chronicling Salvadoran women's experiences of suffering, resistance,
and survival.

The poems with which this section began are representative of
the strategic efforts of many Salvadoran women to place themselves
and their sisters at the poetic center. Nora Méndez, a young mother
and former political prisoner, works with ASTAC, the Salvadoran
Association of Cultural Workers. Although only a few of her poems
have been published, she is gaining an increasingly wide audience
in San Salvador through her connection to ASTAC and her affiliation
with a women's poetry *taller* (workshop) whose members publish in
the alternative weekly newspaper *Diario Latino*. Claiming that Ana
María is a composite of all Salvadoran women in struggle, Méndez

acknowledges as well a personal identification with Ana María's frustrations and accomplishments.

> Ana María enlunecida
> rellenita de futuro hasta los tuétanos
> Ana María de rocío
> pelo liso pelo negro
> Ana María sobrapiedras
> tempranito en el riachuelo
> Ana María enfurecida
> cuando le quieren tocar al hijo

> [Ana María of the moon / filled with future to the core / Ana María of dew / straight hair black hair / Ana María at the washing stones / early at the riverside / Ana María furious /when they would touch her child]

Méndez honors women for their daily strength and determination, for their domestic work as well as their rebellion against authority. "Women here in my country are everything," she asserted in a 1991 interview. "Women have to be mother and father because in so many cases fathers forget their responsibilities. Women have to go out into the streets. We have to take care of the house. We have to fight in the mountains." Her Ana María is also a poet, one in whom enforced silence has long smoldered and at last caught fire to explode into words. She cooks up her poetry in a boiling pot, even as her courage "sows banners" to be carried at the antigovernment demonstrations so prevalent on the streets of San Salvador, despite the risks.

Repetition of the name Ana María underscores, paradoxically, both her individuality and her universality. Furthermore, Méndez's catalog of characteristics functions similarly to reveal the difficult, courageous lives that most Salvadoran women live. Ana María is poor. She is dangerous on her own as well as her child's behalf: "*y pobre aquel que intente deternerla* [and woe to him who would try to hold her back]." She is variously located: in the mountains, by the river Lempa, and always in the streets. She is the emblem and hope of the future.

Ana María siempre
hacia adelante
Ana María enlunecida
rellenita de future
Ana María la Victoria
Ana María se me acerca
Ana María de pié
          de dulce para siempre
Ana María la vida
          madrugando a defenderse

[Ana María always / moving forward / Ana María of the moon /
full of future / Ana María Victory / Ana María draws close to
me / Ana María on her feet / always sweet / Ana María life / rising
early to defend herself][13]

Blanca Mirna Benevides's "'Woman' with a New Accent" also
foregrounds the centrality of women's efforts in the daily fabric of the
Salvadoran revolution. A teacher and a former political candidate
with the UDN (National Democratic Front), Benevides believes that,
whether factory workers, street vendors, secretaries, or activists, Sal-
vadoran women are constantly in motion, fighting misery and de-
spair for their own and their children's sake. Despite their common
exposure to oppression and repression, however, these women bring
to bear a range of experiences and options. Some have little hope and
thus are crushed by silence; others are silent strategically; still others
find it crucial to break silence and speak.

Marchítase la vida en las fábricas
enhebrando hilos de esperanza
cortando el tiempo
cosiendo pedazos de ilusiones rotas.

Inclinada la espalda por el tiempo
vende alegrías para niños
canastos en la cabeza
"frijoles, arroz, guisquiles, papas . . . "

Enscribe líneas negras
envía flores para los amores del jefe

hace café a las diez de la mañana
con una sonrisa ancha y sigilosa.

[Your life withers in the factories / stringing threads of hope /
cutting time / sewing pieces of broken illusions. / Your back bent
over by time / selling joy for the kids / basket on your head /
"beans, rice, squash, potatoes . . . " / You write black lines / send
flowers to the mistresses of your boss / make coffee at ten a.m. /
with a smile that is broad yet silent.]

Benevides's imagery vividly depicts Salvadoran women's complex
roles as both nurturers and breadwinners. The seamstress in stanza
1 attempts to piece together the fragments of her society, to "string
threads of hope," even as she fears that, in the context of her daily
life, hope is illusory. The market woman in stanza 2 cajoles her chil-
dren as she recites her litany of wares. The office worker in stanza 3
must serve her employer as a different kind of mistress, even to the
extent of protecting him in his infidelities. The poet's empathy for
her subjects is evident; these women do what they must to survive.

Other women find ways to challenge their oppressors directly,
Benevides continues, as teachers of Salvadoran children, human
rights activists on behalf of the disappeared, or guerrillas in the
mountains. The "new accent" of which the poet speaks is most in-
tensely manifested in these last three stanzas, in which she pays
homage to women working overtly against political repression and
for the revolution. Stanza 6, which portrays a member of Comadres
(the Salvadoran Mothers of the Disappeared and Missing), illustrates
Benevides's special recognition of those women who refuse publicly
to be silenced:

Grita en las calles
corriendo, caminado
y en catedral cubierta con un manto negro
ruega, suplica, exige
por los hijos desaparecidos
arrebatados por el tiempo y la muerte.

[You scream in the streets / running, marching / and in the
cathedral /wearing a black shawl / you plead, beg for, demand /
your disappeared sons / snatched by time and death.][14]

Benevides's mother is a woman compelled to action, as a catalog of verbs quickly reveals: she screams, runs, marches, to a place of sanctuary no longer safe. Once there she pleads, begs for, and finally demands justice. Like her *compañera*, the woman guerrilla, she devours distances and carries the future of her country to the crest.

Through her use of second-person direct address (*you*), Benevides reveals in "'Woman' with a New Accent" an urgency less evident in Méndez's "Ana María," which is written in the third person. Both poets, however, implicitly critique a patriarchal, militaristic system responsible, at least in part, for the problems of the women they present. This systemic critique, Díaz-Diocaretz argues, is characteristic of a new breed of Latin American women poets who write to counter the "master codes" and the authorities who uphold them. In this anti-authoritarian poetry, "every utterance is set against that system *dialogically*; the woman's strategic consciousness and world view are opposed to patriarchal paradigms, one evaluation responding to another, one accent and one register interacting with another . . . . Woman's authorial intention is a presence at every point of the poem."[15]

The topic of disappearance, central to the experience of so many Salvadoran women, is frequently featured in women's solidarity poetry. These poets mourn their dead and disappeared, who paradoxically seem both present, as witnessed by the body parts that turned up daily in the streets, and absent—denied existence by the state, unable to be located by loved ones. Ana del Carmen de Vásquez, a young mother and student of literature and communications in El Salvador, offers a lyrical elegy of direct address to missing women, men, and children in *"Desaparecido." "De qué eres"* [What are you made of], each stanza opens; *"di"* [tell me], the poet pleads urgently in what becomes a haunting refrain. This poem investigates the topic of identity and subjectivity: What happens to human beings' fundamental, core selves when they lie dead but unidentified, unburied? Most compelling here is the poet's sense of helplessness, her inability to comprehend the incomprehensible, as she strains to see inside the victims' elusive eyes, to locate their missing bodies *"entre laureles mutilados"* [among mangled laurels]. Using a call-and-response technique, she addresses first an anonymous child,

mínima criatura,
entre los elementos,
levantado
de purpura nevada, resurrecto

[least creature, / lifted like bread and wine—purple snowfall,
resurrected].

What are you made of? she again queries, but she is met with silence.
Since, like most Salvadorans, de Vásquez is anguished at the lack of
protection and sustenance her people have been able to afford their
children in this war-torn decade, images of starvation and depriva-
tion dominate this stanza: vinegar, dry bread, long fastings.

Stanza 4, addressed to *mujer* [woman], reveals strong empathy
for those women cut off early from sexuality, childbearing, and the
ambivalent experiences of aging:

De qué eres, di, mujer, cintura cálida,
ausencia que te arde en despoblado,
nudo fértil que teje este presente
con un cierto futuro y un pasado,
dulce arrimo, semilla de dolores
y una nostalgia de años separados
que se sube a tus ojos cuando miras
un horizonte lleno de nublados?

[Woman, what are you made of, tell: skin-warm / belly, loss that
burns you in an emptied / place, rich knot tying the present / to
a certain future and one past, / sweet support, seed of aching
sorrows / and a longing for the split-off years / that comes to
your eyes at the sight / of the storm-wide rim of the sky?]

The most visceral of all the stanzas, this attempt to articulate what
"woman" is reveals the poet's view of women's bodies as the link
between past and future, the site of extraordinary suffering, the fam-
ily's and the society's main source of nurture and compassion. "Loss
that burns you in a emptied / place" may also allude to women's

vulnerability to sexual violation by the soldiers who capture and kill them. The poem ends as it began, with the frustrated plea "tell." When no response is forthcoming, the poet's voice is likewise stilled: *"la boca que te canta, silencioso; / el grito más quemante, silenciado?* [the mouth that sings songs to you, silent; / the most burning cry, fully silenced]."[16]

A professor at the National University and one of El Salvador's most renowned women of letters, Dra. Matilde Elena López writes fervent political poetry expressing solidarity with women and men involved in resistance movement. "Against All Hope Your Hope," written *"a la madre salvadoreña que como Antígona sigue buscando al hijo desaparecido* [for the Salvadoran mother who like Antigone continues searching for her disappeared son]," uses both direct address and an omniscient narrative voice to decry the "angel of death" (the name by which the death squads often identified themselves when making a telephone threat) and to pay tribute to these determined mothers.

> El ángel de la muerte viene armado
> para herir tu sangre.
>
> Oscuro viaje.
> Nadie lo descubre
> nadie su pista
> sus entrañas.
>
> MARIA! BUSCAS A TU HIJO?
> GIMIENDO VAS POR LOS CAMINOS
> DESOLADA!

> [The angel of death / arrives armed / to wound those of your blood. / He's on a dark journey. / No one finds him / neither hide nor hair. / MARIA! ARE YOU LOOKING FOR YOUR SON? /MOANING, YOU WANDER PATHS / DISCONSOLATE]

The poet's empathy with the distressed mother is revealed in her attempt to establish a dialogue, to aid the woman somehow in her quest. In stanza 3, moreover, the parallels with Antigone are made more explicit:

Buscas una pista, un rastro
o tal vez su cadáver
para darle sepultura

[You are searching for clues, a face, / or even a cadaver / so you can give him a holy resting place].

The death squad's activities are a sacrilege on many counts, López suggests, not the least of which is a defiance of the family's right to offer its member a proper burial. Her use of capital letters reveals her outrage at this Salvadoran reality and her admiration for the women who defy danger to shout aloud the death squads' crimes:

MARIA SE ENFRENTA A LOS PELIGROS
COMO SOLO UNA MADRE SABE HACERLO.
YA NO TIENE MIEDO,
HA PERDIDO EL LLANTO
YA NO LLORA.

CUAL ES EL ROSTRO DE ESTE CRIMEN
PARA GRITARLO AL VIENTO?

[MARIA FACES THE DANGERS / AS ONLY A MOTHER KNOWS TO DO. / SHE HAS NO FEAR ANY MORE, / SHE HAS LOST HER TEARS / AND NO LONGER WEEPS. / WHO IS RESPONSIBLE FOR THIS CRIME /THAT MUST BE SHOUTED TO THE WIND?]

This poem intervenes politically and resists discursively by breaking silence about the perpetrators of the crimes. Subverting official discourse, López goes on to provide a gruesome and ironic description of the context in which the death squads did their work. These men drove around at night in Cherokee vans, she asserts, collecting children whose bodies they would throw into ravines at dawn. They would hover over the countryside in planes and helicopters, she concludes graphically, "to wound those of your blood."[17]

An overtly feminist consciousness is revealed by Celia Moran in her poem "*A Emérita, Nena, Mercedes, y las muchas trabajadoras del sexo*"

[For Emérita, Nena, Mercedes, and the Many Other Sex Workers].
In a war-torn country like El Salvador, few stop to consider the casu-
alties of women in the sex industry, subjected to the danger of AIDS
as well as to economic and sexual exploitation. San Salvador's *Zona
Roja* existed long before civil war began in 1979, but the war and its
attendant economic problems contributed significantly to a huge exo-
dus from the countryside, doubling the number of prostitutes in the
zone. It was estimated in 1991 that 19,000 women in San Salvador
worked as prostitutes.[18] Moran, a composer and singer with the
popular group *Teocinte* as well as a poet, was one of the initial direc-
tors of a project funded by the Pastoral Center of the Lutheran Uni-
versity in San Salvador to offer health education and literacy pro-
grams for these prostitutes and to help them figure a way out of the
profession. In this poem Moran addresses directly the prostitutes she
knows and those she hasn't met, calling them sisters, for they have
been raped just as her country has been. She thus draws links be-
tween sexism, nationalism, and militarization:

> Hermana, compañera, amiga.
> Vendedora de amor en la calle Célis.
> Dónde te quitaron el amor?
> La ternura
> La risa
> Tus ganas de vivir
> Dónde están los pedazos de tu corazón?
>
> Sos como mi país . . .
> Tan pisoteada
> tan herida, tan triste
> pero, tan digna.

[Sister, *compañera*, friend. / Seller of love on Célis Street. / When
did they take love from you? / Tenderness, / Laughter, / Desire
to live, too. / Where are the pieces of your heart? / You are like
my country . . . / So trampled / so wounded / so sad / but so
dignified.][19]

Investing these women with dignity is an important aspect of Mo-
ran's strategic discursive awareness: they are no more to blame for

their plight than is her country under siege. Someone has to heal these wounds, the poet concludes, both personal and political; resistance to systemic rape and exploitation, El Salvador's and its women's, is essential if justice is ever to prevail.

Women's solidarity poetry is often read aloud or performed for other women—at urban recitals sponsored by feminist organizations like CEMUJER or IMU, in the countryside at festivals or community gatherings of spirit. At a recent CEMUJER-sponsored cultural evening in San Salvador, for example, Celia Moran sang a poem by Nora Méndez about a woman who leaves her husband because of his battering, thereby raising the once taboo subject of domestic violence for an audience of urban women in a public setting. The solidarity between Moran and Méndez, as evidenced in one's sharing of the other's poem, is thereby extended to all women who listen to and identify with the poem's theme. Later that evening, Moran was joined by teenaged Salvadoran poet Tania Molina and U.S.-born poet and translator Serena Cosgrove, who are sister members of a women's poetry workshop, *Taller de mujeres en la literatura*. Together they performed a poem by Cosgrove exploring the links between street harassment of women by men, domestic violence, and political torture. One hundred fifteen of every two hundred Salvadoran women, a recent study reports, are abused by their husbands.[20] Cosgrove has employed this statistic in the service of her poem, asking, "What then *is* torture, if so many women are hurt each day in their own homes?" The large audience of Salvadoran women—cultural workers, activists, wives, mothers, market women—reportedly responded with great enthusiasm and asked that evenings of women's poetic dramatizations be repeated. Such collective feminist undertakings illustrate the power and poignance of the Salvadoran identity construct that Blanca Mirna Benevides has called "'woman' with a new accent, *"enhebrando hilos de esperanza . . . / cosiendo pedazos de ilusiones rotas* [stringing threads of hope . . . / sewing pieces of broken illusions].[21]

2

>they are bound to kill me
>when?
>I don't know . . .

what I do know is that I'll die soon,
cut down by the enemy.
                    —Delfy Góchez Fernandez, "It Will Be My Pleasure to Die"

. . . algo mi brazo implacable de fuego / para que vivan tus hijos mato de frente

[. . . I raise my arm with resolute fire / so your children can live I serve at the front]
                    —Mirna Martínez, *"Nunca he sabido tus señas"*
                    [I Don't Know What Makes You You]

As is true everywhere, combat has not traditionally been the province of women in El Salvador.[22] Yet the political and social revolution that has occurred there during the past several decades has witnessed wide-scale military participation by women. As they have joined other popular movements—for labor, land rights, food, and peace—so women have taken up arms to defend themselves and their families, to fight poverty and oppression. Founded in 1980, the FMLN was a political-military front composed of five revolutionary organizations operating cooperatively until 1991; 40 percent of its members were women, most of whom were first involved in working-class, peasant, teacher, and/or student protest movements in the 1970s. Although many campesino families at first objected to their daughters' participation in armed struggle, the violence and duration of the war and the relentlessness of governmental repression disrupted family life to such an extent that traditional gender roles were challenged. In 1991 nearly 40 percent of all FMLN combatants were women, many in positions of leadership.[23]

Despite their nearly equal political and military participation, women in the FMLN faced special difficulties, including sexism within their ranks, which some have discussed in interviews and narratives.[24] Most poetry written by women in the FMLN, however, addresses not sexist practices within the organization but, instead, their own internal conflicts and commitments: fear of torture and death, anxieties about combining military struggle and motherhood, sadness at separation from family members on the one hand; yet a fierce belief in the justice of their cause and a certainty of their ultimate victory and their country's eventual reclamation. Despite the fact that these writers have lived for the most part within the borders of El Salvador, their depictions of their experiences reveal a diasporic consciousness. First, they experienced a form of exile/dispersal in that they operated clandestinely. Having relocated in mountainous regions conducive to guerrilla activity, they were unable to move freely outside of the zones of control that the FMLN at various times dominated (up to approximately 40 percent of the countryside). Second, they experienced a psychological diaspora through their dual status as both insider and outsider. Finally, many were cut off from lovers, spouses, children, parents, and friends for long periods of time, nonetheless isolated by having "chosen" their condition. Although difficult, this diasporic experience and the awareness that accompanied it were often empowering, as new territory was claimed and campesinos were buoyed by the "rejuvenating substance of struggle."[25]

In *"Esta es la hora"* [Now's the Time], Reyna Hernández reveals the sense of otherness she sometimes experienced fighting with the FMLN, her alienation and distance from ordinary life, and the terror that can arise in the midst of military preparations. As people in one part of the country kneel calmly in the cathedral, Hernández asserts in ironic contrast:

> mis camaradas
> limpiarán sus armas,
> romperán cercos,
> asaltarán trincheras,
> tomarán posiciones
>
> [my comrades / clean their weapons, break camp / head for the trenches / and take positions . . .].

Her catalog of this secular ritual seems at first glance matter-of-fact, but Hernández disrupts it with an anxious interior monologue: *"habrá muerto mi mejor amigo*? [has my best friend died?] . . . *qué pasará*? [what is happening?]" The guerrilla poet predicts in eerily sensual language the terrible events in which she will soon participate:

> Los A-37 lanzarán sus bombas
> sobre la tierna vegetación de Guazapa
> y el fósforo blanco
> quemará la piel del lago.

[The A-37s will drop their bombs / over the soft Guazapa foliage / and white phosphorous / will put to flame the lake's skin.]

She fears that, as she and her comrades retaliate, not only the lake's skin will burn. Her friend might already have been caught off guard and killed; she might even now lie alone, embracing the cold earth. Hernández's pulsing repetition of "alone" emphasizes her horror at the thought of her friend or herself dying in isolation.[26]

But fears of death and loss constitute only one aspect of women's military experience. As Hernández explains in *"Sexta-Avenida Sur"* [Sixth Avenue South], moments of wry satisfaction do occur, especially when one manages to outwit the opposition. Despite the dangers of sudden gunfire:

> Nos va bien en la montaña!
> Nuestras botas
> resisten los inviernos de Guazapa,
> son botas Yankys
> las tropas del gobierno
> regresan descalzas con La Cruz Roja.

[We fare pretty well in the mountains / Our boots / stand up to the Guazapa rains. / They're Yankee boots. / The government troops / have to go back with the Red Cross, barefoot.][27]

Here Hernández takes an angry stab at both the United States and the Red Cross, which she sees as intervening unethically in the war on behalf of a corrupt Salvadoran military. To steal the enemy's shoes is to humiliate him, she suggests exuberantly, and such humiliation is a valid form of redress.

Much Salvadoran poetry-in-arms directly addresses *el pueblo* [the people], explaining FMLN ideology and expressing determination to continue working for the collective good. Mirna Martínez's *"Nunca he sabido tus señas"* [I Don't Know What Makes You You] illustrates well this genre's colloquial style and absolutist rhetoric:

> No lo sé
> como tampoco sé del vientre que te parió
> ni de la tierra en que agonizas

no sé hacia donde lanzas tus disparos
ni de que lado pesa el dolor sobre tus espaldas
. . . no sé nada de ti
y sin embargo igual edifico mis días
pensando en tu futuro

[I don't know / like i don't know a thing about where you come
from / what patch of land you fret over / I have no idea where
you aim your fire / nor which of your shoulders ache / . . . i don't
know a thing about you / but likewise i structure my days /
thinking about your future].

At moments her language can sound condescending, but on second
reading it seems instead ebullient. It reveal the poet's spirited insis-
tence, to herself and her audience, that the armed resistance move-
ment from which she speaks is heralding a *tiempo nuevo*.[28]

Countermilitant efforts inevitably result in the deaths of some
compus, including some who are survived by their poetry. Amada
Libertad, a young guerrilla with the FMLN in Chaletenango depart-
ment, was killed in mid-July 1991, in combat with the army between
Nejapa and Quezaltepeque near the capital, while negotiations were
taking place in Mexico between the FMLN and the Salvadoran gov-
ernment. Like many poets-in-arms, Libertad wrote poems that ex-
pressed the inevitability of her own untimely death, even as she
affirmed her immortality:

Cuando me muerta
no me iré del todo
quedaré en tus anhelos e ideales
quedaré en las letras que un día
escribí en el odio
estallaré en mil y más auroras
y seguiré amaneciendo
en la conciencia afilada de todos.

[When I die / I won't go completely / I will remain in your desires
and ideals / I will remain in the letters / that I wrote on the wall
of hatred / I will explode in a thousand and more sunrises / and
I will continue to dawn / in the sharp conscience of all.]

It is significant that the image of writing to combat hatred occurs in
this poem. For Libertad, as for Nora Méndez and Blanca Mirna
Benevides, among other Salvadoran women poets, one goal of resis-
tance poetry is to resist hatred, an unproductive and often self-
defeating emotion. Moreover, the phrase "to see the writing on the
wall" suggests to most U.S. readers inevitability, and certainly this
poem's image holds that connotation. But in El Salvador the image
of writing on the wall evokes poems and other forms of revolutionary
testimony literally written on prison walls, as encouragement to one's
compañeros and expression of one's will to remain silent under torture
to the end.

Although guerrillas owe their *compañeros* silence under torture,
their general obligation involves a willingness to speak out collec-
tively. This is especially crucial for the guerrilla poet, who often sees
herself as a channel for voices other than her own. Libertad's *"Dentro
de la voz"* [Within my Voice] captures this theme:

He recogido los pedacitos de voz
que el silencio esconde
en ellos he encontrado
las cicatrices de los mártires,
la ensordesedora plegaría del hambriento,
los estallidos de miseria campensina,
la ardiente e incontenible
sed de Libertad.

[I have gathered up the pieces of voice / which the silence hides /
and among them I have found / the scars of the martyrs, / the
deafening prayer of the hungry, / the explosions of misery in the
campo, / the glowing and uncontainable / thirst for freedom.]

The dead, the starving, the rural poor—all are given witness
through the "pieces of voice" the poet unearths. Her identity is linked
extricably to their identities, her desires to theirs. Their common
bond is *libertad,* "freedom," a word whose resonance is enhanced
here by the fact that it not only represents a fervent goal of the
Salvadoran revolution but is also the poet's surname, a chosen nom
de guerre. Libertad's poetry illustrates well the concept of revolution-
ary subjectivity. Her voice is both personal and communal, even

mythic, in its desire to "explode in a thousand and more sunrises" and survive in "the sharp conscience of all."[29]

Delfy Góchez Fernandez was a young poet involved in a student uprising when she was killed by Salvadoran security forces in 1979. Ten days before her murder she prophesied not the time of her death but, instead, its manner: "what I do know clearly is that I'll die soon, / cut down by the enemy." Unlike Reyna Hernández, this poet evinces no fear at the thought of death, but, rather, a fierce resignation to the certainty of her own martyrdom and an unswerving commitment to her cause. Imagining the aftermath of her own death, she portrays the future as a collective, loving mother happy to be reunited with her once-hungry offspring:

> our mother will laugh with joy
> at being reunited with her child, her people,
> with the child who yesterday begged for a crust of bread
> and today swells full as a river.
>
> the mother who was slowly dying
> and who now is living the dream she yearned after,
> and the eternal militant
> whose blood
> nourishes the day
> that is coming to dawn.

Drunk on the honey of her own vision, Delfy Góchez Fernandez ends with the assertion that self-sacrifice is both a duty and a pleasure:

> I wish to die according to the custom of my times
> and of my country:
> cut down by the enemy of my people.[30]

The seemingly contradictory images of a mother embracing her child and an eternal militant losing life blood are complementary and interchangeable in this poem. The poet's depiction reinforces Latin American scholar Jean Franco's assertion that the role and imagistic resonances of mothers have shifted during the past two decades as countless women in Latin America have become politically active,

protesting against governmental atrocities: "From the signifier of pas-
sivity and peace, mother became a signifier of resistance." Indeed,
mothers are often warriors in Salvadoran women's writing, and
Franco's analysis helps to explain why. Since their government no
longer adheres to the traditional value of protecting the institutions
of motherhood, family, or church, women have experienced a pro-
cess of "deterritorialization," a loss of their conventional immunity
from terrorism and reprisal—an immunity that, Franco argues,
though restrictive, served a vital symbolic and sociopolitical role in
Hispanic societies. "Felicitous spaces" of female sanctuary are no
longer available, yet their loss has made many Salvadoran women
even more determined to continue their revolutionary activism. Delfy
Góchez Fernandez was a victim of this deterritorialization, by virtue
of her gender and the fact that she died seeking shelter in the Vene-
zuelan embassy, another traditional source of sanctuary violated in
war. It seems especially poignant that her parents, themselves noted
Salvadoran authors, gave their daughter's poems to editor Amanda
Hopkinson so that Delfy's silenced voice might be heard. One of
many writers exiled or murdered for her acts of resistance, Delfy
Góchez Fernandez joins Amada Libertad and other women guerrillas
who, in Franco's words, "no longer occupy space but have a place."[31]

Ana Guadelupe Martínez, a survivor of deterritorialization and
today a leading spokeswoman of the FMLN as it attempts to move
toward party status, is committed to revitalizing her country and its
people. As a former combatant, her actions often separated her from
her mate and young daughter. In her interviews and testimonials,
she has been outspoken on the topic of combining motherhood and
militancy: "The birth of my daughter strengthened my identification
with our struggle, because at the moment she was born, I realized
how much I wanted for her: clothes, shoes, medicine, a secure future,
the chances to study, a sane and healthy environment to grow up
in." Certainly, it was difficult to leave her child and go to fight, she
continues, but her daughter stayed with families who love her: "A
deep feeling of solidarity develops in such conditions."[32]

Moreover, an FMLN woman's military duties did not necessarily
end when she became pregnant, nor did her vulnerability lessen her
delight in the child she was carrying, her hope for the future. In
"*Embarazo*" [Pregnancy] Lety, an FMLN *compa*, describes her baby as

a *piqueño transeunte* [tiny wanderer] coming in late winter to herald spring:

> mi niño viene,
> viajero temporal,
> en tiempos de tigres que agonizan
> y huracanes que borran las miserias.
> Astronauto mudo
> siento tu pequeña vida
> enviándome cifrados desde tu tibio espacio
> y los recojo
> para conversar mañana,
> cuando tu piel me toque dócilmente,
> cuando tu llanto me alegre y me acongoje.

> [My baby is coming / temporal traveler / in a time of dying tigers / and hurricanes sweeping away misery. / Mute astronaut / I sense your small life / sending me cyphered messages from your warm space / and I receive them / to converse with you tomorrow / when your skin presses mine quietly / and your tears gladden and sadden me.][33]

Lety's child will arrive during a time of cataclysmic change, she suggests, when traditional authorities are losing their grip and figurative hurricanes rage, their winds "sweeping away misery." Yet any fear Lety might have for her child's well-being is overshadowed here by her pleasure in the signs of life she constantly receives from her "mute astronaut," whose body and spirit are already an inextricable part of her own identity.

Included in *On the Front Line* (1989), a collection of guerrilla poems edited by Claribel Alegría and Darwin J. Flakoll, is verse by several women combatants involved in literacy work during the 1980s in the zones of control. A strategy for personal and collective empowerment, teaching adults to write and read has become a primary societal task that gives its practitioners great satisfaction. As part of the sharing of resources that accompanies the educational process, campesinos often are taught to read and write poetry. As the anonymous Salvadoran woman who wrote the introduction to *Ixok Amar*

Go explains, "*Se el índice general de analfabetismo es del 60% y entre las mujeres aumenta a un 90%, entonces, nuestros poemas van a ser lecciones también*" [If the rate of illiteracy is 60 percent and among women it is 90 percent, then our poems will be lessons too.][34]

In *"A vos"* [To You] a literacy teacher named Carmela addresses her pupil in a rhetoric both tough and gentle:

> Ey compa.
> Sí, a vos te hablo
> a vos que no sabes leer y escribir
> te invito a que abramos juntos
> la puerta que por tantos años
> se ha mantenido cerrado para vos
> y salgás de ese cuarto
> de ignorancia y ceguera
> para aprendar y enseñar tu realidad.

> (Hey, compa. / Yes, I'm talking to you / to you who don't know how to read and write / I invite you to open with me / the door that for so many years / has been closed to you / and move out of that room / of ignorance and blindness / to learn and teach your reality.]

The first stanza's directness gives way to a more empathic tone in the second: "*has caminado un largo camino,* / *lo sé* [you've walked a long road, / I know . . . .]" Although the language here is simple, to some ears even trite, the poem's poignancy is heightened by the dignified portrait its author paints of a valuable mutual collaboration. Since the student's gain is the enemy's loss, the poet urges her *compañera* not to feel sadness or shame that she is just now coming to literacy. Carmela's closing lines reveal both her political ideology and an urgent invocation to her sisters:

> sentite orgulloso
> de poder librar y ganar
> contra el analfabetísmo
> dentro del proceso de la
> guerra pupular revolucionaria

[feel proud / to free yourself and win out / against illiteracy /in
the process of the /popular revolutionary war].[35]

Carmela's associate Karla, a health worker as well as a literacy
teacher, likewise sees links between her militancy and her nurturing
capacities, as revealed in *"Alfabetizar"* [To Alphabetize]. Karla's prim-
ers seem most unorthodox to U.S. readers: with *"nuestras botas / requi-
sadas y nuestros fusiles* [our requisitioned boots and our rifles]," she
teaches the word *enemigo* [enemy]; with *"la convivencia revolucionaria"*
[revolutionary togetherness], the word *compañero*. Repeated massive
withdrawals from their villages imposed on the civilian population
by the Salvadoran army, Karla asserts, have taught the villagers the
word *guinda*. Finally, she concludes, she can teach with pencil and
paper words like *amor* [love] and *victoria* [victory], words that go hand
in hand for both the teacher and her audience.[36] Not all poems about
acquiring literacy are this optimistic. Claribel Alegría's *"Documental"*
[Documentary], for example, ends with a despairing alphabetical ac-
count of El Salvador's myriad problems:

A de alcoholismo,
B de bohio,
C de cárcel,
D de dictadura,
E de ejército,
F de feudo de catorce familias
y etcétera, etcétera, etcétera.

[A for alcoholism, / B for batallions, / C for corruption, / D for
dictatorship, / E for exploitation, / F for the feudal power / of
fourteen families / and et cetera, et cetera, et cetera.][37]

Despite her weariness, however, Alegría recognizes, as do Carmela
and Karla, that literacy is a form of knowledge and power that can
set their people free.

Women guerrilla poets have written, finally, about the promise
of a new El Salvador. This possibility is described by Ilse Margarita
Escobar, a former *compa* who now does organizing work in San Salva-

dor, in a language first of dreamlike surrealism, then of almost erotic love. *"Caminábamos por senderos/poblados de lamentos* [We hiked paths / peopled with laments]" Escobar writes,

> se escapaban
> furtivamente
> los suenos encarcelados
> por la tempestad de
> las horas
>
> [they escaped / furtively / dreams / inprisoned / by the tempest /of the hours].

Her people's wounds notwithstanding, the poet also chronicles the heady impulse of shared desire that arises from communal life and longings in the mountains:

> Caminábamos sintiendo
> el aliento del amanecer
> cuando las hojas
> besaban nuestros rostros
> y el roció
> ungia nuestros labios agitados
> renovando la promesa
> de la sangre
> que nos une
> en nuestro anhelo.
>
> [We hiked / feeling the breath of dawn / when the leaves / kissed our faces / and the dew / anointed our excited lips /renewing the promise / of the blood / that unites us / in our desire.][38]

These poems-in-arms serve as revolutionary edicts, a form of collective identity politics. They subvert notions of the erotic, political, and social self as a discrete entity, affirming instead the power of shared subjectivities, of unity and community in struggle.

3

Madre,
no te asustes
cuando me veas llegar
con un fusil,
como sí fuera a tocar guitarra.

[Mother, / don't be afraid / when you see me arrive / with a gun, / treat it as
though / I were going out to play a guitar.]

El futuro
es un hoy torturado
que aún no tiene alas.

[The future is a tortured today / that doesn't yet have wings.][39]

These two poetic excerpts illustrate the blurred line that exists be-
tween combat poetry, written by women in the FMLN, and revolu-
tionary poetry, written by urban women whose sympathies lay with
the armed struggle but who, during the 1980s, were working for
change in other than militant capacities. November 1989 marks the
date on which FMLN troops entered San Salvador in what is com-
monly known there as "the offensive"; the guerrillas surprised the
Salvadoran military and much of the world by the level and nature
of support they received from thousands of ordinary citizens previ-
ously thought by many in the government to be politically unallied.
Nora Méndez's short poem captures the poignancy of this historical
moment, in which a young girl still living at home attempts to reas-
sure her mother that the gun she carries for the first time is no more
lethal than the guitar with which she usually leaves the house. Ma-
tilde Elena López's poem reveals the anguish perhaps felt by those
who hoped that the offensive would result in a new government with
greater commitment to justice and equality. "*Lloro en la oruga / por las
del mañana* [I cry in the cocoon / for the wings of tomorrow]," López
declares; "*el cielo / que ahora se entreabre / tiene deimones / que la entrada
guardan / con espadas / de fuego* [heaven / opens part way; / demons /
guard the entrance / with swords of fire]." The future's frail wings
are not yet strong enough to permit flight, and the present is tortured
by demonic gate guardians bearing fiery swords—apocalyptic im-

agery, to be sure. All we can do, the poet asserts, is to live intensely in this moment. But is there reason to continue to believe that change will come? The poem's final question hovers between despair and hope:

> yo te pregunto
> grave y triste:
> La plenitud
> de este minuto
> guarda en la oruga
> las alas del mañana?

[I ask you / grave and sad: / Does the abundance /of this moment / hide in the cocoon / the wings of tomorrow?][40]

Since everyone in El Salvador has been directly affected by the war, it is hardly surprising that women poets who are not combatants have often chosen a rhetoric of violence to describe their emotions. Celia Moran's "*Soledad*" [Loneliness] uses personification to depict the loneliness that she feels at her lover's absence as an officer of the Salvadoran military—arresting his victim in the middle of the night, torturing her once she is taken into custody.

> Hoy esta soledad ingrata, vino a capturarme
> arrastrándome, me sacó de mi casa
> me le revelé
> y me dió un culatazo con la tristeza que traía
>
> Me encarceló
> 3 días y noches din dormir
> me preguntaba por vos
> que si te conocía,
> que donde estabas?
> que qué hacías?

[Today rude loneliness / came to capture me / dragging me out of the house / he hit me with the sadness he brought / and I confessed my full name. / He put me in jail / three days and

nights without sleep / he asked me for you, / if I knew you /
where were you? / what were you doing?]

Moran goes on to detail the various forms of torture her interrogator
employs: he forces her to strip, pulls out her fingernails, beats her,
rapes her. But he does not succeed in exacting information from her
about her lover. Still, this experience leaves shaken the speaker's
confidence in her own ability to withstand torture, physical or emo-
tional: "*Fué entonces cuando por primero vez quise realmente / oldivar tu
rostro para no delatarte* [For the first time I truly wanted / to forget your
face so as not to betray you.]"[41]

Blanca Mirna Benevides's *"Reflexiones"* [Reflections], a long
poem in two sections, was written during her recovery from bullet
wounds that she received while posting UDN signs advertising her
candidacy on a street corner in San Salvador the night before the
election in March 1991. As Benevides recounts it, ARENA (the
government party) supporters drove by, yelled something about
being pro-country and anticommunism, fired into the UDN group,
and fled. An explosive bullet ricocheted off the ground and struck
Benevides in the face; she lost an eye as a result of the attack. In the
poem's first section, she portrays herself as a prisoner forever
suspended in that fateful moment and recalls fleetingly her assail-
ants' pale faces, their taunts, her jolting realization that death could
be imminent.

Quedé prisionera
en el día infinito
de una fecha inolvidable
y en los inesperados segundos
de la vida
y la muerte.

Quedé prisionera
en la mirada sorprendida
de rostros pálidos
que pasaron fugaces
borrosos
por mi memoria.

[I was a prisoner / on that infinite day / of an unforgettable
date / in those unexpected seconds / between life / and death. / I
was a prisoner / in the surprised expressions of pallid faces / that
passed rapidly / vaguely / through my memory.]

Benevides goes on to remember intense pain, her own and that of
her *compañera*, who arrived at the hospital shortly after the shooting.
But her overarching memory is that of gratitude to her companion for
being there with her:

que llegaste
con tu mirada fluvial
clara
a entregarme
optimismo y alegría

[and you arrived / with your gaze / clear as rivers / to give me /
optimism / and happiness].

Section 2 of *"Reflexiones"* portrays the wonder of a friendship
that intensified during the author's hospital sojourn. Here Benevides
lays aside her own trauma to chronicle that of her *compañera*, who
kept vigil. The revolutionary consciousness of resistance poets tends
to be communal; thus, it is not surprising that Benevides would use
her personal experience to explore the larger issue of empathy with
her comrades. Salvadorans involved in the struggle have known full
well the risks under which they have lived and worked. Yet when
one pays for his or her activism with a body part or a life, one must
rethink everything, from triumphs gained to loves forgotten.

Te quedaste inesperadamente
prendida de la noche
como contando al tiempo
los triunfos obtenidos
los amores olvidados
los anhelos perdidos
y los caminos no recorridos.

Te quedaste en aquél día
extraño y sin precedentes
en donde el mundo fue tuyo
por último vez
y floreció el amor
sin importar el dolor lacerante
que estremecía tu alma.

[You were caught unexpectedly / alight in the night / counting
the minutes / triumphs gained / forgotten loves, / lost desires,
/paths not taken. / You were caught that day / so strange and
unprecedented / when the world was yours / for the last time; /
love flowered / and withstood the lacerating pain / that shook
your soul.]

The poet realizes that her *compañera*'s pain matches her own, that
their memories and awarenesses, in fact, are inextricably connected.
Both refuse to let the war destroy their hope, yet both recognize that
only a thin line exists between life and death.

Te quedaste presintiendo
que la vida y la muerte
son inseparables
y que nacía otro mundo
del dolor infinito
como un monumento
al amor.

[You stood foreseeing / that life and death / are inseparable / and
another world was born / from the infinite pain / like a
monument / to love.]⁴²

The poet's friend joins her in a community of suffering survivors,
forged from the shared and often reinforced knowledge that love and
resistance can be born of pain.

Two poems by teenage poets Tania Molina and Michele Herrera
illustrate the efforts of young Salvadoran women to combine a

fervent nationalism with an exploration of their own processes of
coming to political consciousness. Both Molina, who was thirteen
when she wrote the poem below, and Herrera, who was eighteen in
1991, spent much of their youth with their families in exile in Nicara-
gua, where they attended school and were supporters of the Sandin-
ista government. A key theme in the work each poet has written since
her return to El Salvador is breaking silence. In *"Prefiero morir"* [I
Prefer to Die] Molina indicates her commitment to the Salvadoran
struggle by radically refusing to maintain four types of silence: poetic
silence, musical silence, political silence, and psychic silence. She
will not imprison her words, hold back her songs of freedom, remain
mute before injustice, or be silenced by fear of death.

> Sin el expresar libremente
> mis ideales y convicciones
> significa la muerte . . .
> prefiero morir, a seguir
> aprisionando mis palabras.
> Sin entonar en voz alta
> un himno de libertad
> significa la muerte . . .
> prefiero morir, a seguir
> reteniendo los sonidos.

> [If expressing freely / my ideas and convictions / means
> death . . . / I prefer to die / rather than imprison my words. / If
> singing out loud / a hymn of freedom / means death . . . / I prefer
> to die /rather than hold back the melody.]

In a 1991 interview Molina explained that, when she returned to El
Salvador from Nicaragua in 1990, she felt that many of her class-
mates, and to some extent their parents and her teachers, had been
frightened into silence; very little acknowledgment of the war and its
commonplace killings and disappearances was made in the course
of her daily educational activities at an urban school in San Salvador.
For Molina, this silence contrasted starkly with the forthright revolu-
tionary proclamations to which she had been accustomed as part of
her schooling in Nicaragua. Thus, she wrote this poem for her class-

mates, to empower them, along with herself, to speak aloud the horrors they were witnessing.[43]

Michele Herrera's *"Rompiendo el silencio"* [Breaking Silence] directly addresses El Salvador, which she personifies as a lover, and explores a theme similar to Molina's—that silence must be broken whatever the cost. It is for you that I live, struggle, and eventually will die, Herrera proclaims:

> eres tú
> palabra,
> pensamiento
> que al viento se eleva
> mi verso libre,
> eterno

[it's for you / word / thought / my free verse / I offer up to the winds].

The poet sees her country as her intimate companion:

> si te amo
> y
> sigo amándote
> será porque eres rayo
> de luz
> que cada mañana
> junto a mi amanece.
> Porque eres noche tibia
> envolviéndome.
> Estrella brillante
> acaso lejana,
> te encuentras,
> más vives en la lucha,
> cada día, con tu gente

[If I love you / and continue loving you / it will be because you are / a ray of light / that wakes up at my side / every morning. / Because you are the warm night / enfolding me. / No bright star far away, / you live in the struggle, / every day, with your people].

No distant lover, El Salvador provides its people with light, comfort, and passion, qualities crucial to their survival. The relationship between the country in turmoil and its people is reciprocal, Herrera further insists; its poets and citizens must also give El Salvador courage and strength to sustain the difficulties of the hour.

> Resiste un poco más!
> Patria Mía!
> No desfallezcas!
> Es tu amor quien nos
> lo exige
> es ahora
> es el momento
> de ir rompiendo el silencio.

> [Hold on just a bit longer! / Oh my country, / don't lose strength. / It is your love / that requires us, / right now, / in this moment, / to begin breaking the silence.][44]

A sense of urgency and immediacy is central to women's resistance poetry, and Herrera's final stanza illustrates this characteristic in its emphasis on the particular moment—*es ahora*. Her country is yesterday, today, and tomorrow, Herrera states elsewhere in the poem; time is fluid and contingent in a revolutionary context. Yet the moment is always ripe for action.

A second poem by Herrera, *"Noviembre"* [November], bears witness to the remorse and self-probing that can occur when a young woman experiences firsthand a casualty of war. Dedicated to her mother, Norma Virginia Guirola de Herrera, killed in San Salvador during the January 1989 offensive, the poem chronicles a daughter's process of coming to terms with both her mother's death and the commitments that caused her death. Like many others by Salvadoran women, this poem uses direct address to bring the dead to life, or, rather, to celebrate the way in which they live on in their surviving *compañeros*. *"Ahí te encontrabas tú* [you found yourself there]," Herrera begins, *"firme, altive / decidida hasta el final* [firm and proud / committed to the end]." The poet goes on to recount her last afternoon with her mother, watching her prepare to leave the house, recalling that, instead of saying good-bye, she merely smiled and left. News of her mother's death came so quickly thereafter that Herrera scarcely could grasp the message—that her mother had been killed by assassins' bullets.

. . . siempre en todo momento
te creí indestructible,
aún cuando trataban
de hacerme comprender
la oscuridad profunda
inevitable sueño
frio misterio,
inaceptable fin: tu ausencia.

[I always believed you indestructible / even when they tried / to make me understand / the deep darkness / inevitable dream / mysterious coldness / unacceptable ending: your absence.]

In subsequent stanzas the poet alternates between reflective and revolutionary voices, as she laments the loss of her mother yet affirms her determination to take up where she left off. Enough crying of tears, she insists; "*a los mártires no les llora, / se les imita!* [don't cry for the martyrs, / try to be like them!]." Her mother is one of many martyrs, and, like countless other Salvadorans, Herrera blames her government for these needless deaths.

Estamos hartos,
nuestra patria llora
sangre de inocentes
y hermanos que tan todo
por el inmeso amor,
llama eterna que vive y crece
en nuestra Pulgarcito
querido y tan herido.

[We're fed up, / our country cries / the blood of the innocents / and brothers and sisters sacrifice / for an immense love /eternal flame that lives and grows / in our *Pulgarcito*, / beloved and wounded.]

Layers of maternal nurture unfold and intersect here, as the mother-less child expresses devotion to her country by using its pet name, *Pulgarcito*, little finger, as well as to its sacrificial victims, on whose behalf the poet must now bear witness. One year after her mother's death, Herrera continues to rage and grieve when she recalls that November afternoon. But she also accepts the mantle that passes on to her:

> Dejando en nuestras manos
> tus sueños,
> anhelos
> de justicia
> libertad
> e igualdad
> por los cuales
> luchaste
> hasta el final.

[Leaving in our hands / your dreams / desires / for justice / liberty / and equality / for which you fought to the end.][45]

In "Poetry and Militancy in Latin America," Salvadoran poet Roque Dalton argues that resistance poetry is a crucial part of a revisionist historical process that eschews disinterest and, indeed, requires taking sides. The gendered voices of Salvadoran women revolutionary poets give credence to Dalton's assertion. Their poems constitute acts of transgression against dominant cultural codes, radical assertions of their own "polemical historicity," as they encode a distinctively female experience of oppression and bear witness to the winds of change.[46]

4

> Write your self. Your body must be heard. Only then will the immense resources of the unconscious spring forth . . . .
>   To write. An act which will not only "realize" the decensored relation of woman to her sexuality, to her womanly being, giving her access to her native strength; it will give her back her goods, her pleasures, her organs, her immense bodily territories which have been kept under seal.
> —Hélène Cixous, "The Laugh of the Medusa"

Y qué importa si yo sólo soy / una niña con un libro de trigonometría entre las
piernas

[And what does it matter if I am only / a girl with a book of trigonometry between
her legs?]

—Nora Méndez, *"Nuevas sensaciones"*

French feminist theorist Hélène Cixous and other advocates of *l'écriture féminine* argue convincingly that the practice of the woman scribe inscribing woman as a sexual being is not merely subversive: "It is volcanic; as it is written it brings about an upheaval of the old property crust, carrier of masculine investments; there's no other way." *L'écriture féminine* encourages women to transgress on the printed page by writing explicitly in a female language of the body.[47] At first glance, this abstract and perhaps essentialist feminist theory might seem to have little relevance to Salvadoran women's poetry, grounded as the latter is in historical circumstance and the materiality of civil war. Yet as Berta López Morales has noted, for an increasing number of Latin American women poets, even those in militarized environments, transforming the language of the body represents an important challenge to the restrictions on women's sexuality imposed by dominant cultural conventions.[48] In El Salvador women's poetic assertions of erotic desire, relational equality, and sexual autonomy constitute a crucial form of resistance to sexist practices and to military appropriation and abuse of women's bodies. In working closely with the women of the *Taller de Mujeres en la Literatura*, I have identified three types of "body-poems" that they have written: those that celebrate female eroticism as intense, spirited, playful; those that insist upon sexual parity between a woman and her male partner; and those that explore abortion as a painful but sometimes necessary part of women's experience.

Nora Méndez's *"Nuevas sensaciones"* links poetry and sensuality. Her art makes her more sexually desirable, the poet claims, and it also arouses her sexual desire. Like Audre Lorde, Méndez views the erotic as an assertion of the life force of women, an aspect of creative energy that empowers us in our writing, our loving, and our daily work.[49] By reinscribing the female body from the perspective of what Morales calls a "feminine subject of discourse," Méndez resists male sexual/poetic codes and asserts her own feminist alternatives.

Estoy desenterrando el hueso
de mis emociones,
se me están cayendo los versos de leche
y mi poema anda descalzo
de jándose llevar por lo fecundo
de este aroma a verde.

Tengo las raices a Flor de Piel
porque es tiempo de palabras
gracias al buen invierno
y voy a hacer con ellas
una canasta de dulces
con la miel de mis sentimientos.

[I am digging up the bone / of my emotions, / verses of milk drip
from me / and my poem walks barefoot / letting herself be carried
away / by the fertility / of this green aroma. / I carry my roots
skin- deep / because it is time for words / thanks to a good rainy
season / and with the roots I'm going to make / a basket of
sweets / with the honey of my emotions.]

Méndez nurtures her verse with what some French feminists
consider woman's signature, the white ink of mothers' milk. The
poem that she births, a girl child, immediately sets out on her own
autoerotic quest, walking barefoot in a garden of fertile green as her
mother, the poet, digs up new words and creates another "basket of
sweets" from her hives of honey. In the third stanza Méndez play-
fully conceals her song as part of an erotic game:

Y es que se me anda apiando la dulzura
y mi canto sale por donde pueda
como fustán saliendo a buscar novio.

[And this sweetness is taking pity on me / and my song comes
out where it can / like the bottom of my slip peeking out / from
the hem of my skirt / looking for a boyfriend.]

This stanza might seem to valorize the traditionally feminine;
Méndez's *canto* is shy, flirtatious, in search of male attention and

affirmation. Yet as Morales argues, even when Latin American women's poems reiterate patterns established by the master codes, they still "break the self-censorship of the subject" by asserting women's right to chronicle a poetics of the body.[50] Furthermore, Méndez's tone is clearly playful: her coy verse may seem stereotypically feminine in behavior, but just beneath the poem's surface lies a strong reclamation of female sexual autonomy and power.

The last stanza of *"Nuevas sensaciones"* establishes the revolutionary context of the poet's sexual and creative awakening. As the days play *arranca-cebolla*, a game in which a child tries to break her friend's grip on a tree, the poet climbs on the merry-go-round of her lover's kisses. Méndez's whimsical images notwithstanding, the links between language and eroticism are profoundly serious to her:

Las palabras se humedecen desde el fondo de la viola
quizás porque El Salvador es un zanate
pasandose la calle
o quizás porque las aves
amanecen recitando en las yemas de los árboles.

Y qué importa si yo sólo soy
una niña con un libro do trigonometría entre las piernas.

[Words moisten themselves from deep inside the viola, / maybe because El Salvador is a *zanate* / flying over the streets / or maybe because the birds / wake up singing in the yolks of the trees /And what does it matter if I am only / a girl with a book of trigonometry between her legs?][51]

Exuberant words emerge from the depths of the poet's being, inspired by the example of her irrepressible country, here portrayed as a tiny blackbird empowered to fly despite its vulnerability. Although Méndez seeks and finds eros in the everyday, she is also fully aware of its mysteries. In her final couplet she celebrates her own sexual complexity by imaging her vagina as a book of trigonometry, incomprehensible to many but well worth learning about. Her casual question "What does it matter? . . ." belies the intensity of her genital and sexual reclamation. In documenting a range of new sensations, Méndez develops "a poetics of the body in whose speech its images and necessities are integrated."[52]

Eva Ortíz also contributes to a Salvadoran version of what U.S. feminist critic Alicia Ostriker has termed a "gynocentric erotics."[53] Inspired by Japanese haiku and by the visual arts, her poem-paintings depict a subtle but nonetheless assertive female sexual desire. *"Desnudaré mi rostre* [I will bare my face]," she declares in *"Entrega"* [Surrender], *"para que el tuyo / se ilumine* [so that yours / be illuminated]. In longer poems she also depicts, painfully and honestly, the excesses of romantic thralldom.

Te esperaba
tú te ibas
tú llebas
yo esperaba.
Y los fuegos se crecían
e incendíaban mi costado.
Tú esperaba
tú te ibas
tú llegabas
yo esperaba.
Grité con toda mi voz
y te esperaba
te esperaba.

[I would wait for you / you would go /you would come / I would wait / And the fires grew / and burned in my side. / I would wait for you / you would go /you would come / I would wait. / I screamed with all my voice / and I would wait for you / I would wait for you.]

Although these poems by Ortíz resist the censorship that Salvadoran cultural mores would impose on frank sexual expression by women, they generally lack the exuberant erotic self-assertion seen in Méndez's work. One exception, however, is "Eva," a self-portrait that affirms a woman's right to love where and whom she wishes:

Eva
quiere sembrar de manzanas
toda la tierra . . .
¡Ciudado!

Las semillas de su mano
es están esparciendo
y sopla el viento.

[Eva / wants to sow apples / throughout the land. / Be careful! /
The seeds from her hands / scatter / and the wind is blowing.]

In a 1991 interview Ortíz claimed that, for her, erotic poetry is revolu-
tionary because it "really shakes people up for a woman to write
it. . . . I have a friend who says to me 'your poetry comes out of your
guts; it's visceral poetry.' That's true, and like Gioconda Belli and
Rosario Murillo [Nicaraguan poets], I believe that to write erotic po-
etry as a woman in Central America is a form of resistance."[54]

Other Salvadoran women write poems exploring the problems
and possibilities of achieving equitable sexual relationships. In "Par-
alelo de amor" [Love Parallel] Celia Moran addresses her lover in the
language of military negotiations, words all the more heightened by
the fact that, at the time the poem was written (June 1991), the FMLN
and the ARENA government were attempting to negotiate a cease-
fire. For Moran, the exigencies of heterosexual love and civil war are
parallel:

Por más acuerdos que tomemos de cese de hostilidades
a posiciones estratégicas, no los cumplimos.

Por más ofensivas que lancemos de. . . .
"Hasta el tope para no amarte"
no hay acuerdos significativos,
y estamos empantanados en los besos y las caricias.

[For all the agreements we reach about a cease in hostilities, /
about strategic positions, we never carry them out. / For all the
offensives we launch / with such slogans as /"Everything to the
limit so as not to love you," / we bog down in kisses and
caresses.]

Sexual difference can be a barrier to effective, mutually sustaining
communication between women and men, Moran suggests, yet she
is committed to continuing negotiations, even in the poorest and

most war-ravaged neighborhoods of San Salvador—Zacamil, Meji-
canos. When their summit meetings fail, however, she and her lover
resort to the only language they do have in common, that of sexual
desire:

> no cumplimos los acuerdos
> y volvemos a enredarnos en el combate do las sábanas,
> en tu territorio controlado en el mío

> [we reach no agreements / and return to tangle in combat among
> the sheets, / in your controlled territory, in mine].

Although the poet indicates dissatisfaction with these negotia-
tions, she is nonetheless insistent not only about continuing the dia-
logue but also about being an equal participant in it: *"tenemos que
sentarnos a la mesa de negociación / en iquales términos* [we have to sit
down at the negotiating table / on equal terms."] Moran determines
to get her relational needs met, and she asserts without hesitancy
which of her partner's behaviors are unacceptable. For her, to meet
on "equal terms" means

> sin pedirnos entregar las armas antes del tiempo,
> sin decirme que mi iqualdad es un tema inconstitucional,
> sin decirme que mi proclama es irreal

> [without asking each other to lay down our arms before it is
> time, / without your telling me my equality is unconstitutional,
> / without your telling me my proclamation is invalid].

Only if such equality can be sustained, the poet concludes, will she
and her *compañero* have achieved love. Clearly a feminist poem, *"Par-
alelo de amor"* illustrates well Berta López Morales's argument that
women deconstruct the derogatory epithets and meanings that patri-
archy has traditionally ascribed to them when they express the right
to their own sexual and relational autonomy.[55] The poem also implies
that the legendary "battle between the sexes" can be demythologized
and disempowered at an equitable negotiating table.

A different kind of poem by Moran contributes to the growing
oeuvre of Salvadoran women's poetry of the body by chronicling,

with bleak honesty and tenderness, a woman's experience of abortion. Given both the Roman Catholic church's traditional taboos on such an act and the widely held revolutionary belief that women must bear children to replenish the population, a Salvadoran woman's exercise of what in the United States is called her "right to choose" is radical indeed. The poem bears witness to four stages in the woman's decision-making process: her confession to her lover that she is pregnant, her association of the fetus with the physical attributes and political convictions of her lover, her decision to abort and the pain of the procedure, and her subsequent efforts to reconcile herself to what has happened.

In Part 1 of this untitled poem, the speaker addresses her lover intimately, reveling in the miracle of procreation. Depicting his penis as *"tu parajo / tejedor de ensueño* [your bird / weaver of fantasy"], she celebrates the fact that this bird found her nest and filled it with his seed:

Lo llenaste de todo tu ser
para que mi marsupia
suave, tibia, dulce
le tejiera la colcha,
antesala de una vida
justa y digna

[you filled my womb / with all your being / so that my kangaroo pouch / soft, warm, sweet, / would weave you a blanket, / a waiting room for life, / just and dignified].

In part 2 she speaks to her fetus of her desire that it have

sus ojos
negros y profundos . . .
sus convicciones libertarias,
la honestidad de su ser,
su espiritu guerrillero

[his eyes / dark and profound . . . / his convictions, / honesty, / guerrilla spirit].

Despite these wishes, however, the speaker decides to abort. Although Moran does not delineate the reasons behind this decision, she does describe graphically the woman's experience of physical violence and emotional pain during the actual procedure:

> Te arrancaban
> de mis entranas.
> En mis oidos,
> resueñan como campanas implacables
> las tijeras
> con quecortaban nuestro nexo

> [They ripped you / out of my womb. / In my ears / the scissors / with which they cut our creation / are implacable bells].

Although she mourns the blood that escapes her body, she affirms her decision by associating this blood with rivers of life. Once her "kangaroo pouch" is empty, she speaks again to her fetus in a gesture of lament and reconciliation:

> No vas a conocer el nuevo día.
> No voy a poder darte
> la mañana fresca
> de una patria nueva.

> [You're not going to know the new day. / I'm not able to give you / the cool morning / of a new motherland.][56]

The poet's revolutionary subjectivity is evident here, as her speaker couches her regrets in terms of that which her fetus will not live to see—the dawn of a peaceful era in her country. This poem, like many by Salvadoran women, reclaims what Adrienne Rich has called "the geography closest in," the female body under siege.[57]

In poems expressing outrage and reconciliation, Salvadoran women extol the role of witness and memory in their daily experience, mourn their own and their country's loss of innocence and illusion, assert their will to survive, and articulate their commitments to collective resistance and a peaceful future. They claim that poetry is essential to the revolutionary process and that women's poetry offers a distinctive perspective in its gendered voicings of Salvadoran realities. According to the anonymous author of the El Salvador introduction in *Ixok Amar Go*, the fact that women are direct targets of military and social repression explains their ongoing commitment to transformation and their personal and poetic quest for peace:

> Por ésto es que gran parte de nuestras mujeres, están entregadas a la lucha por la paz y participan activamente en todas las tareas que esa lucha impone. Solo en este contexto se puede entender como la última generación de poetas, está avanzando a través de su expresión diaria en poesía, en la lucha por la paz y en la vindicación de nuestra pueblo.

> [This is why there is dedicated involvement in the struggle for peace and active participation by our women in all the ways this struggle demands. Only in this context can we understand how the latest generation of women poets are advancing, through their daily expression in poetry, the struggle for peace and vindication of our people.][58]

Chapter 3

"Estrangement from the Center": Salvadoran Women Writing in Exile

> I'm sorry, no, I'm not in voluntary exile. No, I hate it. I have been forced out. . . . Voluntary exile. What a contradiction! What an irony! None of us wants to be anywhere but home. Who would voluntarily choose to be banished and estranged from home?
>> —Marta Benavides, "El Salvador: The Presence Removed"

> Se levantan mis muertos
> tienen rabia
> las calles están solas
> me hacen guiños
> soy cementerio apátrida
> no caben.

> [My dead arise, they rage. / The streets are empty / but my dead wink at me. / I am a cemetery / I have no country / and they are too many to bury.]
>> —Claribel Alegría, "*Eramos tres*" [We Were Three]

Educator, sociologist, and ordained Baptist minister, Marta Benavides directed the Ecumenical Committee for Humanitarian Aid (CEAH) in El Salvador until 1981. Sponsored by Archbishop Oscar Arnulfo Romero, CEAH founded the first refugee centers in El Salvador, thereby incurring the wrath of the Salvadoran government. Unlike the national Red Cross, which, according to Benavides, "abided by the rules" by providing emergency aid only sporadically, at the government's request, CEAH offered ongoing assistance of food and shelter to thousands of homeless campesinos pushed out of rural areas due to militarization—aid that Salvadoran leaders deemed subversive. After Archbishop Romero's assassination in March of 1980 and the murders of the four U.S. churchwomen later that year, Benavides was harassed by the Salvadoran military and eventually forced into hiding, an experience about which she has written, despite the obvious risks: "I must continue to do everything underground. They came after me. They're hunting me down . . . just like most of my friends. . . . I can't go to their funerals; we only help to

97

bury them . . . . The repression continues, but after October 1980, the mountains and cities tremble."[1]

Benavides believes passionately that she and thousands of other Salvadorans like her had no choice during the 1980s but to leave their country, to enter into an exile by no means self-imposed, as the U.S. and her own country's governments would have it. "No, there are no exiles," proclaims the official rhetoric. "El Salvador has not exiled citizens for a while now. They all leave voluntarily." And once in exile, she continues, many Salvadoran citizens have enormous difficulty finding asylum and work, since in the United States, in particular, they are not seen as political refugees unless they can document conclusively that their lives are in danger for political reasons. The concept of "voluntary" exile represents a terrible irony to Benavides, who longed throughout the 1980s to return to her country and her humanitarian work there but feared for her life and for her family should she do so: "No roots—no anything. Except the desire to be back. We have to make it back some day. We are making that day."[2]

Since 1979, one and a half million Salvadorans have been exiled or dislocated—over 700,000 of them homeless in their own country, more than 800,000 living in the United States, Latin America, or Europe. Over half a million Salvadorans continue to reside in the United States, even since the peace accords were signed, in January 1992, between the ARENA government and the FMLN; most of them lack political refugee status, and many are undocumented workers. Many exiled supporters of the FMLN still feel that it would be unsafe to return to El Salvador, since peace is so fragile.[3] The majority of these displaced people are women and children, and a significant number of them have written about their experiences in intense, compelling poetry and prose. Such writing can be seen as a "triologue," to use U.S. feminist critic Jane Marcus's term, a "triple-tongued discourse with her culture" informed by each woman's subjective knowledge and political exigencies. Their nationally and historically contextualized identities, their marginalized status as exiles, and their gender oppression all contribute to these writers' inscriptions of dislocation, of elsewhereness. Yet as Marcus argues, "elsewhere is not nowhere. It is a political place where the displaced are always seen and see themselves in relation to the 'placed.' "[4] Such a vantage point may be paradoxically empowering for the creators of exilic texts, Angela Ingram posits, since state-imposed marginalization frees political exiles to dissect oppressive institutions and educate potential allies. In subverting official versions of reality, Salvadoran women writers in exile also "decenter notions of genre and text and consequently challenge and destabilize the reader's political certainties."[5]

Nonetheless, Salvadoran women's renderings of exilic experience are often fraught with psychic pain and alienation, as the quotation from Claribel Alegría's "We Were Three," with which this chapter began, suggests. One of her country's most prolific and well-known poets of witness and confrontation, Alegría documents with honesty and rigor her survivor's guilt, the feeling that she too should surely have been assassinated, and her overwhelming sense of responsibility to those she possessively claims as "my dead."[6] A theorist of exile as well as a poet who chronicles it, Alegría describes it as an agonizing professional hazard of Central American writers and political activists for over half a century—a fact of which she had firsthand knowledge even before her own exilic status became clear, since her father, a Nicaraguan liberal and a physician, was forced by U.S. marines under the country's former dictator, Somoza, to leave his country for El Salvador when Alegría was a child. After growing up in her adopted nation, Alegría left to continue her education abroad, met and married her North American husband, Darwin J. Flakoll, and settled on Majorca to live and write, planning to return eventually to El Salvador. More than ten years ago, however, she learned that, because Salvadoran officials considered her writings subversive, she could no longer go home without risking her own and her family's lives. Today Alegría lives in her father's country, Nicaragua, happy to be back in Central America but furious at the restrictions placed on her by the Salvadoran government. Still, she explains in an important coda: "I realize that my anger, my resentment, is subjective, and that I would be falsifying if I told you I feel 'exiled' in Nicaragua. Because of that, instead of speaking about my own experience, which is unimportant, I would like to talk about the true political exiles of my country: the refugees, the displaced, the dispossessed."[7]

Alegría's disclaimer and subsequent reconceptualization of what constitutes an exile parallel statements made by Alicia Partnoy, Argentine editor of *You Can't Drown the Fire: Latin American Women Writing in Exile* (1988), in her introduction to that powerful volume. When she first began collecting exilic texts, Partnoy defined *exile* as "the forced departure from a person's homeland due to attacks or threats to her life, her family, or her work." Her contributors challenged this definition, however, as not sufficiently inclusive:

> I soon realized that in countries where repression had taken the most arbitrary, disconcerting and destructive patterns, it was impossible to predict that a woman who had managed to leave before the personal attacks started would not have become a target had she chosen to stay. Internal exile was another issue raised by the women who corresponded with me. What about those who could never leave their country, but had to survive in silence and fear, banished in their own land?[8]

As readers of Salvadoran women's written accounts of exile, therefore, we must recognize that such experiences have taken place in diverse (dis)locations and circumstances: in foreign cities in which they have been forced to relocate, temporarily or permanently; in refugee camps along the Mexican and Honduran borders; in Salvadoran secret prisons and torture chambers.[9] Jane Marcus has claimed that "an exile is a stranger whether or not she has chosen her condition," and in some respects her assertion seems accurate; Salvadoran refugees have been estranged from their homeland, strangers far from home in its many evocative connotations—a material place of shelter inhabited by loved ones, a sustaining community of friends and allies working in their native environs to promote social change, that place in the world that one knows intimately and where one is known. Yet as Benavides has explained, in the context of the Salvadoran political economy and as a result of what Carolyn Forché calls "the longest war in our failing public memory," no Salvadoran exile has chosen her condition.[10] Furthermore, despite Alegría's claim to have no country, many Salvadoran women writers have eschewed the role of stranger, insisting defiantly with the anonymous author of the El Salvador section of *Ixok Amar Go* that *"vivimos en nuestro tiempo, en nuestra tierra (sea en el exilio o no)* [we live in our time, in our land (whether in exile or not)]."[11]

What difference does it make that the poets under investigation here are women, since Salvadoran men have also given testimony to their experiences as exiles and since gender is not the most compel-

ling condition of exile for many political refugees?[12] I would argue
that, although many of these writers articulate foremost their exploi-
tation due to class oppression, cultural imperialism, and/or political
or religious affiliations, gender does represent a significant aspect of
exilic experience for quite a few, especially those who recount mater-
nal loss or sexual torture at the hands of prison officials, the military,
and/or the death squads. Salvadoran women experience discrimina-
tion and brutality not as "Salvadorans" but, more precisely, as "Sal-
vadoran women": that is, they experience forms of oppression that
are simultaneous, interlocking, and mutually determining. Being
raped by a prison guard, fearing pregnancy as a result of that viola-
tion, having one's vagina invaded during political interrogation and
torture, and witnessing the senseless murder of a child one has borne
are all forms of *women's* persecution and, hence, are crucial to the
poems and testimonials Salvadoran women in exile write.

This chapter, then, will examine three conceptualizations of exile
documented in writings by Salvadoran women living outside their
country or under incarceration during the 1980s: exile as forced ab-
sence from one's native land, imprisonment and sexual torture as
forms of exilic experience, and the "elsewhereness" of displaced
women and children in El Salvador's shantytowns and along its bor-
ders. These voices reveal that, despite their "estrangement from the
center," Salvadoran women writers in exile are refusing marginaliza-
tion as liability, as "nowhere," inscribing it, instead, as locus for an
exploratory, contingent identity and an alternative community of wit-
ness. This communal identity, although vulnerable, unstable, and
contextual, offers its affiliates an opportunity for agency rather than
passivity. With Angela Ingram, these writers assert that any pro-
claimed or imagined center is "always shifting, or rather, being rede-
fined, re-placed. Yesterday's place of exile can be tomorrow's cen-
ter."[13]

1

Que aún mi ser se estremece
al pensar en el regreso
a El Salvador

[Still I tremble / when I thinking of returning / to El Salvador].
—Sara Martínez, *"Coordenadas"* [Coordinates]

Y todo esto
es una manera de decir
que me asaltan a veces
unas ganas violentas
de volver

[All of this to tell you / I am desperate to go back]
          —Claribel Alegría, *"Santa Ana a oscuras"* [Santa Ana in the Dark]

In "El Salvador: The Presence Removed," Marta Benavides explains
that like many Salvadorans, she became aware of the term *exile* at an
early age, since military coups d'état were frequent and often re-
sulted in the banishment or sudden leave-taking of government lead-
ers and their families.[14] Although exile could lead to poverty for these
once-powerful officials, a more likely effect was the consolidation of
their stolen wealth: "One has to see the magnificent homes just out-
side Guatemala City on the way to El Salvador to have an idea of how
splendid and glamorous exile can be!" Such splendor is a far cry from
the experience of ordinary Salvadorans—peasants, teachers, trade
unionists, students, religious workers, market women—forced into
exile because they seek equality and justice, democracy and peace.
"We are Salvadoran and we love our country. The rich and the mili-
tary, in alliance with multinational corporations, have tried to banish
us, to prevent us from claiming our right to own our land and forge
a future as a nation. . . . No decisions are ours, and we mustn't try to
change our situation, for we are in exile, and in captivity in our own
land."[15]

Women poets who recount their forced absences from their
country describe similar feelings of frustration and powerlessness.
In *"Coordenadas"* [Coordinates], Sara Martínez explores the shock of
living far from her homeland, in a nation whose language is incom-
prehensible and whose controlling ethical principle seems to be a
self-serving individualism. Like many Salvadorans in exile in the
United States, Martínez is stunned at the poverty and racism she
witnesses in the world's wealthiest country:

que los parques están
llenos de pobreza,
que como sombras miles
deambulan por las calles,
sin un lugar seguro donde ir,

que la discriminación
no tiene limites . . .
que el hambre calcina
los huesos de una mayoria
llamada minoría

[the parks / overflow with the poor, / thousands of shadows /
roving through the streets / without a safe shelter, /
discrimination is limitless . . . / hunger mortars / the bones of the
majority / called a minority].

Despite her dismay and vulnerability, the poet reluctantly acknowl-
edges that she is probably safer here than at home, that she has
nowhere else to go.[16]

A similar sense of helplessness underlies two poems by Reyna
Hernández, a young Salvadoran revolutionary who emigrated to
Sweden shortly after her release from prison. Analyzing "the ethics
of elsewhereness, gender and estrangement," Jane Marcus argues
that women in forced exile are recognized by the state that would
ordinarily ignore them—that unlike most women, political refugees
have been labeled subversive and thus accorded subject rather than
object status.[17] Yet few Salvadoran writers seem initially to adopt
Marcus's perspective that their status as exilic subjects is empower-
ing. In "Me sacaron de mi país" [They Sent Me Out of My Country],
Hernández describes the irony of ordinary citizens, standard-bear-
ers of the spirit, being forced to leave their home while "they," the
military elite, remain in El Salvador as so-called patriots. Dazzled
by the lights of Stockholm and its electric trolley cables, still shaken
from her prison experiences, the poet feels overwhelmed: "Lloré mi
derrota! Cuántos fantasmas! [Defeated, I wept. / So many ghosts!]"
Her only wish is someday to return to her country: "del regreso
/ todos queremos un puñado [about going back / we all want a chance
at that]." Meanwhile, homeless and insecure,

los llevamos en el alma
al otro lado del mundo
al otro lado del alma

[we carry all that we have / packed in our spirit / to the other side of the world / to the other side of our soul].[18]

Despite her depression, Hernández finds implicit comfort in the camaraderie of other exiles, as indicated by the collective pronoun *we*. Her use of the plural here suggests that she, like Marta Benavides, believes that, in their unified resistance, Salvadoran refugees are daring to grab peace and justice, "even by force, from the hands that murder us. We will be home!"[19]

In "San Salvador," Hernández dreams of coming home to her native city, depicted as a once-nurturant mother now violated by drunken soldiers and the decaying dead. Amid the cool of her Nordic summer, the poet evokes the blazing sun of San Salvador and addresses her city directly, imagining

> con colverme a recostar
> un día
> sobre tu falda
> de azafrán planchada . . .
> tomar el agua
> de tú consideración
> entre las mentiras
> de aquel mediodía injusto

[returning / someday / to stretch out / on your saffron skirt . . . / accept the water of your kindness / among lies of that unjust noon].

She goes on to envision Archbishop Romero and other dead heroes walking once more with her through the dirty vegetable markets and bloody streets, but that poignant image is quickly eclipsed by a vision of

> de militares borrachos
> que arrugaban tu falda
> para reirse de tus piernas corvas

[the drunken army / who lift your skirt / to laugh at your bowed legs].[20]

A city under siege, San Salvador offers its nostalgic sojourner no comfort.

What of the exile who does return to her country, by chance or choice? Jacinta Escudos, a young Salvadoran activist and writer now living in Nicaragua, lived in Europe in the late 1970s, working with solidarity organizations and studying at a German university. In 1980, horrified at what she heard of the repression in her country, she determined to go back to El Salvador, join the FMLN, and document her experiences there in poetry. Her prose-poem "To Come Back" is part of a longer sequence written to her East German lover; without Escudos's knowledge, these writings were given to Claribel Alegría in the early 1980s, mistakenly identified as the work of a dead combatant, and subsequently published in London under the pseudonym Rocio America. This mistake was rectified when Escudos resurfaced several years later in Nicaragua and took up writing once more. "To Come Back" explores in greater detail the themes identified by Hernandez in "San Salvador" and "They Sent Me Out of My Country": streets filled with the ghosts of painful memories, confusion and lack of continuity, fear of resumed repression, the sense that nothing remains of one's past life. For Escudos, a haunting question recurs—"Why did I come back?" At moments, her isolation at home is greater than that she experienced elsewhere:

> You don't know who to call first.
> "He's moved and there's no new telephone number."
> "We don't know where she is now."
> "He's left the country."
> "She was killed almost a month ago."
> Nobody wants to give you any details. It seems that these days
> Salvadorans just want to forget everything.

Escudos also acknowledges her fear that her lover abroad will find someone else and her paranoia that her Salvadoran friends view her with reproach for having left at all. "I STAYED HERE," their eyes seem to shout. "But no one can make you back down," Escudos insists, "and you answer—I CAME BACK." The question of why remains unanswered until the poem's final lines. Despite her perception of San Salvador as "a dark, filthy, dangerous blind alley" and her awareness that to return constituted "an unnecessary risk," the poet knows why she has come back. "Your people need you now and forever. / And you will fight for them."[21]

The most thorough and compelling chronicles of the exile's quest for meaning in a world gone meaningless are those of Claribel Alegría. Carolyn Forché, who translated Alegria's *Flores del volcán* /*Flowers from the Volcano*, describes these poems as "testimonies to the value of a single human memory, political in the sense that there is no life apart from our common destiny. . . . Responding to those who would state that politics has no place in poetry, that expressions of the human spirit in art should be isolated in aesthetics, she would add her voice to that of Neruda's: *we do not wish to please them.*"[22] Alegría calls herself a cemetery, a resting place for the unburied dead who call the poet to witness, but she herself can get no rest: safely removed from the brutal scenes of conflict, she can never do enough, say enough. Besides her pervasive guilt and the sharp pangs of loss, Alegría rages with the awareness that displacement camps and exile are a deliberate strategy of the doctrine of low-intensity warfare practiced by her government against its civilian people.[23] From her pain and anger, therefore, the poet insists on revealing to her less-knowing readers that, in Forché's words, "there are lies more believable than the truth."[24]

"Sorrow" is a long poem in eight parts dedicated to Roque Dalton, the Salvadoran revolutionary poet slain in 1975 under circumstances that remain mysterious, and it contains frequent allusions to other dead artists and activists from Spain and Latin America: Chilean folksingers Victor Jara and Violeta Parra, Spanish poet Federico García Lorca, and Argentine-born revolutionary Che Guevara, among others. Section 1 documents the power and elusiveness of memory, disappearing and reappearing voices—voices of friends, other poets, anonymous martyrs in the struggle. Fragments of sound waft about like the pieces of human flesh that turn up on backroads:

> sombras amigas
> que pregonan
> que rompen un instante
> la neblina . . .
> una palabra rota
> pequeñas frases sueltas
> que apenas si adivino

[the dark shapes of friends / crying out / that break the fog an instant . . . / a broken word / small phrases so scattered / I can barely catch them].

Fog is a controlling metaphor here, for so much remains shrouded; the poet's knowledge can only be partial. "*¿eres tú Victor Jara?* [Is that you, Victor Jara?]," she wonders, as fragmented body parts drift by. Alongside these fragments Alegría juxtaposes phrases and lines from her dead friends' writings, words that evoke her own creative spirit and determined will: "*listos para la muerte / listos para vencer* [prepared for death / prepared to conquer death]." This section ends with the poet taking up her pen at the urging of the muses she has invoked: "*Puedo escribir los versos más tristes esta noche* [Tonight I can write the saddest verses]."

Section 2 chronicles the poet's quest in Andalusia for the unmarked grave of García Lorca, dismissed as "*el poeta enemigo . . . / el maricón* [our enemy, the poet . . . / that faggot] by several of the townspeople to whom she turns for help. Like Jacinta Escudos, who lamented that in San Salvador no one wants to give you any concrete information, Alegría encounters only vague gestures and expressions of alarm:

todo el mundo lo sabe
pero nadie es capaz
de un detalle preciso
de decir por ejemplo
allí mismo lo echaron
al borde
de ese olivo
junto al cadáver joven
de un maestro con gafas

[no one is capable / of the precise detail / of saying for example / they flung his body down / at the foot of that olive tree / beside the young body / of a schoolteacher in glasses].

No tombstone, no clues—the poet must imagine the truth, interpret the map on her own. Thus, wrapped in fog, she sets off toward the ravine that swallowed the poet's body. Her sole touchstone becomes

the lone olive tree she encounters on the road, which she envisions
as a silent memorial:

> Cuántos siglos de aceituna
> how many centuries of olives
> los pies y las manos presos
> the feet and the hands prisoners
> sol a sol y luna a luna
> sun to sun and moon to moon
> pesan sobre vuestros huesos
> weigh over your bones,

she asks the dead poet. No stubborn grove of olive trees still stands;
nor does she find a gravestone

> que diga
> aquí yace el poeta
> pero alguien dejó un árbol
> un olivo
> alguien que supo
> lo dejó

> [reading / here lies the poet / but someone left a tree, an olive /
> someone knew and left it standing].

In this solitary tree the poet takes comfort.

Section 3 of "Sorrow" addresses directly the issue of survivor
guilt, as Alegría describes herself and other exiles as hunted animals
marked by shame:

> Se ha dechecho la patria
> se ha podrido
> nos revolcamos en su podredumbre
> y la gente se aparta

> [Our country has fallen apart / it has gone bad / we roll in its
> filth / people avoid us].

The guilty exiles also avoid one another, the poet explains, glancing away during chance encounters. Wandering aimlessly, these homeless chroniclers despise and fear their own helplessness—their poverty, their unfulfilled dreams. Dirty by association, some instinctively congregate at the public baths to wash off their shame. But such efforts to purify themselves are futile: "*el tufo / de exiliado* [the stench of exile]" will not wash off; it persists like the itching fungi that leave their feet bloody.

Section 4 shifts to another aspect of exilic experience, as Alegría recounts how she learned of Dalton's death:

Obstinadas
confusas
me llegan las noticias
hechos truncados
frios
frases contradictorias
que me acosan
así llegó tu muerte
Roque Dalton
la implacable noticia
de tu muerte
en los signos borrosos
de un periódico

[Stubborn /confused / the news comes to me / truncated facts
/ cold, contradictory sentences / that pursue me / that is how
your death arrived, Roque Dalton / the implacable news of your
death / in the smudged headlines].

Again the poet is given no precise details, only a vague account of her comrade's death in fragmented images. Carolyn Forché recalls sitting with Alegría on Majorca during her daily vigil of silence while waiting for the mail to come, a time of despair.[25] Regarding Dalton's death, all Alegría can know is that it happened:

Y nunca sabré quién te mató
pero estas muerto
Roque Dalton

y envolvieron tu muerte
en la neblina

[I'll never know who killed you / but you are dead, Roque
Dalton, / and they wrap your death in fog].

Section 5 returns to depict the wandering exiles, fleeing now to
museums because they are free like the public baths. Pretending to
study the paintings, these dispossessed can sit for hours resting their
infested feet. Among them, the poet hearkens back to her search in
Andalusia, to the olive trees overlooking the unmarked graves of her
compatriot, García Lorca; her mind will not be still, although her
body is. Attempting to find comfort in the maternal arms of the
Virgin portrayed in much of the art, she finds herself recalling the
martyrdom of the slaves who built the cultures documented here, of
the Christ commemorated artistically. As the poet returns to the
streets to wander, she can no longer elude her own tortured memory.
This section ends with a question that becomes a haunting refrain:
"decidme en al alma ¿quién /(tell me in spirit who) / *quién levantó los*
olivos? / (who raised up the olives?)"
    In Section 6 Alegría imagines an encounter with Dalton's assas-
sin, framed in neon on a dark, wet city street. As the poet pauses to
look for matches in her bag,

el rostro se ilumina . . .
una máscara blanca
que me observa
y se vuelve morada
es tu verdugo
Roque

[a face lights up . . . / a white mask / it observes me / it turns
violet / it is your assassin, Roque].

Uncertain what to do, she gives the requested light to this still beard-
less boy, smiling at her; afraid to stop him, she lets him pass and is
then ashamed. This pivotal experience forces the poet to reexamine
her own guilt and complicity rather than be silenced by it. Section 7
captures Alegría's determination *"salir de esta neblina / sacudirme el*

terror [to leave the fog / throw off the terror]" and begin to write. Here she imagines herself a prisoner in solitary confinement, as those fallen friends whom she evokes might once have been, grabbing whatever tool is handy to scratch out her loneliness. But the poet's self-focus and isolation soon give way to communal recollections of imprisonment and torture, as

> comienzan las voces
> a llegarme
> el telón de fondo
> de las voces
> punteado por un grito
>
> [the voices begin coming toward me / this backdrop of cries / punctuated by a scream].

Self-oriented poetry is not acceptable, Alegría implies; her identities must be multiple, her words a collective litany:

> Desde mi soledad
> acompañada
> alzo la voz
> pregunto
> y la respuesta es clara:
> soy Georgina
> soy Nelson
> soy Raúl
> de neuvo el torturado
> su aullido
> el silencio
> con los ojos abiertos
> me recuesto en el catre
> ni una raja de luz
> se apagó el aullido
> empiezo a contar nombres
> mi rosario de nombres
>
> [from my solitude I raise my voice / I ask and the answer is clear: / I am Georgina / I am Nelson / I am Raúl / again the

tortured one / his howl and silence / I stretch out on my cot / with
my eyes open / and not so much as a fissure of light / the screams
are cut / I begin counting the names / my rosary of names].

Reflecting on the next prisoner to sleep on this cot, the poet realizes
she is not alone; only *"una hoja de tiempo"* [a tissue of time] separates
her from her fellow and sister sojourners—Victor, Violeta, Roque.
Writing is a communal act for the Salvadoran poet in exile; her voice
is collective, dialogic, like the screams of prisoners who do not know
whether the sound they hear is coming from within or from another.
    The last section of "Sorrow" further addresses these themes of
multivocality and specificity. The poet at last finds the detail she has
wanted:

> existen los barrotes
> nos rodean
> también existe el catre
> y sus angulos duros

[the bars do exist / they surround us / the cot also exists / with its
hard sides].

As tangible as these, however, is the poem of witness that chronicles
such particularities:

> el poema río
> que nos sostiene a todos
> y es tan substantivo
> como el catre
> el poema que todos escribimos
> con lágrimas
> y unas
> y carbón

[the river poem / that sustains us all / and is as substantial as the
cot / the poem we are all writing / with tears, with fingernails and
coal].

Paradoxically, the poet remains solitary yet not alone, surrounded by the fragmented, sonorous voices of the voiceless dead. She realizes at last that the poetry's role in revolutionary struggle is indeed significant, even if the poet speaks from afar. As in other stanzas, Alegría ends with a resonant query:

> . . . y surge la pregunta
> el desafío
> decidme en el alma ¿quién
> quién levanto los barrotes?

> [the question rises, the challenge / tell me, in spirit, who / who raised up this prison's bars?]

The poet vows to leave this prison of her own making, this exilic guilt. She is fortified by the ghostly presence of her comrades, from whom she feels no longer separate.[26]

In her essay entitled "Talking," exiled Salvadoran Gloria Bonilla, now a legal aide for immigrants in Washington, D.C., asserts that no medicine will cure heartache and homesickness for the refugee, even in the United States, where painkillers abound. Her own antidote has been to keep busy, forcing herself to learn English and complete bachelor's and master's degrees in five and a half years.[27] For Claribel Alegría, Jacinta Escudos, Reyna Hernández, and Sara Martínez, in different ways and to varying degrees, writing poetry from their sites of exile offers a prescription for sanity and survival. "Please accept a sister's suggestion," Escudos wrote to Alicia Partnoy while the latter was compiling *You Can't Drown the Fire*, "do not let this book become a whining sorrowful lamentation. We shouldn't let exile defeat us."[28] As poets of documentation, these exiled women intervene politically to insure that those who have died for peace and justice are not defeated, that voices from the margins will continue to define alternative centers.

2

We called COPPES [Committee of Political Prisoners of El Salvador] "another barricade for the revolution." It's true, we were an enclave of revolutionary supporters. Before I was captured, I hadn't participated in any organization, but

the experience of being a political prisoner soon changes your mind. . . . Now
I've been released and forced into exile, but you can't forget all those people you
have left behind suffering in prison. I'm now working in the Committee of Rela-
tives of the Disappeared and Political Prisoners.
                                                    —Marbel, *Women of El Salvador*

gritos, golpes, preguntas
sólo otra vez,
. . . en el silencio
de la noche eterna

[. . . screams, punches, questions, / you are naked, on the floor, / alone, once
more, / . . . in the silence / of the eternal night]
                                            —Sara Martínez, *"Angustía"* [Anguish]

My shouts were drowned by the walls, and my voice soon gave out. I was still
fighting him when he called in a private to hold down my legs. Two others came
in and stood watch by the door. They were heavily intoxicated and the stench
that filled the cell was revolting. . . . I remained sprawled out on the floor totally
shattered, though I'd been aware that this could happen any day there.
                                —Ana Guadelupe Martínez, "The Secret Prisons of El Salvador"

COPPES, the Committee of Political Prisoners of El Salvador, was
formed in 1980 in two men's prisons and in the Women's Prison at
Ilopango; its primary aims were to secure the release of all political
prisoners and to expose and end the harassment and detention of
their visitors. As the prisoners' elected representative body, COPPES
has staged several successful hunger strikes demanding better food
and living conditions and has initiated educational and social activi-
ties. The Women's Section of COPPES has confronted additional
problems, however, resulting from the multiple rapes and sexual
torture experienced by many female prisoners. One of the organiza-
tion's most meaningful victories was winning for imprisoned women
the right to gynecological treatment. Despite this gain, these women
by all accounts lack adequate medicine and health care and suffer as
well from continued sexual harassment by the security forces and the
inevitable psychological disorders accompanying such maltreatment.
As Marbel's testimony suggests, being a female political prisoner in
El Salvador is a radicalizing experience that makes of an insider an
outsider.[29]

"Anguish" by Sara Martínez, a former National University stu-
dent and political prisoner who later was a refugee in the United
States, documents in poetry the brutal experience of interrogation
and torture in a Salvadoran prison. The dominant images here are

vulnerability and aloneness: roused from her sleep, the solitary victim hears screams, endures punches, and suffers the humiliation of nakedness before her interlocutors, in a scenario that is repeated again and again. Despite her isolation and fear, the prisoner refuses to capitulate.

> Contesta!
> no, no vas hacerlo,
> qué puedes responder?
> y el llanto de silencio
> cae sobre tu cabeza,
> no hay nada que hacer,
> sólo esperar, esparar,
> hasta cuando, hasta siempre,
> Compañero . . .

> [Answer! / no, no, you don't answer, / what can you say? / a
> mournful silence / falls over you, / there is nothing you can
> do, / alone, you wait, you wait / until when, / forever, /
> compañero . . .]

A powerful reversal of the speaker's initial psychological terror occurs in the poem's last words, as she affirms her determination not to break under pressure and defies her isolation by addressing one with whom she shares these experiences: *compañero*—friend, comrade in struggle.[30]

Nora Méndez spent a week in Ilopango as the only "official" political prisoner among the group of women with whom she was incarcerated. The prison experience creates feelings of solidarity among inmates, she claims, regardless of the reason for which they have been arrested. A poem she wrote while in prison, *"Testimonios"* [Testimonies], was written in sand on the prison walls by Méndez's companions, an act of defiance and sisterhood:

> Creimos,
> antes de ser torturadas
> que toda la sensibilidad del mundo
> la cargábamos
> en la llanura adulta de nuestra piel.

Y ahora comprendemos
compañeros
que las convicciones y la fe
no pueden llevarse en la piel
porque sino
hace mucho tiempo
se nos hubiesan muerto.

[We believed / before they tortured us / that we carried / all the
sensitivity of the world / in the soft plains of our skin. / And now
we understand, / *compañeros*, / that conviction and faith / can't
be carried on the skin / because if this were so / they would have
killed us / a long time ago.]

The poem presents the paradox of skin so delicate and vulnerable
that it can be easily mutilated in the process of torture yet so tough
and resilient as to survive because of what lies beneath it: convic-
tions, faith, solidarity.[31]

The preceding poems are inconclusive with regard to gender.
Although I have used *she* to identify the speaker, the poet's account
of the experience of detention and torture does not reveal the
speaker's sex nor mention sexual abuse specifically. In fact, few po-
ems by Salvadoran women that I have read on the topic of imprison-
ment portray this painful dimension of female experience. Numerous
prose testimonials exist, however, in which former prisoners docu-
ment incidents of rape and sexual torture, their own and their sis-
ters', with anguish and outrage. Lydia, a Salvadoran union organizer
now living in the United States, has told the editors of *A Dream
Compels Us* what she witnessed:

During "interrogation," women are beaten and tortured with
electric shock. They are raped with foreign objects. I saw a young
girl, seventeen years old, who couldn't close her legs; when she
was examined by doctors, they found a large piece of wood which
had been forced into her body. If a woman is pregnant when
she's captured, or if she becomes pregnant as a result of being
raped, the constant torture may cause her to abort. The torture
is worse than anyone can imagine. What we women can never
forgive is that even the children are treated in this brutal way.

In analyzing the experience and rhetoric of violence, feminist theorist Teresa de Lauretis asserts that violence is located "somewhere else," outside the social, and that women are among those whose bodies are out there where the violence is—"a space, the territory in which the battle is waged."[32] De Lauretis's thesis seems especially applicable to the exilic experience of Salvadoran women prisoners, triply (dis)located by virtue of their enforced removal from society, their gender with its attendant sexual risks, and their vulnerability as mothers or caregivers. Giving voice to such experience must be simultaneously terrifying and healing. That women recount their prison experiences of sexual violation in prose rather than poetry seems to me understandable, given that, however horrific their subject matter, most poems rely on metaphor, even when the violence under scrutiny defies metaphorization. To metaphorize the violation of one's own most intimate self and sexuality could seem to be an act of complicity in one's assault.

One of the most gripping prison narratives by any Latin American woman is Ana Guadalupe Martínez's essay "The Secret Prisons of El Salvador," written after her release from prison in 1978. Martínez, a student activist who subsequently joined the Popular Revolutionary Army and became its chief of armed forces in the Eastern zone, later worked outside the country with the Political and Diplomatic Commission of the FMLN and its auxiliary organization, the *Frente Democratico Revolucionario* (FDR). Most compelling about her account is its very ordinariness: Martínez recounts the most unspeakable crimes as though they were everyday occurrences, which in her historical and daily context they no doubt are. Yet alongside her seeming equanimity runs a thin thread of rage, spun thicker at pivotal textual moments. When her interrogators are blindfolding her, wrapping tape over her nose so she can scarcely breathe, pushing her down a staircase, and punching her, Martínez identifies them neutrally as "a man in his thirties, dressed in civilian attire," "his sidekick, the soldier." When describing their decision to "put an electrode on her tits," however, Martínez's rhetorical denunciations intensify: the soldiers are "savage beasts of vengeance," "perverse sadists." At this point her narrative becomes almost unbearable, as the electrode is placed in her vagina; we are told, "The jolt makes me double over in pain—but it is more than just pain; it's like a burning coal, an overall shock which blazes through the innermost muscle fiber." Martínez realizes that her persecutors feel special power and pleasure in attacking her sexually—that, in the complex political technology of the prison environment, their goal is to objectify and dehumanize her by appropriating her sexuality.

Martínez's sexual abuse does not end once the torture ceases, just short of death ("they know just how far they can go if they want to keep their victims alive"). When two guards drag her back to her prison cell half unconscious, she continues, they undress her and, "even in the awful state I'm in, these pitiful creatures take advantage of the opportunity to paw me." This description marks another noteworthy rhetorical shift, as the "perverse sadists" are re-identified as the pathetic creatures they are. Such tonal variations are characteristic of many Salvadoran women's prison testimonies, this movement from narrative objectivity to outrage to something resembling compassion, against all odds. Perhaps the most heartrending facet of these testimonials of sexual torture and rape is the women's subsequent fear of pregnancy. Martínez recounts how, a few days before the brutal torture just described, she was raped in her cell at 4 a.m., while handcuffed, by Sergeant Mario Rosales, one of the most hated guards. Her demoralization soon gave way to profound anxiety:

> About a week later, when I was expecting my period, I grew more and more frantic as each day passed and I still hadn't begun menstruating. This was surely the most wicked and ultimately base form of torture they could ever inflict upon their female enemy. It tormented me so fiercely that I had only one idea: to abort if I were pregnant. Just thinking about it provoked unfathomable despair in me.

Martínez's essay is not totally without hope; she also documents her refusal to break completely under torture and her dreams for the new society to which she is committed. And she did survive to continue her revolutionary activity and to claim, in a 1986 interview from the front, that "the incorporation of women has profoundly determined the character of the people in this struggle."[33] Still, her prison narrative captures vividly the enormous burden imprisonment and sexual torture impose upon Salvadoran women and girls.

Another former FMLN commanding officer, Nidia Díaz, has recounted her prison testimony in *Nunca estuve sola* [I Was Never

Alone], a multigeneric document composed of narrative, letters, and poetry—Díaz's own and that of her compatriots. One of the most powerful poems reveals her solidarity with her friend and sister-combatant Yanet Samour, who was captured December 30, 1984, by the Salvadoran National Guard and is believed to have been tortured and disappeared. Díaz writes from her sense of loss and from her remorse at ending up in a better situation than Samour, in prison rather than dead or disappeared. For Díaz, the possibility of freedom remains and thus brings guilt as well as determination to survive:

> Cuando como
> me da tu hambre
> cuando me tapo
> me da tu frio
> cuando me quejo
> de mis heridas y quemada,
> me duele tu piel torturada
> y tus huesos rotos

> [When I eat / I feel your hunger / when I cover myself / I feel
> your chill / when I complain / of my wounds and the burns / I
> feel the pain of your tortured skin / and broken bones].

Díaz's empathy grows as she considers what her friend must have endured, but her poem also pays loving tribute to the values for which her friend stood

> Te recuerdo en la historia
> de la organización campesina
> te pienso en la estructuración
> de las redes clandestinas urbanas

> [I remember you in the history /of campesinas organizing / I
> think of you / in the secret urban network].

Yanet Samour, you are with me in this prison, the poet insists; in impassioned direct address she also claims to be alongside Yanet wherever she may be:

Camarada, no estás sola,
el pueblo y su vanguardia
están contigo y conmigo.
Tú y yo solidariamente.

[Comrade, you are not alone; / the people and their vanguard
/are there with you and me. / You and I together in solidarity].

Díaz evinces a revolutionary subjectivity that is explicitly gendered
as well as communal, a collective consciousness all the more remark-
able for asserting itself in the Salvadoran prison environment, where
objectification and torture of inmates is routine. Despite such treat-
ment, Díaz remains steadfast in her solidarity with her comrades and
her certainty that victory will be attained.[34]

3

Mi gente contenta en el caserio,
los niños cargaban su fusil
y es como
si cargaran una flor en sus manos.

[In my village, the people were radiant, / and children carried their rifles / as if
they were holding tender flowers.]
—Bernadina Guervara Corvera, "*Mi Comandante Federico*"
                                         [My Commandante Federico]

Fue el catorce de mayo
cuando empezamos a correr.
Tres hijos me mataron en la huida
al hombre mío
se lo llevaron amarrado.

[It was the fourteenth of May / when we started running. / They killed three of
my children / in the escape / they took my man away /with his thumbs tied.]
—Claribel Alegría, "*La mujer del Río Sumpul*" [The Woman of the Sumpul River]

Claribel Alegría has claimed that her country's true exiles are its
displaced and dispossessed, in 1991 a staggering 700,000 people left
homeless by aerial bombings and military invasions.[35] By most ac-
counts, such scorched earth tactics took place throughout the 1980s
against civilians living in zones of control, areas held by the FMLN,
as part of an effort to deprive the guerrillas of popular support.[36]

Many Salvadoran refugees moved from the countryside to over-crowded urban shantytowns; others were forced into camps on the Honduran border, where they remained vulnerable to military raids by Honduran soldiers as well as hunger and disease. Despite such adverse conditions, women and children have written remarkable poems describing their life there or recalling their prior lives, poems smuggled out on scraps of cloth or paper so that the rest of the world will know.

Bernardina Guervara Corvera was nine years old in 1981, when her poems were sent out of a refugee camp in La Virtud, Honduras, on small pieces of paper inside a matchbox; they subsequently were published in *Leon de Piedra*, an anthology of poetry and documents of El Salvador. Guervara Corvera has not been heard from since then. "My Commandante Federico" is a nostalgic poem recalling life in Santa Barbara, Cabanas, El Salvador, the zone of control in which she lived before dislocation. In her village the setting was pastoral despite the poverty: children played happily, listening to birds sing and digging holes in the earth to watch the ants work. Recollecting such peaceful community life evokes philosophical reflection, even from a nine-year-old:

> Las hormiguitas para comer no necisitan pisto,
> la tierra les pertenece
> y tienen un gran almacén de víveres
> para estos tiempos de lluvia.

> [Ants don't need money to eat. / The earth belongs to them, / and their fortresses bulge with food / for these nameless days of rain.]

Despite the hunger and want to which she alludes, Guervara Corvera's memories are fond ones, especially of the young man who became her special friend, Federico. This might be any preadolescent crush in any country were it not for one mitigating factor: young Federico is a military commandante, probably with the FMLN. Seeking neither a combatant nor a boyfriend, but instead a playmate, the poet has one poignant wish: "*Yo quisiera que el comandante Federico /viniera a jugar todos los días conmigo.*" [I would like it if Commandante Federico / would play with me every day.][37]

In "The Politics of Exile" Alegría tells the story of Pastora, the child poet of Colomoncagua, a Honduran refugee camp a few miles from the Salvadoran border, whose writings were collected by Alegría's daughter Patricia in 1986, when Pastora was eleven. Like Guervara Corvera, Pastora's whereabouts today are unknown. According to Alegría, Pastora lived until she was eight in the disputed zone of San Vicente, from which she and her mother fled during a search-and-destroy mission conducted by the Salvadoran National Guard in 1983. Having seen her father and two small brothers killed in the raid, Pastora escaped, along with her mother, by hiding in man-made caves called *tatus* during the day and sneaking toward the border at night, single file, with other refugees. When military guards discovered these peasants near the border, they forced them into the Limpa River, where the elderly and very young drowned. Those who could swim or hang on made it to Colomoncagua.[38] Despite such trauma, Pastora found the courage and voice to document her life in the refugee camp, particularly her experience as a literacy worker.

Alegría notes that one remarkable facet of this camp was the incredible success of its grassroots literacy campaign, which resulted in the illiteracy rate decreasing from 80 percent to 30 percent in fewer than five years. Taught to read and write in the camp herself, Pastora evinces obvious pride in her community's collective accomplishments:

> Every single one of the instructors
> we work without complaint
> we aren't better
> than the community here,

she writes in "The People's Teachers." Pastora's most striking recurrent themes are a resistance to hierarchy and an acute awareness of her historical context:

> We aren't intellectuals.
> Because we know how to share
> right now in these moments
> we want to make some suggestions.

Writing for her comrades in the camp, Pastora goes on to assert that learning takes place only if accompanied by love, that educating all citizens is a communal duty, and that teachers learn as much from their efforts as their students do. These same themes appear in "Construction," which reads like a text to accompany Paolo Freire's *Pedagogy of the Oppressed*; its key words are *cooperation, progress,* and *fraternity*.

> We refugees
> don't have an education
> but here we are working on
> the basis of cooperation.

Having survived unspeakable terrors, the young poet is determined to construct a new society based on revolutionary values of equality and collaboration.[39]

Other women poets document not their own experience as refugees but that of compelling women whom they know or imagine. In "Mama Bags Buys Her Clothes," Reyna Hernández pays homage to La Pimpa, a homeless woman who lives in a shantytown and does good deeds for her comrades there. Labeled crazy by some, Mama Bags staunchly rejects the perceptions of her detractors:

> La Pimpa compra su ropa
> al regalado
> en la basurala de Mejicanos
> y grita
> "Todo el mundo está loco menos yo."

> [Mama Bags buys her clothes / for nothing / in the Mejicano
> garbage dump / and yells out / "The whole world is crazy / except
> me."]

Aware of this homeless woman's nurturant capacities, Hernández portrays her with tenderness and respect. La Pimpa comforts lonely Mariona prisoners with lemons and limes and dances for their entertainment. The poem's most striking feature is the repetition of the name La Pimpa, Hernández's effort not to appropriate the woman's identity but to insist upon her right to self-definition on her own terms. For a refugee whom the world considers insane to bring gifts of lemons and limes to the women prisoners, Hernández implies, simply affirms her awareness that, in Emily Dickinson's words, "much madness is divinest sense / to a discerning eye." The poem's last lines present Mama Bags as a seer whose vision offers hope to the downtrodden around her:

> y se va por la tarde
> cantando
> "Y vuela la maripose
> sobre su propio jardín"

[When it's dark she leaves / singing / "Butterflies fly /over their own garden"].

Our human capacity to create love and beauty for one another persists despite dislocation and material want, and, for Hernández, Mama Bags' "crazy" acts exemplify this capacity.[40]

Claribel Alegría's *"La mujer del Río Sumpul"* [The Woman of the Sumpul River], a forceful example of Marcus's triologue, offers three interwoven narrative perspectives: that of the refugee herself, whose words are halting yet powerful; that of the poet as war correspondent and seer, who reports and interprets what she has seen and heard from the river woman; and, more obliquely, that of non-Salvadoran readers, whom Alegría invites to watch, listen, and tell to others in our own uninformed communities what we have witnessed.[41] *"Ven conmigo* [Come with me]," the poet begins, soliciting at once her readers' active participation in the journey;

> subamos al volcán
> para llegar al cráter
> hay que romper la niebla
> allí adentro
> en el cráter
> burbujea la historia

[let us climb the volcano / to reach the crater / we have to break through the fog / history is bubbling there].

As in "Sorrow," a recurring motif here is locating truth despite the inevitable fog surrounding it. On this quest, we must plumb the depths as well as scan volcanic heights:

Desciende por las nubes
hacia el juego de verdes
que cintila:
los amates
la ceiba
el cafetal
mira los zopilotes
esperando el festín.

[Come down through the clouds / toward the play of greens /that scintillates: / *amate* trees / ceibas / coffee groves / look at the buzzards /awaiting their feast.]

Here and elsewhere in her poetry, Alegría uses the color green and its accompanying images, trees and leaves, to suggest not only their conventional meanings of innocence and renewal but also to represent the harsh disjuncture characteristic of life in war-torn El Salvador, where mountain ravines conceal fragmented bodies and exotic foliage becomes a backdrop for buzzards zooming in on their prey. The Sumpul River massacre of 1980 saw more than six hundred campesinos fleeing El Salvador for their lives forced into the river to drown or be gunned down or hacked to death by Salvadoran or Honduran soldiers attacking them from each side of the border.[42] For those unfamiliar with this historical atrocity, Alegría offers through her imagery an implicit warning that readers must bear witness despite our own emotional risk, for we surely cannot remain detached.

"*Yo estuve mucho rato / en el chorro del río* [I was hiding in the river / for a long time,"] explains the woman,

un niño de cinco años
me pedía salir.
Cuando llegó el ejército

haciendo la barbarie
nosotros tratamos de arrancar

[a five-year-old boy / asked me to help him climb out. / When the
army moved in / shooting everything up / we tried to get away].

Like Ana Guadalupe Martínez's prison narrative, the river woman's
testimony begins matter-of-factly with details of time, place, and cir-
cumstance. But as the woman says that she watched three of her
children murdered and her husband taken captive, the poet-reporter
evokes our empathy by revealing that the woman is silently weeping
while holding her baby, still afraid for his life. Of course, the woman
is not truly silent. What unravels in subsequent lines is a harrowing
tale of her journey to safety with her infant, a journey she survived
by pretending to be dead and lying on top of her baby, covering and
distracting him with leaves to conceal and quiet him. This tale is told
partly by the river woman—

cuando llegaron los soldados
yo me hacía la muerta
tenía miedo que mi cipote
empezara a llorar
y lo mataran

[when the soldiers came / I played dead / I was afraid my baby
would begin to cry / and they would kill him]

—and partly by her interviewer, who repeats the story and thereby
creates an echo and a haunting refrain:

Consuela en ensusurros
a su niño
lo arrulla con su llanto
arranca hojas de un árbol
y le dice:
mira hacia el sol
por esta hoja
y el niño sonríe

y ella le cubre el rostro
de hojas
para que él no llore
para que vea el mundo
a través de las hojas
y no llore
mientras pasan los guardias
rastreando.

[She consoles her baby / in whispers / she lulls him with her
tears / she strips leaves from a tree / and she tells him: / look at
the sun / through this leaf / and the baby smiles / and she covers
his face with leaves / so he won't cry / so he will see the world /
through the leaves and won't cry / while the soldiers go past /
mopping up.]

The poet's lyrical recapitulation of this saga captures the river
woman's tenderness and desperation as well as implicitly lambasting
a military so heartless that murdering infants and collecting their
bodies could be presented euphemistically as "mopping up." The
two speakers' roles are thus delineated: the river woman will tell us
what happened, and we will listen and respond; the poet/*periodista*
will help us visualize and interpret the horrors, so we will see and
understand.

It is significant that the river woman speaks only a few lines,
however; the narrative is dominated by Alegría as war correspon-
dent, who observes the woman helping the five-year-old child, hers
and not hers, who has seen the soldiers and knows enough to remain
silent. This devout peasant woman feared she would die by the river,
the poet tells us, and remains convinced that she was saved only by
the divine intervention of the Virgin of Carmen. Spellbound as read-
ers, we are invited to watch a buzzard fly around the woman and
children, providing eerie entertainment for the bored and frightened
little ones. We witness the river woman covering her wounds with
leaves, now poultice and bandage as well as protective shield. As
compelling as her photographic catalog of imagery is the poet's ability
to evoke the universal as well as the particular. Without dishonoring
the individual traumas experienced by the river woman and her

children, Alegría ritualizes and spiritualizes her encounter with the
maternal earth of her country. The woman *"se ha vuelto transparente
[has turned transparent]*," we are told,

> se confunde su cuerpo
> con la tierra
> y las hojas
> es la tierra
> es el agua
> es el planeta
> la madre tierra
> húmeda
> rezumando ternura

[her body mingling with the earth / and the leaves / is the earth /
is the water / is the planet / mother earth / soaking wet / oozing
tenderness].

This mother's wounds become the repeated violations of the sacred
earth, her deep fissures those created by El Salvador's volcanic erup-
tions, which spew blood along with ash. The blood is that of her
people, Alegría proclaims; this woman's tragedy is multiplied a thou-
sandfold:

> nuestra historia
> en pueblo incandescente
> que se confunde con la tierra
> en guerrilleros invisibles
> que bajan en cascadas
> transparentes

[our history / has turned into lava / into an incandescent people /
mingling with the earth / into invisible *guerrilleros* / who flow
downward / in transparent cascades].

The poet goes on to pay homage to El Salvador's guerrilla fight-
ers, dead and living, unseen by the soldiers, military pilots, and
Yankee advisors who govern. Incandescent, the rebels defy the light,
disguising themselves as sentinels, jailers, priests, and beggars to spy

on the soldiers. The official story in El Salvador is that most citizens support the government, that the rebels constitute a small, armed minority of communist terrorists. The truth, Alegría whispers, is that resistance is widespread and guerrillas are working everywhere, in all shapes and forms. Among the resisters is the woman of the Sumpul River, no one special yet someone profoundly worthy of attention in her quiet dignity, there with her infant and the river orphan she adopts. One of the children *"duerme en sus brazos* [sleeps in her arms]," we are told, *"y el otro camina* [and the other walks beside her]." The poem ends with Alegría's characteristic understatement. Having come full circle, we as readers must now interpret for ourselves what the river woman can teach us, what the war correspondent has recorded in her diasporic consciousness:

Cuénteme lo que vio
le dice el periodista.
"Yo estuve mucho rato
en el chorro del río."

[Tell me what you saw / the reporter says. / "I was hiding in the river / for a long time."]⁴³

Adriana Rodriguez was forced to leave El Salvador in 1982 after working for several years as a student nurse at the San Jose de la Montana Refuge, a camp twenty miles south of San Salvador that housed elderly people, women, and children who had fled from the war zones in the countryside. According to Rodriguez, two thousand refugees lived here without toilets, cooking or bathing water, or adequate medical care. Besides food, shelter, and basic health care, she and the three nurses with whom she worked tried to provide psychological counseling and support to the refugees, most of whom had experienced the violent death of a husband, child, or parent. Expelled from nursing school by a supervisor who claimed that Rodriguez's work was subversive, she continued her efforts despite the abduction of one of her colleagues by heavily armed men, her own subsequent harassment by the government, and the persecution and eventual murder of her fiancé and her father, who was burned alive. After these tragedies, Rodriguez wanted to leave and work with Salvadoran refugees in Honduran refugee camps, but, aware of the Sum-

pul River massacre in 1980, she feared she would never make it
across the border. Her written testimony recounts her journey out of
Salvador, first to Guatemala, then to Mexico, and finally to the United
States, where she later worked in a New York health clinic run by the
Committee of Central American Refugees (CRECEN). Like Ana
Guadalupe Martínez, Rodriguez insists that her story is not unusual:
"The other nurses who worked in the clinic were all basically in the
same situation. We had all been threatened and had to leave our
country." Yet all of them are undocumented workers. Rodriguez
makes an eloquent case for recognition by the U.S. government and
its citizens that Salvadoran refugees deserve political asylum: "We
left our country because of the war, because it's dangerous to live in
the middle of a war, even if one is not actively participating in it.
Providing health care to people who need it the most is a crime in El
Salvador. It is because of the war that we had to leave. That makes
us political refugees."[44] Like many other displaced Salvadoran
women, Rodriguez asks her U.S. sisters for support and solidarity.
Until all of us are free, all of us remain in exile.

4

> Particular stories call us to accountability. As dangerous memories of conflict,
> oppression, and exclusion, they call those of us who are, often unknowingly,
> complicit in structures of control to join in resistance and transformation.
> —Sharon D. Welch, *A Feminist Ethic of Risk*

In her recent book, U.S. feminist theologian Sharon Welch critiques
Western notions of what constitutes responsible action by progres-
sives and addresses the need for a newly constituted ethic of risk.
This ethic would acknowledge that communities of feminists and
activists have multiple and divergent principles and values and that
such difference is essential to open dialogue, which, in turn, is essen-
tial to the growth of a coherent politics and a just society. Most
activist groups have difficulty accepting challenges to their own pur-
poses, Welch claims, but believing one's own group possesses the
prerequisites for solid moral judgment, especially when one has First
World privilege, is arrogant and shortsighted. "Foundational ethical
critique requires difference," she argues; "we cannot be moral alone."
A communicative ethic of dialogue between "concrete others" can
lead to just action; stories of resistance and pain must carry particular

weight as the privileged recognize the limitations of our/their own perspectives. In time, "an emancipatory politics emerges from an epistemology of solidarity."[45]

Salvadoran women's writing in and of exile asks that its U.S. feminist readers acknowledge difference: in our literary strategies, our political exigencies, our lived experiences. As the anonymous author of the El Salvador section of *Ixok Amar Go* reminds us, Salvadoran poets "cannot afford to be enamored with the moon"; in many instances, social and political immediacies take precedence over traditional Western literary notions of aesthetic distance.[46] Yet these poems and testimonials offer distinctive, alternative literary strategies that reveal an aesthetic not lesser but different. The Salvadoran women whose writing I have examined here illustrate several noteworthy characteristics of both resistance and exilic literature. First, these writers challenge the static identities imposed by First World powers upon oppressed people. They do this by describing new, gendered political and cultural subjectivities that are being claimed collectively by the once-silenced dispossessed. Second, they assert an alternative chronology and temporality that defy what Barbara Harlow calls the "Western calendar of events." Third, they reclaim the past dynamically, without nostalgia or conservatism, by constantly emphasizing historical specificity and context. Fourth, they intervene in the process of political transformation by writing for *el pueblo*, attempting to educate the people for their own liberation. Finally, they reject despair in favor of the joy of community and a shared commitment to a better future. Salvadoran women's writing in exile is an important part of what Harlow calls "the ideological foundations of the new social order, personal as well as public. . . . Neither armed struggle alone, nor cultural resistance by itself, can provide the necessary resources."[47]

Chapter 4

"You Have Struck a Rock": Black Women's Resistance Poetry in South Africa, 1972–88

> You have tampered with the women; you have struck a rock. You have dislodged a boulder; you will be crushed.
> —Song sung by African women during anti-pass demonstrations, Pretoria, 1956

> Say No, Black Woman
> Say No
> When they give you a back seat
> in the liberation wagon
> Say No
> Yes Black Woman
> A Big NO
>
> —Gcina Mhlope, "Say No"

In South Africa, as in other countries in which indigenous people have been colonized and resistant, poetry has emerged as a vital arena of struggle: a means of reappropriating and re-presenting history from the perspective of the dispossessed; of chronicling dead, exiled, or imprisoned heroes; of refusing any inherited, Eurocentric notion of literature as objective or dispassionate. In discussing protest poetry of the 1960s and 1970s, Nadine Gordimer claims that black South Africans writing during that period were forced, for survival's sake, to be implicit or cryptic rather than explicit; hence they turned to poetry, a more indirect than direct form of resistance.[1] Piniel Viriri Shava argues, further, that in South Africa resistance poetry has served not only to challenge the racist hegemony by accusing, warning, and exhorting but also to reeducate and regenerate an audience of activists subject to feelings of discouragement, fear, and internalized oppression. By providing comfort in struggle, poetry has contributed to the formation of a collective consciousness and to renewed political commitments.[2]

133

That black women have contributed meaningfully to the struggle against apartheid and colonization in South Africa is historically documented in academic studies, oral histories, and well-known chants such as "You Have Struck a Rock" that survive from specific historical milestones.[3] Despite this widespread recognition of women activists' achievements, however, a misconception flourishes in South Africa and elsewhere today that black women did not contribute significantly as poets until around 1988, when academic and grassroots organizations started publicly to lament the absence of their voices and a newly formed publishing house, Seriti Sa Sechaba, dedicated itself to foregrounding black women's work. In fact, many black women were writing resistance poetry in English during the 1970s and 1980s, and some managed to publish their work, albeit mostly outside the country. The result is a substantial body of gendered revolutionary poetry—dating roughly from Gladys Thomas's 1972 co-authorship (with James Matthews) of *Cry Rage!*—that has been largely overlooked, due in part to sexism and racism, sometimes even among otherwise liberal or radical writers, publishers, and critics.[4] My goal in this chapter is to analyze and evaluate black women's resistance poetry of this period as it contributes to a collective, militant ideology and/or to societal continuity and as it documents the revolutionary subjectivity of the writer herself.

First, however, I would like to examine why and how the myth that there were no black women poets writing before 1988 has been perpetuated. One writer who has been particularly vocal on this subject is the progressive Afrikaner poet Antjie Krog. At a historic meeting in Senegal in 1987 between exiled African National Congress leaders and writers and academics (mostly Afrikaners) sympathetic to the movement's goals, Krog spoke angrily of the suppression of black women's voices. When "I wanted to hear the poetry of the doubly oppressed . . . the sound I heard was *one big silence*," she protested, going on to list an array of poetry anthologies that had omitted black women altogether. "Am I to conclude that black women do not write poetry, or do I have to suspect the collectors of considering their duty done when they have included the work of a few white women?" Krog went on to argue passionately for the inclusion of black women's writings in such collections, to decry the stereotypical portrayals of black women in literature by black and white men, and to examine courageously the vexed question of whether Afrikaner women poets, many of whom have received extraordinary critical attention during the 1970s and 1980s, have been "doubly privileged" *because* of black women's double oppression.[5]

Yet, even as Krog rightly challenged racist and sexist publishers and critics for their discriminatory policies, she contributed to the misconception that black women were, in fact, silent during these decades. "Why doesn't the oppressed woman use poetry today as a survival strategy?" Krog asked the audience of ANC supporters then attempted to answer her own question with a series of rhetorical questions:

> Why should a woman who already has to meet so many de-mands, try to fulfil the requirements of poetry? Why should a woman whose life is already fragmented between children and labour to such an extent, fragment it even further with meta-phors? Why should she choose a medium which can mobilise a situation with a seizure, while she is going under precisely be-cause of the mobilisation of her total being? She should write prose, her mother and children and literate neighbour would all understand her clearly. If she should choose to write poetry, she immediately loses half or more of her audience.

Krog's comments, I submit, reveal both myopia and condescension toward her subject, as is evident in her monolithic characterization of "the oppressed woman." She assumes, incorrectly, that, because black women have not been widely published—a fact she herself attributes to sexism and racism—they have not written. Furthermore, she assumes that, because their lives are more precarious than those of white women, they *should* not attempt to meet the rigorous formal and intellectual demands of poetry but should turn, instead, to prose. Yet later in her speech she criticizes the black woman for "preferring" to write prose when "she has the soul of a poet, like Bessie Head."[6] Krog's assumptions and prescriptions seem especially inappropriate considering her audience, which included black women in the ANC who wrote and published significant poetry during the period that Krog found lacking: Barbara Masekela, head of the ANC Cultural Affairs Division; Baleka Kgositsile, then a representative of the ANC Women's Section; and Rebecca Matlou, the nom de guerre of Sankie Dolly Nkondo, then a member of the ANC's militant wing,

Umkhonto we Sizwe (Spear of the Nation).[7] It seems odd that Krog would deduce that a dearth of publication meant a dearth of poetry written by black women; it is startling that she would lament the absence of black women's poetry in the presence of poets of stature, each of whom had just spoken eloquently about the issues and goals facing women writers.

Krog is no more culpable on this score than a host of other progressive South African writers and critics, both white and black; she at least acknowledges the need for black women's voices to be heard poetically. In contrast, renowned poet and Communist party activist Jeremy Cronin, also at the 1987 meeting of writers and the ANC, recognized as significant only black men and white women writers, claiming that, in regard to South African poetry, "a very interesting thing about the last 15 years has been that the sources of vitality, of real impact, of meaningful change have come from two sorts of voices. The one has been black poets, mainly male, unfortunately, but black, writing in English. If one turns to the Afrikaans language . . . virtually all the major poets . . . who have emerged since the mid-seventies are in fact women."[8] Again, black women are conspicuously absent from the progressive writer's discourse, as though ("unfortunately") they had not written meaningfully or, indeed, at all. Liberal critics also perpetuate this error. Of the three best-known critical analyses of black South African resistance poetry to be published in the 1980s—Ursula A. Barnett's *A Vision of Order* (1983), Jacques Alvarez-Peyeyre's *The Poetry of Commitment in South Africa* (1984), and Piniel Viriri Shava's *A People's Voice* (1989)—only one critic, Barnett, discusses any women's poetry at all; she includes three women among the twenty or so poets featured.[9] Thus, it begins to seem more comprehensible that politically committed writers such as Krog and Cronin could actually believe that no body of black women's resistance poetry has emerged from these tumultuous decades.

Alongside the names of distinguished black male poets who have challenged apartheid and enhanced their audience's will to struggle and survive—names like Dennis Brutus, Achmed Dangor, Mafeka Pascal Gwala, Keorapetse Kgositsile, Mazisi Kunene, Don Mattera, Oswald Mtshali, Njabulo Ndebele, Winston Nkondo, Arthur Nortje, Essop Patel, Cosmo Pieterse, Sipho Sepamla, Mongane Wally Serote, Adam Small, and Christopher Van Wyk—I propose a catalog of noteworthy black women poets, among them Gertrude Fester, Amelia House, Baleka Kgositsile, Lerato Kumalo, Lindiwe Mabuza, Ilva Mackay, Nise Malange, Zindzi Mandela, Barbara Masekela, Gcina Mhlope, Boitumelo Mofokeng, Jumaimah Motaung, Roseline Naapo, Sankie Dolly Nkondo, Portia Rankoane, Heather Robertson, Mavis Smallberg, Gladys Thomas, and Phumzile Zulu. To avoid the hierarchies and implicit assumptions of canonicity that any such lists suggest, however, and in the interest of fairness and accuracy, I would add for consideration women practitioners of "orature" and indigenous language poets: Zulu writers of *izibongo*, praise poems, whose traditional form of "publication" is communal performances for other women; African songwriters and singers, whose power of the spoken word and capacity to rouse audiences politically belie simplistic Western binary notions about literacy and illiteracy; and countless women poets, published and unpublished, who write in Xhosa, Zulu, Sotho, and other indigenous languages. Most of these poets are beyond the scope of this study; performers of *izibongo*, however, will be considered later as practitioners of women's resistance poetry.

The women poets noted above have not produced the extensive oeuvres of their male counterparts; most have not published collections of their poetry until the last five years, if at all, and few have more than one collection in print. Most who have published have done so sporadically in small literary and/or women's magazines or in anthologies produced outside of South Africa; the poetry of others has been performance oriented. Some generously answered my call for unpublished poetry by black women when I visited South Africa in the summer of 1992. Nonetheless, I believe that, taken collectively and judged by the same aesthetic and political standards as the men's work, this body of poetry represents a substantial literary achievement.[10] It reflects a revolutionary consciousness and commitment that enhances our collective knowledge of black South African life, and especially women's experiences and emotions, during the country's most turbulent years of antiapartheid activism.

My argument is supported, I believe, by Boitumelo Mofokeng's challenge, in "Where Are the Women? Ten Years of *Staffrider*," to the editors of a 1988 anthology of the best poetry from that literary journal, an anthology that excluded black women's voices. According to Mofokeng, this collection suggests that women's contribution to *Staftrider* was almost nonexistent, but she knows otherwise and sees no justification for this erroneous presentation. "The international world has been denied the opportunity of knowing and understanding the role of women writers, especially black women writers, in South Africa," Mofokeng claims. She argues that this omission seems especially inexcusable when one considers the strengths of women writing during the period on which the anthology focuses, 1978–88: the women's "strong political awareness," their vital accounts of protests and uprisings, the "spontaneity, truth, and authenticity" of their poetry. After listing eleven women, including herself, whose poetry might have been included in the anthology, Mofokeng offers this indictment: "We have heard much in the last few years, about the importance of women's 'Breaking the Silence'; these women who wrote and performed their work have broken it. But this anthology, which ignores or forgets their work, has been reimposing silence on them." She concludes by inviting poets whose poetry is anthologized to insist on an equitable representation of black women in any work in which their writing appears, and by exhorting black women to keep writing, denounce all racial and gender discrimination, and establish networks with other women writers.[11]

I hope to contribute to breaking this silence by examining four thematic/political categories of black women's resistance poetry in South Africa written from 1972 to 1988: (1) poetry in arms, written by participants in Umkhonto we Sizwe (known in South Africa as MK) and by the ANC's exiled supporters; (2) prison poetry, written surreptitiously by and about black women political prisoners and detainees; (3) resistance poems by and about domestic workers, black women traditionally among South Africa's most oppressed, who have risked their jobs to write about their lives and their treatment at the hands of white women, white men, and, in some cases, black men; and (4) women's *izibongo*, Zulu praise poems, which invite us to redefine the term *resistance*. These poems document the power and commitment of millions of African women who, as Gcina Mhlope urges them to do, "say No / When they give you a back seat / in the liberation wagon / . . . A Big NO."

1

> Suddenly there are women poets from South Africa. Phenomenal, some might
> want to acclaim. Praise and accolades is not what these women are after. They
> clearly want your heart, eyes and nerves to move your mind to what they know,
> so that understanding afresh, you might be inclined to act accordingly.
> —Sono Molefe, editor, *Malibongwe*

> Today
> the sons and daughters of Africa
> embrace the weapons of our struggle
> with guns and truth
> and swear
> that our mother shall be
> returned to us
> —Ilva Mackay, "Mayibuye"

A significant body of poetry-in-arms written by South African women
was published in 1982 by the ANC in Sweden in a collection entitled
Malibongwe [In Praise of Women].[12] As part of the ANC's celebration
of the Year of the Woman, this publication reveals in its subtitle—
ANC Women: Poetry Is Also Their Weapon—both the secondary status
that women and their writing had been accorded, even within the
antiapartheid movement, and the organization's belief in the power
of poetry as a weapon to challenge the status quo and construct
counterhegemonic knowledge. The choice of the third-person pro-
noun *their*, instead of *our*, reflects the volume's overall deemphasis
of gender issues, of women's proclaiming the need for their own
emancipation, in favor of an emphasis on the struggle for national
liberation. Some poems in *Malibongwe* offer no overtly gendered per-
spective—for example, poems warning the oppressors that justice
and the ANC will prevail, encouraging comrades to keep the faith,
celebrating the founding of the ANC or MK, or honoring the move-
ment's fallen or imprisoned male leaders. Other poems, however,
do reveal the women poet-combatants' sense of themselves as
women. This is especially evident in their tributes to heroic women
and children, in the use of childbirth imagery throughout the volume,
and in their portrayal of South Africa as a maternal figure. The an-
thology's editor, Sono Molefe, emphasizes the women's collective
voice: "Who are these women? As any of them will tell, they are no

striking personalities individually." Their collaborative goal, she explains, is to engage their readers' eyes and hearts and nerves, to change our minds, to move us to support or join in revolutionary action.

Despite Molefe's emphasis on the collection as "solidly communal," she does identify the poets by the myriad roles and activities in which they have participated, thus challenging traditional literary presentations of black women as objects rather than subjects by presenting them as agents of change: "There are those who battled police, their dogs and bullets on the streets of their country in 1976. There are students and former school-teachers. There are trained soldiers, daughters of workers; militant patriots fully engaged in the continuous act of liberation, one and all, struggle is their chosen path." The women range in age from fifteen to fifty; they are lovers of the African revolution who "speak as one." The editor also addresses the thorny question of a revolutionary aesthetic, making no apology for the overtly political, even propagandist, nature of the poems; their themes are justice and its aberrations, she claims, their aesthetic "thrillingly new: nerve-filled and public" (4–5).

Ilva Mackay's poem "Mayibuye" [Come Back] illustrates well the collective revolutionary awareness of which Molefe speaks:

> Mayibuye . . .
> the sons and daughters of Africa remain hopeful
> one day
> some day
> our mother will be returned to us,

the first stanza begins. The language is strikingly optimistic, even idealistic; the key image is that of the lost mother whose children long for her embrace and feel certain they will be reunited. The second stanza, in contrast, reflects a harsher reality and offers a searing cultural critique:

> Yesterday
> armed with stones
> and determination
> the voices of freedom
> echoed from

Soweto to Cape Flats
Gelvandale to Kwa Mashu
as Vorster's henchmen
murdered man and child.

This stanza reveals the power of memory as a revolutionary tool, as
the speaker evokes the reader's anger at the government's atrocities
and her pride in the people's rebellion. Naming townships and
"homelands" (Soweto, Cape Flats, Kwa Mashu, etc.) as sites of resis-
tance—rather than as sites of oppression, as the government and its
lackeys ("Vorster's henchmen") would dictate—represents a form of
collective empowerment of African people. The poet ends with a
strong, if predictable, statement of militant determination: "with
guns and truth," the people will triumph (46).

Certainty about the justice of their cause also pervades two po-
ems about the formation of Umkhonto we Sizwe; the two are similar
in thematic purpose—the assertion of what Barbara Harlow calls
"their own polemical historicity"—but strikingly different in idiom
and tone.[13] Lindiwe Mabuza's "December 16" is a historically rich
account, directed to her comrades-in-arms, of what took place on
December 16, 1961, when ANC leaders, having heretofore embraced
nonviolent strategies, felt compelled to take up the spear in their own
defense. Mabuza acknowledges her goal of providing a revolutionary
education, for, like herself, many of her MK peers were too young
to be present at that vital historical moment:

We neither heard Mandela's trumpet
Stirring and mustering to national duty
Millions of poised waiting lions
Nor were we in Tambo's mind
As he carried us around the globe
Dissecting for the world to see
Our lands and fields overflowing
With rivers and rivers
Of our own precious blood.

As Nelson Mandela called up the lions—the ANC's favorite meta-
phor for its militant agents, especially its youth—Oliver Tambo took
his country's cause around the world. Mabuza goes on to pay hom-

age to other elder statesmen: Walter Sisulu, whose heart hammered
as he helped to forge MK; Chief Albert Luthuli, the first president of
the ANC, who justified the move from nonviolence as essential self-
defense. Even those not present in 1961, the poet exhorts, can thrill
to Luthuli's historic words:

> I am an African
> And if the enemy comes into my home
> To attack both myself and my family
> Then I as an African
> Must take up my spear and fight.

The poem's final stanza rests on the paradox of presence and ab-
sence, for surely the spirit can be where the flesh was not.

> Absent we were there
> Because we all now agree
> That this pain
> Will not repair
> Before the sharpening of all our spears
> Deep inside racist and fascist bones.

A vengeful reckoning is essential to eliminate racism and fascism in
South Africa, Mabuza declares; MK's goal, the restoration of stolen
land to its rightful owners, must, of necessity, be militant. "Decem-
ber 16" reveals the role of resistance poetry as part of a noncanonical
historical process that requires taking sides: building allies and nam-
ing enemies. Mabuza employs a technique described by Nicaraguan
militant poet Ernesto Cardenal as *exteriorismo*, the documentation of
daily historical events and the key actors in struggle as a contribution
to creating an alternative history (19–20).

Baleka Kgositsile's "Umkhonto" offers less a historical catalog of
leaders and events essential to the formation of MK than an emotion-
ally intense praisesong honoring its existence. Where Mabuza con-
cerns herself with the organization's history and goals, Kgositsile
celebrates its spiritual power. Her controlling metaphor is rhythm,
her intent the evocation of ancient drums still present, though threat-
ened by agents of colonization. The poem itself pulsates on the page,
an urgent dance in which readers are invited to participate.

Rhythm
feet so precise
to the left
to the right
to the songs
we sing now
our voice beckoned
from the past of the future
will be pronounced
medicine or poison
rhythm
this dance is our future
moving with the clumsy
or graceful vigour of the present
to the song of today
echoed in our tomorrow

The "dance" extolled here may well be the carefully regulated steps of MK military trainees; the poet, in any event, portrays their movement as alternately fluid and regimented. Her tone quickly becomes didactic, as the poet urges her comrades never to stop this dance, which joins the present to the past and the future.

In the dance's forceful rhythms, Kgositsile continues, can be found "my child's motive," which she reveals as the "anxiety to live." Determined to protect her child, the poet experiences

brutality
anger
and resolve
flowing in her maternal veins:
through this umbilical cord
rhythm
to the sound of those heavy drops
from millions of black bodies
to the tears of emaciated children
to the endless sweat of the toiling parents.

The poet's vision is inextricably linked to her viewpoint as a mother, preserver of life for her children and her people. As a mother, however, she is also a revolutionary, aware not only of her own children's struggle for liberation but also those of other African people with whom she is in solidarity. Hence, Kgositsile displays her consciousness of the larger historical arena in which she writes:

> only yesterday my brothers
> from Angola and Mozambique
> danced a protracted step
> to the song
> of exploitation.

Today, in contrast, a fresh smell pervades

> the morning air of Africa
> the beginning of the end
> of the stench of colonialism.

RESISTANCE, one of twelve words capitalized for emphasis in this lengthy poem, is identified as

> the rhythm that gave birth to us
> and the dance we bear
> . . . this is our dance to the
> rhythm
> of centuries of NO!

Resistance, for Kgositsile, is

> the dance of now
> in the bush
> in the city
> in the ghetto
> in the kitchen
> in the factory.

It is resistance to the murder by police of unarmed African workers at Sharpeville in 1961, the event that led to the formation of MK; resistance to the killing of Hector Peterson, the first schoolchild shot in Soweto in 1976; resistance expressed through affiliation with other

African movements for self-determination—ZAPU, ZANU, SWAPO, PLO, POLISARIO. In these final stanzas, "Umkhonto" is stringently polemical, as Kgositsile catalogs acts of racist violence that have compelled her people to dance to "rhythms spat out by the gun"—to form MK, the source of

> grenades and guns
> that sing the song
> my people want to hear.

Until South Africa is free, the poet concludes, the only "motive song" available to her people is self-sacrifice, "our right to / DIE TODAY TO LIVE TOMORROW" (15–18).

Other poets from *Malibongwe* address directly the white, colonial oppressor and thus fulfill the dual role of lambasting the enemy and provoking their comrades to retribution. Phumzile Zulu's "You Are Mad: And I Mean It" illustrates well this subgenre of outrage. "What did you mean when you called me benighted / Savage pagan barbarian," the furious speaker begins, cataloging the insults hurled against her across time.

> You must have been mad
> I know now
> I say it and I mean it.

This poem and its counterparts are characterized foremost by fury, followed closely by a refusal to back off or down: the poet must express, and the oppressor hear, the full weight of injustice. Zulu goes on to indict those Christian hypocrites who called themselves "Good Samaritans" but wished only to steal her people's fertile lands:

> You had come here to explore my wealth
> Bloody spy in camouflage of a missionary
> Did you think you would succeed forever and ever?

The main thrust of this poem and similar poems is to warn the oppressor that his game is over, his time is up, the lies exposed. The poet's strategy is to hurl angry truths as weapons, via rhetorical questions and absolutist assertions:

You have failed with your BANTU EDUCATION
. . . You stole my forefathers' land
. . . I am not going to stand your lie
. . . You requested that I give you fresh water and vegetables
. . . my blood has become your water
My body your vegetables.

Like many black South Africans, the transgression that most infuri-
ates Zulu is the theft of her communal identity, her people's claims
to nationhood and self-determination on the land that is rightfully
theirs. Her poem ends with a fierce denunciation of colonization:

You tell me you are going to give me scattered portions
Of my own soil
And now you claim that this is a whiteman's country
You forget how you came here
You are a fool
You are mad
And I mean it!

(116–17)

Lerato Kumalo's "No More Words Now" challenges another
form of white oppression, that of well-meaning liberals in the United
States who agree that apartheid is wrong but who attack the ANC's
commitment (from the 1960s through the 1980s) to militancy. This
poem's controlling strategy is irony: How can the ladies and gentle-
men of America, who acknowledge so readily that "apartheid is a
crime against / humanity" and that they are complicit in this crime,
pale at the thought of countermilitant action? "I read but scorn your
logic," the poet insists,

that violence begets violence
when you supply guns and money
to those who had them, have had them and have them,
that two wrongs don't make a right
when countless times
you veto my freedom
at the United Nations

that diplomacy works wonders
when you fatten on the blood of my people.

The U.S. policy of constructive engagement, operative throughout the Reagan and Bush years, provokes the poet's disgust and fury; she counters it by offering its proponents a logic of her own, which emerges "from piles of dead bodies / and the necks struggling under the yoke." The true litmus test of whose logic makes sense is a survey of the oppressed themselves:

ask them what they think of me
"a nice girl like you" as you put it
when I shoulder with pride
this AK 47.

Enough of your "cocktail party wisdom," Kumalo concludes bitterly, you who were also silent as Hitler exterminated the Jews. She prefers her actions to the liberals' empty words:

No more words now
till our Nuremberg trials
judge the rallies
and weigh Munich.

(118–19)

The militant women poets of *Malibongwe* perform certain functions that black women have traditionally performed in rural societies: they tell stories meant to be passed on from one generation to another, and, in so doing, they encode the cultural, social, and spiritual values of the group. Their poems, furthermore, are similar in many respects to the protest poetry of black men of the 1970s and 1980s, which is characterized by a strong political awareness, catalogs of heroes and martyrs, angry repetition, and the promise of retribution. In Harlow's terms, these poets have responded to the catastrophic disruption of their cultural and literary traditions under colonialism by reappropriating history. Part of any such reappropriation, notes poet Ingrid de Kok, is to challenge the Nationalist government's silencing of atrocities, to "concretize subjects that too often have been left vague and generalized and therefore historically un-specific and safe."[14] Also, since it is difficult to be individualistic in a traditionally oral society, these poets deemphasize individual subjec-tivities in favor of collective consciousness. As Harlow puts it, private poetic identities are dismembered only to be "re-membered" and reconstructed in solidarity.[15] Allegiances forged in MK, and among ANC activists in exile, were stronger for having been illegal—so strong that leaders incarcerated on Robben Island were for years forbidden in speaking to use the pronoun *we*.

ANC women's determination to defy this ban may be one reason why many of their poems do not deal with gender-specific issues, leading feminist scholar Lynda Gilfillan to argue that the *Malibongwe* poets relate totally to the ANC men's agenda for struggle instead of formulating their own.[16] Although I agree with Gilfillan that these poems invite readers to problematize and redefine the concept "women's writing," I would emphasize that parts of *Malibongwe* do contrast sharply with sections such as "Birth and Genocide," in which the poets portray themselves as mothers and wives of male soldiers, or "Our Men Who Fought and Died and Fight," where they extol male heroism. In the section entitled "Women in Struggle," for instance, their revolutionary reclamation is gendered *and* liberatory, as women are honored for their centrality in the struggle and for their efforts as revolutionary agents.

The ten poems that constitute this section pay homage to the collective strength of women activists from 1913, the inaugural year of the ANC, to 1982, as well as to individual women whose heroism the poets find praiseworthy. Among the women leaders foregroun-ded are Charlotte Maxeke, a founding member of the ANC and the primary organizer of the 1913 women's anti-pass campaign; Lilian Ngoyi, prime mover of the 1954 protest against passes, in which 20,000 women of all races confronted Prime Minister Strydom in Pretoria; Helen Joseph, a white ANC freedom fighter who was the first person ever to be placed under house arrest by the Nationalist government; and Dorothy Nyembe, who served two prison sen-tences during the 1950s Defiance campaigns and, in 1956, led a con-tingent of women from Natal to protest at the Union buildings in Pretoria.[17] Also honored are the poets' resistant mothers and grand-mothers, especially rural South African women, who perform tradi-tionally female nurturing tasks as well as heavy physical labor once done, before homelands and poverty necessitated urban migration for rural men, by their male counterparts.

Jumaimah Motaung's "The Great Day—August 9th" (now the date of Women's Day in South Africa) will serve to illustrate the concern for gender issues prevalent in the "Women in Struggle" section of *Malibongwe*. Here the poet pays tribute to "Our mothers, / marching" on Pretoria in 1956, resistant to the government's insistence that they, like African men, take up the pass:

> They heard the call
> They came together and shared ideas
> They all had one aim in mind
> To show the regime
> They were not what the regime thought they were—robots.

These women chose to challenge not only the Nationalists' stereotypical notions of them, however, but also their husbands' resistance to their wives' entrance into the political sphere.

> One husband might have reprimanded the wife,
> "What do you people think you are up to?"
> And the wife might have answered bravely,
> "We know our aims and objectives
> We mean to carry them out."

As Gilfillan has noted, especially telling in this poet's imagined recreation of a dialogue between husband and wife is her decision to have the husband speak in the language of the oppressor, addressing his wife and her comrades-in-struggle as "you people."[18] Women's defiance of patriarchal oppression, Motaung implies through the wife's response, has never been restricted to the public venue. The poet ends by heralding again these valiant mothers, who marched

> carrying us on their backs
> Gallant heroes of the time
> . . . Your Mother, My Mother
> Our Mothers

(58)

Despite a tendency to conflate women and mothers throughout
Malibongwe, this poem and others that focus on women's resistance
reveal that the volume's emphasis on liberatory politics rather than
feminism should not belie the fact that ANC women poets did and
do write from a gendered consciousness.

    Gcina Mhlope, a writer, an actress, and a performer at the Mar-
ket Theatre in Johannesburg, has not been a member of MK, but her
poem "We Are at War" offers one final example of a gendered call-to-
arms by a woman poet committed to struggle:

    Women of my country
    Young and old
    Black and white
    We are at war
    The winds are blowing against us
    . . . But do not despair
    We are the winning type
    Let us fight on
    Forward ever
    Backward never.

Mhlope's poem employs a strategy typical of revolutionary poetry
by women and men, that of direct address to her comrades. Signifi-
cantly, however, those comrades are here defined exclusively as
women of her country, "mothers and daughters / workers and
wives." "We Are at War" is an urgent call to solidarity by a woman
to women—those most negatively affected by laws that are sexually
exploitative as well as racist. Mother Africa is as degraded as her
daughters are, Mhlope contends, but, if we drink her tears, we can
consume her courage. Like many other revolutionary poets, Mhlope
links South Africa's struggling women to those throughout the conti-
nent: "women of Egypt and Libya / . . . women of Zambia and Zim-
babwe." Mother Africa's tears race down all her countries' rivers,
Mhlope's catalog reveals, as she names the Nile, the Congo, the
Zambezi, the Limpopo, the Thuleka, and the Kei, waterways con-
nected by injustice and exploitation. If women do unite against sex-
ism, racism, and imperialism, her poem concludes, the "chained
women of Africa," linked, are "bound to win."[19]

    Despite these poets' commitment to militancy, they acknowledge that it exacts a high price, especially for the lonely exile attempting to combat isolation and despair. The world of the exile is one of simultaneously expanding and contracting horizons, notes South African scholar J. U. Jacobs; outside the country, resistance poets are less susceptible to their government's repressive maneuvers but may be plagued by cultural alienation, psychic anxiety, and creative debilitation.[20] For ANC women exiles, this exilic consciousness often takes the form of acute introspection coupled with intense feelings of connection with comrades. Baleka Kgositsile's "Exile Blues" attempts to effect catharsis through the time-honored black strategy of singing the blues. "Let them roll / let the blues roll out," the poet begins, insisting at once that, as a woman, she has as much right and power to sing the blues as any man. " 'This load is heavy it requires men' / has nothing to do with baritone or beard." A prescription for staying sane that transcends gender, singing the blues helps any militant to reduce "the unaccountable miles / between you and home," to grapple with whether "it was worth your leaving the loved ones."

The poet's exilic consciousness forces her to be frank in cataloging the ways in which separation from home, in all its powerful evocations, can threaten one's revolutionary resolve. Paralysis can set in; addiction to gossip or masochism can emerge; inferiority complexes can reign. "You put the stamp / on your own death certificate," Kgositsile warns her comrades and herself,

> . . . when you drink yourself insensible
> into the gaping void
> . . . when you feel trapped
> suffocating cornered
> at a cul de sac
> and your tears roll down uncontrollably
> as memories invade you daily.

The most effective solution to the pain of exile, she asserts, is to "let them blues roll out / . . . till oblivion sneaks to your rescue." Later, when your load is lighter, you can "retrieve the zeal that made you leave home." Only once the blues have been expressed can an exile in despair again affirm her resolve.[21]

Malibongwe is not the only source of South African exilic women's poetry from the 1970s and 1980s. Three poems by Barbara Masekela, published in 1982 in the U.S.-based anthology *Somehow We Survive*, echo Kgositsile's concern with combating despair and interrogating the revolutionary consciousness of the exile. In "Demon Exile" the speaker likens herself to an insect mounted to a wall and subjected to intense, painful self-scrutiny. "My resolve is outstared," she begins,

> Mother-hunger
> Father-craving
> Sister hankering
> Myriad blood longings
> Mushroom
> Mount me here
> On needle point
> Labeled self reliance.

Pain of loss, guilt, and feelings of inadequacy stalk the exiled poet; despite her intention to be strong-willed and autonomous, her speaker longs incessantly for the family members she has left behind. Furthermore, like Salvadoran poet Claribel Alegría, Masekela finds that, outside the known contexts of family and home, she has difficulty recognizing herself:

> My scarred face alien mask
> Shaded and rouged
> Jumps at me
> In crowded windows
> Concealed mirrors
> Reflect eyes raised in inquiry
> At an imposter rushing towards me.

The image of this imposter blurs as the speaker fights back tears, only to merge with her own troubled reflection as the glass splinters at the impact of this untimely union.

As Masekela reveals in "Uthekwane," however, the exile sometimes evokes her pain deliberately, for in the memories it signals can be found remnants of sweetness and sensuality as well as the complex rhythms of exorcism. Having "fetched" the pain, the speaker proceeds to

waft in and out of it
Exorcizing demon memories
And a bloody fetus of love.

It is striking that in both poems Masekela demonizes her exilic consciousness as an other with whom she must wrestle, who threatens her sanity and survival. In the second stanza of "Uthekwane" she addresses directly a lover left behind, whose imprint can still be found upon her bereft body:

Your absence is a thorn
Quick and sharp
On my left heart
In between my breasts
Where your head
Used to nestle.

Along with "mother-hunger" and "father-craving," perhaps more insistent even than those "blood longings," comes sexual desire for the absent beloved.

A third exilic poem by Masekela, "Where Are They Now," expresses public, political sentiments rather than private griefs, though certainly the poet's sense of physical and psychic distance from home informs this poem as well:

Where are they now
My people surrounded by the waters
At the Cape-of-no-Good-Hope
The lifers at Robben Island
Whose words banned by order
Travel in sudden choirs
Of adolescent voices
Raising apartheid death a dare?

More than "Demon Exile" or "Uthekwane," this poem reveals the poet's anger at the racist system that has provoked her leaders' resistance and imprisonment as well as her own banishment. It also pays homage to the youth of South Africa who rejuvenate their incarcerated leaders' songs and deal a death blow to apartheid. Primarily, however, it honors the Robben Island prisoners themselves, "the silenced ones," whose years of agonized waiting far exceed her own. At the back of their eyes, she claims,

> Years leap up
> Stand at attention
> Abandoning them
> In the rigid minutes of waiting.

Here Masekela alludes to the terrible conflation and expansion of time for the imprisoned or the exiled—hours that fly away as memories align today and yesterday, excruciating minutes that drag on like decades. Her controlling theme and image is that of waiting: for the leaders' release, for the revolution to succeed, for society to be transformed. Implicit in her portrait of the waiting leaders is Masekela's own exilic dilemma, a stasis born of distance and forced detachment from the center of the struggle. Her words remind us that exiles are both products and determinants of South African history, the victims of apartheid and its potential executioners.[22]

2

> I've been endorsed out of my community
> Into the Homeland of my cell—
> Dark dull grey dreary—where even a
> Smile is scarce!
> —Gertrude Fester, "This Is the Reality"

> Toilet paper! / Ya comrade / Manna from heaven
> —Jessie Duarte, "Toilet Paper"

Another type of forced removal that black South African women poets document is political imprisonment.[23] Three poems by ANC activist Gertrude Fester, written while in police detention and in solitary confinement at Pollsmoor Prison during 1987-88, reveal the range of emotions and thoughts this poet experienced during her incarceration. "This Is the Reality," the most documentary of the three, combines *exteriorismo* with internal scrutiny as the poet describes her daily life in prison, explores her identification with the poor, with and for whom she struggles, and asserts her unwavering commitment to societal transformation. A so-called colored woman from Cape Town, and thus relatively economically privileged, Fester acknowledges the particular oppression of Africans under apartheid, likening her sentence of solitary confinement to the government's removal of Africans to distant homelands under the Group Areas Act, an experience that thousands have suffered in South Africa since the formal imposition of apartheid in 1948:

> I have been forcefully removed
> From my cosy and cushioned cocoon
> To a Group Area reserved for terrorists:
> Solitary Confinement.

In ironically naming herself a terrorist, Fester implicitly challenges the apartheid regime for its failure to admit its own terrorist actions, especially the theft of African people's lands and their forced dislocations and relocations. This label, and her identification with other banished folk, gives the poet courage. Thus, when she is watched closely by guards looking for one false move, she takes heart in recalling the daily scrutiny to which her African sisters and brothers are subjected when they

> enter a supermarket or shop.
> The floorwalkers are on guard!
> These are the people who steal!
> Their every twist, each turn is carefully perused.
> And here—my every turn, twist too is controlled
> A recording is made of what I eat, how much
> . . . Where and when I sit, stand, shit or sleep!

Her indignities are no worse than those suffered daily by others, she realizes; like them, she lacks the government-mandated "pass to humanity." The difference is that her suffering is finite:

> Thousands, millions
> Drudgingly eke out
> This degradation all
> Their lives.

What she describes here, the poet concludes on a note of anger and retribution, is "the South African Reality. / BUT NOT FOR LONG!"

A second poem by Fester, "It's Carnival Time," explores the moments of relief that sounds from the outside world afford the prisoner in an urban jail. On this particular Saturday night, a carnival is in progress, and the speaker is heartened by its blaring music,

> first harsh and strident, then softer, then
> Crackling with interference
> Depending on how the wind blows.

In depicting the vagaries of the carnival sounds, the poet alludes to the caprice of her captors, whose noises seem as arbitrary and riotous as those of the vendors she overhears. But the vivid sounds of a robust humanity also induce the poet's nostalgia:

> I can almost see lovers walking hand in hand
> Eating either ice cream or mielies.
> Parents indignantly digging in their pockets
> As children swear this is the umpteenth last round;
> And the more fastidious in some dark corner
> Trying to eat enormous hamburgers in a delicate fashion,
> Onion rings dangling down the sides of their mouths.

Fester's irrepressible humor is evident here, as nostalgia gives way to ironic pleasure in the implacable human quest for dignity, even when combating one's hamburger. Her humor is short-lived, however, as she strains to hear an unintelligible announcement and recognizes in its wake the pain of isolation:

> This cacophony
> Bombards me where I sit
> Alone
> In my dark dreary cell.

A third poem, "The Spirit Cannot Be Caged," reveals the political prisoner at a resolute moment, reveling in what it means to be human, to be resistant, and to survive. "This is a celebration to life," the poet claims,

I want to sing   shout   dance   whirl   twirl
teasing the sunlight
My spirit effervesces champagne
in finely cut crystal glasses.

Outside her cell in her mind's eye, she imagines herself free to indulge in spirited rituals of hope—communal ones like drinking champagne with friends, solitary ones like gazing at "the moon in azure skies." "I stretch my arms out wide," the poet concludes exuberantly,

I grow tall as trees
And take a deep breath of beauty
I embrace the whole world wantonly
Become one with it
red sun
turquoise moon.

Here Fester joins a distinguished lyric tradition in promoting the theme of the spirit that cannot be captured; prison, however, occurs not just in the imagined world, as she reveals by signing and dating her poetic document: "Gertrude, Pollsmoor 3/11/88."[24]

In 1992 COSAW (the Congress of South African Writers) published the first collection of women's writing from prison, *A Snake with Ice Water*. Its editor, Barbara Schreiner, an ANC activist from Cape Town, describes South Africa correctly as a "criminalized society" due to political resistance and economic disparities between blacks and whites under apartheid. She notes that, in 1989, there were 111,557 South Africans in prison per day, 4,500 of whom were women. Seventy percent of accused persons were not represented by lawyers, and, despite the Nationalist government's claims of the best rehabilitation rates in the world, between 60 and 80 percent of all prisoners return to jail. Because of such extraordinary incarceration rates, Schreiner notes, South Africa has a long tradition of prison literature, a tradition from which women's voices, especially black women's, have usually been excluded.[25] For this reason, she includes in this collection interviews with black women prisoners along with poems, stories, and essays by women of all races.

Two poems from this book convey with particular poignancy what it meant to be a female political prisoner in South Africa during the 1980s; these poems, like many, treat also the theme of writing as subversive activity. The first, Arona Dison's "Pollsmoor, 15 July, 1986," was written on a tissue with the pen of a detainee with study rights and later smuggled out of prison in a packet of sanitary pads. The author, a white woman activist detained for fifteen days for illegal pamphleteering on behalf of a progressive political organization, recognizes both her privilege and her ignorance as she watches and listens from her cell to the resistance efforts of her black cohorts. The poem begins with an epigraph from the *Cape Times* newspaper, dated August 11, 1986: "On the 14 July black women detainees in Pollsmoor were tear-gassed through the bars of their communal cell by prison authorities when they demanded to see the security police to furnish a reason for their detention."

> A Pen is a dangerous weapon
> You may not have one in your cell
> here in Pollsmoor
> where the white women detainees
> are treated oh-so-well
> by South African standards.

Dison's opening lines portray ironically the government's realization that the prisoners' written revelation of the atrocities they experience is their most powerful tool; hence, they forbid writing instruments to all but a few whites and to every black woman. When supper is served at 3:30 (to meet the wardens' needs, not the prisoners'), the poet continues,

> the depression from the realisation
> that you'll soon be locked in
> for the night
> starts sinking in.

Isolation and immobility cripple and silence prisoners of conscience; especially difficult for Dison is hearing women's screams nearby and being able to do nothing. When the screams stop— screams of black women, the poet implies—they begin to sing

    songs of freedom
    but we
    white women
    don't know the words
    don't want to lose the slight rights and privileges
    that we have.

Thus, the white women lie in their cells in solitude and silence. Most
compelling about Dison's poem is the tension it reveals between her
envy of the black women prisoners' solidarity and her inability or
unwillingness to forgo white privilege to achieve community, an
awareness she treats with bitter irony in her final stanza:

    And we lie and listen
    to the other dangerous,
    locked away sonder trial, sonder lawyer
    detainees
    singing
    "let there be love spread amongst us . . .
    . . . Nkosi Yam—My God"

                                                            (167–68)

The poet foregrounds racial difference in her use of the plural pro-
noun we, situating herself with other white women, outsiders to the
spirit of song; in her choice of the Afrikaans preposition sonder, in-
stead of without; and in her inclusion of the Xhosa language celebra-
tion of "Nkosi Yam" sung by the black women. Her sense of alle-
giance with black women struggling against the government, despite
racial barriers, is evident in her ironic labeling of the women as "dan-
gerous" in their call for brotherly and sisterly love. Still, it is clear
that her identification with black women prisoners is far more tenu-
ous than that of Fester, herself a woman of color. This poem is note-
worthy for its candid account of racist complicity, even on the part
of those white women who have themselves been jailed for further-
ing the antiapartheid struggle, and its unequivocal portrait of the
strength and community of incarcerated black women.
    Jessie Duarte's "Toilet Paper" portrays the futility that prisoners

sometimes experience when their efforts to speak on their own behalf
fail to evoke change. Simply to receive toilet paper in a South African
prison is miraculous, especially if one is black and female:

> Now we use it to wipe
> arses, then to blow noses
> or to write a poem on . . . .
> or better still . . . .
> we use it to write
> an impassioned plea for
> release to minister of law and order
> and then he stuffs it in
> his ear!

                                                                    (178)

Duarte's wry poem touches indirectly upon a concern Barbara Schrei-
ner raises in her introduction to *A Snake with Ice Water*: the psycho-
logical damage incurred by women political prisoners, whose isola-
tion from family ties, years of condemnation to boredom and often
meaningless labor, and lack of privacy in communal cells often result
in what one analyst has termed "the gradual disintegration of the
individual's sense of self worth and personal identity." Furthermore,
Schreiner notes that many women prisoners, once out, recall with
horror that the sterile grey prison environment and the hostilities
between wardens and prisoners were especially unnerving (3–4). It
is this latter issue that Duarte's poem addresses, since wardens often
exert their authority by withholding toilet paper and other "ameni-
ties" (with women, it frequently is sanitary napkins) from rebellious
prisoners, particularly if they are black. To have access to toilet paper
is "manna from heaven" for the black female political prisoner, Du-
arte asserts, yet to invest in it not only one's intimate words of self-
expression but also one's hopes for freedom, via mercy by the op-
pressor, may well be an act of self-delusion.

    Poetry about incarceration is also written by women who have
not themselves experienced prison but have heard the narratives of
their sisters. Mavis Smallberg's "June" illustrates this type of poem,
in which the poet serves as mediator, juxtaposing the storyteller's
account with her own (and other listeners') reflections and response
in a manner akin to Coleridge's speaker, who recounts with horror

and awe the rhyme of the ancient mariner. English Romantic tradition, however, cannot adequately document the atrocities of which South African activists speak. The narrative is starkly realistic, framed on either end by brief descriptions of the narrator herself—her husky voice, dark and gleaming skin, inner strength—and of her audience, whose pained anticipation is matched only by the tension in the woman's own face. Smallberg uses the stylistic device of the inverted sentence to dramatize the incipient tale and invoke her reader's suspense:

> Everyone remained quite still
> When slowly, out of nowhere,
> Her tale this pregnant space
> Began to fill.

The metaphor of pregnant space, of nothing waiting to be filled with something, is of course intensely maternal; the syntactic inversion prefigures the monstrous distortion of human decency to which the female political prisoner is subjected. Within Smallberg's frame lies her speaker's narrative, an ominous tale of "two huge men / with deadened eyes" who invade her prison cell at night and force her from already violable space into a waiting car, toward an unknown destination. Shock and fear beset the prisoner, who recalls a warning that,

> If they take you from the prison
> To the Square,
> Beware!

When at last she sees a sparsely furnished interrogation room and six burly men, she knows her worst fears have been realized.

Smallberg goes on to present, via dramatic monologue, her speaker's harrowing account of her repeated beatings, of tufts of hair littering the floors, of hearing from a distance her own screams of pain. Most important to the speaker is her revelation of refusing to beg for mercy or reveal the information sought:

> My legs swelled up in protest
> My knees wobbled in sheer pain

My back was sore and aching
My head was cracked and bleeding,
Bleeding
Yet I still stood.

She attributes her resolve to feelings of solidarity with sisters and
brothers in struggle and to her commitment to her cause:

The cause I fight is just.
I do it through the people
I cannot do it on my own.

As the narrative continues, the speaker remains resolute, despite
hurled bottles, cigarette burns, a nearly broken neck. At last, con-
vinced that their violence will not cause her to break, the disgusted
interlocutors return her to her cell, where concerned inmates try to
treat her wounds. As she worsens, however, her comrades rebel
against their incarcerators, insisting that the prison guards hospital-
ize her. Later, misogyny emerges as a tool of systemic oppression and
deception when the guards respond to the doctors' queries with a
sexist lie:

These women always fight amongst themselves,
And then complain,
Trying to give us the bloody blame!

But the speaker refutes this lie. Despite her semiconscious state, she
mutters her interlocutors' identities to the doctors, who, subse-
quently, see that the men are brought to trial.

In the poem's final section the speaker recounts her experience
of identifying her torturers in a police lineup, despite their threats of
reprisal:

One of them returned my look,
And slowly drew his finger past his throat.
But my mind was calm;
I felt so calm!
I did what needed to be done

And placed my hand upon the shoulder
Of each and every guilty one.

Smallberg's use of occasional rhyme adds a ballad quality to this saga, and, like the traditional ballad, its ending is not triumphant. The speaker concludes her story by revealing that her life is once again endangered as she awaits her captors' trials, threatened by the authorities who should protect her: "I fear the guardians of the state." Still, her determination is fierce, as her refrain reveals: "'I do it through the people / I could never do it on my own.'" Smallberg's external frame returns near the end of the poem, portraying an audience rapt until the speaker's desolate sigh and subsequent tears break their silence. Rising up as one to comfort her, her listeners heal with words as well as gestures; they sing the liberation songs so central to their people's struggle:

> . . . And echoes of the people's song
> We sang
> Permeated the air,
> Out into the Cape Flats night.[26]

A poem by Smallberg published in *A Snake with Ice Water* addresses a special concern of many South African women poets who write on imprisonment: the plight of the child detainee. The detainment, often without trial, of politically active children—and of children who happen onto a demonstration and thus find themselves in the wrong place at the wrong time—has been well documented since the Soweto uprisings of 1976, when thousands of children shouted down and threw rocks at police with tear gas and weapons in protest against the inequities of "Bantu" education. These children are generally treated as adults and thus have been subjected to the standard forms of abuse and torture used by the police during interrogation and incarceration.[27] In "Agreements" Smallberg speaks on behalf of child prisoners and castigates a government so fearful of its black population that it considers a refusal to do schoolwork a crime. "Each day brings a new sorrow," the poem begins,

> a new death
> a new deadened child

inconspicuous reports on page three
page four
page five:
"Boy, thirteen, must stay in detention"
says Supreme Court
"No work written in school books
since March"
what a hideous crime
what a villainous deed.

The poet's outrage is barely suppressed as she goes on to challenge
her government and its white citizenry to "look at all these sweet
young things / bright black blonde beautiful." All children should
be loved and seen as vital national resources, the poet implies, yet

some blacks are shoved in a cell
no spring flowers, no bright sky
no books, no pictures
no family
nobody.

The injustice of depriving a child of her or his freedom and family
speaks for itself, the poem suggests tersely; this is a crime for which
the society will pay for generations. Meanwhile, countless black im-
prisoned children experience each day

only buttoned brass
popping questions
popping heads

—the ruthless control of racist magistrates, judges, and welfare
agents collaborating in the determination that these children should
remain in prison. At times even God seems to be part of the conspir-
acy, Smallberg's ending implies, with its poignant question:

and you
lord, and
you?

(157–58)

The title *A Snake with Ice Water*, Schreiner tells us, comes from an interview with a woman who served several consecutive sentences for criminal rather than political offenses; "it symbolises the torture, monotony and myth that twine through and around the prison experience." Unlike Salvadoran women's prison narratives, which often chronicle rape and sexual abuse along with physical deprivation and psychological stress, the narratives offered in this collection document primarily the mental and physical, rather than sexual, torture of incarceration. Nor have South African poets yet taken up as subjects rape and sexual torture during incarceration. This is perhaps because most of the South African women whose prison experiences have been published are white, Indian, or so-called colored; under apartheid, even the most politically resistant white women have generally been protected from sexual violation, and in some instances Indian and "colored" women might have been similarly exempted, especially if they are middle-class. As Schreiner points out, however, the amount of material written by African and working-class women about incarceration "in no way matched the overwhelming majority of South African women that these sectors represent"; indeed, the apartheid system has silenced (or refrained from publishing) the voices of "the women at the bottom of the pile," those most vulnerable to sexual abuse. In *Barred* (1992) Barbara Harlow argues convincingly that "women detained by the security forces in South Africa are indeed held and interrogated in the 'cells of rapists,'" albeit rapists as yet unconvicted, despite international censure.[28] Once one person–one vote takes effect and black women feel safe to break this silence, it seems probable that accounts of sexual abuse and rape at the hands of police and prison guards will become subject matter for South African women's prison poetry.

3

Some call me Maid
Some call me Mary.
Is it so hard to be called Lekhutso?
                              —Roseline Naapo, "Alone I Sit in My Cell"

I am only human
give me what you want
for your sons and daughters

. . . I am not asking for your
mink coat Ma'am.
                        —Boitumelo Mofokeng, "Domestic Worker's Plea"

In examining the relationship between art and politics in South Africa,[29] the Natal Culture and Working Life Project has proposed an alternative aesthetic standard to both the militant precept that culture is a weapon of struggle and Eurocentric views of "quality" as detached, "pure" art. "Will the times we are living through be *remembered* through our work?" they wonder, suggesting an important criterion for evaluating artistic productions. As a project related to black workers, women, and youth, this project's investigators have been especially concerned with principles of participatory education that facilitate and promote grassroots creativity.[30] Among the population with whom the project has worked most closely are domestic workers and their union, the South African Domestic Workers' Union (SADWU); their goal is to insure that these times are accurately remembered through the creativity of their society's most oppressed. One of the best-known domestic worker poets, and also a staunch advocate of empowering women workers to write, is Roseline Naapo, now an organizer for SADWU. "I was not born with the knowledge of writing," Naapo admitted at a 1988 COSAW conference on women's writing; " . . . when I started going to school I learnt to have a little notebook to write about whatever problems I had on a particular day. These writings made me compile them into small poems, or plays." When she left school to become a domestic worker, she resolved to document the profession that, because of much suffering, she had been forced to undertake. "In the field of domestic work," Naapo explains, "it's not happy. It's not nice. You live in a beautiful room which they call a home. But you live alone. You are not allowed to have visitors, you are not able to live with your husband. You are separated from your family for many months. And your employer expects you to smile each morning when you come into her house."[31] Domestic worker poets like Naapo have chronicled their experiences of racism, discrimination, and economic exploitation along with the empowerment they have discovered through solidarity and writing. They have urged readers to realize that a truly just South Africa cannot be fully envisioned until the conditions of domestic workers improve dramatically.

A representative poem by Naapo, "Alone I Sit in My Cell," reveals the irony in her assertion that a typical domestic worker's room is "beautiful." The "cell" in which the speaker sits feels like prison, partly because of its size and partly because of her isolation:

> Alone I sit in my cell
> thinking of my poor children
> and husband.
> No-one to talk to
> nor listen to.

A frequent lament by domestic worker poets is how tired they become and how much they have to do; Naapo is "nurse, doctor, cook / you name it, I do." But most disturbing is the racial and gender politics of domestic work, which for many poets centers on the interrelated issues of identity and naming. How difficult can it be for an educated employer to say "Lekhutso," Naapo's speaker muses; why is it that the "madams" call us by their preferred title for us, "maid," or by Christian names they impose on us, she wonders wryly. The poem goes on to expose the country's rulers for the "reward" they have given for such good service: theft of the land of the workers' forefathers.

> How can you forget one
> who sacrificed her children
> to be with yours?

Naapo concludes her poignant indictment.

> Oh rulers of our country
> how can you forget me in your house
> how can you forget the lonely worker?[32]

It is important to note that Naapo indicts white women as well as men under the label "rulers of our country." The history of tensions and betrayals between white and black women under apartheid raises serious questions about whether and how nonracial sisterhood might ever be attained.

Inspired by Naapo's work, Boitumelo Mofokeng has written two poems in the voices of domestic workers in different situations. Mofokeng has never worked as a domestic but identifies with their plight as well as their resistance strategies; her poems also reveal her interest in the ways in which domestic work has changed over time. The first poem, "Inside a Domestic Worker," is set in the 1950s, when countless African women from the countryside left their homes due to poverty and starvation to seek a living wage in the cities and help their families. Fear of the unknown dominates the emotional landscape of this interior monologue:

> Where I am going
> I know no one
> My friends have gone there,
> they never returned
> I am sure they found work
> "God be with me and
> my ailing parents"
> I say as I pack my clothes
> and venture into the world
> which I know nothing about.

Aware of her lack of formal education, the young worker knows not what she will become, but she knows what kind of work she will be assigned:

> If I don't know arithmetic
> my hands will save me
> I can work in the "kitchens"
> My back can be a rocking horse
> for *kleinbassie*
> *Restig, Missus soek vir hardwerkers.*

The terrible truth of poverty and racism is told at the poem's end in the oppressor's language, Afrikaans: as a domestic worker, she will become a beast of burden as well as a toy the master's young son can enjoy. By validating the domestic worker's inner turmoil, Mofokeng contributes to the feminist project of breaking silence about women's historical exploitation.

"Inside a Domestic Worker (in the 1980s)" presents the voice of a more aggressive worker, yet her options for employment are more limited even than her predecessor's. An exterior rather than an interior monologue, this poem has two parts, an initial telephone call to a potential employer and an interview in her home. Part 1 is somewhat matter-of-fact until the last line, which conveys the twin themes of racism and erasure of identity:

> Good morning Madam
> I am responding to
> your advert in todays
> newspaper.
> I would like to come in for an interview.
> Thank you, Madam, I'll be there.
> Remember my name is Sophie.

As did the domestic worker in Naapo's poem, this woman identifies herself to her prospective employer by a Christian given name only; she knows that her own given name and her surname will be erased by another woman. Part 2 emphasizes further the racial and class divisions of women under every racist system, divisions most striking under apartheid. The worker must call the employer "Mrs. Vlak," a formal title and a solid Afrikaner surname, and must catalog her own capabilities in terms of what she does, not who she is:

> I can do general household cleaning
> washing and ironing
> cooking and baking
> babysitting
> telephone answering
> I can read and write
> I am learning to drive
> My hobbies include loving pets
> Is there anything else
> you would like to know?

At this point, and only here, does the madam speak, to ask the question foremost on her mind: "How much do you want?" The worker's response is eminently reasonable but, to the employer,

cheeky: "Pay for my every skill and service, / it all adds up to a living
wage." The woman in power delivers her response immediately and
emphatically: "NO, SORRY, YOU ARE OVERQUALIFIED."[33]

One of the first poems published by a black South African
woman on the plight of the domestic worker was Gladys Thomas's
"Leave Me Alone," from *Cry Rage!* (1972). Vacillating in tone between
plaintiveness and outrage, the poem addresses directly the madam
from the perspective of the maid.

> I tear my hungry babe from my breast
> To come and care for yours
> Yours grow up fine
> But, oh God, not mine
> From school and beach yours I fetch
> And wonder if mine school did reach.

The contrast between the certainty with which any white woman
may reflect on her children's well-being, largely because of the
black domestic worker's capable care, and the insecurity experi-
enced by most black women about the welfare of their own children
is striking, and it has been one of the most widely addressed
inequities in domestic workers' poetry. Thomas, however, also
examines here a topic often silenced, that of the domestic worker's
sexual deprivation:

> Your man comes home at night
> A welcome and delight
> Wine glass in hand
> Red chair in front of fire bright
> To bed you go and make love
> My bed is empty and cold
> For all my energy is drained away
> My man and I too soon feel old

The poem's simple language, its singsong rhythm and rhyme
scheme, belie the complexity of the problem of racial and class injus-
tices, perpetrated even by white women who are self-defined political

liberals against the black women whom they employ. Thomas confronts this tension directly in her last stanza, in which the domestic worker challenges her employer to examine her oppressive behavior:

> Can you still look me in the eye
> And ask me what's wrong
> After you've stripped me to the bone
> . . . What have I done that you won't leave me alone?[34]

The final poignant question reveals a degree of internalized oppression on behalf of the worker, whose tendency toward self-blame emerges even as she castigates the employer.

Some domestic workers have written and/or performed their work collectively, an experience that empowers through solidarity and provides a needed respite from their often sterile and exhausting daily routines. One such group, the Thula Baba Collective, has published a book of poems written down by Ntombi, a domestic worker who is also a literacy teacher. One poem, "Domestic Workers," raises the issue of who has the power to name and reveals this power as a source of workers' resentment:

> We are called girls. We are called maids.
> It is like we are small.
> It is like we are children.
> We are told what to do.
> We are told what to say.
> We are told what to think.
> We are told what to wear.

The poem's singsong, childlike repetition reinforces the hateful theme of adult women treated like children; it also reminds readers that for none of these women is English an indigenous language but, instead, the language of colonization, in which they are now forced to tell their stories if a wide audience is to hear. Claiming their right to name themselves, even in an alien tongue, lies at the heart of the collective's poem.

We are women.
We are mothers.
Our bodies are strong from hard work.
Our hearts are big from suffering.

This is who we are, the women insist upon revealing, and they are stronger because of their solidarity and resistance.

But we find friendship if we meet together.
And we find answers if we talk together.
And we find strength if we work together.
And we find hope if we stand together.[35]

The Progressive Arts Project (PAP) of the Market Theatre in Johannesburg, under the leadership of playwright and actor Irene Stephanou, also focused, in the mid- to late 1980s, on empowering domestic workers through performance of their own stories and poems. The original PAP group, composed of ten women and one man, originated through the friendship of Stephanou and Mary Thibedi, a domestic worker who "makes tea and generally has a hard time at a doctor's surgery" that Stephanou, a white woman of Greek origins, had occasion to visit. Having grown up with a domestic worker in her household, Stephanou felt that here is "the very real apartheid at work"; after exchanging stories at length with Thibedi, and through her meeting another domestic worker, Thandi Khoza, Stephanou suggested forming a writers' group to focus on these issues. A third domestic worker, Irene Mvelase, wrote the first work to be performed, and the group went on to entertain and move large audiences at several National Women's Day celebrations and to perform together for two years. Of special concern to these women is bad treatment by faithless men, as Khoza's "Women's Warning" reveals:

He can say to you: Make our baby, if you make
it we will be married.
After you have the baby he will disappear like
water into the ground.
You will never see him again.
Then you will suffer alone.

And then the person you work for will say there
is no more work because you are pregnant.

One problem caused by an errant man will inevitably lead to others,
she insists; "lots of women fall in the same deep hole." The prose-
poet sees it as her duty to warn young women not to make these
same mistakes, to listen to and learn from older women and consider
other options:

I say to young girls:
Do not run with the boys
Run with your education because it is your
future these days.
I say devils are hunting us,
but we can run from
them now, because we have seen them.

There is hope and strength in solidarity, Khoza concludes, even if the
outcome of collective efforts to outwit faithless men is not entirely
clear. "I wish we can run away from them all, all of us /women."[36]
    The women of PAP have also written a rap song that reinforces
the theme of Khoza's lament and exposes irresponsible men:

He says: "look dear—I don't mean to moan
I can't look after children—I've a life of my own."
He says he wants five kids—I've given him three
I say: "who goes into labour?—not you but me!"

Freedom of reproductive choice and freedom from sexual harassment
by police are two of the rap song's overriding themes.

The policeman says: "No money woman? well sleep with me
Do what I say and you can go free!"
I say: "Freedom?" and look in his eyes
"Freedom means equality—and no more lies."

Mary Thibedi, a major contributor to the rap and a songwriter, ex-
plains that she sees her songs as tools of education for the privileged:
"People are dying in South Africa. Some people don't even know

what is going on, so I would like to sing a song so that people can know what is happening." Another group member wishes to challenge sexism in her poems: "I wrote the poem because I wanted everybody to know about how the men treat the women. How men take us as slaves. I hope it will make people change how they behave—especially the men. I want them to understand that women can be friends." Women's liberation can no longer be sidelined until after national liberation, declared Barbara Schreiner, another PAP member during the late 1980s; this collective of black and white women, domestic workers and professional actors, was an attempt to insure that it would not be.[37]

The issue of domestic workers' exploitation arises also in poems by young black women who respect their mothers who did domestic work yet who have used their educational access to reject this profession for themselves. Roshila Nair's "But Oneday Madam" is a case in point. Nair, a black student at the prestigious and until recently segregated University of Cape Town, recounts in her poem a conflict with a white classmate, who challenged the poet's institutional loyalty when she questioned the meaning of her studies. "Do you remember that day," Nair asks her classmate, when

> I was ranting
> raving about how boxed-in I feel
> in class,
> that I want to snort
> on the words to analyse
> that very moment a life's being born
> and somebody's burning?

What is the value of all this when more people are dying than surviving, the poet wonders, to the dismay of her haughty friend:

> Then,
> your dark glasses enquired,
> why are you here?

At the time the poet evaded her colleague's question, but now she wants to set the record straight:

What I really wanted to say
is for to reduce the odds
my just becoming your maid,
oneday madam.[38]

The divisions of women under apartheid must be chronicled along-
side the quest for solidarity, Nair reminds us, and racism and class-
ism are terrible chasms to attempt to cross. "Maids and madams,"
the controversial subject of numerous analyses by women involved
in the South African liberation struggle, might be assisted in their
efforts to communicate across these canyons of difference by the
development of a feminist theory that "emerges from within the
ranks of those whose life is theorised."[39] Meanwhile, the efforts of
domestic worker advocates such as Roseline Naapo and Boitumelo
Mofokeng, along with the collaborative poetry of groups like Thula
Baba and PAP, remind women readers that any effort toward solidar-
ity "must rest on a simultaneous, mutually liberating recognition of
other women's difference."[40]

4

What is it smelling at Zenzele?
The pepper is smelling.
The pepper is words that stab,
They carry spears and arrows,
They stab the husband's heart
And they stab at his in-laws' home as well.

—MaCele of Zenzele, Melmoth

Sensitive one, easily moved.
I wonder, father, if the deceitful creature over there hears my words?
The broad-lipped woman pursued unmercifully, the one with labia like a puffed
adder.

—Silomo of the Mdlalose clan, composed for and
recited by her daughter, Princess Magogo

Unlike South African women's poetry of militancy, of incarceration,
or of domestic work, Zulu women's praise poetry, or *izibongo*, seems
on the surface to have little link to politics or resistance as heretofore
defined.[41] Thus, from the outset, it is necessary to problematize its
inclusion in this study. First, it does not fit with precision the time

frame of 1972-88, nor is it written in English. *Izibongo* is a form of oral literature that has been written and performed for centuries as part of Zulu language and culture. Praise poems have generally been associated with war and with male authority, and traditional *izimbongi* (bards), performers on public occasions, have always been men. Women, however, have long written *izibongo* and performed them in private circle ceremonies, as a means of exploring issues of daily life, personal identity, and domestic conflict.[42]

Second, for readers who do not speak or understand Zulu, myself included, the issue of mediation arises in attempting to determine the purpose, nature, and significance of women's praise poems. The scholar and oral historian Elizabeth Gunner, the best source I know on this subject, collected women's *izibongo* from October 1975 to September 1976 in KwaZulu. In my discussion I draw heavily on her insights and use her translations as my texts; my thinking has also been informed by conversations with Lauretta Ngcobo, a novelist of Zulu origins who is not herself a composer of *izibongo* but who kindly shared with me anecdotes and memories of her grandmothers' compositions.[43] My point, then, is that this poetry is available to literary scholars primarily through the linguistic and cultural study of scholars like Gunner, who entered the Zulu women's rituals as an informed outsider after apparently winning the women's trust, since she was allowed to observe and record their performances over a long period of time; we, in turn, place our trust in the accuracy and validity of a mediator's translations and insights.

Finally, the inclusion of Zulu women's praise poetry here expands the definitions and connotations of resistance heretofore suggested. What does *izibongo* resist, how does it resist, and what does praise poetry offer to a study of South African women's resistance poetry of the 1970s and 1980s? First, the poetry's content itself might be considered resistant in that it uses highly figurative language and private allusions to *act*—that is, to celebrate the author's own character and accomplishments in a strong poetic statement of identity; and to *react*—to lodge and perhaps, indirectly, to resolve complaints and conflicts between the poet and her husband, his parents, or other co-wives. *Izibongo* frequently serves, in Gunner's words, as "an effective and socially acceptable way of publicly announcing one's anger or grief. Once a complaint has been made in a praise poem it remains long after the incident is past, acquiring its own artistic objectivity and serving as an expression of its owner's identity; in this way life is turned into art."[44] Second, through its private nature via "in-house only" performances and its use of an indigenous language, *izibongo* resists appropriation by the forces of apartheid, which since 1948 have attempted, through forced relocations, Bantu education, and a thousand other overt and subversive means, to rob African peoples of their culture heritage and distinction. Proponents of apartheid have devalued or ignored orature, just as they have marginalized the people who create it, yet orature thrives across African cultures and languages and might be considered the most authentic voice of the people. Any study of South African women's poetry would be remiss in failing to look at an example of its orature.

Furthermore, women's praise poems also resist appropriation by Zulu men, whose roles as public bards determine the stylized, formal nature of their own *izibongo*, and who, in any event, do not normally have access to women's recitations, which traditionally have been open only to other women and children. In contrast, women's praise poems *invite* appropriation by this other audience, in that other women present collaborate by adding lines to a poem as it is recited; revising passages in an ironic, a bawdy, or a serious way; and introducing running commentary of any sort on the text. According to Gunner, "the interaction between individual performer and the seated group of participants is constant and essential; the seated participants provide the background singing, clapping, and calling out *izibongo*. It is in this performance that a woman's praise poem is completely realised" (17). The poems also invite appropriation by the poet's children, for whom she writes *izibongo* in order to secure their identities and to pass on a cultural and personal legacy from generation to generation of rural Zulus.

An analysis of Zulu women's praise poetry is therefore important to this study, in that it offers a counterhegemonic historical portrait of rural African women's lives and issues as well as an alternative poetic of resistance based on: (1) an implicit rather than explicit challenge to the political status quo (i.e., it marginalizes the architects of apartheid by ignoring them altogether and assuming instead its own cultural and literary authority); (2) a collaborative aesthetic of performance that reveals women's collective skill at composition-in-process and challenges the notion of the poet as one who creates autonomously; and (3) a recognition of rural African women's oral

poetry as equally valuable and aesthetically pleasing as written po-
etry, which often is created by women who are bi- or multilingual,
highly educated, and/or urban. The two praise poems with which
this section began can be used to illustrate the genre. The first is a
short, allusive poem by a married woman upset with both her hus-
band's cold behavior and that of her in-laws, who she feels are under-
mining her marriage; the second, a longer daughter's poem inherited
from her mother, foregrounds the mother's hostility toward a vicious
co-wife but proclaims as well the royal identity of her child, for whom
these lines are written.

In analyzing the first poem, which opens "What is it smelling at
Zenzele?" Gunner notes that "the praise poem as a whole is built on
a number of progressions formed by linking": for example, lines 1
and 2 are linked by the motif of unpleasant smell, lines 2 and 3 by the
metaphor of pepper, lines 3–6 by the image of stabbing, directed first
at the husband's heart and then at the home of his intrusive parents.
She further asserts that such a complaint would be viewed not as an
insult, as it would be if stated in conversation, but, instead, as an
invitation to restore healthy relationships (17—18). Considering the
poem further from the perspective of resistance literature, we might
add that the poet addresses not only family politics but also what the
U.S. poet Adrienne Rich has called a "politics of location": she identi-
fies herself by her place of origin and residence, Zenzele, and by her
identity as a maker of words, through poetry, that stab as harshly as
those spoken by her husband and his family.[45] This poetic identity,
however, is part and parcel with her domestic identity; she is a
wronged wife and daughter-in-law and an experienced cook (who
recognizes bitter pepper when she smells it). Furthermore, she as-
serts a public and generally male-possessed identity, metaphorically,
as a warrior who brandishes and uses weapons effectively, someone
whose words can be dangerous and can act in self-defense. Gunner
explains that "the emphasis in Zulu rural communities on one's social
identity as a married woman is very clear. The imposition of such a
social identity is in some ways restrictive, yet Zulu women have a
corporate strength, an assurance, an ability to act cohesively as a
group, that could well be the envy of their western sisters" (16). It is
perhaps this corporate strength that gives MaCele the courage to
resist abusive treatment and use praise poetry as a means of taking
action to change the circumstances of her life.

The second poem, an example of *izangelo*, or praise poems of infancy, would be recited with other women at a social event or to the poet's child in the privacy of her home, though perhaps loudly enough for others to overhear; it would later be recited by the child for whom is has been written and of whose ongoing identity it becomes a part. Its primary stylistic characteristics are indirection and private allusion, its major motif is confessional, and its composition is singular rather than collaborative. Princess Magogo's mother illustrates in her poem's first three lines her hostility toward an unnamed other woman, probably a co-wife, that woman's aggression toward her, which presumably motivated the speaker's hostility, and the genre's reliance on references to male and female sexuality and appearance as a point of approval or insult: "the broad-lipped woman . . . the one with labia like a puffed adder." Lines 4–9 catalog a series of insults the speaker has suffered at the hands of this woman and others in "the royal household," who she claims angrily, "turned in disdain from me." The reason for this scorn, and the reason for the poem, is the birth of her own regal child: "I have come out with the great mother of the royal line." For this "I was mocked by the vultures, / I was mocked by the cuckoo shrikes" at harvest time, the speaker asserts, employing as insults the animal imagery that often so functions in *izibongo*.

In the last five lines, as Gunner notes, the poet offers a "bitter invective" that is "scorching but controlled" as well as quite humorous:

And what could you say to me? You with a twig for offspring,

With your lop-sided head.
You're like this and I will insult you like this:
You're like the shrivelled-up buttocks of my brother-in-law,
You're like the shrivelled-up buttocks of Zinyo. (32–33)

One striking feature of this poem that Gunner did not discuss is its shifting subjects of direct address. "Sensitive one, easily moved," it begins, and continues, "I wonder, father . . . ?" The references are ambiguous: is the "sensitive one" the child for whom the poem is written or the father named in the second line? Is the "father" the poet's own father or her husband, the father of the child, who could perhaps overhear her lament? I speculate that the poem's first nine lines are addressed to the daughter, Princess Magogo, the sensitive one, who is also, more obviously, the child of the royal line; and less directly to the listening husband, the royal child's father, whose polygamous status would grant him knowledge about whether the "broad-lipped woman" of whom the poet complains has heard the poet's accusations. The last five lines, in turn, are addressed to this woman herself, clearly with the assumption that she has by now overheard and is continuing to listen and perhaps preparing to respond: "And what could you say to me?" This poem treats the subjects of power politics between women as mothers and co-wives (and, indirectly through the references to labia, as rival sexual partners) and competition between blood lines of a royal clan; it thus addresses issues of gender, class, and sexuality from the perspective of a woman restricted by patriarchal convention from discussing these issues outside of the purview of poetry. The term *poetic license*, it could be argued, here reaches new heights. I view Silomo's poem for Princess Magogo, and for that matter most of the *izibongo* translated by Gunner, as a means of conflating the public and private spheres and resisting conventional taboos on women's anger, competition, and defiance. Thus, these poems invite readers to expand our definitions of a women's poetics of resistance.

5

> What other role can we say the woman writer has? She also has to project the woman as acting and perceiving. Much literature has been written. We have women characters portrayed, but most of the time they are being acted upon . . . .
> —Rebecca Matlou, in Coetzee and Polley, *Crossing Borders*

> I am, firstly, a woman and millions of my kind are oppressed today, both by the political dispensation and by the oppressed male. Secondly, I am a poet in a South African literature which oppresses the black woman as a voiceless being.
> —Antjie Krog, in Coetzee and Polley, *Crossing Borders*

Having taken Afrikaner poet Antjie Krog to task earlier in this chapter for her claim that black women poets of merit were not to be found in South Africa of the 1970s and 1980s, I wish now to reposition her in creative political dialogue across differences with black woman poet and ANC activist Rebecca Matlou, the nom de guerre of Sankie

Dolly Nkondo.[46] Both women presented their views on the status of women writers in South Africa, and the relationship of writing to political struggle, at a 1987 conference, sponsored by the Institute for a Democratic Alternative in South Africa (IDASA), that brought together exiled artists and political strategists from the ANC and progressive Afrikaner writers and academics.

Matlou claims that at this historical moment it is necessary to discuss women's writing in racial terms, but the ANC is working for a future in which racial designations will be superfluous. She does not view sexism as black women's main problem in managing to make themselves heard; black women, she asserts, know that it is possible to work for liberation and at the same time write. She acknowledges, however, that published poetry by black women has been limited, largely because more pressing demands interrupt their work, and suggests that what does exist is poor. The black woman's poetic production, "most of the time, can only be of inferior quality, not because she cannot rise to high levels of craftsmanship, or craftswomanship, but because . . . there are other immediate issues to relate to." Matlou further asserts that black women have been seen as objects rather than subjects in their own right, and she calls upon women and men to change this by portraying and accepting black women as literary and political agents.

Krog, whose speech followed Matlou's at the conference, begins with a cogent plea for more attention to black women's poetry, only to undercut it with assertions that there has not been significant poetry written thus far. On both points Krog and Matlou agree. Most sympathetic readers today, of course, as in 1987, would concur that more black women's poetry should be published. But why might an articulate black woman poet such as Matlou describe her own poetry and that of her cohorts as inferior in quality? Krog offers one possible explanation when she challenges black men in her audience to consider whether they oppress black women by claiming to speak on their behalf, but Matlou clearly rejects sexism as an explanation. Instead, Matlou puts the blame for what she characterizes as the dearth and inferiority of black women's poetry on their circumstances under apartheid—their exile, their busy lives as workers, activists, maintainers of families, and writers. Neither Krog nor Matlou evidently was familiar in 1987 with the substantial body of black women's written poetry that, as this chapter has shown, did exist. This lack of awareness might well remind readers of a problem we face in 1994 in attempting to understand why black women's poetry has been so underrecognized and devalued in South Africa, even by other women: it is easy to forget how much information and art was closed off, even to educated and informed South Africans, in 1987. Access to poetry by black women has opened up in the past few years as apartheid has loosened its grasp, and, as we shall see in the next chapter, the rise of a public discourse on gender and feminist issues in South Africa since 1990 has affected women poets positively.

Both Matlou and Krog prefigure this feminist discourse in calling for a new consciousness regarding South African women's art and activism. Matlou encourages black women's equal political participation, alongside a reclamation of their right to represent themselves poetically on their own terms: "What kind of consciousness as women do we look forward to? Are we going to continue to be projected through the eyes of men? Or a political system that tends to reject or devalue women? That is where our role is. We should take part in transforming society." Krog's final challenge to the women and men present is more imagistic and more overtly feminist in nature. Furthermore, she extends the referential context from South Africa alone, calling for "a Third World space in which the woman can lift her head high and look her sisters in the eye; a space in which she can shape a spiritual independence from her exploiters. How does one start to form that space? How else than shaping one's tongue and spitting out the subversive words: my body and my voice belong to me alone."[47] That two South African women poets divided by race, class, and role in the liberatory struggle could agree, finally, on the importance of articulating what a women's poetic consciousness might look like, despite their very different ways of formulating this vision, offers hope that more women can begin dialogues across differences and heal wounds. Meanwhile, it is clear from the voices of black women represented in this chapter—militants, prisoners, domestic workers, and composers of *izibongo*—that this rich body of poetry has been too long devalued or ignored.

Chapter 5

Redefining Resistance: South African Women's Poetry and Politics in the 1990s

Can we say that we have begun to grasp the full dimensions of the new country and new people that is struggling to give birth to itself, or are we still trapped in the multiple ghettoes of the apartheid imagination?
—Albie Sachs, "Preparing Ourselves for Freedom" (1989)

We cannot ignore the fact that apartheid and patriarchy in unholy wedlock have begotten a vicious system of subordination of women in this country.
—Frene Ginwala, "Women's Future, World's Future: Transforming the Nature of South African Society" (1992)

Where women are concerned, I write from a region I can't reach.
—Lauretta Ngcobo, personal interview, June 1, 1992

As South African writers and cultural workers struggle to redefine their roles in a postapartheid society, the term *resistance literature* has become a site of contestation. Frank Meintjies, a member of the Transvaal Regional Executive Committee of the Congress of South African Writers, explains that for decades the concept "culture of resistance" has been used in a similar way to terms like *alternative, oppositional,* and *anti-:* "to rouse and embolden the oppressed." As the country and its people prepare themselves for the end of apartheid, however, a new language is needed, "one imbued with the promotion of life, a celebration of democracy building on creative grassroots energy."[1] Exiled novelist Gillian Slovo agrees with Meintjies that the term *resistance writer* might be retrogressive at a time when censorship seems no longer operative; she is joined by feminist scholar Lynda Gilfillan, who studies women's writing in "what might tentatively be described as a post-resistance South Africa."[2] For Cape Town poet Ingrid de Kok, resistance poetry must be balanced by lyric poetry in the 1990s, for it has been difficult to write

183

about the self in a cultural environment that understandably has
privileged overtly political poems, that has demanded of poets that
each poem counter the government's doublespeak. Poet and student
Lisa Combrinck concurs, noting that resistance poetry still needs to
be written but that it must be different, more ambiguous and open-
ended, less capable of "glorifying death and horror."[3]

Other writers, however, embrace the concept of resistance litera-
ture even as they reconceptualize it. Brenda Cooper, academic coor-
dinator at the Center for African Studies at the University of Cape
Town, advocates a new cultural consciousness, "a joy and sensuality
that defies oppression, *not* one that substitutes for resistance."[4] Sta-
cey Stent of the Cultural Workers Congress argues that, in order for
culture and its creators not to become a mere political afterthought
in this time of transition, artists must redefine resistance not only in
terms of race, class, and economics but with concern as well for
"new" issues such as gender and ecology.[5] And Natal worker poet
Nise Malange, writing collaboratively with other members of the Cul-
ture and Working Life Project, claims that cultural workers will con-
tinue to present struggle as an essential part of their art: "it is about
surviving, being resilient, living, singing *and* fighting."[6]

As the preceding chapter documents, black women contributed
significantly to South African resistance poetry of the 1970s and
1980s. Yet even though their voices, when lifted, were among the
most vital and compelling, many were marginalized; others were
completely silenced, as the triple oppression of race, class, and gen-
der forced them to contend with the poverty and/or with the physical
and psychological displacement caused by exile and migration. Tal-
ented but hard-pressed to write, Nise Malange asserts, such women
have been "like shadows only to be heard during the night, whisper-
ing their stories to the children"; they have too often been positioned
not as creators but as audience, "ululating when the praise poets
praised the chiefs and the izinduna."[7] In the 1990s, however, a pro-
cess underway in South Africa is challenging the "politics of space":
the struggle for democracy and against apartheid, a movement to-
ward one person–one vote, efforts toward reterritorializing and re-
possessing colonized land, a reconsideration of what art should be
and do. As feminist scholar Annemarie Van Niekirk notes, in such a
context of change it is hardly surprising that both black and white
women's social and cultural positions are being reexamined by most

of the country's major political and intellectual leaders and move-
ments, as well as by its artists. How, then, can South African women,
in her words, "claim cultural ground"?[8] Have women poets, in par-
ticular, begun to carve out new cultural and literary space for their
writing in the late 1980s and early 1990s? If so, what types of cultural
interventions do their poems offer, what meanings do they produce,
and how do they differ from women's resistance poetry of earlier
periods?

In this chapter I will examine three internal political and cultural
debates that I believe have contributed significantly to the growing
body of black and white women's resistance poetry in English, albeit
resistance redefined. The first of these centers on a controversial series
of articles and discussions sparked by Albie Sachs's 1989 paper "Pre-
paring Ourselves for Freedom," presented as an in-house document
for an ANC seminar in Lusaka, Zambia, shortly after the organiza-
tion's unbanning. Sachs's paper, which questions whether South Af-
rican writers and artists have "sufficient cultural imagination" to
guide them during the transition to democracy, proposes with some
irony a five-year moratorium on the idea of culture as a "weapon of
struggle." This view of culture, widely held by activists and revolu-
tionaries, has produced an impoverished art and a diminished critical
vision, Sachs argues. Responses to his paper, especially those col-
lected in a volume entitled *Spring Is Rebellious* (1990), range from
endorsement of Sachs's position as one freeing to artists to rejection
based on an interrogation of his authority as a political exile.
Women's and gender issues are not raised prominently in these dia-
logues, a topic I shall take up later. Nonetheless, this challenge to the
apartheid imagination and its "multiple ghettoes" has had an impact
on women's poetry. Has it helped to empower the once-silenced or
contributed to their continued marginalization?

The second internal debate surrounds several national political
projects designed to combat sexism and enhance women's options
for leadership and full equity in the social, political, economic, and
cultural spheres. This discussion is ongoing within the highest ranks
of the ANC and, most recently, among members of a 560-member
organization, the Women's National Coalition (WNC), representing
women's groups from across the political spectrum. Initiated by the
ANC Women's League to further dialogue among women about gen-
der rights and the new constitution, the WNC has as its goal the

development of a Women's Charter to accompany a proposed Bill of Rights. The charter would reflect the views of *all* women, including black rural women, domestic workers, women activists with the ANC and the Pan-Africanist Congress (PAC), white members of the Conservative and Nationalist parties, and women affiliated with the Inkatha Freedom party, to name only a few. Led by Frene Ginwala, WNC members share a commitment to challenging the "unholy wedlock" of apartheid and patriarchy, to eradicating sexism in its many forms. They also hope to influence the negotiations toward a postapartheid government that have taken place under the auspices of the Convention for a Democratic South Africa (CODESA), negotiations from which women were at first conspicuously absent.[9] How might these debates free oppressed women to find voice in poetry?

The third series of internal debates, spearheaded by academic as well as grassroots women, black and white, focuses on empowering women to write and on assessing the value of feminist discourse as a critical and theoretical tool. These subjects have been foregrounded at several literary conferences of recent years, most notably the COSAW-sponsored forum "Buang Basadi / Khulumani Makhosikazi / Women Speak," held in November 1988, and the COSAW / New Nation Writers' Conference, held in December 1991. Because of an upsurge in women's writing, especially black women's, and the challenges their texts pose to traditional canons and critical theories, leading South African scholarly journals have also taken up feminist debates. The October 1990 issue of *Current Writing: Text and Reception in Southern Africa,* for example, is dedicated to feminism and writing; its editor, M. J. Daymond of the University of Natal's English Department, argues that gender is a key concept in constructing a new nationhood, that raising women's voices is crucial to this construction, and that, "within feminism itself, claiming the right to name oneself must rest on a simultaneous, mutually liberating recognition of other women's difference."[10] South African women poets are interrogating their own literary voices and critical stances vis-à-vis feminist identity politics; with Lauretta Ngcobo, they are plumbing the depths of womanhood, regions heretofore difficult to reach.

An understanding of the nature and goals of these three debates will enhance our analysis of South African women's resistance poetry in English from the late 1980s and 1990s, poetry in which the concept of resistance extends beyond the parameters of the struggle for racial and national liberation. As the ANC's current guidelines call for a "non-racial, non-sexist democratic South Africa," so contemporary women's poetry foregrounds issues of gender as well as race, class, and colonialism. In the second half of this chapter I will examine three categories into which women's recent poems of resistance can be seen to fall: (1) poems that take up Sachs's aesthetic challenge by blending the political and the lyrical and are also written with overt gender consciousness; (2) poems that explore with honesty and ambivalence women's sexualities and sexual relationships in a changing South Africa; and (3) antisexist, antipatriarchal poems that offer feminist critiques and assert the importance of women's solidarity and mutual empowerment. "Creativity begins with disobedience," dissident Egyptian novelist Nawal el-Saadawi told a riveted audience at the 1991 COSAW / New Nation Writers' Conference.[11] South African women resistance poets have become increasingly disobedient, not only toward an oppressive apartheid regime but also toward those institutions and individuals within their own ranks that have contributed to their marginalization. "Disloyal to civilization," they join black poet Boitumelo Mofokeng in a passionate exhortation to her sisters: "Let us remove the barriers! Let us break the silence! Let us stand up and speak our minds before the men do it for us!"[12]

1

> Culture is not something separate from the general struggle, an artifact that is brought in from time to time to mobilise the people or else to prove to the world that after all we are civilised. Culture is us, it is who we are, how we see ourselves and the vision we have of the world.
>
> —Albie Sachs, "Preparing Ourselves for Freedom"

> Until the creation of peace and free political life in our cities, the squatter camps and countryside, we cannot but accept the inevitability of competing hegemonic projects *and* the necessity to change violent behaviour into structured criticism, discussion, and protest.
>
> —Culture and Working Life Project, "Albie Sachs Must Not Worry"

When Albie Sachs's ANC paper on cultural change in a postapartheid South Africa was published in the Johannesburg *Weekly Mail* in February 1990, it received both enormous praise and immediate challenge.[13] An ANC revolutionary-in-exile who had lost an arm in what many believe to have been a government-sponsored bomb attack,

Sachs had credentials for questioning his country's cultural impera-
tives that were accepted by many liberal and radical readers. Further-
more, his status as a writer and a lawyer, a member of the ANC's
Department of Legal and Constitutional Affairs then engaged in writ-
ing the party's proposed Constitutional Guidelines, gave additional
weight to his concerns. As a former supporter of armed struggle,
Sachs clearly views art as inseparable from politics; certainly his argu-
ment does not endorse the Eurocentric notion of art as politically
unaffiliated, pure. Instead, he proposes that a rigid definition of art
as a weapon of struggle has resulted in too narrow a range of themes
and styles; such a definition does not allow contradiction or ambigu-
ity, where he believes the power of art lies. Writers in the 1990s
would be well advised to "shake off the gravity of their anguish and
break free from the solemn formulas of commitment that people (like
myself) have tried for so many years to impose upon them." Sachs
is self-critical, even as he challenges the ANC's tendency to support
"culture by decree." Although broad parameters would continue to
define what is "acceptable" art—is it, finally, pro- or anti-
apartheid?—he argues that the ANC should take a leadership role in
freeing *all* people's voices to depict a rich diversity of cultures and
languages. Such a role, he continues, requires affirmative action in
terms of class: "We can envisage massive programmes of adult edu-
cation and literacy, and extensive use of the media to facilitate access
by all to the cultural riches of our country and of the world." As both
the producers and the audiences of art expand, Sachs concludes,
South Africans must work to write better poems, make stronger
films, compose finer music.[14]

Ari Sitas, a poet, labor organizer, and academic from Durban,
claims that respondents to Sachs's argument fall into four categories:
conservative upholders of literature as separate from politics, who
want to view Sachs as having switched to their position; radical intel-
ligentsia, who argue for both political art and academic standards;
grassroots writers, who argue for internal standards "*within* the
grassroots energy of oppositional and/or resistance formations"; and
cultural workers, who may feel attacked because they consider art
their weapon and propose to continue using it strategically. The
twenty-two responses to Sachs collected in *Spring Is Rebellious* repre-
sent voices from the last three groups.[15] Published in newspapers
and journals or presented at cultural forums during the six months

following the publication of his piece, these articles raise issues that continue to be fiercely debated. Those who support Sachs's stance do so primarily in the interest of artistic openness and aesthetic scrutiny. Brenda Cooper, for example, heralds his criticism of humorless, one-dimensional, dictatorial art while simultaneously praising his rejection of the bourgeois concept that, in art, anything goes. Kendell Geers, a free-lance art critic, agrees that art today "should remain critical of apartheid, but at the same time become critical of itself as well as its own history"; he advocates a return to the avant-garde, which he claims is always revolutionary in its subversiveness. Karen Press, a poet and co-editor of *Spring Is Rebellious*, purports that artists should surprise their audiences by celebrating a reality and vision that could not have been anticipated in advance. Decrying "church art" approved by cultural priests or commissars, Press emphasizes that, when artists are free to produce what they want, they must assume full responsibility for their content and audiences.[16]

Other respondents are more measured in their endorsement of Sachs's vision, more inclined to defend cultural workers and the last decades' art and to be wary of a renewed emphasis on aesthetics. Frank Meintjies emphasizes that the definition of aesthetics is determined by those in power; he asserts that "any critical assessment of an artist, whether white or black, liberal or radical, does not end with the aesthetic; it necessarily takes account of the specific milieu and how the artist engages with, relates to, is influenced by social circumstances and the issues of the times." Junaid Ahmed, national executive director of COSAW, chronicles the strengths of viewing culture as a weapon of struggle: art, then, challenges hegemonic power structures, gives voice to many indigenous languages that might otherwise remain static, and honestly documents the violence endemic to South African society. The Natal Culture and Working Life Project acknowledges that some grassroots creators and publishers have lacked critical capacities, that a sometimes oppressive notion of "revolutionary style" was developed by alternative media, and that some artists were marginalized because of these problems. Nonetheless, they agree with Ahmed that a marvelous and powerful body of grassroots resistance art has appeared in recent decades and believe that these artists are to be congratulated and supported. "Structured criticism, discussion and protest" are essential, they conclude, to the ongoing struggle for liberation.[17]

Those who oppose Sachs's position are fewer in number but scathing in their critiques. Most vocal is writer and COSAW member Rushdy Siers, who questions the efficacy of Sachs's vision, given that he has lived outside the country for so long, and claims that, if artists followed his prescriptions to write more of love and connection, a bizarre scenario would ensue: "bouquets of roses on casspirs and ratels, ozone-friendly labels on mustard gas, greeting cards on bullets, . . . kwashiorkor and TB riddled infants singing 'all we need is love.'" Until injustice and poverty end, Siers concludes sardonically, art must continue to shout "vivas" and "amandlas." Sculptor and academic Gavin Younge, though less negative than Siers toward Sachs's questioning of politically monitored art, agrees that Sachs is out of touch with sentiments inside the country and wonders why an exile still living abroad feels qualified to make decisions for artists living in South Africa. A return to asthetics implies a return to tradition, after all, and "all artists who have loved their tradition," he concludes, "have had to disrupt it."[18]

Sachs and numerous respondents lament that many artists have been marginalized in past decades, and they express a desire to make amends. However, the language and content of these debates are striking in their failure to discuss the empowerment of women artists or to foreground gender concerns. Sachs does give passing mention to "the whole issue of women's liberation," which he sees as "finally forcing itself on to the agenda of action and thought"; his ambivalence toward this subject is revealed in his verb choice ("forcing itself"), even as he asserts, perhaps grudgingly, that this is "a profound question of cultural transformation." Of the twenty-two contributors to *Spring Is Rebellious,* only five are women, including the two editors, and only two raise gender issues. Orenna Krut of Transvaal COSAW is explicit in foregrounding gender along with racial discrimination; she notes that writing by politically oppressed groups has always been suppressed, including that by people of color and women, and that, in a world in which the "great" writers are presented as white and male, any writing by other groups constitutes an important political act. Ari Sitas joins Krut in identifying the need to free the voices of black working women. Nise Malange, herself a black worker poet, also laments the lack of poetry by women workers, "lost in the vast buildings" at night in South Africa's cities, polishing floors and risking rape or murder as they make their way home to the townships in the wee hours. Such women "are beginning to strut out and to struggle to define their own identity," many of them through poems, Sitas and Malange assert, and they deserve recognition. Yet despite these important interventions, most of the discussions of art and struggle published in *Spring Is Rebellious* do not seriously address black and/or white women's cultural production.[19]

What has been the impact of the "Albie Sachs debates" on women artists in general and on resistance poets in particular? Have Sachs's article and the controversies it sparked opened up creative space for marginalized writers, including white and black women, as Brenda Cooper and others allege, or has a renewed attention to aesthetics (conventionally defined) limited such space? Has Sachs's injunction to write poems about love and sexuality freed some women to address subjects traditionally assigned to them but forbidden to anyone in a climate in which revolutionary themes were privileged? Has the emphasis on women's poetry, gender sensitivity, and black women's oppression espoused by Krut, Sitas, and Malange helped to bring to voice any women previously silenced? These questions will be addressed when we examine women's lyrical/political poetry of the late 1980s and early 1990s and when we turn to their poems about sexuality.

2

> The liberation of women is central to our people's struggle for freedom.
> —Statement of the National Executive Committee of the
> African National Congress on the Emancipation of Women
> in South Africa, May 2, 1990

> Our men, both black and white, have to be educated to realize we're not chattel. . . . Other women—often our white sisters who have been spoiled by apartheid—have to be educated, too.
> —Albertina Sisulu, deputy president, ANC Women's League, June 1992

Founded in 1912, two years after the Union of South Africa was established, the African National Congress determined to resist colonization in its myriad forms, from land seizures to pass laws to the elimination of African parliamentary voting rights.[20] Eighty years later the ANC, widely believed to have the support of 60 to 70 percent of the people of South Africa, continues in the vanguard of struggle.[21]

With regard to women, however, the ANC has a complex and troubled history. For the first thirty years of its existence, the organization was open to women only as auxiliaries, despite the fact that they were leaders in resistance efforts during that period. In 1913 African women in Bloemfontein successfully resisted having to carry passes (already carried by men) that would restrict their movement from recently established "reserves"; in the 1930s they organized passive resistance against curfew regulations that the government wished to impose. In the 1950s many African women joined the newly expanded ANC; they also banded together with their "colored," Indian, and white sisters and brothers to participate in the 1952 Defiance Campaign, in which 8,500 were arrested for civil disobedience. Women also resisted without the aid of men. In 1954 they founded the Federation of South African Women, whose goals were articulated in a Women's Charter that became the model, one year later, for the famous Freedom Charter urging the establishment of an equitable, nonracial democracy in South Africa. In 1955–56 thousands of women of all races demonstrated in Pretoria against the pass laws the government again sought to institute. Furthermore, women were among the 156 leaders charged but ultimately acquitted in the 1956–61 Treason Trial. Women participated in the 1961 founding of Umkhonto we Sizwe (Spear of the Nation), the militant arm of the ANC, and served throughout the next three decades as combatants and strategists in what South Africans call MK. In 1975 women formed the Black Women's Federation to strengthen ties among African, "colored," and Indian women who had long been pitted against one another under the arbitrary and divisive guidelines of apartheid; this federation worked closely with the Black Sash, an organization of white women dissidents established in 1955, which became increasingly radicalized during the upheavals in Soweto and elsewhere in the mid-1970s. The Women's Section of the ANC was centrally involved in all of these resistance efforts, often in conjunction with members of the South African Communist Party (SACP), and women leaders like Lilian Ngoyi, Helen Joseph, Frances Baard, Albertina Sisulu, Winnie Mandela, Fatima Meer, and Ruth First were and still are honored as "mothers of the struggle."

Nonetheless, ANC women today, along with some men, have begun to recognize and acknowledge their organization's struggle over the emancipation of women; with ANC Women's League representative Gertrude Shope, they are insisting that "the question of women's emancipation be written into every document of the ANC."[22] As justification for this request they frequently cite Mozambiquan president Samora Machel's statement from the early 1970s: "The emancipation of women is not an act of charity. . . . The liberation of women is a fundamental necessity for the revolution, the guarantee of its continuity and the precondition for its victory."[23] Despite Machel's call for women's liberation and similar cries from male ANC leaders such as the late Oliver Tambo, resistance by many ANC men and some women to feminist issues as "bourgeois," as well as the overarching needs of the national liberation struggle, kept women's emancipation on the back burner until the mid-1980s, when concerned women again began to lobby their leaders for change. Many of these women were exiles: members of Umkhonto we Sizwe and other exiles living in progressive African countries like Mozambique, Zambia, and Namibia, where women's rights were being addressed; or political exiles working or studying in England, Europe, or the United States, where feminist consciousness was on the rise. In 1985 ANC president Tambo joined with Namibian president Sam Nujoma to pledge to the women of South Africa and Namibia that the struggle for national liberation would not be complete until women were no longer oppressed. In 1987 the Second National Congress of the ANC Women's Section, meeting in Luanda, Angola, proposed that the ANC National Executive Committee (NEC) establish a special commission to address the issue of discrimination against women in the ANC and to establish policies designed to solve this problem. Still, this proposal did not go immediately forward; it was not until 1990 that the NEC issued a position paper on women's emancipation and not until 1991 that it formally established a National Commission for the Emancipation of Women, chaired by Oliver Tambo and co-chaired by Frene Ginwala.[24]

The 1990s thus far have generated an enormous surge of interest in women's liberation in the ANC and the democratic movement as a whole, and, while many women remain concerned that policy has not yet translated into practice, the attention now given to combating sexism and empowering women is heartening. The document produced by the ANC's NEC in 1990 states its goals strongly and clearly:

The ANC's commitment to eliminate racism, oppression and exploitation from our society cannot fail to address also the question of the emancipation of women.

The experience of other societies has shown that the emancipation of women is not a by-product of a struggle for democracy, national liberation or socialism. It has to be addressed in its own right within our organization, the mass democratic movement and in the society as a whole.

The majority of South African women, who are black, are the most oppressed sector of our people, suffering under a triple yoke of oppression. The liberation of women is central to our people's struggle for freedom.

This document goes on to analyze what gender oppression is and how it works, concluding that all women have lower status than all men of the same social group, in both law and practice, and that this lower status puts women at economic, political, cultural, and domestic disadvantage. Furthermore, it links gender oppression to apartheid and acknowledges that black women have suffered most greatly under these interwoven systemic inequities: "The manipulation of gender relationships has been an important feature of state control over, especially, the African people and the effects have impinged most harshly upon women. Their mobility has been rigidly controlled, and the unpaid labour of African women in the rural areas has underpinned the migrant labour system and subsidised the profits of the mining industry." But the ANC does not shift the blame for women's oppression fully to the apartheid regime; it also accepts its share of the burden. It proposes that the ANC Constitutional Guidelines be amended to state that South Africa is an "independent, democratic, non-racial and non-sexist state," that laws and traditions and practices discriminatory toward women be made unconstitutional, and that women be fully supported in claiming their rights to education and other resources that will insure their "democratic participation in all decision making." ANC women are urged to take the lead in creating a nonsexist society and a charter of women's rights, but men are not exempted from responsibility; the document makes clear that eliminating sexism is everyone's task. It concludes on a didactic note with an implicit warning to ANC men to avoid the temptations to power to which proponents of apartheid succumbed:

"Although the dominant always find it difficult in the short term to give up age-old privileges and habits, in the long run they only stand to gain from living in a world in which the health, happiness, and welfare of all is guaranteed."[25]

Despite the important political advances for women that this and other ANC documents signify, many women in the ANC continue to challenge their organization and the mass democratic movement for their sexist practices. This problem was most evident during the 1992 CODESA negotiations between the Nationalist party, the ANC, and other participating bodies. According to Baleka Kgositsile, executive secretary of the ANC Women's League and a poet, debates within the ANC revealed resistance to women's taking leadership roles at CODESA 1 (April 1992); as a result, the ANC was the only organization not to have a woman in its official delegation.[26] One ANC leader, Frene Ginwala, who participated in an advisory capacity, initiated contact with women representing other parties present and learned that all of them were concerned about the dearth of women. Out of more than four hundred official representatives, less than 7 percent were women, and the nineteen-member steering committee remained all male. Determined to tackle this problem directly, Ginwala took action on three fronts. First, after CODESA 1 she joined with other women to convince CODESA leaders to institute a gender advisory committee (GAC), which worked with the management committee at CODESA 2 (held in May 1992) to create more gender-sensitive policy. For example, when the management committee discussed how to end violence in the townships, the GAC insisted that rape, sexual harassment, and attacks on sex workers be added to the agenda. Second, she and other members of the ANC Women's League brought their protests to the ANC National Executive Committee, insisting that at least 30 percent of that body (fifteen members) be women; the result of this dialogue was the appointment of thirteen women to the NEC.[27]

Finally, and perhaps most important, Ginwala and the ANC Women's Committee joined with other women and women's groups from forty sectors to form the Women's National Coalition, a group "united in one cause—to get women's rights codified in the Bill of Rights of a new constitution."[28] This time, the women agree, they will not depend on male leaders to insure that their needs are met. According to Ginwala, CODESA 1 and 2 evoked remarkable discussions about how to end apartheid, what the nature of democracy is, and what the new South Africa will be; still more remarkable, she explains with irony, is the fact that they occurred among a minority population—men, who constitute 47 percent of South African society—and that these men did not find the absence of women worth noting until angry women brought it to their attention. Male dominance was reflected, she argues, in the language, style, and content of the debate as well, most notably in the emphasis on one man–one vote. Women will continue to be marginalized, she claims, unless the WNC manages to bring together successfully women long separated by race, ethnicity, language, poverty, and privilege, "divisions entrenched in law and sanctified by practice." Its specified goal is to write a Women's Charter to present alongside the Bill of Rights that CODESA hopes to produce, a document designed to insure women's full legal rights and address practices that prevent women from exercising these rights.[29]

Furthermore, according to several WNC members, the coalition has as a second and equally important unstated goal, that of forging women's solidarity across differences. Because it would be easy for educated white women to control the WNC and thus to determine myopically what "all women" need, the organization has determined that each represented body will canvass as many of its female constituents as possible, asking them to set their own agenda. The ANC Women's League, for example, has sent out one hundred field workers to all areas of the country, including the so-called homelands and other rural areas in which women have lacked adequate health care, housing, education, and economic options, to listen to these women's assessments of their needs. This information will be incorporated into the Women's Charter to insure as truly democratic a process and a product as possible.[30] According to Albertina Sisulu, if women in the WNC can learn to communicate across their differences and unite in developing a Women's Charter, they will be better equipped to agree on other issues. "We're really all together," she asserts, "because as South African women the same things oppress us—our men and our government." An additional advantage of the coalition's bipartisan efforts, Sisulu concludes, will be preparing women for the nonracial elections to come—empowering women to speak and to vote on their own behalf.[31]

What are the connections between women's increasing political visibility and the upsurge since the late 1980s in women's artistic productivity and public recognition of it? Has discrimination against women under apartheid but also within the ANC contributed to the past silencing of women's voices in the arts? How might the attention CODESA has been forced to give to women's experiences of rape, harassment, and sexist practice free women poets to write about these experiences? Might the process undertaken by the Women's National Coalition empower women in the townships and the home-lands to write what is on their minds? We will take up these questions when we investigate women's poetry challenging patriarchy and sexism in the home, in organizations, and at work.

3

> Years of conditioning had taught us that only men have a voice and are worth listening to. This, over and above the intolerance engendered by Apartheid South Africa in all spheres of life. That tutored feeling of "less worthiness" has been a crippling factor in all my creative thinking.
> —Lauretta Ngcobo, "My Life and My Writing"

> I can think of no reason why black patriarchy should not be challenged alongside the fight against Apartheid.
> —Zoë Wicomb, "To Hear the Variety of Discourses"

The anger at sexism and patriarchy articulated by Sisulu, Ginwala, and other women leaders in the ANC and WNC has been echoed of late by women writers, both established and aspiring, and by feminist academics in South African universities.[32] The issues most often raised by women writers, especially at the grassroots levels, involve silencing and empowerment. Lauretta Ngcobo, a prominent novelist who lives in London but travels frequently to her homeland, speaks for many in acknowledging the psychological oppression she has suffered as a black woman writer living first under apartheid and then as a political exile after the 1960 Sharpeville massacres; her poignant coinage "less worthiness" reflects both the power of hegemonic discourses, whether racist or patriarchal or both, and one woman writer's stubborn refusal to divest herself of self-worth. At two COSAW-sponsored conferences on women's writing, in 1988 and 1991, many women from diverse races and walks of life chronicled their struggle to write through phrases like "breaking the silence," "removing the barriers," "speaking our minds," and "refusing marginalization." They spoke as often of women writers' strengths and solidarity, of "closing gaps" among women, "sharing with each other," "making women strong," and together "exploring issues of race, gender and language."[33]

The topics taken up by academic women overlap with the concerns of writers outside the university context but grapple also with competing definitions of feminism, the role of feminist literary studies in the new South Africa, how feminist discourse can be theorized, and by whom. A special issue of the *Journal of Literary Studies*, edited by Pam Ryan in 1988, was dedicated to feminism and literary studies, and the second issue of *Current Writing*, edited by M. J. Daymond in 1990, took up the topic of South African women's writing and feminist criticism. The articles in *Current Writing* are especially compelling in their investigation of the "competing" discourses of womanism, as defined in the United States by Alice Walker and in Africa by the Nigerian critic Chikwenye Okonjo Ogunyemi, and feminism, as defined by U.S. gynocritics, by French advocates of gynesis, and in different ways by South African critics Cecily Lockett, Sisi Maqagi, and Zoë Wicomb.[34] Examining these cultural interventions will enhance our understanding of recent poetry by women and feminist poetics in South Africa today.

That COSAW chose to sponsor a conference in its prominent Transvaal region on women's writing in 1988, one year after its inception as a cultural organization, attests to the significance of this subject and the debates it generates. A publication that resulted from the conference, *Buang Basadi / Khulumani Makhosikazi / Women Speak*, bespeaks the conference's success; it has been sold out virtually since its publication by COSAW in 1989. It is important to note COSAW's commitment to fostering women's writing and scholarship in indigenous languages, as the tripartite conference and book title in Xhosa, Zulu, and English reveals, as well as the active participation of men writers along with women, particularly among poets. The conference clearly sought to be inclusive in terms of language, race, culture, and gender. Featured at the conference were panels on women worker poets, liberating learning through literacy movements, and images of women in South African literature, along with readings by well known and aspiring poets; audiences participated actively in discussions after all three panels. Although each panel was provocative, the one most relevant to the empowerment of women poets was "Breaking the Silence," a dialogue among three African women worker poets.

Panelist Boitumelo Mofokeng, a member of the Federation of Transvaal Women who works as a journalist for the South Africa Council of Churches, has long been an advocate of women's resistance art. An African poet who came of age in the Soweto uprisings of 1976, Mofokeng expressed distress that so few of her female compatriots from those days are still writing. Citing a number of possible inhibiting factors, from the lack of a writers' network to problems in their marriages to the alleged lack of support for women writers by *Staffrider*, the national COSAW journal, Mofokeng explicitly challenged marriage as a patriarchal institution and her male hosts for their sexism. Such forthrightness was typical of the women on this panel and at the conference in general, who saw as one of their tasks the reeducation of potentially sympathetic male compatriots. But Mofokeng also called women to action, urging them to take responsibility for their own empowerment by writing about their experiences of discrimination and their struggle to survive. Black women, in particular, suffer from oppression because of race, gender, and legal status as minors, she noted; they are economically abused under apartheid along with their brothers, and they are also sexually abused and harassed. "A literature from these women, or about their experiences, would provide an important social documentation of their lives," she concluded, "and provide further study materials for addressing women's issues and their role in the struggle."[35]

On the panel with Mofokeng were two other worker poets and advocates: Roseline Naapo, a former domestic worker who is now an organizer for the South African Domestic Workers' Union, and Nise Malange of the Culture and Working Life Project. Having begun writing poetry out of her own suffering, Naapo has gone on to document the difficult lives of domestic workers, most of whom live alone and can have no visitors, are grossly undercompensated in time and money, and are expected to care for white children but rarely see their own. She urged other domestic workers to tell their stories, whether or not they are literate: "Say whatever you can say without knowing how to write. The next person will write it down for you, and it can be compiled into a book."[36] Malange echoed Naapo's sentiments and called upon grassroots working women to share writing

skills and to challenge patriarchy along with apartheid, thus building
an alternative cultural agenda.

> There is a long history of women's resistance against apartheid
> and capitalist exploitation. Increasingly working class women are
> becoming part of the organised labour force and are effecting
> changes within their communities. The struggle to change patri-
> archal attitudes, share the double shift and achieve higher wages
> and better working conditions, is being forced onto the agendas
> of organisations. As long as culture is not part of the same
> agenda, women miss one of the most powerful tools for bringing
> about cultural transformation.[37]

Differences in viewpoint between these worker poets and their
sisters in the academy are worth noting, since they highlight alterna-
tive visions and discourses that exist among black women in South
Africa, too often lumped together as though they agree on all issues.
Mofokeng's emphasis on black women's writing as social documenta-
tion, for example, has been implicitly challenged by Zoë Wicomb, a
black novelist and an academic who complains that such descrip-
tions, which reveal some black women's discomfort with feminist
strategies, may inadvertently further racist assessments of black writ-
ing as valuable only for sociological reasons, not for artistic merit.[38]
Nise Malange's claim that "you do not have to be . . . specially gifted
to be able to tell or write a story" strikes Sisi Maqagi, also a black
woman and an academic, as "symptomatic of the successful way in
which black women have, in spite of their conscious resistance, im-
perceptibly absorbed devalued images of themselves."[39] Wicomb also
is concerned with naïveté on the part of black women writers, as
revealed in her challenge to Roseline Naapo's assertion that illiterate
women can still write by having someone else do it for them. "Far
from offering a new paradigm for art and writing (who would recom-
mend illiteracy for the writer?), it tells us something about the condi-
tions of textual production, about naive attitudes towards the medi-
ated text and points to an area of enquiry where the voices in texts
struggle for dominance. Our culture boasts of a number of such am-
biguous biographies-autobiographies of illiterate servants written by
white women whose voices cannot be effaced."[40] In advocating atten-
tion to how meaning is produced in texts as well as to their content

and themes, academics like Maqagi and Wicomb will no doubt be seen by some grassroots writers as elitist and overly theoretical, by others as contributing meaningfully to a complex, ongoing, and sisterly debate.

The COSAW / New Nation conference, entitled "Making Literature: Reconstruction in South Africa" and held in Johannesburg in December 1991, did not focus exclusively on women's writing but did provide another forum for "exploring issues of race, gender and language and the emergence of a new culture in South Africa." In an article on the conference in *Die Suid-Afrikaan*, scholar Annie Gagiano notes that, among the many politically engaged and prominent writers present—"locals" such as Nadine Gordimer and Njabulo Ndebele, exiles such as Dennis Brutus and Lauretta Ngcobo, and a host of international writers—the most powerful presences were the women writers.[41] Like the conference participants at *Women Speak*, many of these women deplored the virtual absence of rural women and of writers of indigenous languages other than Afrikaans. They also decried sexism and spoke frankly of their own struggles as writers who are also gendered beings. "Sexism differs markedly from classism and racism," Ngcobo asserted, "for it is the only condition where the oppressor and the oppressed share space intimately in love relationships." She went on to call for an end to theoretical debates about feminism and sexism and an emphasis, instead, on addressing the wounds of sexist oppression and empowering women writers to speak of these wounds.[42]

Poet and chief ANC representative to Germany Sankie Dolly Nkondo argued that most writing by African men shaped woman as the other, a portrait that reflects the patriarchal and neocolonial nature of the culture, and that women's writing challenges this "outsider status" for women and its accompanying stereotypes.[43] Scholar Annemarie Van Niekirk urged South African women to reclaim cultural ground by sensitizing women and men to the problem of women writers' marginal status, questioning the notion of a "gender-neutral" literary aesthetic, freeing children's literature and education of gender stereotypes, exploring the strengths of oral literature, much of which has attracted women, and working to insure more women's leadership in cultural organizations and decision-making bodies.[44] And Afrikaner poet Welma Odendaal attacked the title of her panel, "Creating a Gender-Sensitive Culture," proclaiming that she did not

want to be sensitive about gender issues; she preferred, instead, to
be offensive! Too much protection of men's sensitivities has already
occurred, Odendaal asserted wryly; to strengthen women's art, "let's
make sexism a punishable crime."[45]

The feminist issues raised at these two conferences have also
been taken up by prominent literary journals, as the October 1990
issue of *Current Writing* attests in its focus on feminism and writing
in South Africa. Daymond, the journal's editor, justifies the special
edition in light of a marked increase in the publication of women's
writing, especially black women's, in anthologies and journals, as
well as the current political debates about the role of women in a
democratic society. The topic's controversy stems from its potential
to be seen as exclusive or divisive. Some prominent women writers
and scholars have rejected feminism as irrelevant to their lives and
work; some men and women argue that it diverts essential energy
from the national liberation struggle; still other women have been
angered when conference coordinators asked them to participate in
sessions on women's writing, which they see as an attempt at ghet-
toization. As Daymond notes, however, many grassroots women
have begun to claim "I am a woman writer," a statement of personal
and political identity that she thinks must be distinguished from the
potentially dismissive statement "She is a woman writer." Further-
more, many women academics believe that careful negotiations be-
tween feminist and political concerns are essential for the 1990s and
that literary criticism is enhanced by feminist analysis of women's
texts and textual production.[46]

Among these academics is Randse Afrikaanse University profes-
sor Cecily Lockett, a white academic and a feminist, who asks, "What
exactly is feminism and how does a feminist critic locate herself
within the arena of competing discourses that constitute the field of
South African English literary studies in the 1990s?" Lockett goes on
to support the development of a feminist critical perspective that
gives equal weight to gender and race, a perspective that she claims
must differ significantly from both U.S. gynocriticism, which empha-
sizes a "prescription for action" yet fails "to go beyond the challenge
of the white middle-class text," and French gynesis, which privileges
a "masculine" theory and establishes no "concrete political agenda."
While both can be useful, neither fully addresses the realities of Third

World women's lives; thus, each is inappropriate to the South African context, in which First and Third worlds coexist. A theory that could be especially applicable to black women's texts, she asserts, is womanism, which she endorses without significant interrogation.

Lockett's model has been convincingly challenged by Maqagi and Wicomb for its unconscious assertions of white privilege and its reliance on womanism rather than feminism as an effective tool of analysis for black women's writing. Both critics invite Lockett to interrogate her own positionality when she claims that "perhaps we will have to develop a more sympathetic discourse for considering the work of black women . . . ," or that it is "our place" (white feminist critics?) to "listen to them" (black women writers?) "as *we* formulate approaches to *their* work."[47] As Maqagi argues in "Who Theorizes?" the question Lockett raises of whether white women have the right to speak for black women "should not even arise," and her advocacy of a "sympathetic" womanist discourse in evaluating black women's writing is both presumptuous and condescending. Lockett's contradictory language reveals her "unconscious impulse to assume initiative," Maqagi concludes, her inappropriate desire to "do the work" for black women.[48] Wicomb criticizes Lockett on somewhat different terms, asserting that her uncritical reliance on womanism as defined by Alice Walker and Chikwenya Okonjo Ogunyemi raises problems. Although Walker defines womanism as a strong black alternative to feminism, Wicomb points out that womanism's failures to take on black patriarchy led to the diminishing of Walker's own text *The Color Purple* (1982) in the film version, which "artlessly othered" Africa and distorted the book's woman-centered discourse. As for Ogunyemi's assertion that "the intelligent Black woman writer, conscious of black impotence in the context of white patriarchal culture, empowers the black man," Wicomb sees it as "alarming" in its failure to recognize that upholding black patriarchal power might well lead to a mimicry of white patriarchy's practice of unequal power relations. "The necessary linking of race and gender," Wicomb concludes, which both she and Lockett support, "is not adequately theorized in the concept of womanism."[49]

Despite their different perspectives, Maqagi, Lockett, and Wicomb agree that feminist analysis can heighten readers' understanding and appreciation of women's texts, especially those of black women, which have traditionally been critically ignored or devalued, and that any feminist perspective must challenge hegemonic power structures. Maqagi believes that a collective effort is needed to build feminist criticism, one that must emerge from those whose lives have too often been theorized by white women. Lockett warns similarly that "we cannot discount race and class in our investigations and we cannot allow our perspectives to become overly Eurocentric." And Wicomb, in what is to my mind the most cogent argument of the three, urges a poststructuralist feminist approach that would examine the black text's structures as well as its themes and sociological importance. Such an approach could interrogate a writer's "stealthy negotiation of race and gender" in order to explore the "fissures" in her discourse, and it could contribute to a critique of black patriarchy as well as challenge white women's racism and the oppressive structures of apartheid.[50]

It is hard to gauge whether these debates among South Africa's artists and intelligentsia have had a direct impact on aspiring women writers who are newly literate, live in rural areas, and/or lack practical or educational access to such interventions. Certainly, they have opened up space for educated women, black and white, to explore feminist issues in their poetry. Furthermore, one can only assume that, if debates about feminism and literature have occurred because of an upsurge in women's writing, the reverse is also true—that more women of all classes and races have been able to write and publish more work because of the attention given to women's writing in these forums. The two conferences, in particular, received widespread news coverage, and the concerns they generated continue to be discussed in COSAW branches and in newspapers all over South Africa, including those in many outlying areas. Challenging sexism and patriarchy, linking women's liberation to national and racial liberation, and empowering women to write about their struggles and strengths are all part of the redefinition of resistance in which, I believe, many contemporary South African women poets are participating. In the spirit of indigenous storytellers and praise poets, whose oral presentations command direct and enthusiastic audience participation, these women resistance poets are inviting readers to their work with a simple question: "Are you ready to listen?"[51]

4

> In this country you may not
> suffer the death of your stillborn
> remember the last push into shadow and silence
> . . . in this country you may not
> mourn small passings.
>
> —Ingrid de Kok, "Small Passing"

> Dear, dear Mama
> they tell me I am a funeral dancer.
>
> —Gcina Mhlope, "The Dancer"

In "Preparing Ourselves for Freedom" Albie Sachs proposes that art-
ists lay down their cultural weapons and, instead, create art that
reveals society's contradictions and tensions as well as "the emergent
personality of our people."[52] Writing is best when it reflects conflict-
ing emotions—"struggles and torments and moments of joy"—rather
than being all fists and spears and guns. What Sachs seems to be
calling for, and what several of his respondents endorse, is a renewed
emphasis on aesthetics, which, according to traditional Western po-
etic discourse, suggests a return to lyricism. After all, Sachs notes,
"what are we fighting for, if not the right to express our humanity in
all its forms, including our sense of fun and capacity for love and
tenderness and our appreciation of the beauty of the world?" Lyrical
poetry need not be politically dispassionate, he argues; in fact, the
ambiguities it chronicles can lead readers to a richer appreciation of
struggle, to an awareness that there is bad in the good and good in
the bad.[53]

A number of outstanding South African women poets writing in
the late 1980s and 1990s have chosen to blend the lyrical and the
political in powerful poems of resistance redefined. These poems are
not overtly feminist—that is, they do not attack patriarchy or choose
gender as their central issue or theme—yet they clearly reflect the
poets' gendered resistant consciousnesses. A girl child's first encoun-
ter with racism and sexual shame, a white woman's experience of
stillbirth, her solidarity with black mothers who have lost children in
more violent ways, an African daughter's honoring of her mother's
creative legacy: such subjects demand both lyricism and political in-

tensity, and such subjects have been written about convincingly from women's perspectives.

Ingrid de Kok's "Our Sharpeville" combines autobiography, lyricism, and antiapartheid sentiments in the saga of a young white girl whose political and sexual awareness is heightened by events that occur near her home on the day of the historic Sharpeville massacre of 1960, when sixty-seven unarmed black anti-pass demonstrators were shot dead by police. The poem also interrogates the complex concept of home as a site from which to confront the painful legacies of apartheid and sexism, difficult negotiations for the child re-membered in the poem as well as for the adult speaker struggling for insight and reconciliation. The poem opens with a young girl

> playing hopscotch on the slate
> when miners roared past in lorries,
> their arms raised, signals at a crossing,
> their chanting foreign and familiar.

The miners, of course, were participants in the PAC-sponsored workers' strike that resulted in police violence; to the child, however, they appeared part of a great dramatic caravan like the kind she had seen in her Sunday school book, which showed men in wagons stopping at a deep jade pool to rest. The girl's reverie on this "foreign and familiar" sight is abruptly broken by her grandmother's call from just inside the front door, "her voice a stiff broom over the steps": "'Come inside; they do things to little girls.'"

This command, which occurs at the middle of the poem, marks not only the first half of the text but also an epiphanic moment, a shift in the child's political and gendered awareness. The light of noon, the center of the day as the grandmother's words are the poem's center, evokes the girl's painful awareness that "there was no jade pool," as in her Bible story fantasies. "Instead, a pool of blood that already had a living name / and grew like a shadow as the day lengthened." That name, of course, was Sharpeville, and what the child reluctantly recognizes is the stark contrast between hegemonic white history, which will erase and/or distort the massacres, and the alternative histories of the oppressed. In her family's closed white community the dead of Sharpeville,

buried in voices that reached even my gate,
. . . were not heroes . . .
but maulers of children,
doing things that had to remain nameless.

The metaphor of namelessness has a double function in the poem: it
signifies the anonymity of the dead to the unconcerned white towns-
people as well as the "unnameable" crime, female sexual abuse,
against which the grandmother has euphemistically spoken. The
stiffness in her grandmother's voice and her misrepresentation of the
men's intentions, which the child intuitively recognizes, makes the
girl doubt for the the first time the truth of her grandmother's admo-
nitions. The poem's central themes, the silence and concealment en-
forced by a powerful racial minority and the girl's ambivalent com-
plicity in this suppression, are revealed in the last two lines of the
penultimate stanza: "And our Sharpeville was this fearful thing / that
might tempt us across the well swept streets."

One set of doubts gives way to another, however, for the child,
after all, is a product of this racist and myopic environment as well
as its implicit critic. Could her grandmother possibly be right about
the miners? The adult poet knows better, but the child remains uncer-
tain:

If I had turned I would have seen
brocade curtains drawn tightly across sheer net ones,
known there were eyes behind both,
heard the dogs pacing in the locked yard next door.
But, walking backwards, all I felt was shame,
at being a girl, at having been found at the gate,
at having heard my grandmother lie
and at my fear her lie might be true.
Walking backward, called back,
I returned to the closed rooms, home.[54]

The last stanza puts forth a powerful image cluster to reinforce the
theme of narrow-minded protectionism: tightly drawn curtains, peer-
ing eyes, pacing dogs, closed rooms. It also presents a final, inter-
related thematic concern, an almost silent subtext, that of gendered

shame—"shame, / at being a girl" and, thus, by definition requiring warnings such as her grandmother's, at bringing the danger on herself by having dared to wander to the gate and look. The repetition of "walking backwards" suggests the speaker's adult awareness of the skewed perspective on gender and race that she received as a white female child in apartheid South Africa. Despite her return to the closed rooms of home—for what else, then, could she do?—the speaker reveals her ambivalence toward this physical and emotional site. In fact, the entire volume from which this poem is taken interrogates the concept of home from the perspective of a politically conscious white South African, fully aware of the oppression and privilege this construct can be used to conceal.

The complex legacy passed on through generations of women is also the theme of Gcina Mhlope's lyrical homage to her mother, "The Dancer." Here the daughter-speaker is black, and she celebrates her maternal inheritance unambivalently even as she mourns the societal violence that keeps her from fully realizing it.

> Mama,
> they tell me you were a dancer
> they tell me you had long
> beautiful legs to carry your graceful body
> they tell me you were a dancer
>
> Mama,
> they tell me you sang beautiful solos
> they tell me you closed your eyes
> always when the feeling of the song
> was right, and lifted your face up to the sky
> they tell me you were an enchanting dancer

The poem's mesmerizing quality arises partly from the daughter's repeated direct address to the mother she never knew, partly from the compelling images of grace and enchantment conjured by the bereft child and the "they" who wish to impart the legacy. The speaker goes on to imagine her mother as a wedding dancer performing for an audience of celebrants but not, alas, for her child as well:

> tshi tshi tshitshitshitha, tshitshi tshitshitshitha
> o hee! how I wish I was there to see you
> they tell me you were a pleasure to watch.

A storyteller and performer as well as a poet, Mhlope draws heavily on orality and onomatopoeia in this stanza, as she brings the mother's wedding dance alive by imitating the swishing of her graceful feet and imagining her own delight, had she been there to witness the scene.

In her final stanza Mhlope reveals a terrible irony that connects mother and daughter even as it delineates the different parameters of their lives and art: one chronicles life in her dance, the other death. Simple language and understated grief combine to give this poem its aesthetic and emotional power:

> Mama,
> they tell me I am a dancer too
> but I don't know . . .
> don't know for sure what a wedding dancer is
> there are no more weddings
> but many, many funerals

Since celebrations in black communities in South Africa can rarely be fully joyous, nascent dancers must instead use their feet for "running fast with the coffin / of a would-be bride," their tearful eyes "filled with vengeance." The poet's use of the stark word *vengeance* near the end of an otherwise lyrical poem reveals her political purpose: to expose the atrocities to which black families are subjected and to document their angry resistance. "Dear, dear Mama," Mhlope concludes softly, "they tell me I am a funeral dancer."[55]

Karen Press's "When your child is born, mother" employs two of Mhlope's poetic techniques—direct address and a lyrical refrain— to depict women's maternal grief during war and to urge women to "unlearn the old lessons / your mother taught you," lessons of passivity and despair:

When your child is born, mother
place a songbird at your nipple
and fix the child's mouth to the rationed tap.
Bitter water its comfort, dust of the streets its cradle.

When your child is born, mother
give your heart to a piece of land,
and when the child goes out
to fight, sing out across the land
and when they bring the body back
clutch the land to your breast, and build your house there.

In the context of apartheid violence, Press suggests gently, mothers
must inure themselves to the inevitability of the loss of children, but
they need not accept this loss without resistance. Mothers must also
continue to sing, to be politically committed, and to rebuild.
Women's traditional resourcefulness emerges during times of strug-
gle, she continues:

When your child is born, mother
pour your love into a clay pot,
bury it in a corner of the house.
If the future comes, there will be wine for the feast.
If the future does not come, there will be water for a small grave.

Female despair cannot longer be tolerated, Press insists; the contem-
porary African mother must actively engage in preparation for the
future, whether or not it will come. "Do not sit waiting over the
supper pot," the poet concludes in her final series of imperatives;
passive femininity must be unlearned. In this process one's children,
not one's mothers, can be the teachers:

mothers, look at your children, these small stones
building a road through the country,
these graves like footsteps towards the harvest.[56]

This is a politically risky poem, given that Press, a white woman,
could be accused of "doing the work" for black women in chiding

them about what they must unlearn. I see it, rather, as a poem of solidarity and encouragement toward the construction of a mutually empowering nonracial future.

What one mother can learn from other mothers both like and different from herself is the subject of Ingrid de Kok's "Small Passing," a lyrical tribute to women's potential solidarity across racial lines during times of struggle and loss. The poem's epigraph reveals its dedication to "a woman whose baby died stillborn, and who was told by a man to stop mourning, 'because the trials and horrors suffered daily by black women in this country are more significant than the loss of one white child.'" This epigraph raises at once the gendered issue of men telling women what they have the right to feel, the racial issue of blaming or bonding between black and white mothers, and the overarching issue of "political correctness" in the context of apartheid's bitter legacy. Who does have the right to mourn the loss of a child in this violent society? Does one's gender or race grant one the license to draw emotional parameters for another? Can one's private grief ever be simultaneously public, collective, and can this collectivity be nonracial? It is with these questions that de Kok's poem grapples.

Section 1 of the poem poses its central problem in language as absolute and final as the man's dictum, yet it also conveys lyrically the numbing despair of a woman whose child is born dead:

> In this country you may not
> suffer the death of your stillborn
> remember the last push into shadow and silence,
> the useless wires and cords on your stomach,
> the nurse's face, the walls, the afterbirth in a basin.
> Do not touch your breasts
> still full of purpose.
> Do not circle the house,
> pack, unpack the small clothes.
> Do not lie awake at night hearing
> the doctor say "It was just as well"
> and "You can have another."
> In this country you may not
> mourn small passings.

The doctor's callousness matches that of the man in the epigraph, the poet implies, yet for all her resentment she knows their partial truths. Children in South Africa do suffer enormously, as do their mothers, if they are black. De Kok's second stanza offers miniportraits of bereft Africans—a homeless newspaper boy sleeping in a doorway in the rain, a city woman removed by force to a homeland that was never her home, a baby whose parents cannot afford her care sent to an aunt. Nor are the famous exempted from the pain of separation and dislocation: "Mandela's daughter tried to find her father / through the glass. She thought they'd let her touch him." Other black women, the poet continues, are forced to care for white women's children at the expense of their own: one woman's

> hands are so heavy when she dusts
> the photographs of other children
> they fall to the floor and break.

Elsewhere, nannies meet on sidewalks in what the poet tells us, in an ironic aside, are "legal gatherings" and talk "about everything, about home."

Part 2 of the poem pans the South African landscape in a frenzied movement from one suffering child to another:

> Small wrist in the grave.
> Baby no one carried live
> between houses, among trees.
> Child shot running,
> stones in his pocket,
> boy's swollen stomach
> full of hungry air.
> Girls carrying babies
> not much smaller than themselves.

The societal disruption and pain that these children reveal is reflected grammatically by the poet's use of fragments; one short image piles atop the next to reveal "Erosion. Soil washed down to the sea." In this country, de Kok suggests, the unimaginable is true. Yet there is hope in the power of mothers to help one another, across racial lines, through these traumas. In the final stanza, the poet asserts her alter-

native, woman-centered vision of potential healing. Black mothers
who "dream / headstones of the unborn," whose "mourning rises
like a wall / no vine will cling to," will refuse to be the arbiters of
white mothers' grief, she alleges.

> They will not tell you your suffering is white.
> They will not say it is just as well.
> They will not compete for the ashes of infants.

On the contrary, these mothers will reject privileged suffering and
patriarchal judgment—or so, the poet is careful to tell us, she be-
lieves:

> I think they may say to you:
> Come with us to the place of mothers.
> We will stroke your flat empty belly,
> let you weep with us in the dark,
> and arm you with one of our babies
> to carry home on your back.[57]

Even as she deftly presents women's solidarity, the speaker casts
doubt upon her perspective; "the place of mothers" *may* exist, and
the black women there *may* respond with generosity to the new white
visitor. The mixed reception of de Kok's poem among black women
attests to the controversial nature of its theme, since some criticized
her for presuming connection between black and white women in
their grief, while others praised her compassionate vision.[58]

Can a poem be, finally, both lyrical and political? Can black and
white women's lyric poems about the contradictions and tensions of
their daily lives under apartheid, a subject Albie Sachs and many of
his respondents view as needing more attention, be aesthetically
pleasing as well as meaningful to the struggle? The poems discussed
above suggest that, indeed, they can. Acknowledging that lyric po-
etry may not always make a "daily difference," Ingrid de Kok argues
convincingly that it nonetheless does "make a sort of a difference in
some contexts, sometimes." Whether the written lyric is also politi-
cal, that is, depends upon whether it reflects its historical context in
a conscious, accountable way. Lyric poems by the women cited above
are politically conscious in that, as de Kok suggests, they are "put to

the service of the historical moment in all its urgency."[59] As apartheid groans to a weary end in the 1990s, the link between art and politics is further complicated, for the creation of new political space requires the creation of a new language.[60] De Kok, Mhlope, and Press are among the many women poets in South Africa who employ a rejuvenated lyrical aesthetic and a gendered consciousness in poems that seek to dismantle apartheid as they herald the possibility of change. They also challenge any notion of a gender-neutral aesthetic by privileging women's experiences of girlhood initiation and maternity as subjects worthy of both poetic and political scrutiny.[61] Finally, in their subtle criticisms of apartheid society from women's perspectives across differences, they contribute to the kind of world the ANC document on women's emancipation calls for, "a world in which the health, happiness and welfare of all is guaranteed."[62]

5

> I am weary of weaving words
> into another torn, tattered tapestry of the times
> we live in . . .
> It so happens that I want to be a woman undeniably
> who writes erotic love poetry.
>   —Lisa Combrinck, "Concerning the Subject Matter of this Poetry"
>
> Love is a liquid feeling
> in the milky way of dreams.
>   —Heather Robertson, "Love"

One of the most controversial topics in the Albie Sachs debates has been his injunction to resistance poets to write more about love.[63] "Can it be that once we join the ANC we do not make love any more, that when the comrades go to bed they discuss the role of the white working class?" Sachs wonders wryly; what are they fighting for if not the right to feel and express love? Nise Malange agrees that it is necessary to write about love but reminds readers that, when one makes love while fearful that her house will be firebombed, as she has done, art and struggle *must* intersect. For Lesego Rampolokeng, too, lovemaking occurs only in the context of challenging injustice: "I do make love, comrades, but the love I make is of babies born in prisons not hospitals: if they are, it is on top of other people . . . [because of the shortage of beds]. Augustinho Neho made love and

Angola was conceived."[64] South African women poets who write
about love in the late 1980s and 1990s wrestle too with the issue of
whether love and politics are ever separable. Lisa Combrinck, a
COSAW member from Cape Town, rejects "the tedium of producing
political patches" in her art and, instead, embraces sexuality as the
subject of her latest poetry, admitting all the while that "most of my
poems . . . / shape words into the slogans we shout" even as she
foregrounds the erotic.[65] Heather Robertson, formerly COSAW coor-
dinator in Cape Town and now a journalist and poet in Johan-
nesburg, declares that lovemaking provides fleeting pleasure before
the next meeting or rally to which the activist must inevitably rush.[66]
Along with Sobhna Poona, Deela Khan, Meryl Coetzee, Ingrid de
Kok, and Gertrude Fester, Combrinck and Robertson have chosen to
explore their sexuality and sexual relationships in poems that leave
the weapons of struggle, however momentarily, at the door to the
bedroom.

In a poem entitled "To the Reader," Combrinck begins with the
query "Why should a woman not write erotic love poems?" True, she
continues,

> most of my poems are about the struggle: shaping words into the
> stones we throw at the oppressor
> . . . But these cold stones, these slogans of struggle,
> these wounds, these spears will not be free
> until they come to terms with femininity
> and feel the freedom of love.

Combrinck's affiliation with Sachs on this point is evident; her poem
reads like a poetic version of the request he makes in prose. But her
question also has a feminist tone of resistance, insisting that women
now claim the right to write of sexuality as men have long since done:

> In this struggle, let us leave some space
> for people in love, love's bleeding lips, a blushing face.
> And allow this woman unconditionally
> to write lines and lines of erotic love poetry.[67]

Combrinck asserts this right in numerous poems in *Unfolding
Petals*, whose title reveals its emphasis on sexuality, but she ad-

dresses it most self-consciously in the previous poem and one other. "Concerning the Subject Matter of this Poetry," like "To the Reader," is an apologia that refuses to apologize; instead, like the U.S. poet of democracy Walt Whitman, she celebrates herself and sings herself. "Simply being a person / in the political melting-pot," "aborting all talk of sex," no longer is acceptable to Combrinck as a woman or a poet. "I declare emphatically for you and all the world to see / that I shall sing openly and honestly of sexual love." Furthermore, she asserts that her song will differ when sung "through the lips of a woman," yet it will be as vital as a man's. Her goal is "to let the poem throb furiously / with an urgent, persistent femininity."[68]

When Combrinck writes a poem for her lover, however, she writes frequently of resistance to apartheid and the desire for a new and just world. "My love / you have lost your way," she declares in "The Journey";

> put your finger deep within me
> return to the source
> and confirm your route
> the spoors of the struggle
> are difficult to identify
> and dangerous to follow.

Her body can be a guidepost, she claims, their lovemaking "moistening the present / mapping out the future." In another poem, anticipating a new lover, she creates an experiential prototype:

> when at last we love
> all existing texts will fall away
> like black sheets we'll meet
> create a new world
> invent the first day.

Making love is recreation and re-creation for Combrinck:

> like children we'll scrawl
> give birth to wondrous words
> . . . rise and fall time and again
> pattern our new page of life.

Sexuality and writing are closely aligned, and often, as in this poem, her erotic need is strongest when she is creating:

> I write with wide-open legs
> waiting for the sun
> to pounce
> and fuck me furiously.
> . . . Only this desire to write
> turns me on.[69]

In her frank expressions of desire as resistance and resistance as desire, Combrinck represents a new breed of South African women poets who view eroticism as powerful aesthetic and political terrain.

Like Combrinck, Heather Robertson links lovemaking to creating a different world, but she also foregrounds its playful dimensions. She and her lover

> swim in love's pool
> splash
> laugh
> dive
> then rise
> to fly
> to the next meeting
> where we pour our love
> into the calabash
> of a new society.[70]

The image of the calabash emphasizes the earthiness of this project and reinforces Sachs's point that the new society must be receptive to the pleasures of love after decades of having to focus on its losses. But apartheid is not yet eradicated, and the loss of a lover to the struggle is not yet a problem resolved, Indian poet Sobhna Poona reminds readers in "They Came at Twilight." This poem is written in the voice of a young woman whose lover is detained just after their first sexual encounter:

> They came at twilight
> seconds after

my first act of love
they came
with weapons at their side
and dense folds of paper
they took you away.

That this police raid is recalled from a distant vantage point is evident
when the speaker reveals that she now has a son, whose loss, she
admits to her lover, she dreads as well:

everyday
at twilight
i write you a poem
. . . your son
will want to know
he will ask questions
and i will lie
for fear
of losing him too.

Here Poona poignantly depicts the dilemma of the black single
mother whose partner is imprisoned: if she tells her child the truth
about his father's whereabouts, he will want to join the children's
resistance effort and she will no longer have him either. Significantly,
Poona's speaker is a poet, one who writes of both love and resistance.
Her poetry, Poona implies, contributes to both her child's and her
lover's well-being as well as to the speaker's own peace of mind.[71]
    Other South African women writing of love and loss resist an
individual man and/or a patriarchal institution other than apartheid.
Deela Khan, an Indian poet from Cape Town, rejects love altogether
in "Cocktail Party Effect," for overhearing another woman's tale of
betrayal evokes her own cynicism:

My ears pricked as his name slithered
through the drone of cafeteria chatter.
"He's a walking cock . . . "
she said, convinced.
"I hurled him right out of my life but
as always, he landed on his feet

unscathed."
He was my friend.
Colliding with hurt, I was forced to
admit that the tale was true.

Khan's speaker's reluctant realization leads her to empathize with the angry woman and reflect upon her own relational dilemmas. Her liaison will be with no man, she concludes, but with life and poetry:

I walked away
hardened,
upright and strong.
It's to life that
I belong.
No man
will shatter my song![72]

Four years later, however, Khan's speaker is singing a bitter song of lost love and betrayal. "I carried your face with me like a talisman," she laments; "it seasoned my life with herbs I'd never / tasted, with spice it sorely lacked." Naively, she had believed this love would "outlast / the sphinxes," but such a dream, she realizes now, "eludes us all." Now, instead of her lover's talismanic face, she sees "a thorn-tattered mask." What is left of their love is depicted finally through the surrealistic image of

a mangy mongrel trapped in a minefield—
Cursed with eternal life, it totters the
Death-strip, skipping the fatal blast to
Stardom with every tread.[73]

This bizarre scenario takes on a harsh realism, however, when one considers the South African landscape from which it is written, where a half-dead dog wandering aimlessly, through what was once a township but is now a minefield, constitutes a grimly common sight.

Meryl Coetzee's "Institutions" indicts marriage as an institution leading painfully but ineluctably to adultery and divorce. The speaker's rage is evident in her assertion that, even though she and

her lover defined marriage as "only a piece of paper," it assumed a
seamy life of its own:

> the institution swallows us
> with its rottenness
> as it has swallowed
> most who went before us.

Some of this rottenness she ascribes to her unfaithful husband, who
not only rationalizes his infidelity as "only a much-needed fling" but
tries to convince her to stay with him and experiment with

> the self-made institution
> of liberated 20th-century
> polygamy.

Although the speaker wants to believe his assertions of love for her,
and even wants to stay, she realizes finally that she lives in bondage.
Thus, she embraces bitterly

> the best intitution of all
> invented as it is by man
> but God's gift to woman
> the welcome institution
> of divorce.

Despite her fierce rejection of her husband and their marriage, the
speaker reveals her ambivalence in the jolting final lines: "—now
maybe we can love each / other, I say."[74]

A problematic sexual partner is also the subject of Ingrid de
Kok's "To a Would-be Lover," which chronicles the sort of lover the
speaker prefers as well as addressing one whom she rejects. "I once
knew a man who made love / with pockets of iron filings," begins
de Kok with a line sure first to shock and then to amuse. "The ma-
chines were oiled, the pistons shone, / we were stapled together and
sent through a shute." Callous, dangerous sex is not to the speaker's
liking, but neither is performance art:

> And you would probably balance
> like a gymnast on the cross-bar,
> just before the triple turn,
> with the air still, the audience still,
> energy parallel with intention.

Disgusted with men whose egos are insatiable, who watch themselves in an imaginary mirror during sex rather than attending their partners, the poet goes on to inform her "would-be lover" in some detail about her preferences. First off, she rejects the stereotypically masculine:

> I cannot love athletes or makers of metal things
> or anyone associated with the Concorde.
> I like the sillier body, earthbound,
> with its many joints and dents:
> a squat figure on a sweaty mat.

This homely, earthy man "whose shirt hangs out" is paired with a clumsy "heroine who trips over the bed / because her contacts are lost under the sink." De Kok's lovers are unpretentious and flawed.

The fourth stanza offers a lyrical praisesong to "the inelegance of ordinary love," with its soft pillows and cold feet and interrupting doorbells. With characteristic attention to language and structure, de Kok here plays with grammatical and literary terms in a governing image cluster. Love, that "delicious fiction," must

> dangle its infinitives,
> forget to close its clauses,
> offer alternative endings.

The "pyrotechnic suitor" to whom her poem is addressed would never be so careless or carefree, the poet concludes; he thus must be not only rejected but also mocked with the image he reflects in *her* mirror:

> So, pyrotechnic suitor,
> your skin is far too sleek,
> your arms too architectural,
> your timing much too neat.
> I'm sure you'll find another
> to watch you in the mirror
> but I must refuse your offer
> and decline to conjugate.[75]

The poet's delight in word play is evident here, as is her pleasure at putting this suitor in his place. Still, her theme is serious for all that, as she celebrates love in the classic comic mode, as a form of imperfect celebration.

Women's poetry about sexuality, desire, and betrayal fits uneasily into any resistance paradigm, but, in the context of the Albie Sachs debates and the injunction to write of love instead of (or along with) spears, poems about heterosexual experience can help to redefine culture and struggle. For lesbians writing of their sexuality in South Africa, however, the link to resistance is more obvious, since the police continue to harass gays and lesbians, and homophobia flourishes despite the ANC's recent inclusion of a clause outlawing discrimination on the basis of sexual orientation in its draft of a proposed bill of rights. Although there is a small body of lesbian poetry published in Afrikaans, lesbian poets writing in English appear to be few, indeed. A prominent item of graffiti found in Cape Town, however, calls upon lesbians to "unite in armed snuggle," and in October 1990, just eight months after the government lifted its ban on demonstrations, eight hundred people rallied in Johannesburg central for the country's first lesbian and gay pride march. Carrying balloons and signs that read "Black Gays Are Beautiful" and "God Let Almal Lief" (God Loves Everyone), the marchers insisted on their right to visibility and justice.[76]

Given this changing but still repressive environment, Cape Town activist-poet Gertrude Fester's nonchalant presentation of lesbian experience in "Really Woman" is all the more striking. A call to women activists to reexamine their priorities when the struggle starts to overwhelm their personal lives, the poem uses irony and humor to suggest that "real women" need sex and love as much as demonstrations and meetings and that sometimes their sexual partners are women. "Really Woman," the poem begins,

> if you're awakened with a phone call
> in the wee wee hours of the morning
> it's not your lover telling you about
> a hot hot dream she's just had . . .
> it's some comrade or other;
> the venue or time's been changed
> for the meeting, workshop or whatever . . .
> Then, woman, you should take a good look at your life.

That Fester's speaker's rollicking admonition is self-directed can be seen when she turns to her own diary, "mottled with appointments," and realizes she has left no time for anything "as ordinary / as walking with Sandra" or "movies with Pam." No, her time must be devoted to her duties:

> Women's League
> what fatigue!
> it's resolutions, draft proposals, workshops, nominations,
> pamphleteering, picketing, some door-to-door for sure.

Where will she find the time for frolicking with her lover, the poet laments? "Really woman," she concludes in exasperation, "you've got to take a good hard critical /analytical look at yourself!"[77]

Poems by South African women about sexuality and the relational world, as well as those that unveil the institution of marriage or propose lesbianism as a viable alternative, must take their place along the continuum defined as resistance art. They are resistant to patriarchal traditions that would deny women sexual expression, resistant to cultural edicts that deem love inappropriate revolutionary subject matter, resistant to men who disappoint and betray, resistant to apartheid's restrictions on love, and at times resistant to any internal impulse to remain silent on such private matters. Although not all women's love poetry is feminist, furthermore, it is useful to examine this body of work from a feminist rather than a womanist perspective. Lockett's assertion that womanism is the best lens through which to examine black women's writing falls short when applied to the poems discussed above. Neither Combrinck, Robertson, Poona, nor Khan—all black, Indian, or so-called colored women poets—empowers men who are sexist, as the Nigerian womanist critic Chikwenya Okonjo Ogunyemi endorses, nor do they hesitate to challenge black patriarchy alongside apartheid. With Zoë Wicomb, these poets see no reason *not* to challenge both at once. In fact, as the next section will show, both black and white women poets have written overtly feminist poems that reveal that sexism, patriarchy, and the apartheid mind-set are inextricably linked.

The impulse that most fiercely quickens women's poetry about love and sexuality, I would argue, is their subtle recognition of what the U.S. poet Audre Lorde has called "the erotic as power":

> The erotic is a resource within each of us that lies in a deeply female and spiritual plane, firmly rooted in the power of our unexpressed or unrecognized feeling. In order to perpetuate itself, each oppression must corrupt or distort these various sources of power within the culture of the oppressed that can provide energy for change. For women, this has meant a suppression of the erotic as a considered source of power and information within our lives.

For women confronting oppression under apartheid as well as sexism, and for women living under the scrutiny of the powerful and conservative Dutch Reform church, erotic power has been especially difficult to assume. But in South Africa today, more and more women poets are endorsing Lorde's view that claiming the power of the erotic in their lives can increase their artistic energy and strengthen their commitment to change. For in embracing the erotic, Lorde concludes, "not only do we touch our most profoundly creative source, but we do that which is female and self-affirming in the face of a racist, patriarchal, and anti-erotic society."[78]

6

All I hear is "women are nuisance."
Is it not time to give me a little respect?
—Boikhutso Siane, "I Am a Woman"

And then this quick critic,
at the last moment, shot out of the blue
Well, what kind of feminist are you?
It took me till supper time to retaliate
out loud to the kitchen wall—
What kind of fucking man are you?

—Joan Metelerkamp, "Poem"

Although there is a great deal of overlap between South African women's poems about sexuality and their antisexist poetry, the latter category encompasses poems that challenge not only lovers but employers, colleagues, the entire male-dominated system.[79] Like the women leaders in the WNC, no longer willing to assume that the male hierarchy will address their concerns, a number of poets are airing their gripes against patriarchy with poignancy, humor, anger, and passion. With grassroots poet Boikhutso Siane, they demand respect for who they are and the work they do; with academic Joan Metelerkamp, they retaliate against invisibility, trivialization, and exploitation. Not all feminist poetry is antipatriarchal, nor is all antipatriarchal poetry feminist. But the feminist debates, both in the academy and in organizations like COSAW and the ANC, have cleared space for women to "negotiate between lived experience and feminism, awareness and knowledge."[80]

In a poem published in the women's fashion magazine *Tribute*, Boikhutso Siane speaks for many women in a plea for justice and equality. "I am craving to be respected / I am crying to have my rights," she begins, then continues to tell the truth about her life. Although she works twice as hard as any man, both inside and outside the home, "all I hear is 'women are nuisance.'" Despite this overt condemnation of sexism, in a maneuver that might suggest her affiliation with Ogunyemi's brand of womanism, Siane addresses not men but, rather, "African people." This choice of address reveals as well what Zoë Wicomb has called "the prohibitions that govern a black woman's discourse."[81] Still, Siane speaks loudly and clearly. "Listen to my voice," she insists;

I cannot afford to be a slave
As a woman I do not deserve that
I have my hands and brains and action
A woman of substance and a mother.

Like many contemporary African women poets, Siane refuses to elide womanhood and motherhood; both identities are important to her, and both she sees as deserving respect. Yet her decision to mask her intended audience with the generic label African people illustrates how concealment can become "a trope for the woman writer who has to negotiate the conflicting loyalties of race and gender."[82]

Sexist exploitation within marriage is the subject of Boitumelo Mofokeng's "With My Baby on My Back," a working wife and mother's lament at her domestic servitude in her own home. Using simple language and her title as a refrain, the poet catalogs the household responsibilities she must shoulder singlehandedly and thus exposes her husband's sexism:

> With my baby on my back
> day in and day out I toil
> with my baby on my back.
> Hour after hour I count undone chores.
> I'll have to stop at 6 p.m. to prepare meals
> with my baby on my back.

Why is it her job to contend with "all cries of hunger," to sing their child lullabies, to do housework alone with her husband watching? The final irony, Mofokeng suggests, occurs at bedtime, when at last he does

> help to remove my baby from my back
> because it is time to make love:
> the only chore I do without
> my baby on my back.

When sex is more a duty than a pleasure, she concludes, something at home must change. In an article in *Speak*, a grassroots feminist magazine in South Africa, Mofokeng urges other black women to be courageous enough to write about domestic problems and to raise their sons not to be sexist. "Let us bring up our children without treating girls and boys differently. Because then when males have grown up, they will give their wives a chance. Let us express our true feelings about the things which keep us down. If we don't speak for ourselves, men will accept that things are okay."[83]

Nise Malange's "Nightshift Mother" addresses a concern related to both Siane's and Mofokeng's, black women's double work shift and economic exploitation. This poem is typical of workers' poetry in its use of a first-person account, its kinetic quality, and its reliance on nonstandard English (the second or third language of most Africans); its poignancy comes from the power of the woman's voice and her frustrated call for resistance:

> Left with a double load
> > at home
> > > my children left uncared
>
> Anxiety
> > at work
> > > my boss insists we should
> > > be grateful for the opportunities
> > > he gives women to be exploited
>
> Anxiety
> And I am stranded with these loads,
> this "nightshift job" which brings home pittance

As a poor single mother in an apartheid state, the speaker goes on to explain, she has no choice but to take this terrible job. Because she has "no other training," "no place to place my children in the day," she cares for her kids by day and cleans office floors at night,

> lost in these vast buildings
> forgotten and neglected
> exploited as you sleep.

The "you" reveals the speaker's intended audience: the exploiter himself and those more privileged than she. This angry worker speaks not only for herself but for other women like her, "unmarried mothers, widows, / elder women, migrants, but always" Malange concludes, "mothers." As the poem ends, she calls upon black worker women to act in solidarity and refuse further oppression:

We are
        cleaning and cleaning
            lift each other off our knees
            and fight our exploitation[84]

This poem is feminist in its interweaving of gender, race, and class issues to reveal the realities of African women's lives and to challenge white patriarchy on multiple levels simultaneously.

South African women poets are also confronting men's sexual objectification of women and some women's complicity in that objectification. Ingrid de Kok's "Woman in the Glass" refuses sexualization by cataloging a series of male fantasies and disassociating herself from them:

I am not the woman in the train
who pulls your hand between her legs
and then looks out of the window
. . . Nor am I the woman in the glass
who looks at you look at her
and the glass smokes over.
. . . Nor am I the woman in the dark
whose silence is the meteor
in the sky of your conversation.

Your ego is no doubt salved by that self-effacing woman, the speaker continues to an unidentified man, but she is a traitor to other women. "That woman, bent over, offering her sex to you / like a globe of garlic, asking for nothing" participates in her own and other women's oppression, de Kok implies; she is the "widow-virgin" who "burns on your pyre." The speaker takes perverse delight in watching the woman burn, as

her mouth drips wax,
her eyebrows peel off,
her sex unstitches its tiny mirrors.

Yet even as she condemns "that woman," de Kok acknowledges an uncomfortable identification with her. "Your woman: cousin, sister, twin," the first line of the poem's last stanza, reveals the poet's empathy; the missing pronoun, the fissure in the text, is *my*. Your fantasy woman, she tells her male listener reluctantly, is my cousin—no, closer than that, my sister, no, actually my twin, my shadowy double. The poem's last lines assert the contrast between a patriarchal attitude toward this complicitous woman and the poet's own ambivalent perspective: "You want her burning, distant, dumb. / I want to save, and tear, her tongue."[85]

Interrogation of identity is also the theme of Joan Metelerkamp's "Poem," which details an academic woman's enraged response to a male professor who challenges her feminism.

> People surprise me by asking
> what kind of feminist are you
> concisely, what's your specific stand?"

The speaker's ironic narrative perspective (for this is a prose poem written in colloquial language) quickly reveals her resentment of these "people's" call for precision, which she sees as masking their desire to trivialize; thus, she throws precision back in their faces: "What kind of people precisely? / . . . oh, academics maybe, and critics." Metelerkamp is not unwilling to enter into dialogue with her pompous interlocutors, but it must be on her terms; she barely conceals her desire to beat them at their own game. "Judging by my way of acting," she retorts with precision,

> by the way you see my passion
> articulate with the discourse,
> what kind of feminist do you think I seem?

The language of contemporary academic literary theory is parodied by Metelerkamp here. Eventually, one particularly reprehensible colleague—a man of some reputation, we are told—emerges as the target of her most juvenalian satire. "What kind of critic do you think you are / I might as well say," the poet continues, practicing her slicing and dicing; "what kind of a man are you?" At lunch just yesterday with "X," who invited her out but then brought his own sandwich and offered her none, she tried to see him as he sees himself, "genial and well intended." Her effort fails, however, when she confronts his inability to communicate authentically and his carefully masked but transparent disdain of who she is. "And then this quick critic," the poet concludes, "shot out of the blue / Well, what kind of feminist are you?" Her furious response, delivered with pro-verbial hindsight to her kitchen wall later that evening, recasts her afternoon's ironic musings. "What kind of fucking man are you?"[86]

How can feminist theory enhance our understanding of antipa-triarchal poems by South African women writing today? An extended anecdote will perhaps help to answer this question. Zoë Wicomb begins her essay "To Hear the Variety of Discourses" by narrating an incident that occurred at a political gathering she recently at-tended at the University of Cape Town. Before the scheduled speaker, Albie Sachs, took the podium, as a group of young black men from the townships played rousing music, four bikini-clad Afri-can women leapt onto the stage, gyrating, to sing with the band about freedom. Hoarse cries from the crowd followed, Wicomb con-tinues, followed by *amandlas*, vivas, and longlives. Sachs went on to speak about "the need to enshrine the right to be the same as well as the right to be different" in any new constitution, but the spectacle that preceded him was more interesting to Wicomb, a feminist, than the main speaker. Her attempt to "read the evening's discourse" in terms of womanism failed, she explains, because to subjugate gender issues to racial ones is to overlook the contradictions of the incident in question. Womanism, by Ogunyemi's definition, can only "meet the spectacle with silence." In contrast, a feminist "reading" of the evening's discourse might reveal that revolution "can be a pretext for domination," as black women, by coercion or choice, "participate in their own degradation."[87]

Similarly, feminist analysis reveals that the poets represented above refuse also to meet the spectacle of sexist oppression with silence, despite their commitment to revolutionary changes and/or their awareness of some women's complicity in their own oppres-sion. Jenny de Reuck, a South African teaching and writing in Austra-lia, argues that feminists in her homeland could contribute signifi-cantly to a theory of social justice if they would deconstruct "the 'edifice' of patriarchy" and thereby liberate the oppressed "from ide-ologies of race or class or gender": "In so doing . . . we would find, in the process of articulating our positions as subjects in a South African feminist aesthetic, 'our measure exactly, / Not the echo of other voices.' "[88] I would argue that the women poets cited here—in merging the lyrical and the political, in exploring women's sexuality, and in challenging sexism—contribute to social justice in their deconstructions of patriarchy's edifices. They also participate in creating a feminist aesthetic, by finding their own measure, exactly.

Chapter 6

"Lust for a Working Tomorrow": U.S. Women's Poetry of Solidarity and Struggle

So where is true history written
except in the poems?
—Audre Lorde, *Our Dead behind Us*

One cannot disown one's own culture. One can reconstruct it in struggle.
—Maria Lugones, in Anzaldúa, *Making Face, Making Soul*

For many Salvadoran and South African women, poetry is a site of contestation linked directly to acts of economic, political, and social resistance that have taken place in their countries in the past two decades. Because their writing offers a radical cultural critique and sets out to reappropriate history, to give voice to the dispossessed, it often uses noncanonical forms and strategies. In Barbara Harlow's words, "formal criteria yield to political ones." These resistance writers challenge such traditional Western aesthetic concepts as "emotion recollected in tranquility" (Wordsworth) and "the pleasure of the text" (Barthes), asserting, instead, a counterhegemonic aesthetic: poetry is a weapon of the struggle, even when disarming or disarmed. Thus, they call into question or dismiss altogether Eurocentric notions that poetry should be "objective" or politically detached. Instead, taking sides becomes artistically requisite as well as ideologically strategic for many dissident poets. In revolutionary contexts, conventional dicta against the merger of politics and art are exposed as "the political declarations of privilege."[1]

Several critical studies have documented the creative strategies and discursive interventions employed by contemporary Latin American women resistance poets.[2] In an essay in *Knives and Angels*, for instance, Myriam Díaz-Diocaretz asserts that the most powerful Latin American women poets today "transgress stylistic decorum and tend to subvert the authority of the dominant discourses and the

official values." Characterized by a polemic against postcolonial and
military repression, this writing sometimes mimes linguistic/expres-
sive cultural codes but simultaneously "generates a mimetic displace-
ment" through the poets' gendered and politicized consciousnesses.
To be a woman poet writing in Latin America typically involves a
process of "reterritorialization," a complex subversion/reclamation of
discursive practices in a culture that traditionally has denied or ap-
propriated her words.[3] Many of Díaz-Diocaretz's points apply as well
to dissident writings by South African women, who come from all
echelons of society to participate in and/or sing about revolutionary
transformation, denounce the racist regime, and defy the muteness
their culture has imposed on them because of their race, class, and/or
gender.

This process of reterritorialization, however, is not unique to
women living in El Salvador or South Africa; U. S. women poets also
engage in discursive protests and reclamations. Barbara Harlow has
asserted that many Third World resistance poets call upon U. S.
writers not to take responsibility for others but, instead, to acknowl-
edge their own perspectives and limitations.[4] Despite the validity of
this injunction, one of its implications is that U.S. poets cannot /
should not identify as poetic subjects people and events in the Third
World. Yet an examination of U.S. women's writing from the 1980s
reveals a strong tradition of solidarity poetry, especially by women
of color, lesbians, working-class women, radical feminists and activ-
ists—writers who have been marginalized due to race, class, sexual
orientation, or political affiliation; who have the greatest stake in
challenging U.S. politics-as-usual and the most pressing desire for
change, globally and locally. These women have written poems of
connection with Third World people in struggle, especially with dis-
located women and children, with whom they identify. With Audre
Lorde, they believe that true history can and must be recorded in
poetry. The atrocities committed in South Africa and El Salvador, in
particular, have moved U.S. women to poetic resistance—against
those countries' repressive governments, against their own govern-
ment's financing of apartheid in South Africa and the decade-long
civil war in El Salvador. Alongside their "sisters in arms," these poets
oppose poverty, hunger, racism, sexism, and institutionalized vio-
lence while exposing those responsible for the casualties of war and
dislocation.[5]

A coherent and cogent feminist theory of resistance has developed in the United States during the past fifteen years, much of it written by women of color and radical poets. Cherríe Moraga and Gloria Anzaldúa describe political writing by women of color as acts of defiance whose goals are to "cultivate our colored skins" and to "brew and forge a revolution."[6] Maria Lugones warns white women of the perils of disengagement, which she defines as "a radical form of passivity toward the ideology of the ethnocentric racial state which privileges the dominant culture as the only culture to 'see with' and conceives this seeing as to be done non-self-consciously." White women practice disengagement when they act or write without naming themselves white, thereby presuming their universality. Women of color may risk disengagement too, Lugones suggests, if they attempt to disown their culture rather than reconstruct it.[7] Adrienne Rich, in turn, chronicles with rigorous honesty her efforts to resist "white circumscribing," the arrogance of placing her own privileged racial group at the center without evaluating who she means when she says *we*, without interrogating her own "politics of location."[8] Chela Sandoval advocates for U.S. women of color an "oppositional consciousness," which would allow no single conceptualization of empowerment but would process how power circulates; the literature and acts emerging from such a stance would recognize that "a new morality and effective opposition resides in a self-conscious flexibility of identity and of political action which is capable, above all else, of tactically intervening in the moves of power in the name of egalitarian social relations."[9] These women and others view their poetry and theory as contested but crucial terrain for rewriting histories and reexamining cultural institutions.

U.S. women's resistance poetry both builds upon and illustrates these theoretical concepts. It shares many characteristics of Salvadoran and South African women's poetry: it is politically charged, ideologically committed, contextually aware, overtly gendered, and always visionary. Yet some strategies distinctive to U.S. women's poems of resistance are also worth noting. These poets often criticize their government's support of South Africa's and El Salvador's oppressive policies and institutions, their crimes against humanity, and, along with this harsh criticism comes a rigorous self-examination, a struggle for accountability as U.S. citizens. When she visited Central America, Adrienne Rich explains, she felt for the first time "what it means, dissident or not, to be part of that raised boot of power," to be inadvertently complicitous. "I come from a country stuck fast for forty years in the deep-freeze of history," Rich asserts; with that knowledge comes responsibility for exploring in depth one's own cultural particularities and myopias.[10] Moreover, U.S. women's resistance poetry draws grim parallels between racism in their country and apartheid in South Africa, between the decadence and greed of the Salvadoran military and the power hunger of the Reagan and Bush administrations. "Don't ever tell me that South Africa makes America better by comparison," cries Michelle Cliff in her prose poem "Constructive Engagement," which extols the courage of black children everywhere and lambastes U.S. governmental policy at home and abroad as hypocritical and destructive.[11]

Like Salvadoran and South African women's resistance poetry, that of U.S. women acts as a consciousness-raising tool for its audiences—not for the people in war-torn countries themselves so much as for those who need to listen at home. These poems express solidarity with women in struggle and simultaneously call upon U.S. readers to act politically, to "learn new syllables of revolution," as June Jordan asserts.[12] For many Salvadoran and South African women, resistance poetry documents countermilitant efforts and therefore is participatory, crucial to the struggle. Such poets may see themselves as outsiders in sexist societies, but they are "inside" the revolutionary context. For U.S. women poets, the issue of insider/outsider status is problematized by their complex positionalities: as citizens of the wealthiest nation on earth, they are in one sense privileged, potential agents of oppression, while, as women marginalized by gender, race, class, and/or sexual orientation, they suffer discrimination and exile. Thus, their poetry offers a unique blend of *exteriorismo*, the chronicling of daily revolutionary acts, their own and those of others, and what we might call *interiorismo*, the documentation of personal, internal conflicts over which forms of resistance and solidarity are most effective.[13] Many U.S. women poets interrogate their own individual identities and responsibilities even as they endorse the collectivity celebrated by the poets whose struggles inspire them.

Finally, feminism may be more central to the agendas of U.S. women resistance poets, who tend to link race, class, and national identity conflicts directly to concerns they face as women fighting sexism. This is not to say that Salvadoran and South African women resistance poets do not reveal strong gender identification; the preceding chapters clearly reveal otherwise. Myriam Díaz-Diocaretz has documented a long history of gendered and feminist consciousness in Latin American women's poems, despite the fact that "the *given* is imbedded with a collective cultural muteness as far as women's active role as producers of discourse is concerned";[14] theorists like Cecily Lockett and Zoë Wicomb have likewise traced the parameters of an emerging feminist consciousness among South African women writers.[15] Nonetheless, women writing out of revolutionary contexts during the 1980s have been less likely to *foreground* gender oppression than their U.S. counterparts, more likely to see women's issues as part of a larger struggle for liberation yet secondary in a given historical moment to issues of race, class, and/or nationalism. U.S. resistance poets, in contrast, have often made feminism central to their texts, employing their identity politics explicitly in the service of their art.

Audre Lorde's "Holographs" illustrates many of these characteristics of U.S. women's resistance poetry. A handwritten document typically signed by its composer, the holograph acts as the poem's controlling image and, as such, proffers a double meaning. Lorde's poem is itself a holograph, a statement of witness; the keenings of the bereaved South African parents, whose words and feelings she can only begin to imagine, represent another form of holographic testimony. In the first stanza, the U.S. speaker watches the evening news on TV as "150 million truth seekers in South Africa" riot "against Pik Botha's belly." Immediately, we see several qualities crucial to this type of poetry: an angry, polemical tone and stance, through which the speaker berates the South African government's racism and greed; a sense of solidarity with the demonstrators, described as "truth seekers"; and an awareness of a historical context larger than the poet's own. Lorde goes on to mourn children needlessly dead of malnutrition and to empathize with the mothers who have lost them. The stanza ends with a poignant and pointed rhetorical question:

and how does it feel
to bury this baby you nursed for a year
weighing less than when she was born?

The second stanza reveals the enormous scale of violence and
sorrow that has characterized life for many black South Africans and
presents another historical event in their struggle against apartheid:

> 60,000 Pondo women keening
> on the mountain
> the smell of an alley in Gugelito
> after the burned bodies are dragged through.

One atrocity gives way to another, as Lorde evokes memories of the
1976 Soweto uprisings, in which countless thousands of schoolchil-
dren, armed only with rocks, marched on police demanding an end
to the inequities of inferior Bantu education in the townships, only
to be gunned down by their adversaries as they ran away. The
speaker extols the courage of these

> deadly exuberant children
> stones in their kneepants pockets
> running toward Jo'burg
> some singing   some waving
> some stepping to intricate patterns
> their fathers knew tomorrow
> they will be dead.

Here Lorde extends her feminist empathy to men in struggle, to
fathers of "our dead," as well as mothers.

This focus continues in the poem's final stanza, which is domi-
nated by another searing question, this time more personal:

> How can I mourn these children
> my mothers and fathers
> their sacred generous laughter . . . ?

Lorde struggles in these lines with her own accountability as a distant
witness to the horrors; neither the poet, comfortably ensconced in
her New York home, nor the language in which she writes is fully
adequate to the task. Yet while the poet is an outsider by virtue of
her nationality, her intense identification as a black woman with the

suffering she witnesses gives credence to her lexically implicit claim of insider status. *"My* mothers and fathers" are invoked, not only as the poet's political allies but also as her parents and teachers, the family from whom she would learn. The poem's final line rejects lyricism and metaphor in favor of a shockingly violent but contextually realistic image: "The only dependable warmth / is the burn of blood." In its graphic description and complex emotional resonances, "Holographs" serves as a call to political action and solidarity for U.S. readers of conscience and as Lorde's chronicle of her own introspection.[16]

Speaking of Raymonda Tawil's *My Home, My Prison,* a compelling autobiographical/political narrative by a Palestinian woman living under Israeli occupation, Barbara Harlow identifies the writer's major themes as "flight, exile, loss, struggle, steadfastness," terms that describe as well the primary subjects of Salvadoran and South African women's resistance poetry.[17] Most of the U.S. women poets examined in this chapter are thematically concerned with the last three: loss, struggle, steadfastness. Articulating the losses accrued by those who suffer from U.S.-endorsed atrocities, documenting their own struggles against oppression at home and their solidarity with other struggling women, remaining steadfast in their beliefs that change is possible and requisite—these discursive stances characterize U.S. women's poetic interventions. Like many resistance poets elsewhere, these women acknowledge their "hyphenated identities, hybrid realities," their multiple and fluid "terrains of consciousness."[18] In so doing, they refuse to disown their culture but insist on reconstructing it.

1

Creative acts are forms of political activism employing definite aesthetic strategies for resisting dominant cultural norms and are not merely aesthetic exercises. We build culture as we inscribe in these various forms.
  —Gloria Anzaldúa, *Making Face, Making Soul*

Every night Winnie Mandela
Every night
  —June Jordan, "To Free Nelson Mandela"

Tell me if I saw what I thought I saw. Tell me if you will whether this happened in New York or Pretoria, L.A. or Johannesburg.
  —Michelle Cliff, "Constructive Engagement"

Anzaldúa's equation of creative acts and political activism suggests a cultural/aesthetic philosophy shared by many radical U.S. women writing resistance poetry. The nature of their subversive inscriptions varies, from June Jordan's elliptical lyricism to Michelle Cliff's compelling direct address.[19] These poets have expressed anger at the genocide occurring in South Africa and solidarity with their sisters and brothers there; constructed complex identities and subjectivities, individual and communal; committed politically subversive acts and written out their political commitments. Some U.S. women of color have chosen to identify themselves as "Third World women," although this designation has been controversial. As Chela Sandoval notes, women at a 1981 National Women's Studies Conference who argued for this label saw themselves as "working politically to challenge the systems that keep power moving in its current patterns, thus shifting it onto new terrains," as well as underlining similarities between their own oppression and that of women elsewhere. Others feared that using this term would be seen as appropriative by their counterparts living in Third World countries and/or that it would diffuse any sense of the particular oppressions experienced by U.S. and other women. Those on each side of the debate warned against the claiming of a falsely simple unity, which they distinguished from solidarity with other women in struggle.[20] As Norma Alarcon explains, "the pursuit of a 'politics of unity' solely based on gender forecloses the 'pursuit of solidarity' through different political formations and the exploration of alternative theories of the subject of consciousness."[21] A politics of solidarity with Third World people must explore gender, race, class, sexuality, and national or ethnic identities as interwoven and overlapping categories of analysis. A poetics of solidarity must interrogate identity, difference, complicity, and agency as aspects of its practitioners' discursive interventions.

South Africa is the country whose political situation has been most often chronicled by U.S. women poets of color, especially by African-American women, who have connected apartheid there to slavery and racism here. These poets combine *exteriorismo*—an emphasis on specific historical events such as the Sharpeville massacre, the Soweto uprisings, the incarceration of Mandela—with a fierce brand of *interiorismo:* identifying with Winnie Mandela's loneliness or with a bereaved daughter's grief; exploring personal feelings of guilt for being safe, for not doing enough. Not all of their introspection is painful or negative, however; like many black South African poets, writing and living on the edge and against all odds, they sometime evince euphoric moments of hope as they witness, for example, a child warrior's stunning courage or celebrate a political detainee's release. "We were not meant to survive," Audre Lorde has asserted, yet the determination to survive and effect lasting change is evident in much U.S. resistance writing about black South Africans' struggle.[22]

June Jordan has written "everything I knew how to write against apartheid," including several aesthetically innovative and politically charged poems commemorating both acts of courage by South Africans and her own journey toward political consciousness.[23] "To Free Nelson Mandela" features a chant, or mantra, whose haunting refrain depicts Mandela's wife, endlessly waiting. Such a depiction might seem to foreground passivity rather than activity, but in their poetic context these recurring lines resonate, becoming more powerful with each repetition:

> Every night Winnie Mandela
> Every night the waters of the world
> turn to the softly burning
> light of the moon
>
> Every night Winnie Mandela
> Every night

Interspersed between these poignant stanzas, and in stark contrast to them, is an aggressive catalog of rhetorical questions designed to expose the daily atrocities suffered by black South Africans at the hands of their government.

> Have they killed the twelve-year-old girl?
> Have they hung the poet?
> Have they shot down the students?

The poet goes on to reveal specific crimes: "They have murdered Victoria Mxenge." Like many resistance poets, Jordan relies on her audience to comprehend her allusions, to know who Victoria Mxenge is and to identify the "they." Her frequent historical and contemporary references become a call to self-education for many U.S. readers. Mxenge was a lawyer and black consciousness activist allegedly murdered by government forces; Jordan honors her memory by depicting graphically both her untimely death and her symbolic triumph:

> They have murdered her
> victorious now
> that the earth recoils from that crime
> of her murder now
> that the very dirt shudders from the falling blood
> the thud of bodies fallen
> into the sickening
> into the thickening
> crimes of apartheid.

Mxenge's murder was no isolated incident, the speaker asserts, but one of the repressive regime's many politically motivated slayings, so brutal that they make the earth shudder.

The second half of the poem envisions an end to all the slaughter, a time when the oppressors' tactics backfire and the oppressed rise up. Again, the poet's main stylistic strategies are repetition of a resonant key phrase, "at last," and an assertive catalog, this time not of questions but of resounding exclamations. The tables are turned, and ordinary people are empowered in this futuristic scenario:

> At last the bullets boomerang
> At last the artifice of exile explodes
> At last no one obeys the bossman of atrocities
>
> At last the carpenters the midwives
> the miners the weavers the anonymous
> housekeepers the anonymous
> street sweepers . . .
>
> At last the diggers of the ditch
> begin the living funeral
> for death

Two phrases give the first stanza its primary intensity: "artifice of exile" and "bossman of atrocities." Involuntary exile is an artificially imposed status, Jordan implies; there is no rightful banishment of indigenous people. "Bossman," or *baas* in Afrikaans, the hierarchical term some white South Africans have insisted upon being called by their black employees, occurs in this phrase as an ironic reminder of who has had the power and how it has been misused. In subsequent stanzas the poet eschews punctuation so that all the anonymous workers she lists are equally foregrounded, a collective mass for change. Paradoxically, it falls to the grave diggers, often perceived as society's most lowly, to bury death itself as life triumphs and Mandela presumably is freed. As of the writing of this poem, however, that time had not arrived; thus, Jordan ends as she began, coming full circle, expressing her solidarity with Winnie Mandela and her hopeful compatriots: "Every night Winnie Mandela / Every night."[24]

"A Song for Soweto," set to music by Adrienne Torf, echoes "To Free Nelson Mandela" in its polemic of rage and its structural and linguistic experimentation. Speaking of Latin American women poets who write against patriarchal paradigms, the "master traditions," Myriam Díaz-Diocaretz claims that "every utterance is set against that system *dialogically* . . . one accent and one register interacting with another. If they come to be in opposition, it is in a dialogic tension between specific evaluations and belief systems. Woman's authorial intention is present at every point of the poem."[25] Such dialogic tension and overtly gendered authorial intention also characterize much of Jordan's poetry, including "A Song for Soweto," whose main theme is the seizing of the oppressor's language by a young Soweto girl set up to be its victim.

> At the throat of Soweto
> a devil language falls
> slashing
> claw syllables to shred and leave
> raw
> the tongue of the young
> girl
> learning to sing
> her own name

The poet cleverly employs traditional devices of rhyme and alliteration to illustrate how easily words can roll off the tongue, yet her thematic content reveals just how much damage a "devil language" can do. Her description of a young girl singing herself evokes U.S. feminist ideology as well, which emphasizes the importance of self-naming for women. Self-named women are "New Women," Jordan suggests in a recent essay: "What I see for myself is New Women everywhere in the world discovering each other with a happiness and a resolute purpose of survival that will surpass all the weird and fatal bewitcheries of traditional power, traditional insanities of conflict."[26]

Jordan goes on to foreground, via italics, this inevitable reversal of the status quo; "they" hold the power and dominate the subject position in the poem's first half, while "she," the new young woman, claims autonomy and subjectivity in the second:

Where she would say
                    water
They would teach her to cry
                         blood

. . . .
Where she would kiss with her mouth
                                   my homeland
They would teach her to swallow
                              this dust

But words live in the spirit of her face and that
sound will no longer yield to imperial erase

Where they would draw
                    blood
She will drink
             water

. . . .
Where they would teach her to swallow
                                   this dust
She will kiss with her mouth
                        my homeland

Despite its awkward sound when read rather than sung, the phrase "imperial erase" epitomizes all that is under siege in Jordan's new order; as death must die, so erasure of the silenced must be eradicated and language reclaimed. "If we collaborate with the powerful then our language will lose its currency as a means to tell the truth in order to change the truth." What remains, when the truth is changed and told, is the girl from Soweto, singing.[27]

Jordan's "War and Memory" reveals a different set of discursive strategies, and hence a different type of resistance poetry, from the two works just discussed. More autobiographical in nature, and more concerned with political awareness in general than with South Africa per se, it personalizes the process of attaining radical consciousness by linking the poet-speaker's childhood experience with domestic violence to her commitments as an adult. A long poem, "War and Memory" is divided into seven sections, ranging in length from two lines to ninety-four. In section 1, the ninety-four-line stanza, Jordan documents with painful exactitude the terrible fights a child witnesses between her abusive father, here called Granville, and her passive and often distraught mother, named in the father's frequent invectives only as "you damn Black woman!" The slam of drawers, the hurl of epithets, are the sounds of the speaker's childhood; to her falls the task of rescuing her mother from her father's violence and thereby becoming its recipient.

> And he
> berserk with fury lifted
> chair or frying pan
> and I'd attack
> in her defense: "No
> Daddy! No!" rushing for his knees
> and begging, "Please
> don't, Daddy, please!"
> He'd come down hard: My head
> break into daylight pain
> or rip me spinning crookedly across the floor.

Her mother's silence echoes in the speaker's memory, as does her father's curse to her, which again reveals his internalized racism: "You damn Black devil child!"

Subsequent stanzas trace the speaker's emerging awareness that other wars took place outside the boundaries of her domestic world. In section 2 she recounts having learned about the Holocaust through pictures in *National Geographic* and, upon questioning her parents about their meaning, having gotten brutal honesty from her father and protective evasion from her mother. Section 3 consists of two ironically evocative lines: "The Spanish Civil War: / I think I read about that one." Her memories of Korea are framed in a neighbor's photograph of her soldier-lover there, as section 4 reveals. The last three sections chronicle the now-grown speaker as she protests against Vietnam, makes war on poverty, expresses her ambivalence toward the police, who, like her parents, were supposed to protect her but didn't. Life for her has been one long war: "peace never meant a thing to me."

The last forty lines of "War and Memory" are explicitly self-creative; like the young girl from Soweto, Jordan's speaker must combat a devil language and malignant memories in order to name and thereby heal herself. The word *I* recurs twenty-one times in twice as many lines:

> And from the freedom days
> that blazed outside my mind
> I fell in love
> I fell in love with Black men White
> men Black
> women White women
> and I
> dared myself to say The Palestinians
> and I
> worried about unilateral words like Lesbian or Nationalist
> and I
> tried to speak Spanish when I travelled to Managua
> and I
> dreamed about the Fourteenth Amendment
> and I
> defied the hatred of the hateful everywhere
> as best I could.

Without ever quite planning to, the speaker implies, she became a writer and an antiapartheid activist. Still, who is she, really? The statement "I / thought I was a warrior growing up" reveals her lingering doubts about the accuracy of her own perceptions; her account of burying her abusive father suggests an ongoing ambivalence toward this patriarch who, in spite of everything, loved his daughter and was loved. Her speaker's language and tone vacillate between self-denigration and self-affirmation even as the poem ends:

> and I
> lust for justice
> and I
> make that quest arthritic/pigeon-toed/however
> and I
> invent the mother of the courage I require not to quit[28]

The allusion to Bertolt Brecht's Mother Courage, whose pragmatism determined her survival at the cost of her children, is at best an ironic and ambivalent self-descriptor, yet the verbs in the final lines—*lust, quest, invent*—suggest an incipient integration of the speaker's personal and political subjectivities.

Jordan is one of many renowned African-American women poets to write South African solidarity poetry. Two short but suggestive poems by Alice Walker explore the controversial issue of U.S. complicity in apartheid. Walker uses gentle didacticism to persuade privileged U.S. women, in particular, not to buy or wear diamonds and gold, the most vivid symbols of the oppression of black workers in South Africa. "The Diamonds on Liz's Bosom" juxtaposes the jewels' brilliance with the superior brightness of the miner who unearthed them. The rubies in "Nancy's" jewel box, the poet claims, are less vivid than the sorrow and want evident in the miner's children's faces. Although Liz and Nancy are not explicitly identified, U.S. readers of the 1980s easily recognize them as Elizabeth Taylor and Nancy Reagan, both known for their emphasis on fashion and jewelry. "Oh, those Africans!" Walker concludes ironically; what trouble they cause,

> crying and bleeding
> on some of the whitest necks
> in your town.

Not only famous or wealthy women are complicitous, the poet suggests; *all* women readers must assess whether they are doing enough to combat racism and capitalistic oppression.

This poem's companion piece, "We Alone," offers an alternative to gold and diamonds, which, after all, are only as valuable as their investors make them.

> We alone can devalue gold
> by not caring
> if it falls or rises
> in the market place.
> Wherever there is gold
> there is a chain, you know.

This quiet reminder of the price exacted of the miners and their families is designed to convince readers to adopt different valuations—for instance, to select jewels from nature:

> Feathers, shells
> and sea shaped stones
> are all as rare.
> This could be our revolution:
> To love what is plentiful
> as much as
> what's scarce.[29]

The phrase "our revolution" and her use of the inclusive pronoun *we* keep Walker from alienating defensive readers and suggest a way that once-complicitous U. S. citizens can contribute to South Africa's struggle for liberation.

Michelle Cliff's "Constructive Engagement" also examines issues of complicity, through her title, which refers to the Reagan-Bush administrations' euphemism for their "hands-off" policies in South Africa, and through her angry assertion that the two countries are equally racist. Her style is somewhat reminiscent of June Jordan's in its aggressive catalogs and fierce rhetorical questions, but Cliff's writing is more experimental; Díaz-Diocaretz has called her intermingling of poetry, prose, documents, and visual effects "metacommentaries."[30] This poem reclaims the term *constructive engagement* as a metaphor for her own racial and feminist alliances with a long list of "ordinary" Africans:

the sisters and brothers on the sun-blasted dried-out
    bantustans
the gold-miners
the white-baby minders
the diamond miners
the forced laborers
the Ford auto workers
the house workers
the urban dwellers.

She also offers a shorter catalog of "extraordinary" South Africans about whom we have read in U.S. papers, people like Sisulu and the Mandelas and Biko, with whom she likewise feels solidarity. Yet the poem's central focus is on one little-known person. Its longest stanza explores an event documented in a newspaper photograph, a "Black girlchild" testifying in court about an "accident" in which her young friend was run down on his bike by a car driven by a white man. The child's quiet courage and the senselessness of such an act obsess Cliff, who, in anger and frustration, hurls a series of hammering questions: "Did anything stop in her when she saw her friend die? Does she dream about that afternoon? Is she afraid? Does she feel guilty for not saving him? Did she think she could save him? . . . Does she think about enemies? That the enemy has shown his face to her? Can she realize that there are people who will hate her without ever meeting her? What will happen in her life?" The poet's queries hang suspended, and, along with them, another question: Where did this take place? "Tell me if you will whether this happened in New York or Pretoria," Cliff commands her readers. But no answer is forthcoming. The only thing she knows for certain is that South Africa does not "make America better by comparison."[31] This resolute assertion intervenes politically by forcing U.S. readers into examination of themselves as citizens of conscience and their "democratic" system of justice.

The plight of South Africans in exile in the 1980s, and the alternative knowledge offered to U. S. citizens fortunate enough to interact with them, is the subject of Sonia Sanchez's prose poem "A Letter to Ezekial Mphahlele." Her poem pays tribute to an African novelist and autobiographer who left his country in 1957 for political reasons and, at the time of her writing, was planning to return. Sanchez composes her letter just after having a "dinner of peace" at Mphahlele's house with her young son and the writer's wife, Rebecca. Their meal, as well as her awareness of "two centuries of hunger" for black Africans and African Americans, leads her to explore the exigencies the Mphahleles face as they prepare to leave: "now you are returning home. now your mother's womb cries out to you. now your history demands your heartbeat." Sanchez's characteristic eschewal of capitalization gives her writing a quiet understatement that is especially appropriate for musing on the power of the construct "home" and the courage of this exiled couple: "sonia," Zeke explains to her, "i must be buried in my own homeland, my bones must replenish the black earth from whence they came, our bones must fertilize the ground on which we walk or we shall never walk as men and women in the 21st century." The writer's sense of duty to his native land, his identification with its "black earth," and his fierce belief that only by returning can he and his wife contribute to the process of change evoke in Sanchez empathy and admiration. Heroes are not found only in Bruce Lee movies, she tells her son on their drive home: "you have just sat and eaten amid bravery. relish the taste. stir it around and around in your mouth until the quick sweetness of it becomes bitter, then swallow it slowly, letting this new astringent taste burn the throat. bravery is no easy taste to swallow." The reader, too, must consider the implications of this lesson if she or he is to have empathy and solidarity with those in struggle and exile. To label exiles brave is too simple unless one considers also the bitterness of their situation, the danger that attends the Mphahleleses' need "to breathe again their own breath suspended by twenty years of exile."

The poem's introspective final stanza asserts Sanchez's fears for Zeke and for herself: "it is 2 a.m., my children stretch themselves in dreams, kicking away the room's shadows. i stare at the night piling in little heaps near my bed. zeke. maybe you are a madman." Her momentary panic that her friend risks too much gives way to an assessment of her own willingness to take risks for a better future. Seeking to understand her own multiple and contingent identities, the poet labels herself successively a madwoman, a child-woman, and a lost woman. Her vulnerabilities thus exposed, yet under the cover of night, Sanchez calls on Mphahlele as a father returning to claim his political/ethnic space and hers. She also honors him as a

muse enabling her to break silence and write: "i love the tom-tom
days you are marching, your feet rooted in the sea. save a space for
me and mine zeke and rebecca. this lost woman, who walks her own
shadow for peace."[32]

Interrogating the construct "home" is also the subject of Audre
Lorde's long poem "On My Way Out I Passed over You and the
Verrazano Bridge," which opens up ideological questions of censor-
ship and accountability. As the poet leaves her lover and New York
home by plane and flies over them on her voyage out, she reflects
intently on how best to effect revolutionary change: must they bomb
the Verrazano bridge to insure their future? The cause of this militant
reflection, it appears, is the *New York Times,* whose scanty and dis-
torted coverage of racist oppression in South Africa comes under fire
in several of Lorde's poems in *Our Dead behind Us:*

Wintry Poland survives
the bastardized prose of the *New York Times*
while Soweto is a quaint heat treatment
in some exotic but safely capitalized city
where the Hero Children's bones moulder unmarked
and the blood of my sister Winnie Mandela
slows   and her steps slow
in a banned and waterless living
her youngest daughter is becoming a poet.

Lorde's bitterness over the newspaper's suppression of the details of
the Soweto uprisings gives way to rage at Winnie Mandela's banish-
ment to Brandfort in the Orange Free State, a dry Afrikaaner outpost
far from Mandela's home in Johannesburg. The poet feels affinity
with Mrs. Mandela in her isolation and identifies strongly with her
remarkable daughter Zindzi, who writes poetry against great odds.

Lorde, too, considers herself a poet-in-exile, moved to create a
blueprint for herself and others—exiled as an African-American
woman, a radical feminist, a lesbian, a cancer survivor, and a political
writer. The poem reveals her strong sense of solidarity with other
exiles, her communal identity. Poetry is not a luxury, Lorde has ar-
gued elsewhere; it is critical to the survival of oppressed peoples, a
crucial tool for resisting what the poet in another context has called
the "myth of sameness." Poems produce alternative historiographic

knowledge, for, after all, "where is true history written / except in the poems?"

In stanza 8 Lorde takes up a subject that has troubled many U.S. women writing about Third World sites of conflict: women and militancy. Like many women, Lorde endorses nonviolence yet supports countermilitancy as a last-resort strategy. Thus, she presents sympathetically images of mothers carrying both baby and rifle, "small boned dark women / gun-belts taut over dyed cloth." She wonders who these women are, what their life experiences have been, if one carries out her commitments by "activating plastique near the oil refineries / outside Capetown," thus combatting violence with violence. Or perhaps another woman was driven out of the Crossroads squatters' camp, "perched on the corrugated walls of her uprooted life," by a government determined that she would be banished to a bantustan or live no-place. Still another of the women Lorde imagines and particularizes has suffered maternal loss as well as dislocation, having seen

> her two-year-old daughter's face
> squashed like a melon
> in the pre-dawn police raids upon Noxolo.

Others, she asserts, are like her; they write poems, are lesbians. Lorde's interrogation of multiple, particularized identities reveals her commitment to women's connection across difference.

As the poem ends, Lorde again advances the twin agendas of rewriting history and redefining sisterhood. "History is not kind to us," she asserts, speaking of black women in both the United States and South Africa; "we restitch it with living." Women struggling across cultures can be linked by their commitments to a more just future:

> And I dream of our coming together
> encircled   driven
> not only by love
> but by lust for a working tomorrow
> the flights of this journey
> mapless   uncertain
> and necessary as water.[33]

The sense of fragmentation that Lorde's writing sometimes reveals gives way here to a visionary statement of interdependence. Still, her lyricism does not mask her sense of urgency: "Our dead line our dreams, their deaths becoming more and more commonplace," she insists in her essay "Apartheid U.S.A."[34] U.S. and South African black women must realize, now as never before, that their survivals are linked and act accordingly. To participate in the silences and separations endorsed by racist governments and their institutions, Lorde suggests, will surely be to perish.

U.S. women who are not African-American have also written poems expressing solidarity with South African women in struggle, often evoking gender or shared political commitments rather than race as their primary source of connection. In "The Name of This Flower Is the Same," poet-activist Sara Miles links the struggles of U.S., Central and Latin American, and South African women through the figure of an exhausted waitress who serves the poet and her Spanish-speaking companion in a restaurant. After discussing words that are the same in Spanish and English, like *petunia* and *boycott*, the two activists order coffee and strategize about a labor strike they are planning. At first they do not notice the woman who serves them. But as the waitress clears the table and brusquely requests her tip, the two women's attentions shift to her: "*Oreja? No, waitress—/ pobrecita,* you whisper, in my country too." The speaker's companion, presumably the Lupe of the poem's dedication, recognizes after a first suspicious moment that the waitress is not a spy but a poor *compañera*. She understands that waitresses deserve empathy, that women worldwide are linked as exploited workers, and that poets must intervene discursively and politically on behalf of all oppressed women.

> The name of this woman
> wearing her tiredness
> is universal language
> in the camps
> in Soweto
> cleaning offices in Washington her call
> comes the same:
> don't forget us
> keep planning

arm the women
arm the women—
we rise
and this flower blooms
one name.[35]

The poet and her friend acknowledge responsibility for supporting cross-cultural revolutionary actions and, especially, for helping poor women get arms. The poem implies that women's social and economic conditions are desperate and that collaborative resistance is crucial if change is to occur.

Ikon editor Susan Sherman's "Facts" is a long, heavily ironic poem that bears some resemblance to Audre Lorde's "Verrazano Bridge" in its equation of U.S. and South African racist atrocities and its castigation of the *New York Times* and other media sources for distorted coverage of political atrocities in both countries. Part 1 proclaims that

what you see is what you get
What you hear is
often lies.

In the United States, for example, people in cities hear a great deal about the successes of neighborhood gentrification projects, yet the poet knows that such accounts fail to acknowledge people still living among the burnt-out ruins on Ave. C, where such projects come last if they come at all. The very concept of gentrification is illusory, the poet argues:

The neighborhood hasn't "gone up"
since then
regardless of what the papers say
It's gone down
Down to money
& greed
disregard for human needs
& illusion
That "things are getting better"
At least for some.

Sherman's colloquial diction and style, especially her pointed use of cliches to expose the rubbish of such pretense, underscore her outrage. She acknowledges her own privilege, too, as a former resident of Ave. C who was lucky, who could find housing elsewhere.

Part 2 shifts gears to discuss a *Times* report on twenty-eight South Africans dead and six hundred detained for demonstrating at their friends' funerals,

> black people moved again
> as they were before
> and before
> and continue to be
> (except in our press)
> to action.

As these demonstrators resist lies, the U.S. press conspires to disinform through lies of omission, as in the caption "Police Quell a Riot" placed beneath a photo of a South African political demonstration. Such distorted captions imply that the police were acting commendably, the angry poet objects. Too few bother to analyze the news, to move beyond "how" and ask the crucial question "why?" Sherman goes on to focus her criticism on students in her writing classes. When she asks them what a fact is, they reply, naively and to her mind irresponsibly, "what you hear on the 5 o'clock news"; she is shocked that no one laughs ironically except her. The poem's remaining stanzas explore how so many U.S. youths have come to be so ill-informed and apathetic, why they have never learned to ask

> why that gun was there at all
> why she was in front of it
> why that policeman's finger pressed the trigger.

Apartheid means separation, Sherman goes on to assert; it stands to destroy everyone by making people think they aren't connected. She ends with a dramatic juxtaposition of young people's rebellious actions in Soweto with the passivity of students at her university in New York:

> *In Soweto*
> *the people continue to rebel*
> *in Soweto*
> *The people continue to fight back*
> In Manhattan
> My student looks at the 5 o'clock news
>
> His head is filled with facts
> He knows nothing
> He learns nothing
>
> He doesn't even know "Why?"[36]

Sherman's outrage is matched by her frustration and guilt. After all, this is *her* student, *her* country; this uncompromising indictment extends, implicitly, to herself as well as others. As in Lorde's poetry, *exteriorismo* blends here with *interiorismo*, the writer's exploration of her own ambivalent quest for reconciliation.

New York / Puerto Rican poet Sandra Maria Esteves also compares New York and South Africa in "Fighting Demons for South Africa," but her poem reveals a broader multicultural context than does Sherman's. As Sherman juxtaposes "how" and "why" as crucial interrelated questions, Esteves interrogates "here" and "there":

> What is the difference between there and here?
> Between what is seen and the elusive face
> Fascism or imperialism
> South Africa / New York
> South Bronx / Soweto / Harlem / East Harlem / Namibia
> Lower East Side / Sharpeville / Williamsburg / Watts /
> Johannesburg

The poet not only compares New York's black ghettoes with South Africa's townships but also extends her comparison of the sites of fascism and imperialism to Namibia and Los Angeles. Here and there people are hungry, enslaved; banks fund racism and greed; continents deny their rich inheritances. Neither North America nor Africa acknowledges fully its cultural multiplicity: Yoruba incantations, Mayan astrology, Cherokee wisdom, Hopi sungods, all hold legacies forgotten or devalued.

In every stanza Esteves repeats her central question, "What is the difference?" to emphasize that for her there *is* little difference in the oppression of people of color in New York and Johannesburg, Vietnam and Chile:

South Africa / New York
What is the difference of the face of greed?
How does it construct its smile
From the burning bones of Vietnamese families
Or the music of Chile
Of a million martyred students
In a stadium filled horror
That witnessed the slashing of the poet's tongue
The murder of Victor Jara

The same type of imperialistic greed that sent the United States to Vietnam in the 1960s and 1970s, the poet argues, orchestrated the public murder of Chilean singer Victor Jara in 1973. The poet laments these deeds, yet, despite her anger and frustration, she refuses to abandon her quest for "the perfect equation / That brings food to every table," for a world of justice in which all people have dignity and hope. Art provides one possible resource for change, she implies, if resistance poetry can be effectively transmitted.[37]

Nigerian playwright Wole Soyinka has claimed that African writers are more concerned with "visionary projections" of social change than with "speculative projections" on the nature of art, an assertion that applies as well to U.S. women's resistance poetry.[38] Women writing about South Africa politicize their acts of interpretation and artistic production; they preserve and redefine cultural images in and for particular historical moments.[39] No mere aesthetic exercises, these poetic inscriptions challenge structures of domination, both political and literary, and affirm connections among struggling people, especially women, everywhere.

2

> The movement for change is a changing movement, changing itself, demas-
> culinizing itself, de-Westernizing itself, becoming a critical mass that is saying in
> so many different voices, languages, gestures, actions: *It must change; we ourselves
> can change it.*
> —Adrienne Rich, "Notes toward a Politics of Location"

> Go after that which is lost
> and all the mass graves of the century's dead
> will open into your early waking hours.
> —Carolyn Forché, "Ourselves or Nothing"

> I have written these few remembrances of a country my country won't leave
> alone because the faces of the people I saw in those short days do not leave me.
> —Grace Paley, preface to *A Dream Compels Us*

U.S. women's resistance poetry is part of a large and growing move-
ment for change, a critical mass of workers, activists, and writers
who increasingly monitor and condemn their government's actions
at home and abroad and examine as well their own unwitting com-
plicity.[40] There are, of course, intellectual and emotional risks inherent
in devoting one's artistic energies to writing about injustice and the
need for change. In her poem "Ourselves or Nothing," Carolyn Forché
explores affinities between her work on El Salvador and that of her
friend, the late Holocaust historian Terrence Des Pres, who warns
that the written quest for "that which is lost" will likely unearth "the
century's dead," ghosts who will populate the poet's consciousness.
In writing about her short sojourn to El Salvador, Jewish writer and
activist Grace Paley echoes this line of thought when she asserts that,
despite the brevity of her visit, the faces of the women she encountered
there stay with her. With these risks comes responsibility for creative
and political leadership in challenging atrocities sanctioned by the
U.S. government and funded with its taxpayers' money.

El Salvador has offered fertile soil for cultural and creative arti-
sans of resistance to till. Writing in April of 1989, the editors of New
Americas Press urged concerned U.S. citizens to take a stand against
continued repression there:

> With the rise of ARENA on the one hand and the resurgent
> popular movement and FMLN/FDR on the other, the U.S. gov-
> ernment and the American public are presented with a clear

choice in El Salvador. We can continue to bankroll a government which is now in the hands of an extreme right-wing party that promises to solve the country's problems through increased bloodshed. Or we can heed the broad-based popular movement's plea for an end to U.S. interference, and for a national dialogue, involving *all* sectors of Salvadoran society. Every day of U.S. funding, every day of delay, means more bodies to bury, more wounds to heal, more homes to rebuild.[41]

Statistics widely endorsed by human rights organizations in the 1980s confirmed this argument. Between 1979 and 1991, more than 75,000 Salvadorans were killed in politically related violence, and over 7,500 disappeared. Nearly a million fled their country, and more than 600,000 spent part of the decade in refugee and relocation camps within El Salvador or on the Honduran border. A majority of the dislocated were women, children, and the elderly. Primarily to women, furthermore, fell the tasks of caring for refugees and the wounded and for protesting the incarceration and disappearances of their loved ones. The Comadres and other Salvadoran women's groups who document governmental and military atrocities have continued, since a fragile peace was negotiatied in January 1992, to work in solidarity with women's and international monitoring organizations. They have called for nonreprisal against the demobilizing FMLN, sought the freedom of all political prisoners, gathered information on disappeared persons, and challenged the government to account for its human rights abuses and purge its military.[42]

Although fewer U.S. women poets have written in solidarity with Salvadoran people than have written to support South Africans in their struggles against apartheid, the poems of Grace Paley, Jessica Hagedorn, and especially Carolyn Forché reveal strong identification with the sufferings and longings of Salvadorans. Like the New Americas collective, these poets have chronicled Salvadorans' experiences of death and disappearances, refusing to rest until their stories are told.

Paley's "In San Salvador I" pays tribute to the Comadres for their courageous persistence and joins them in mourning their losses:

Come   look   they said
here are the photograph albums

these are our children

We are called the Mothers of the Disappeared
we are also the mothers of those who were seen once more
and then photographed   sometimes parts of them
could not be found
a breast   an eye   an arm is missing
sometimes a whole stomach
that is why we are called   The Mothers
of the Disappeared   although we have these large
heavy photograph albums full of beautiful
torn faces

Paley's dominant image is the photograph albums, graphic documentary sites of both resistance and lament. Ironically, their heaviness indicates their worth; the horrors that they at once conceal and reveal speak more forcefully than any monitoring group ever could. The fragmented body parts depicted therein become for the poet and her readers synecdoches, symbols of the cultural and familial fragmentation experienced in the daily lives of these protestant mothers.

"In San Salvador II" Paley is inspired by one particular member of Comadres, who recounts the murder of her son:

I heard a cry   Mother
mother   keep the door closed   a scream
the high voice of my son   his scream
jumped into my belly   his voice
boiled there and boiled until hot water
ran down my thigh

Abandoning her own voice for the more authoritative one of the lamenting mother, Paley uses elliptical spacing to emphasize the halting nature of this horrific revelation and, by implication, to reveal her empathy with this grieving woman. The woman's story becomes parabolic, as she recounts successively the disappearances of a second, third, and fourth son. "Mother quickly / turn your back to the door," cries the second son protectively.

> Oh mother please
> hurry up   hold out your apron   they are
> stealing my eyes,

demands the third son, seeking her intervention.

The fourth part of her saga breaks at several key points, revealing the poet's awareness that this disjointed story is many stories; this could be any woman's, many women's, tale of loss. Continuing in the parabolic mode, Paley chooses, as an analogue to the suffering Salvadoran woman, Mary, the mother of Jesus:

>   And then in the fourth week my
> fourth son   No
>
> No   It was morning   he stood
> in the doorway   he was taken right
> there before my eyes the parts of
> the body of my son were tormented   are
> you listening? do you understand
> this story?   there was only one
> child   one boy   like Mary I had
> only one son[43]

Carolyn Forché has claimed that the twentieth century demands a poetry of witness, and this is precisely what Paley's poems attempt to be.[44] The mourning speaker interrupts her tale to foreground the reader-listener's accountability, reminding all who hear of their responsibility to attend closely, remember what they are told, and act accordingly.

Asian-American poet Jessica Hagedorn's "The Song of Bullets" assesses further the U.S. resistance poet's responsibility

> to commit
> those names to memory
> and stay angry.

Protected by the vicissitudes of middle age, the safety of a middle-class home, and the wonders of a young daughter learning her first

words, the poet finds it all too easy to fall prey to apathy, to "count
the dead" each day "with less surprise." Still, as her daughter sleeps,
the speaker and her companion "memorize / a list of casualties":

> The photographer's brother
> the doctor is missing.
> Or I could say:
> "Victor's brother Oscar
> has been gone for two years . . .
> It's easier for the family
> to think of him as dead."

The allusion to disappearance and the names Victor and Oscar alert
the reader to a probable Latin American context, and in the next
stanza Hagedorn reveals that the setting is El Salvador:

> Victor sends
> a Christmas card
> from El Salvador:
> "Things still the same."

Like many resistance poets, Hagedorn uses ironic understatement to
emphasize that, as Carolyn Forché has claimed, the political particu-
lars in El Salvador may shift slightly from year to year, but, between
1979 and 1991, repression continued its reign.[45]

The poet goes on to catalog a list of "others / who don't play by
the rules" in Third World countries and are subsequently punished:
"someone else's brother / perhaps mine" languishing in a hospital,
"someone else's father / perhaps mine" awaiting execution, "some-
one else's mother / perhaps mine" lamenting her lost husband, mad
son, suicidal lover. Repetition allows Hagedorn dramatic emphasis
as well as allegations of affinity; these could be her own relatives.
Still, it is difficult to maintain an immediate sense of identification,
the poet acknowledges, when confronted with

> the sight
> of my daughter's
> pink and luscious flesh,

the living proof of her own well-being. Like friends who send a very different kind of postcard from Victor's—enjoying the nightlife in Manila and the rural splendor of Sagata—Hagedorn is tempted to repress her knowledge of the political exigencies that disrupt ordinary people's lives in many countries of Asia and Latin America. Yet she knows all too well that, even as North American sunbathers loll on exotic beaches, "assassins cruise the streets / in obtrusive limousines."

The last four stanzas reveal the poet's commitment to support militancy as a last resort. It is easy for U.S. citizens to deny their government's complicity in upholding repressive regimes, to believe that war is something around the corner rather than a lived reality—something

    predicted
    in five years
    ten years
    any day now.

Hagedorn, in contrast, "always thought it was already happening." As a woman whose cultural roots are Asian, she chooses for her own sake and her daughter's to embrace a revolutionary heritage in which "snipers and poets secretly embrace," in which passionate women and men dance "to the song of bullets."[46]

Carolyn Forché first went to El Salvador in the late 1970s, posing as a journalist. A working-class white woman then in her mid-twenties, Forché has described herself as "ideologically vague" at the time of her journey, arranged by friends who wished her to document her findings there. Over a period of nearly two years, Forché received an invaluable political and social education, working alongside nurses in the understaffed, undersupplied shanties that passed for hospitals, visiting the solitary confinement unit of a political prison and emerging with hives from what she smelled and saw there, dodging bullets designed to insure that she saw nothing. As a result of this experience and her close affiliation with Salvadoran poet-in-exile Claribel Alegría, whose volume of poetry *Flores del vólcan / Flowers from the Volcano* Forché has translated, Forché has dedicated much of her own poetry to telling U.S. readers about El Salvador's political exigencies.[47]

An eight-poem sequence in Forché's Lamont Prize-winning volume *The Country between Us,* "In Salvador 1978–80," most fully and eloquently articulates the poet's experiences there. The first of these, "San Onofre, California," invites readers to come with her on a journey far south, past

> the oldest women
> shelling limas into black shawls
> Portillo scratching his name
> on the walls, the slender ribbons
> of piss, children patting the mud.

Forché's tone gradually becomes ominous; if we go far enough, she warns,

> we might stop
> in the street in the very place
> where someone disappeared.

The dangers of such a journey are manifold, for if we travelers hear too much,

> we would
> lead our lives with our hands
> tied together.

To escape this fate, the poet and her companions listen only to "the wind jostling lemons, / to dogs ticking across the terraces." Still, they know full well that these benign sounds are misleading, that they conceal "the cries of those who vanish," cries so long denied that they "might take years to get here."[48]

Dedicated to Alegría, "The Island" offers an account of the months Forché spent living with Alegría and her family in Deya on the island of Majorca while Forché was translating the elder poet's work. In this three-part poem the younger poet pays tribute to Alegría as her muse, a source of inspiration due to both her artistic and her political integrity. In part 1 Forché observes closely as Alegría gestures, explaining "what she would do with so many / baskets of bread," and she describes in detail Alegría's petiteness and her "violent" black eyes and hair, as dark as the violent mornings she has spent each day of her fourteen-year exile on Majorca. As a developing poet who is politically naive, Forché looks to the elder poet for guidance. "She wears a white cotton dress," the poet says of Alegría;

> tiny mirrors have been stitched
> to it—when I look for myself
> in her, I see the same face
> over and over.

This assertion is ambiguous, since the poet goes on to admit that there are no physical nor experiential similarities between the two. Forché has

> the fatty eyelids
> of a Slavic factory girl,
> the pale hair of mixed blood.

She has never been hungry or had to fight for something to eat. "But we are not unalike," she claims of herself and Alegría; each has empathy for others and a need to interrogate official history. "When I talk to her," Forché explains, "I know what I will be saying / twenty years from now."

Part 2 describes Alegría's return to El Salvador the summer before, her first visit since her book *Ashes of Izalco* was burned publicly. Having gone back primarily to visit her mother, Alegría went also to find herself, "to flesh out the memory of a poet / whose body was never found." The weight of this culture, with its buried nightmares, presses on Alegría. Salvador was different from what the poet remembered, Forché explains, but had not actually changed, for "in Salvador nothing is changed." Part 3 shifts from Forché's voice to Alegría's, as the elder poet gently tells her young colleague that she cannot help her understand Salvador, that in Deya she is too far removed from her homeland to comprehend its exigencies herself, that Forché will have to figure this out on her own:

> To my country I ship poetry instead
> of bread, so I cut through nothing.

> I give nothing, so you see I have
> nothing, according to myself.

Exilic guilt is implied here, as Alegría, speaking through Forché, acknowledges her nagging fear that poetry is not enough to offer people who need food. Yet she cannot change her exilic circumstances. The poem closes by revealing Alegría's frustration at her enforced separation from her land and its struggling people: "Carolina, do you know how long it takes / any one voice to reach another?"[49]

Forché describes "The Colonel" as a poem *trouvé*, the recounting of her actual experience when invited to dine with a prominent military officer during her sojourn in El Salvador in the guise of an unaffiliated reporter. "What you have heard is true. I was in his house." The poet's terse opening lines set the tone of this prose piece, which catalogs the morbid incongruities between the "civilities" of the colonel's family life and the atrocities for which he is responsible. Much of his life-style seems at first glance mundane, if privileged: his daughter filed her nails, his son left for the evening, the maid brought bread and mangoes. Yet just beneath the surface is an ominous note, struck vividly in Forché's juxtaposition of the ordinary and the horrific: "There were daily papers, pet dogs, a pistol on the cushion beside him. The moon swung bare on its black cord over the house. On the television was a cop show. It was in English. Broken bottles were embedded in the walls around the house to scoop the kneecaps from a man's legs or cut his hands to lace." The colonel lives in a prison of his own making, the poet implies; even the moon is threatening to one who threatens so many others.

The poem goes on to document the colonel's greed and inhumanity, as the evening took a sickening and dramatic turn. After an elegant meal of rack of lamb and good wine, "his wife took everything away," and the officer began to talk "of how difficult it had become to govern." As tensions around the table built, the poet was warned by her friend's pointed look to say nothing:

> The colonel returned with a sack used to bring groceries home. He spilled many human ears on the table. They were like dried peach halves. There is no other way to say this. He took one of them in his hands, shook it in our faces, dropped it into a water

glass. It came alive there. I am tired of fooling around he said. As for the rights of anyone, tell your people they can go fuck themselves.

Forché's short, staccato sentences add to the intensity of her recitation. Despite her recognition that metaphor is a limited tool in poetry of witness, Forché makes brilliant use of the severed ears that come alive in water to represent El Salvador's listening dead and disappeared.[50] "Something for your poetry, no?" the colonel laughs ironically, sweeping the ears to the floor. And indeed, he does unwittingly proffer to the poet a sacred gift: "Some of the ears on the floor caught this scrap of his voice. Some of the ears on the floor were pressed to the ground." Forché knows that she must speak now for these voiceless; her North American readers, in turn, must hear.[51]

"Return" deals with the poet's culture shock when she comes home at last to the decadent United States, with its iced drinks and supermarkets and relative safety. In dialogue with her more politically experienced compatriot, presumably Josephine Crum, to whom the poem is dedicated, Forché chronicles the horrors she has witnessed and attempts to process what she has learned and to determine where she can go from there:

> Afraid more than
> I had been, even of motels so much so
> that for months every tire blow-out
> was final,

the poet documents her struggle "to remember things impossible to forget." As Alegría inspired Forché through her writing, so Crum nurtures yet challenges her through her rigorous questioning and listening to her younger friend's accounts: "You took / my stories apart for hours," Forché tells the older woman,

> sitting
> on your sofa with your legs under you
> and fifty years in your face.

So now you know, Crum replies, how machetes mix with whiskey at cocktail parties, what happens to imprisoned men and women left to starve for days in pits, how complicitous the U.S. government is in all of this.

> Go try on
> Americans your long, dull story
> of corruption, but better to give
> them what they want,

Crum advises, cynically but no doubt wisely.

What they want, the older woman continues in poetic mono-logue, are graphic documentations of atrocities; they will be moved to action only by accounts of such survivors as Lil Milagro Ramírez, who could not walk without aid

> and was forced to shit in public.
> Tell them about the razor, the live wire,
> dry ice and concrete, grey rats and above all
> who fucked her, how many times and when.

Forché uses a catalog of victims to offer moving testimony to particu-lar Salvadorans whom she met there and because of whom she will never be the same. Like many U.S. poets writing about South Africa, Forché here combines the mantric recitation of atrocities with fierce introspection:

> Josephine, I tell you
> I have not rested, not since I drove
> those streets with a gun in my lap,
> not since all manner of speaking has
> failed and the remnant of my life
> continues onward.

The poet's previously held beliefs in physical safety, political secu-rity, and the power of language have been exposed as naive illusions. She goes mad in the Safeway, she explains, with all the choices of lettuce, papayas, sugar, and coffee, "especially the coffee"; she can no longer talk to American men, put off by

their constant Scotch and fine white
hands, many hours of business, penises
hardened by motor inns and a faint
resemblance to their wives.

They remind her too painfully of the U.S. military men working with
the government in El Salvador, men she cannot respect.

In the poem's final stanza, Forché draws again upon Crum's
voice to offer wisdom and perspective to her struggle for accountabil-
ity. "And so . . . you've learned a little / about starvation," Crum re-
plies, cautioning Forché not to think of herself as a victim when so
many in El Salvador suffer to a degree she will never know. Use this
experience and learn from it, assess your country's greed and with it
your own, and do something meaningful with what you discern, the
poet's friend advises forthrightly:

It is
not your right to feel powerless. Better
people than you were powerless.
You have not returned to your country,
but to a life you never left.

What Crum forces Forché to confront, finally, and what Forché im-
plicitly urges her readers to admit, is the weight and responsibility
of privilege, which, according to Adrienne Rich, is always "ignorant
at the core."[52]

"Message" seems to be Forché's address to those Salvadorans
who "fight / for the most hopeless of revolutions." Her pessimistic
assertion of affiliation designates several combatants as particular
allies: Pedro, who handles religious rites for the dead and dying;
Margarita, who makes bombs to avenge her friend, who languishes
unindicted in prison; Lionel, armed only with a few guns and "an
idea for a water pump and / cooperative farm." Despite her pessi-
mism, the poet makes a lifelong commitment to tell their stories.

You will fight
and fighting, you will die. I will live

and living cry out until my voice is gone
to its hollow of earth, where with our
hands and by the lives we have chosen
we will dig deep into our deaths.
I have done all that I could do.

In these poignant lines, the poet justifies her literary work as inade-
quate yet all she can offer. She commends the revolutionary actors
for their efforts, whether or not they are ultimately successful. Arms
linked, joined tenuously together, they can hold fast now only to

a belief that became
but small light
in the breadth of time where we began
among each other, where we lived
in the hour farthest from God.[53]

Taken as a group, Forché's El Salvador poems illustrate an important
interventionist strategy of resistance poetry: the dismemberment of
the poet's individual identity and its subsequent reconstruction in
solidarity. "The resistance to terror is what makes the world habit-
able," she claims in her introduction to *Against Forgetting*, an anthol-
ogy of twentieth-century poetry of witness. "The protest against vio-
lence will not be forgotten and this insistent memory renders life
possible in communal situations."[54]

What, finally, does U.S. women's poetry resist, and how does it
resist? I want to suggest three answers to each question, although I
am aware that there could be many more. These poems first and
foremost resist the self-aggrandizing manuevers and genodical prac-
tices of the U.S. military-political machine. "America" has contrib-
uted economically and ideologically to war in El Salvador and apart-
heid in South Africa, these poets assert, and "Americans" can not
ethically afford to remain silent. They thus refute the lie that racism
in South Africa differs altogether from racism at home, that the Pen-
tagon budget is not linked to military oppression of the Salvadoran
poor. This point connects directly to a second: this poetry demands
of its readers a painstaking and often painful self-analysis for signs
of apathy and complicity. It cajoles and instructs its audiences to
refuse any privilege they might otherwise accrue as U.S. citizens

and, instead, to add their voices of protest to those of the poets. Finally, these poems resist any temptation to appropriate the voices of Third World people; they speak *of* and *with* them but not *for* them. Through documentation and empathy, they encourage readers to listen across the borders of difference, to learn from those in struggle as well as to express their solidarity with them.

How these poems resist is, of course, more difficult to articulate than *what* they resist, but I find that they employ three key rhetorical, stylistic, and ethical devices. First, they refuse the pretense of objectivity, instead asserting polemically the terms of their engagement with the topic at hand. In so doing, they claim as their own the task of historiographic reconstruction. Second, they violate poetic decorum in order to invite conflict and confrontation. They express anger stylistically via capital letters, exclamations, profanity, and arguments ad hominem; they hammer readers with aggressive catalogs, lengthy repetitions, and fierce rhetorical questions designed to evoke discomfort. For the reader's initial resistance will contribute ultimately to the success of the resistance poem. Finally, and simultaneously, they call forth from their audience an alternative complicity, a willingness to participate in a re-visionary project—ethical, political, literary—that could actually make a difference in the lives of the marginalized. These poems solicit our solidarity with not only the oppressed of South Africa and El Salvador but also with the poets who recount these people's struggles. By saying "listen," "come with me," "tell me," or "don't tell me," these poets engage our active participation in the intervention process, as we too join a community of resisters.

Chapter 7

"Sisters in Arms": The Warrior Construct in Writings by Contemporary U. S. Women of Color

The women say they have learned to rely on their own strength. They say they
are aware of the force of their unity. They say, let those who call for a new
language first learn violence. They say, let those who want to change the world
first seize all the rifles. They say that they are starting from zero. They say that a
new world is beginning.

—Monique Wittig, *Les Guérillères*

We are Black people living in a time when the consciousness of our intended
slaughter is all around us. People of Color are increasingly expendable, our
government's policy both here and abroad. We are functioning under a govern-
ment ready to repeat in El Salvador and Nicaragua the tragedy of Vietnam, a
government which stands on the wrong side of every single battle for liberation
taking place upon this globe. . . . Can anyone here still afford to believe that
efforts to reclaim the future can be private or individual? Can anyone here still
afford to believe that the pursuit of liberation can be the sole and particular
province of any one particular race, or sex, or age, or religion, or sexuality, or
class?

—Audre Lorde, *Sister Outsider*

Although Wittig's epic celebration of women warriors eradicating
male oppressors in *Les Guérillères* differs generically from Lorde's
impassioned speech to the black North American left in *Sister Out-
sider*, the two writers share certain radical themes and goals. Both
address the politics of oppression, decrying injustice and urging
strong, immediate action in global battles for freedom. Both believe
in unity as the guiding spirit of such action, in communal resistance
as the strongest force and greatest resource for making fundamental
change. And both dare to imagine, in feminist terms, the raw, excit-
ing possibility of a truly liberated world.

Their intended audiences, liberatory tactics, and rhetorical strategies differ significantly, however. Wittig creates a woman-centered utopia of rebellion and revenge, a fantastical landscape populated by "the women"—raging furies fully armed, handily eliminating patriarchal adversaries. Her warriors resort to conventional military language and methods: they learn violence, seize all the guns, start from zero. Rhetorically, Wittig uses repetition aggressively to dramatize the authoritative power of women's voices raised collectively: "the women say . . . they say . . . they say . . . they say." Lorde, in contrast, writes to and for people of color—women and children in particular, but men as well—though certainly her final question raises the hope that individuals of all colors, classes, etc., will work together to combat oppression. Further, she decries militarization (as reflected in the U. S. government's imperialistic policies) rather than embracing it, for "the master's tools will never dismantle the master's house."[1] Like Wittig, she relies on repetition to strengthen her audience's resolve, but her repetition reverberates as a troubling rhetorical question: "Can anyone here still afford to believe . . . ?" For Wittig, a white radical feminist, and her idealized revolutionaries, the tough decisions have apparently been made: violence is being met with violence, women are destroying men, gender is the controlling agenda of struggle. For Lorde, as a woman of color, and for the real-life revolutionaries she addresses, the painful question of who unites with whom to wage what kind of battle is still very much in process.

The passage from Wittig illustrates what Teresa de Lauretis has labelled a "rhetoric of violence." It posits as utopian feminist strategy a totalizing patriarchal model for attacking and defeating "the women's" enemies, presumably men of any and all colors and classes. Lorde's statement critiques violent patriarchal rhetoric and practice and confronts that "othering" that de Lauretis describes as "the violence of rhetoric," here depicted by the U.S. government's purposeful acts of erasure against those whose race, gender, sexuality, or class make them marginal and, therefore, disposable.[2] Lorde's rhetoric calls for collective resistance against the state rather than violence against "the men"; her political consciousness "stems from an awareness that the public is *personally* political." Aída Hurtado further clarifies strategic differences in political praxis of white women and women of color: "The political skills of feminists of Color are neither the conventional political skills of white liberal feminists nor the free-spirited approaches of white radical feminists. Instead, feminists of Color train to be urban guerrillas by doing battle every day with the apparatus of the state."[3] For Wittig's fictionalized women, rebellion takes an apocalyptic form; for Lorde's people of color, resistance occurs as sustained acts of daily confrontation, part of what Patricia Hill Collins has called "a self defined standpoint on their own oppression."[4]

Political theorist Jean Bethke Elshtain has critiqued Wittig (along with Mary Daly, Susan Griffin, and other "hard-line feminist realists") for creating a "Manichean narrative" of oppressor/oppressed that "reiterates rather than deconstructs a patriarchal model of armed civic virtue"—a model that reinforces the "congealed typifications" she finds prevalent in both feminist and antifeminist writing about women, men, and war.[5] Although I do not completely agree with her argument, Elshtain's assessment of the dangers feminists have encountered in writing on women and violence raises some thorny issues. How is it that U.S. feminists of color have claimed warrior identities, even when their proclaimed goal has been to eliminate oppression, injustice, ultimately war itself? When they have claimed such identities, how have they avoided essentializing (men as Evil Enemies, women as Just Warriors) and, instead, problematized this construct, thereby increasing its accuracy and effectiveness? And what distinctive re-vision of warriors and warring, of the rhetoric of violence and the violence of rhetoric, have women of color offered in the 1980s from which white feminists have learned?

The dilemmas about essentialism, dichotomous thinking, and competing feminist theories—dilemmas suggested by Elshtain's critique and my questions—are further illustrated when we examine Mary Daly's treatment of warriors in her *Wickedary* (1987), purportedly a radical feminist "metadictionary." Here she defines *necrophilia* as "the most fundamental characteristic and first principle of patriarchy: hatred for and envy of Life." The Necrophilic State, she argues, is upheld by rape, genocide, and war, "the logical expression of phallocentric power." In contrast to these violent manifestations of phallic lust, she presents a woman-centered *biophilia:* "the original Lust for Life that is at the core of all Elemental E-motion; Pure Lust, which is the Nemesis of patriarchy."[6] Although Daly presumably means to include all radical women in her "crone-ological" vision of Hags and Witches weaving a new language on the boundaries of patriarchal

space, she sometimes oversimplifies and/or essentializes: dystopian
patriarchal terrain is countered by utopian, Amazonian borderlands.
While most U.S. feminists would have some understanding of what
Daly means by patriarchal space, not all would agree about the de-
gree and nature of its malignancy or about which men (or women)
inhabit it. Elizabeth V. Spelman has rightly criticized Daly for "white
solipsism" in relying on an "additive analysis" that argues that sex-
ism is the root and paradigm of other forms of oppression, while
racism is "a deformity within patriarchy." Since U.S. women of color
experience racism and sexism simultaneously, Spelman concludes,
Daly implicitly asks them to compartmentalize their struggles.[7]

Furthermore, women-controlled borderlands are more ambigu-
ous territories than Daly suggests. As Gloria Anzaldúa has explained,
for Chicana/*tejana* feminists, borderlands are places of contradiction
in which "keeping intact one's shifting and multiple identity and
integrity is like trying to swim in a new element, an 'alien' element."[8]
Since Daly does not identify explicitly what kinds of Crones inhabit
her boundaries—that is, she does not acknowledge fully the impor-
tance of differences among women—readers must wonder: Where
in her borderspace do U.S. women of color live? Doubly displaced
by institutionalized racism as well as sexism, women of color have
traditionally been marginalized, whether on the boundaries of the
borderlands or in the institutions of the heartlands. There they have
often had to fight not only white patriarchs but some white women
and men of color as well—to proclaim their centrality in any struggle
for liberation, indeed to assert their very presence. There they have
become warriors, raging against their own invisibility.

Nowhere in the *Wickedary* does Daly gloss the word *warrior*, how-
ever, perhaps because she recognizes its complexity. At first glance,
it may seem necrophilic, to use Daly's term, an "anti-biotic" meta-
phor identified with self-justifying patriarchal rhetoric. Men love
war, Vietnam veteran William Broyles informs readers of *Esquire*,
because it allows them to intuit the intimate connection between "sex
and destruction, beauty and horror, love and death."[9] Given this sort
of masculinist reasoning, many U.S. feminists have viewed with am-
bivalence or rejected outright the term *warrior*, as creative identity
and/or theoretical construct. Furthermore, many Third World women
have realistically feared that naming themselves warriors would
make them more vulnerable to dictators and torturers in their coun-

tries. Hence, the editor's disclaimer in the "Woman as Warrior" issue of the U.S. feminist journal *woman of power:*

> Throughout this issue, the word warrior is used as a metaphor. It is not intended to mean that the women profiled or pictured are involved in military activity of any kind, or in the bearing or transporting of arms, or in armed resistance, insurrection or attempts to overthrow any government. This material should not be understood to mean such things or used against these women for purposes of persecution, interrogation, incarceration or further oppression.[10]

Yet many U.S. women of color have claimed a warrior identity, especially in their poetry and essays—an identity re-visioned not as a necrophilic zest for destruction but as an ongoing commitment to radical change and political intervention. Toni Cade Bambara, for example, has called herself and other writers of color "creative combatants." Cherríe Moraga wars with her words, "to clarify my resistance to the literate." June Jordan declares herself "a woman searching for my savagery / even if it's doomed." Nellie Wong wants to "approach enemy lines, link arms with my people, to guard our dead." Similarly, Chilean exile Marjorie Agosin has described Third World women as silence breakers, storytellers, global warriors for change:

> Our own history obliges us to speak, to loose words of fire. Thus we come out of the silence and darkness to show ourselves as we are: free women, warrior women. We are washers of clothes, teachers, lawyers, journalists, poets. We are mothers, sisters, wives, daughters. . . . We wage our war every day in the country called Chile or Guatemala or the United States. We are new women with new stories to tell.[11]

My examination of poetry and essays by contemporary U.S. women of color reveals three main ways in which they have used the warrior construct. Some poets have identified themselves explicitly as warriors, as in Audre Lorde's claim to be a "Black lesbian feminist warrior poet."[12] Others have named themselves war correspondents, narrators from the front rather than active combatants, as in Ntozake

Shange's assertion that "the front lines aren't always what you think they are."[13] A third group of poets have invoked a warrior-muse: a bellicose mother, historical foremother, goddess, or mythic hero who inspires the writer's art—as in Maxine Hong Kingston's invocation of the Chinese warrior Fa Mu Lan.[14] In the sections that follow, I will examine each of these constructs and analyze why and how the warrior represents for many women of color a powerful force for global transformation.

1

> On worn kitchen stools and tables
> we are piecing our weapons together
> scraps of a different history
>
> —Audre Lorde, "Call"

> Now among the alien gods with weapons of magic I am.
> —Navaho protection song

The struggle to claim her racial, sexual, feminist, and warrior identities forms the core of Audre Lorde's poetics and politics.[15] As she explained in a 1982 interview with Claudia Tate, her creative energy comes from being outspoken about these diverse parts of herself:

> With respect to myself specifically, I feel that not to be open about any of the different "people" within my identity, particularly the "mes" who are challenged by a status quo, is to invite myself and other women, by my example, to live a lie. In other words, I would be giving in to a myth of sameness which I think can destroy us.[16]

Women must acknowledge our multiple identities and our differences, Lorde believes, if we are to remain strong.

Many of Lorde's poems contain images of women as warriors: "warrior queens" ("Harriet"); "like a warrior woman" ("Chorus"); "like my warrior sisters" ("125th Street and Abomey"); "Assata my sister warrior" ("For Assata"). At times the epithet *warrior* becomes an emblem of hope for future generations: "I bless your child with the mother she has / with a future of warriors and growing fire" ("Dear Toni instead of a Letter").[17] For Lorde, the term *warrior* evokes centuries of history of African women's resistance to white authorities and other forces of suppression. Foremost among such warrior women were the legendary Amazons of Dahomey, about whom Lorde writes in "The Women of Dan." Here she enacts a strong revisionist impulse, for she insists that women's warring be not stealthy but open, visible:

> I come as a woman
> do not come like a secret warrior
> with an unsheathed sword in my mouth
> hidden behind my tongue
> slicing my throat to ribbons.

Dangerous to others but not to herself, the poet names her new weapons, erotic heat and poetic words, a combination vital for continued growth and vision.[18]

> I come like a woman
> who I am
> spreading out through the nights
> laughter and promise
> and dark heat
> warming whatever I touch
> that is living
> consuming
> only
> what is already dead.[19]

Like Mawulisa, a peace-loving Dahomean goddess about whom she has often written, Lorde resists war as a deceptive, vindictive enterprise. She refuses to be silenced or to destroy unnecessarily. Instead, she openly warns contemporary oppressors of her watchful presence and embraces her warrior identity through a passionate, ritualistic celebration with her sisters of Dan.

Lorde does not reject retribution altogether, however, nor is her presentation of women as warriors always ritualized or celebratory. Her 1986 volume of poetry, *Our Dead behind Us*, is rife with horrific war imagery: arms, guns, battles, massacres, limpet mines, flames, explosions, blood, corpses, mournings for the dead. If unjust wars against indigenous peoples continue to be waged around the world by U.S. and other imperialistic governments, Lorde believes that radical women must spearhead the resistance; "this is the way in which the philosopher queen, the poet-warrior leads." Lorde is especially determined to speak of and for the voiceless, for "all those feisty, incorrigible black women who insist on standing up and saying 'I am and you cannot wipe me out, no matter how irritating I am, how much you fear what I might represent.'"[20] Many of her poems, therefore, support women and children engaged in global struggles for liberation—in South Africa, Grenada, and Chile, to name only a few.

"Sisters in Arms" illustrates well the complexity of Lorde's use of the warrior construct; in fact, it interweaves related images of the poet-warrior, the war correspondent, and the warrior-muse. Sexuality and political struggle intersect, as Lorde describes sharing her bed and her arms (in both senses of the word) with a South African woman who learns that her fifteen-year-old daughter has just been brutally murdered near Durban, her body "hanging / gut-sprung on police wheels." The poet feels agony and helplessness:

> I could not return with you to bury the body
> reconstruct your nightly cardboards
> against the seeping Transvaal cold
> I could not plant the other limpet mine
> against a wall at the railroad station. . . .

So Lorde does what she can: buys her lover a ticket to Durban (ironically, on her American Express card) and comforts her physically before her departure.

Written retrospectively, the poem reveals Lorde's fury at both the South African government's continuing atrocities against its black people and the *New York Times'* scant coverage of what it euphemistically deems the "unrest" there. As a war correspondent, she reports graphically the horrors the *Times* chooses to hide:

> Black children massacred at Sebokeng,
> six-year olds imprisoned for threatening the state . . .
> Thabo Sibeko, first grader, in his own blood
> on his grandmother's parlor floor.

The newspaper's evasions and these terrible truths haunt Lorde as
she gardens haphazardly and recalls moments of intimacy and pain
with her South African sister:

> we were two Black women touching our flame
> and we left our dead behind us
> I hovered   you rose   the last ritual of healing
> "It is spring" you whispered
> I sold the ticket for guns and sulfa
> and wherever I touch you
> I lick cold from my fingers
> taste rage . . .

Lorde knows that the sisters who lay in each other's arms may also
bear arms together one day, stronger for having shared erotic experi-
ence; "someday you will come to my country / and we will fight side
by side?" Since she cannot go to South Africa, Lorde invokes, in her
stead, the African warrior queen Mmanthatisi, who led the Sotho
people during the *mfecane,* an earlier black South African uprising.
As this warrior-muse "dresses again for battle, / knowing the men
will follow," the poet chronicles her preparations, dreaming of Dur-
ban and the possibility of revolutionary change.[21]

Lorde shared the energy and fatigue of battle not only with her
South African sister but also with the white woman with whom she
lived for many years. In "Outlines" Lorde explores the complex inter-
nal wars that divide women, that raise not only our enemies' hands
against us. Despite their private conflicts, however, the two women
in the poem fight together against the forces of racism and homopho-
bia:

> We rise to dogshit   dumped on our front porch
> the brass windchimes   from Sundance   stolen
> despair offerings of the 8 a.m. news
> reminding us we are still at war
> and not with each other.

As the Klan burns a cross ten blocks away, one woman exchanges
concern with their neighbors while the speaker registers a shotgun,
searching for courage. The poem's concluding lines present both

women as warriors in an ongoing battle—for their survival as lesbians, as interracial lovers, and for the survival of women and the planet:

> we have chosen each other
> and the edge of each other's battles
> the war is the same
> if we lose
> someday women's blood will congeal
> upon a dead planet
> if we win
> there is no telling.[22]

Radical women must begin to imagine what is possible, Lorde reminds us, when we piece our weapons together and assemble a different history.

Sometimes, however, conflicts between women are not soluble. Lorde points out in "Equal Opportunity" that not all women, not all women of color, are sisters in arms.

> The american deputy assistant secretary of defense
> for Equal Opportunity
> and safety, is a home girl.
> Blindness slashes our tapestry to shreds.

The deputy is blind to her own tokenism and, most appallingly, to the terrible irony of her complicity in her department's invasion of Grenada. Against the deputy's naïveté and self-interest, Lorde juxtaposes the victimization and quiet resistance of Imelda, a young Grenadian woman whose sister has been missing for ten days, whose hut has been destroyed by "armed men in moss-green jumpsuits /searching for weapons." Along with M-16s and rapacious soldiers, Imelda fears her child's death from malnutrition and dehydration, yet her prior experience with nervous armed soldiers has taught her how to talk to invaders, how to remain calm and dissemble: "no guns, man, no guns here. we glad you come. you carry water?" Back in the United States the deputy flexes her newly acquired muscle ("when I stand up to speak in uniform / you can believe everyone takes notice!"), extols her department's fine record of equal opportu-

nity hiring for women, and, Lorde concludes searingly, "swims to-
ward safety / through a lake of her own blood."[23] This sister's viola-
tion of justice obviously pains the poet, as does her own obligation
to present and condemn this home girl as a tool of the U.S military
machine. For Lorde, however, irresponsible actions against Third
World people by co-opted women are surely indefensible.

The importance of personal accountability for the warrior-poet,
an issue raised by Lorde in this poem and throughout her work, is
one of several characteristics that Patricia Hill Collins considers cen-
tral to an alternative black women's epistemology drawn from both
feminist and Afrocentric standpoints. The other traits she enumer-
ates—concrete experience as a source of knowledge and wisdom,
dialogue as crucial to any struggle, and an ethic of caring grounded
in empathy—characterize Lorde's poetic practice and theory as well.
Lorde's aesthetic-political goals parallel those that Collins ascribes to
black feminist scholars who move among multiple epistemologies in
complex acts of political translation, affirming alternate truths. Such
writers and scholars "rearticulate a preexisting Black women's stand-
point and recenter the language of existing discourse to accommodate
these knowledge claims."[24]

The knowledge that Gloria Anzaldúa advances in her poetry and
prose also emerges from a self-articulated standpoint of her oppres-
sion as a Chicana/*tejana* lesbian and her culturally specific forms and
historias of rebellion. Anzaldúa's self-conceptualization as warrior-
poet differs from Lorde's in several ways. For Lorde and other Afri-
can American women, a root source of oppression is racism, whether
manifested in the nineteenth-century U. S. system of slavery or in
South Africa's apartheid laws. For Anzaldúa and other Chicanas,
historical conquests and thefts of their native tongue are the foremost
offenses. "Who is to say that robbing a people of its language is less
violent than war?" Like hundreds of women before her, Anzaldúa
refuses for her "wild tongue" to be tamed.[25] "My Chicana identity is
grounded in the Indian woman's history of resistance," she explains.
For centuries the mestiza has been silenced, threatened, imprisoned
in abusive marriages, bludgeoned by the system; "for years she hid
her flame but stoked and tended it." At the end of the twentieth
century, Anzaldúa asserts, this warrior is coming into her own. "The
spirit of the fire spurs her to fight for her own skin and a piece of the
ground to stand on."[26]

For Anzaldúa as for many contemporary U.S. women of color, ground to stand on, a place to claim safely as home, constitutes a complex piece of racial and feminist identity invention. "There is nothing more important to me than home," Barbara Smith states in her introduction to *Home Girls* (1983), a black feminist anthology, and many of Anzaldúa's poems and essays imply a similar valuing of her ethnic milieu.[27] But a fierce ambivalence permeates her "politics of location," because her homeland is neither clearly delineated nor completely safe. She was raised in the borderlands, that physical/psychical terrain "wherever two or more cultures edge each other, where people of different races occupy the same territory, where under, lower, middle and upper classes touch."[28] Anzaldúa's particular home is the U.S. Southwest–Texas Mexican border, with its heavy Indian influence, its constant state of transition, its sense of itself as a separate country. Living in the interfaces between worlds, the Chicana must discover and use her mestiza consciousness.

Anzaldúa's war is both internal and external: to understand her multiple identities despite enormous insecurities and obstacles; to combat racism, sexism, heterosexism, elitism in their many forms. Constantly juggling multiple cultures, "*la mestiza* undergoes a struggle for flesh, a struggle of borders, an inner war." On the one hand, Anzaldúa argues, this psychic unrest helps poets create; on the other, any cultural collision takes its toll. Attacks on indigenous peoples and their values demand a counterstance, yet, as Anzaldúa notes, any counterstance risks replicating the polarized models of binary opposition she and other mestizas wish to reject.: "A counterstance locks one into a duel of oppressor and oppressed; locked in mortal combat, like the cop and the criminal, both are reduced to a common denominator of violence."[29] Yet a self-defined stance of resistance can also represent proud defiance, a necessary step toward liberation.

In her poem "To live in the Borderlands means you," Anzaldúa explores this multifaceted Chicana identity and its warrior context. *En la frontera,* she finds it difficult to speak or be spoken to: "the wind steals your voice"; parts of her feel betrayed by other parts. Her racial identity is uncertain:

> you are neither *hispana india negra espanole*
> *ni gabacha, eres mestiza, mulata,* half-breed
> caught in the crossfire between camps.

Likewise, she struggles with an ambiguous gender identity as the

> forerunner of a new race,
> half and half—both woman and man, neither—
> a new gender.

The poet must be a crossroads, both a victim of war and its soldier.

> In the borderlands
>   you are the battleground
>   where enemies are kin to each other;
>   you are at home, a stranger,
>   the border disputes have been settled
>   the volley of shots have shattered the truce
>   you are wounded, lost in action
>   dead, fighting back.[30]

In this milieu, survival is a key issue; the poet thus imagines herself fighting back even from death to insure a future for her selves and her people.

One characteristic of Anzaldúa's warrior poetry that distinguishes it from Lorde's is its hybrid style: "Poetry, description, essay—we cross genres, cross the borders. It's a new poetics. It's a new aesthetics. And I don't even know if it's new. It's probably not new. . . . What's new is bringing it to the forefront and giving it a name. And making it part of the dialogue." Code switching is a means of honoring her native tongue, Spanish, though she recognizes that it, too, has been historically the "oppressor's language." Still, she points out that "ethnic identity is twin skin to linguistic identity—I am my language"; to be denied it evokes both anger and shame. Poverty and classism further contribute to her feelings of internalized exile. For Lorde, black warrior writing requires transforming silence into language and action. For Anzaldúa, this endeavor is further problematized by her desire to use politically and aesthetically her Spanish, Indian, and English voices, her "serpent's tongue."[31]

Because of the risks inherent in resistance, both Lorde and Anzaldúa have claimed, women of color must work collaboratively to combat their multiple oppressions; in community lies power. Change "requires both the alchemist and the welder, the magician and the laborer, the witch and the warrior, the myth-smasher and the myth-maker."[32] As warrior-poets, Lorde and Anzaldúa are committed to this collective defiance.

2

> Here, supposedly, we do not have "dissident" poets and writers—unless they are well rewarded runaways from the Soviet Union. Here we know about the poets and writers that major media eagerly allow us to see and consume. And then we do not hear about the other ones. But I am one of them. I am a dissident American poet and writer completely uninterested to run away from my country, my home.
> —June Jordan, *On Call*

> I am a war correspondent . . . in a war of cultural and esthetic aggression.
> —Ntozake Shange, 1985 interview

Many feminist writers in the U.S. have grappled with issues of censorship, external and internal.[33] How much can they say, and how angrily, and still be published by university or commercial presses? How strongly should they defend freedom of the press when pornography and sexist exploitation of women are at issue? How rigorously should they conceal or reveal their most intimate truths when they write autobiographically? But as June Jordan points out, for the North American writer who is black, female, and dissident, censorship requires daily confrontation. In her introduction to *On Call* (1985), a stunning collection of political essays, Jordan addresses directly her own rejection by mainstream media:

> If political writing by a Black woman did not strike so many editors as presumptuous or simply bizarre, then, perhaps, this book would not be needed. Instead, I might regularly appear, on a weekly or monthly schedule, as a national columnist. But if you will count the number of Black women with regular and national forums for their political ideas, and the ideas of their constituency, you will comprehend the politics of our exclusion: I cannot come up with the name of one Black woman in that position.[34]

Jordan goes on to assert that, in the United States, black people are systematically silenced, as evidenced by the *New York Times'* failure throughout the 1980s to cite on its op-ed page, frequently and regularly, any African-American writer on the topic of South Africa. Such "whitelistings" necessitate the writer's taking matters into her own hands, addressing her constituency through radical/alternative presses, asserting her right to honest, informed reportage on global struggles for liberation.

As a political poet and essayist, Jordan has focused particularly on Third World sites of turmoil and transformation: South Africa, Lebanon, Palestine, Guatemala, Nicaragua. She has traveled to these war-torn countries and has brought back eloquent, angry reports from the front. At times, she struggles with her confusion over whether or how to become an actual combatant. "I must become a menace to my enemies," Jordan proclaims in a poem dedicated to Agostinho Neho, poet and former president of Angola; "I must become the action of my fate." The time for silence, passivity, and fear is past, she warns her oppressors:

Be afraid . . .
I plan to blossom bloody on an afternoon
surrounded by my comrades singing
terrible revenge in merciless
accelerating
rhythms.[35]

The poet asserts here the bellicose power of her poetic meters and words. Despite efforts to censor her, Jordan insists on documenting her political efforts and views in a rhetoric and a poetics of anger, insight, and compassion.

Her essays on South Africa illustrate Jordan's role as an embattled war reporter attempting to bear witness to international struggles. For Jordan, "South Africa was how I came to understand that I am not against war. I am against losing the war. But war means that you fight. Who is fighting South Africa here, in my house? . . . I know my life depends on making this fight my own." In a sense, Jordan has been a correspondent, rather than a participant, by default; she

has wanted to be more active in South African liberation struggles
from her U.S. vantage point but has been uncertain how best to do
so in an apathetic environment. "What can I join? Where are the
streets side-to-side jammed with Americans who will not be moved,
who will shout until the windows shatter from the walls? Is there a
picket line that blocks the South African Embassy? Do the merchants
dealing diamonds and gold loudly deny the blood on the
counter? . . . No and no and no . . . . What is the difficulty? Has no-
body heard the news?" Jordan's furious questions accumulate relent-
lessly, hammering readers of conscience with the awareness that
concerned U. S. citizens have been derelict in not protesting more
rigorously our government's complicity in apartheid. She speaks to
and for many of us when she confesses her horror at the Reagan and
Bush adminstrations' policies and acknowledges her own uncertain-
ties: "I yet look for the dignity of an effective, defiant response."[36]

Jordan's commitment to struggling with this complex political
issue is also apparent in her poetry. Here, too, she uses rhetorical
questions and fierce irony to expose the political absurdities and
atrocities of our times. "How many of my brothers and my sisters /
will they kill," she wonders in one poem, "before I teach myself /
retaliation?"

> Shall we pick a number?
> South Africa for instance:
> do we agree that more than ten thousand
> in less than a year but than less than
> five thousand slaughtered in more than six
> months will
>
> WHAT IS THE MATTER WITH ME?
>
> I must become a menace to my enemies[37]

Elsewhere Jordan speaks of and for African women engaged in mili-
tant efforts toward liberation. Working for freedom in Mozambique
or Angola

> lifts
> the head of the young girl

formerly burdened by laundry
and yams,

she asserts; collective action brings dignity and hope. Paradoxically,
killing is sometimes the only means of preserving life. Jordan refuses
to present maternal nurture and possession of weapons as contradic-
tions.

She
straps the baby to her back
and
she carries her rifle
like she means
means to kill
for the love
for the life
of us all.[38]

The war correspondent's task, Jordan believes, is to foreground such
complexities in solidarity with women of color worldwide. Thus, her
work documents both global movements for self-determination and
the poet's own political struggles.

Like Jordan, Ntozake Shange has traveled in the Third World
and chronicled the efforts toward liberation she has witnessed. But
more explicitly than Jordan, she embraces her role as a war corre-
spondent, something she wanted to be from childhood on. At first,
her goal was romantic and frivolous, she explains, an idea she got
from watching *It Happened One Night* with Clark Gable and Claudette
Colbert. When her father dissuaded her from pursuing this occupa-
tion (because girls didn't do it), Shange turned to writing as a logical
alternative. As a feminist poet-playwright with strong leftist political
convictions, Shange has recognized that her current vocation and her
fantasy one have merged: "I figured out that I am a war correspon-
dent after all because I'm involved in a war of cultural and esthetic
aggression. The front lines aren't always what you think they are."[39]

Shange's lyrical reportage and idealistic vision are evident in
"Bocas: A Daughter's Geography." Her lyricism contrasts sharply
with Jordan's pained, raw questionings, her uncertainty about the

appropriate reportorial stance for the feminist war correspondent.
Shange's speaker is embattled, but she asserts herself as powerful
and victorious. As a mother, she embraces an identity global in its
parameters:

> i have a daughter / mozambique
> i have a son / angola
> our twins
> salvador & johannesburg / cannot speak
> the same language
> but we fight the same old men / in the new world.

Her litany of places in which poor people are rising up continues,
haunting and incantatory: Habana, Guyana, Santiago, Managua. The
patriarchs who dominate the world's peoples are tunnel-visioned,

> unaware of . . . all the dark urchins
> rounding out the globe / primitively whispering
> the earth is not flat old men.

The poet juxtaposes ironically the men's flatness, their one-dimen-
sionality, with the round, wholesome humanity of the embattled
daughters and sons. People of color have power in both their num-
bers and the justice of their causes, Shange implies; if they but perse-
vere, these men who lack empathy and vision will fall off the edge
of the earth. This utopian victory will make possible mass and mas-
sive revolutionary nurture, "feeding our children the sun."[40]

Aída Hurtado's assessment of women of color's resistance strate-
gies helps us understand both the particularities of Jordan's and
Shange's rhetorical stances and the common concerns that may dis-
tinguish their poetry and praxis as black U.S. women from those of
white feminists. According to Hurtado, many women of color have
more and earlier experience in developing effective ways of using
anger to promote sociocultural change than have middle-class white
feminists, who are often protected by classism and racism. As a con-
sequence, many white women do not acquire their political con-
sciousnesses until they become adults. Because their childhoods were
"safer," white women may have less anger (or be less strategic in

expressing and using the anger they feel) at gender-related and other oppressions. White feminists and feminists of color today may experience differently, for example, the rampant loss of children in our culture to poverty, police brutality, drugs. Hurtado quotes Audre Lorde's address to white feminists: "Some problems we share as women, some we do not. You fear your children will grow up to join the patriarchy and testify against you, we fear our children will be dragged from a car and shot down in the street and you will turn your backs upon the reasons they are dying."[41]

Hurtado claims that women of color are often more effective than white feminists in expressing their rage—in Jordan's and Shange's cases, in political poetry and essays. Even so, their expressions of fury may take different forms according to their particular experience of racism, classism, and gender oppression. The slaughter of innocent children drives a pessimistic Jordan most often toward the prosaic, it seems to me; the horrors she witnesses are too stark to be rendered metaphorically. An angry optimism, in contrast, underlies Shange's lyric intensity and rich metaphors; for her, "dark urchins" are the hope of the revolution as well as its casualties. Shange also seems to believe in an "essential" women's inclination toward peace and nurture, a viewpoint I see no evidence of Jordan's sharing. Patriarchal forces do not understand, Shange asserts, that women "see the world in a way that allows us to care more about people than about military power. The power we see is the power to feed, the power to nourish and to educate. But these kinds of powers are not respected, and so it's part of our responsibility as writers to make these things important."[42] As Adrienne Rich has said, even common words must be reconsidered, laid aside, recast with new meanings.[43] At the head of this list of re-visioned words, for Shange as for Rich, is *power*.

With other writers who identify themselves as warriors or war correspondents, Jordan and Shange support the last-resort strategies of countermilitancy that women are evincing throughout the Third World. Specifically, U.S. women of color have honored their sister-combatants in their dedications, prefaces, and introductions. Shange, for example, dedicates *See No Evil* (1984), her collection of revolutionary essays, to "the 30 million african women/in the NEW WORLD OF WHOM I AM A PROUD SURVIVOR" and to the armed women of Nicaragua, Guatemala, El Salvador, Mozambique, Angola, Namibia, and

South Africa. Jordan describes with admiration seeing all the Nicaraguan people armed, "nine year olds, Black women, elderly men . . . people forming volunteer militia to defend the revolution they had made." Combatting cultural aggression requires global consciousness raising, these two poets believe, and it is the writer's responsibility to instill this awareness through her art. *"When will we seize the world around us with our freedom?"*[44]

3

> My mother taught me the song of the warrior woman, Fa Mu Lan. I would have to grow up a woman warrior.
> —Maxine Hong Kingston, *The Woman Warrior*

> Find the muse within you. The voice that lies buried under you, dig it up. Do not fake it, try to sell it for a handclap or your name in print.
> —Gloria Anzaldúa, *This Bridge Called My Back*

White male poets have traditionally imagined the quintessential source of poetry as a female muse, an inspirer whom they have invoked through the ages and by whose aid they claim to create.[45] This figure has been described as the male poet's inspiring anima, who influences him in her roles as shamaness, sibyl, priestess—as the power that kindles his vision. Whether wise woman or human lover, the muse has existed for man as a series of opposites: he is subject, she is object; he is lover, she is beloved; he is begetter, she is begotten upon. As divine inspirer and sexual/creative stimulus, the muse has been a central symbolic aspect of the male literary imagination.

In many respects, the concept of the muse has been a luxury of race and gender privilege, a metaphor of colonization. Yet a surprising number of U.S. women poets have reimagined the muse in nonhierarchical ways, rejecting the passive, objectified version of men poets and re-visioning her, instead, as an active source of inspiration, a force born of their own artistic energy and will. Feminist poets often name as muses women from their lives—mothers, sisters, lovers, friends. Some women invoke goddesses and mythic women, especially in poems about creative process: Ishtar, Isis, Astarte, from Eastern myths; Demeter, Artemis, Eurydice, from ancient Greece; Seboulisa and Mawulisa, from African lore. A striking number of women focus on figures traditionally viewed as evil or dangerous to men: Kali, Circe, Medusa, Helen of Troy, the Furies, the Amazons. Unable or unwilling to idealize their inspirational sources as passive others, many women poets employ powerful muses as extensions of their own imaginations and partners in their creative endeavors.[46]

For U. S. women of color, the muse is often depicted as a warrior or a goddess of war who guides the poet in her cultural as well as creative battles. The reasons for choosing such a muse seem obvious when we consider the ravagings women of color throughout the world have undergone from poverty, starvation, war, and dislocation. Many U. S. writers recognize that they write from a position of relative security, a recognition that fuels not complacency but, rather, empathy with and rage on behalf of their sisters. To invoke a militant muse is, therefore, to add their voices—angry, impassioned—to others speaking out against oppression. Yet the muses of women of color differ according to a given poet's particular material and cultural circumstances. Contemporary African-American poets such as Audre Lorde and Ntozake Shange honor powerful goddess-mothers from African oral traditions, legendary figures who pass on an Afrocentric spiritual legacy. Chinese-American writers such as Maxine Hong Kingston and Nellie Wong pay tribute to their biological warrior-mothers, whose particular immigrant experiences on Gold Mountain forced them to resist with strength they did not know they had.[47]

In "Call," for example, Audre Lorde invokes as muse the African mother-goddess Seboulisa, said to ride through the world on the back of the Rainbow Serpent Aido Hwedo. This goddess sustains not only Lorde but also her African sisters in struggle.

> I am a Black woman   turning
> mouthing your name as a password
> through seductions   self-slaughter,

Lorde claims in her address to the goddess:

> . . . I believe in the holy ghost
> mother
> in your flames beyond our vision
> blown light through the fingers of women
> enduring   warring
> sometimes outside your name

we do not choose all our rituals
Thandi Modise   winged girl of Soweto
brought fire back home in the snout of a mortar
and passes the word from her prison cell   whispering
Aido Hwedo is coming[48]

Although Seboulisa is a peace-loving goddess, she does not shrink from warring when there is no alternative. Here the poet suggests that the goddess's spirit is being served in her own art and in counter-militant "crimes" by South African rebels such as Thandi Modise, an ANC guerrilla fighter who has become a legendary figure. By invoking a muse who supports countermilitancy, Lorde can mourn "our dead behind us" and affirm their revolutionary zeal.

For Chinese-American writers Maxine Hong Kingston and Nellie Wong, the warrior-muse is connected not to African history but to the marginalization experienced in the United States by their immigrant families. In *The Woman Warrior* (1975), Kingston names her mother shaman and revels in her subversive wisdom, though she also suffers from the "talk stories" her mother forces upon her: "My mother has given me pictures to dream. . . . I push the deformed into my dreams, which are in Chinese, the language of impossible stories." From her mother's endless tales come Kingston's inspiration and creative ambition but also an internalized sense of shame and loss. "When we Chinese girls listened to the adults talk-story, we learned that we failed if we grew up to be but wives or slaves. We could be heroines, swordswomen." Her mother's chant of Fa Mu Lan, the Chinese swordswoman who, according to legend, replaced her father in battle, was especially compelling to the young Kingston. "She taught me the song of the warrior woman. . . . I would have to grow up a woman warrior." Yet the same woman who taught her daughter such songs confessed to her, "You have no idea how I have fallen coming to America." As an adult Kingston finds she hates armies and prefers, instead, to use words as weapons. Like Shange and Jordan, she will challenge racist and classist oppressors via her reportage. "The swordswoman and I are not so dissimilar. What we have in common are the words at our backs. The idioms for revenge are 'report a crime' and 'report to five families.' The reporting is the vengeance—not the beheading, not the gutting, but the words. And

I have so many words—'chink' words and 'gook' words too—that they do not fit on my skin."[49]

Nellie Wong's "From a Heart of Rice Straw" also pays homage to her mother as warrior-muse, and, like Kingston, she reveals both shame and inspiration at the heart of her homage. Ostensibly, this poem chronicles two combat stories, a family quarrel in which Wong's father was accused of theft and assaulted by his angry brother and a San Francisco newspaper's condescending account of this unfortunate incident as just "another Tong war" in Oakland Chinatown. But Wong recognizes that the main warrior in this saga, her mother, has been silenced and made invisible, due in part to the stereotype of the Asian-American woman as the "ideal minority."[50] Thus, she retells this family story, reclaiming her mother as muse and as mouthpiece.

When her father was stabbed, Wong's mother chased the offender through the streets of Oakland Chinatown, oblivious to her own danger, finally to capture him.

> The cops said you were brave. The neighbors said
> you were brave. The relatives shook their heads,
> the bravery of a Gold Mountain woman unknown
> in the old home village.

But this courage was soon forgotten by everyone except Wong's mother. As a younger woman the poet had tired of her mother's tale of vengeance: "Ma, you've told this story one hundred times." As a feminist thinking back through her mother, however, the poet honors the rebellious and self-naming mother whose inspiration she once denied:

> Well, I'm not ashamed of you anymore, Momma.
> My heart, once bent and cracked, once
> ashamed of your China ways.
> Ma, hear me now, tell me your story
> again and again.[51]

Chinese-American women turn not only to biological mothers as muses but also to revolutionary activists from their country of origin. One warrior Wong honors is the Chinese writer Ding Ling, whom she discovered during the 1970s and reveres as an artist and a fighting woman imprisoned during the Cultural Revolution for her radical beliefs. Wong's epigraph to *The Death of Long Steam Lady* (1986) quotes Ding Ling: "Our joy is a battle within a storm and not playing the harp under the moon or reciting poetry in front of a flower." Poetry is subversive and defiant, Wong claims, and to brave any battle feminist writers must learn how our literary mothers have survived. Ding Ling provides such inspiration: "Ding Ling, imprisoned for expressing her anguish, her love and compassion for China's women, for recording the conditions of their lives. . . . Now there is information trickling out that she is writing again, silenced for so many years. Now you want to search for more of her work . . . jewels you want to hold in your hand. Now you want . . . to find the grandmothers you wish to adopt."[52]

Naming their own muses, adopting bellicose grandmothers, has empowered U. S. women of color to chart new courses of battle. Fear of reprisal when they break silence, the ambivalence that accompanies marginalization, inchoate rage at the forces of oppression—all can be debilitating emotions unless they speak as individual and collective resisters, artistic as well as political transformers. "Put your shit on paper," Gloria Anzaldúa exhorts her sisters. "We are not reconciled to the oppressors who whet their howl on our grief. We are not reconciled."[53]

4

This is the profound paradox of the feminist speaking in our contemporary culture: she proceeds from a belief in a world from which . . . Truth has disappeared. This paradox, it seems to me, can lead to (at least) three possible scenarios: a renewed silence, a form of religion (from mysticism to political orthodoxy), or a continual attention—historical, ideological, and affective—to the place from which we speak.

—Alice Jardine, *Gynesis*

Not knowing
what deaths you saw today
I've got to take you
as you come, battle-bruised
refusing our enemy, fear.

—Cherríe Moraga, *Loving in the War Years*

We can return now to the questions I posed earlier in this chapter.[54] Why has the warrior construct been so prevalent among U.S. women of color? Have they simply reversed the patriarchal paradigm of the Just Warrior versus the Monolithic Enemy, thereby replicating the dominant discourse's binary oppositions, or have they reconceptualized warriors and warring from a multiconscious feminist perspective that acknowledges the political and creative complexities of such metaphors and identities?

Several U.S. feminist theorists, white women and women of color, have suggested that, in reconsidering the construct "woman," a necessary departure point for any feminist politics or poetics, we pay closer attention to the place(s) from which we speak. Alice Jardine has rejected silence, mysticism, and political orthodoxy as essentialist stances antithetical to a dynamic feminist enterprise and has stressed, instead, a constant reassessment of our historical and ideological contexts. Similarly, Linda Alcoff has critiqued both cultural feminists (whose stances have often implied an innate female essence) and poststructuralist feminists (whose nominalist views have sometimes theorized women out of existence) as providing retrogressive models of gender analysis and feminist praxis. As an alternative to these self-defeating theoretical-political positions, Alcoff has posited the concept of identity politics as defined and practiced by U. S. women of color. Identity here is acknowledged as a sociocultural construct but serves also as a necessary political point of departure: one's particular experience of the intersections of gender/race/class/sexuality inform a position from which to act and speak. For Alcoff, identity politics can thus avoid the pitfalls of cultural or poststructural feminist theory: "The position that women find themselves in can be actively utilized (rather than transcended) as a location for the construction of meaning."[55] As Diana Fuss has warned, however, it is crucial that feminists constantly interrogate the meaning of identity politics, even as they use it strategically, so that the political is not reduced merely to the personal.[56]

Some women of color have used what Fuss calls a "repoliticized" identity politics as a means of problematizing such feminist concepts as "sexism" and "enemy." Alcoff cites Chicana feminist Cherríe Moraga as one U.S. writer who has spoken to the simultaneity of oppressions for women of color and their need to resist essentialist formulations. "When you start to talk about sexism," Moraga asserts, "the world becomes increasingly complex. The power no longer breaks down into neat little hierarchical categories, but becomes a series of starts and detours. Since the categories are not easy to arrive at, the enemy is not easy to name. It is all so difficult to unravel."[57] As maleness cannot be wholly other for women of color, neither can the enemy be wholly other.

Instead, diverse and multiple sources of oppression have contributed to the appropriation of the warrior construct by these women: internal "enemies" such as guilt over their own perceived inactions or inadequacies, alienation from some members of their racial/ethnic group or from white liberal feminists, fear of military reprisals against them; and external "enemies," as embodied in white patriarchs and imperialists, women who deny their white-skin privilege, men of color who perpetuate sexist ideologies in their movement work. As warriors using words to combat simultaneous oppressions, women writers of color have not claimed to be always redemptive, ever just, always clear about the source(s) of a particular oppressive act or the "rightness" of a decision at hand. Certainly, the warrior aspect of their identities has remained, in Moraga's phrase, "difficult to unravel." Yet many women of color *are* clear that both discursive and political resistance is essential—that, as Alcoff argues, "their position within the network lacks power and mobility and requires radical change."[58] Operating from complex and particular historical contexts, they have used the warrior construct to articulate an impassioned feminist politics and poetics and to inspire them to undertake the attendant sociocultural transformations.

Examined from this vantage point, Cherríe Moraga's assertion that "I love women to the point of killing for us all" can be seen as neither hyperbolic nor malevolent; it reflects, instead, the historical, ideological, and affective locus from which she spoke at the time that she wrote.[59] Moraga and her lesbian lover had to learn to love in the war years, to receive each other battle-bruised, to combat a racist/sexist death machine "out there" and an internal enemy, fear, at home. Women warriors' rage and retribution are facets of their identity politics—in Moraga's case, part of her class-related and culturally specific distrust of the formal English language. (She has claimed that "words are a war to me.")[60] Similarly, Lorde's assertion that

> I am a bleak heroism of words
> that refuse
> to be buried alive
> with the liars

constitutes an aesthetic as well as a political stance of defiance.[61] Finally, the warrior construct offers a metaphor and an identity by which white feminist poets, especially those who have experienced ethnic, religious, or heterosexist marginalization, can delineate a position of camaraderie and affiliation with their sisters of color. "There must be those among whom we can sit down and weep, and still be counted as warriors," Adrienne Rich proclaims in her long poem *Sources,* in which she explores the intersection of her lesbian feminism and her once-denied Jewish identity.[62] For U.S. women of color and for many of their white sisters, the warrior construct resonates, multifaceted.

Conclusion

> Writing often becomes the context through which new political identities are forged. It becomes a space for struggle and contestation about reality itself.
> —Chandra Talpede Mohanty, *Third World Women and the Politics of Feminism*

> I am writing these words as a route map
> an artifact for survival
> a chronicle of buried treasure
> a mourning
> for this place we are about to be leaving
> a rudder for my children   your children
> —Audre Lorde, "On the Way Out I Passed over You and the Verrazano Bridge"

> Do not be wedded forever
> To fear, yoked eternally
> To brutishness.
> —Maya Angelou, "On the Pulse of Morning"

When Chandra Talpede Mohanty asks, in the introduction to *Third World Women and the Politics of Feminism*, whether women from Africa, Asia, Latin America, and the Middle East share a history, she concludes that they instead are joined in a "complex relationality" based on five distinct "socioeconomic, political and discursive configurations." The shared configuration most relevant to this study is the intersection of *consciousness, identity,* and *writing,* specifically poetry. Questions of political consciousness and subjectivity are crucial to understanding the experiential texts of the women poets examined in this book, poets who designate their writing as a site of struggle from which competing realities are contested and new identity politics are forged. Inventing "spaces, texts, images for encoding the history of resistance," these poets from El Salvador, South Africa, and the United States intervene politically and create new strategies for dissenting, subverting, and re-membering.[1]

Women's production of alternative knowledge and their inven-
tion of new norms for encoding resistance can perhaps best be seen
in their self-reflexive poetry, which interrogates both themselves as
poets and the role of poetry in revolutionary praxis. This poetry raises
questions of self-representation, audience, and ideology. As the first
chapter of this book has illustrated, critiques of resistance poetry
abound from the political Right and from academic traditionalists on
the grounds that it is too polemical. But many women poets also
evince troubled awareness of critiques from their peers on the Left—
militants, activists, even writers of other genres who consider poetry
writing a marginal activity at best when there is a revolution to be
won. Such judgment makes some women momentarily or chronically
ambivalent regarding the viability of their art as an act of political
intervention. Other women who write self-reflexive poetry of resis-
tance, however, reveal full confidence in the centrality of their writ-
ing to their cause; with Myriam Díaz-Diocaretz, they insist that "dis-
cursive practices are resistance," asserting their own agency as gen-
dered revolutionary subjects and challenging us as readers to reject
dominant hegemonies.[2]

As Third World or First World women scholars, feminist theo-
rists, and/or political activists, or as men of these descriptions, what
do we make of these resistance poems, finally, and of their poets?
What do they invite us to believe, think, write, do? In the words of
Audre Lorde, "What do we want from each other / after we have told
our stories?"[3] Women's poems about the contributions of poets and
poetry to resistance movements reveal at least three common charac-
teristics. First, they present poems as guidebooks, route maps, strate-
gies for negotiating the complex, painful, daily exigencies of the
struggle for revolutionary transformation. As Lorde asserts, poetic
words can constitute "an artifact for survival." Second, these poems
present poetry, and indirectly the poet herself, as a conduit to the
future—a fragile thread or a hearty rope tying together generations
of dreamers who have and claim the right to peace with justice: for
Lorde, "a rudder for my children   your children"; for Angelou, a
rejection of fear and brutishness. Third, as part of their visionary
tones and imagery, these poems invoke what Adrienne Rich has
called "the spirit of place," the particular locus of war zone, prison,
exile, or home that situates the poet historically, geographically, and
materially and impels her to speak. Although this locus shifts from

person to person, country to country, struggle to struggle, readers of resistance poetry—like readers of testimonials—are made complicit in the poet's vision through an invitation to view, on the poet's terms, the site of resistance as a shared location. Thus, Lorde urges and expects readers to mourn along with her "this place we are about to be leaving."[4]

An examination of poems by six emerging poets who explore the meaning and purpose of resistance poetry, two from each of the countries foregrounded in this book, will further illustrate the power of this genre to encode new syllables of revolution. Each of the six poets—Patricia Jones and Kate Ellis from the United States, Lisa Combrinck and Frances Hunter from South Africa, and Mirna Martínez and Jacinta Escudos from El Salvador—is an activist as well as a writer; none is, as of yet, well known as a poet in her own country or internationally. Martínez and Escudos have participated in their country's armed struggle, while the others have encoded resistance with their activism and their words.

Patricia Jones's "Buckets of Music" begins with an allusion to the early twentieth-century Russian dissident poet Anna Akhmatova as she sits at her writing table and "precisely / conjures winter," waiting for war to end. Like Akhmatova, Jones herself struggles with the temptation toward muteness and despair as she reflects upon the horrors that the century has produced and witnessed. "What a poet offers," she asserts,

> is the hard realities
> a drama of the interior
> mutable as real estate.

Both interior and exterior dramas are constantly shifting, the poet suggests; thus, it is crucial for poems to situate readers in a particular time and locus, to chronicle rigorously "where we are now / rattling billions of bones."

Poetry can be a revolutionary tool linking women poets in solidarity and struggle across generations, around the globe, as Jones goes on to suggest:

> A poet in Guatemala
> in South Africa

or perhaps Korea
wages her lonely battle
as mother
in her fierce regard
for a new day
"the revolution"
or
the remainder of
misbegotten dreams:
three meals a day
a soft bed to lie upon
a roof that does not leak
police who do not bang
loudly
at two a.m.

What resistant women poets in many countries in turmoil battle for, Jones claims, are basic human rights to life, food, shelter, privacy—rights violated frequently in the countries she enumerates and in countless others. They struggle to find effective words as mothers, as revolutionaries; like Akhmatova before them, they envision and call for a better world in which no roof leaks, no home or family suffers nocturnal invasion, and all are fed. Jones's conflict in this poem pivots on whether poetic vision has, finally, a viable place in any revolution, whether it really contributes to meaningful change. Akhmatova "dreams of stars / far flung, cosmic," but the husband for whom she waits experiences a harsh, endless winter of imprisonment and torture and weeps "buckets of music," the tears that lie at the heart of Akhmatova's lyric-political poetry. Does the poet as documenter of that interior drama, "mutable as real estate," help to eliminate oppression, a ruthless external force that appears to continue unabated? "Has anything changed?" this poem concludes ambiguously, inviting readers to ponder its purpose and merits.[5]

Kate Ellis's "The Secret Life of Plants" also addresses the issue of waiting, and through this metaphor the tension between activity and passivity inherent in the poetic process and in movements for social change. "What am I waiting for, here in the quiet / center of the whirlwind?" the poet wonders in self-interrogation; why do I write instead of fight, since "metaphors like this no longer heal"? In need of healing, the poet reflects, are the black residents of Cape Town, where shots ring out at night through lace curtains; the disappeared of Santiago, where a person—the poet herself—could be seized from her own home before dawn. Yet, miraculously, humanity continues its daily routines; "the center does not crack open." Thus, Ellis turns to her own seemingly protected environs: "My plants need extra water. The Sunday paper's heavier than usual." The paper's emotional weight matches its bulk, as the poet-activist reads about South Africa and Chile and determines once again to use words as a means of fighting alongside the wounded and disappeared. The resistance poet's task, Ellis concludes, is to make ropes of words that refuse to break under the people's weight, her own and those with whom she writes in solidarity, as together they carry "the six-sided coffin / of a two-month-old black child."[6]

Lisa Combrinck's "Birth of a Poem" is set at a particular historical moment and locale: early 1987, Belgravia Road in Crawford, a so-called colored section of Cape Town, just after an army attack on ANC demonstrators in the poet's neighborhood. The poem begins by establishing as its context this military atrocity that the poet, having left her home to join the demonstrators, has experienced firsthand:

> When the fires were smouldering,
> the casspirs still patrolling, the mourners going home,
> ominous echoes as drums and barricades were removed from the
> street,
> the disappearing drone of a helicopter returning to the base,
> I returned to my smoke-filled room
> and picked up a poem I had written earlier.

Its innocence lost, the poem—

> buried in ash and dust,
> yet filmy, and membraneous
> like caul

—reminds the poet nonetheless of a newborn child. This child needs little tending from its mother, however, for it has lived through an eternity of smokebombs and resistance. Combrinck goes on to describe her poem-in-process, in its more mature incarnation, as a

red-hot poem
fertilized with mud—
the singeing African earth.

Months of the most frenetic dusting could not purify this raging
page, the poet concludes,

contaminated,
as it were,
with the fires
of everyday life.[7]

Combrinck's initial poem is simultaneously victim, witness, and sur-
vivor of a particular act of repression by the perpetrators of apartheid;
in the fires of daily life, she suggests, lie the flames of injustice. The
singed but singing poem remains, for Combrinck, a beacon to that
truth. Furthermore, that poem and the events surrounding its com-
position inspire a second poem, Combrinck's metacommentary about
revolution's effect on poetry and poetry's effect on revolution.

Frances Hunter's "In a Poem Is Life Hereafter" attempts to jus-
tify her stealthy power to those who consider her inadequately com-
mitted to the antiapartheid effort because she spends so much time
writing poetry:

Their faces contort when they think
i am not involved in the struggle
i hold my irrelevant breath against
the burning rubber in their eyes.

In this poem the scorching heat comes not from military bombs or
teargas but, instead, from the poet's comrades-in-arms, who trivial-
ize her work, perhaps even threaten her ("burning rubber" alludes
to the necklacing of traitors at the hands of certain South African
revolutionaries). These detractors thus evoke the poet's bitterness.
As the struggle "creeps in the streets" and "whispers of boycotts" are
overheard in kitchens, the poet goes about her daily business in the
township as an ordinary worker, a shopper, a resister imagining a
less violent future:

> All the while holding my breath
> against rolling clouds of acrid smoke
> i collect my pay packet
> (subsidy's delayed)
> shop for bread
> milk
> insurance
> a new basin . . .
> then furtively breathing i write a poem.[8]

Is poetry a luxury, as Hunter's acquaintances obviously believe, or is it, as Audre Lorde insists, as necessary to our lives as bread? Hunter's answer is implied in part in her title: poetry provides an essential cord to the future; "in a poem is life hereafter." Yet poetry documents as well the daily difficulties of life under apartheid: delayed subsidies, acrid smoke, threats of boycotts, rejection by people with whom the poet might otherwise feel solidarity. This poem raises a similar issue to what Adrienne Rich addresses in "Poetry III," the issue of whether the "criminal joy" a poet feels "when the thing comes   as it does come" would be any less suspect if all the prisoners were free, all the children fed.[9] Although neither Hunter nor Rich offers a definitive answer to this question of whether poetry diminishes or extends the quest for justice, the fact that both keep writing stands as an homage to the power they ascribe to poetry.

Mirna Martínez does not seem to experience the ambivalence toward the viability of poetry that Jones, Ellis, Hunter, and Rich do, perhaps because she has the credentials of a militant. A combatant with the FMLN during her late teens and now a poet and cultural worker in her twenties, Martínez creates exuberant poetry that illustrates well what Lorde has called the "lust for a working tomorrow."[10] "Si alguna vez pudiera" [If Only Someday] features a motley catalog of words that the poet considers crucial for assembling "el poema más hermoso" [the most wondrous poem] yet to be written about the Salvadoran revolution:

> calle
> paredes
> rojo

radioactivo
misil
. . . 1932
vanguardia
historia
. . . etc.

[street / walls / red / radioactive / missile / . . . 1932 / vanguard /
history / etc.]

These words, many of them prohibited by the government but whis-
pered clandestinely by campesinos, urban guerrillas, and combat po-
ets, will lie at the heart of what will be, Martínez insists, *"el poema
precisado por las contradicicciones de la historía"* [an essential poem /
borne from historical contradictions].[11] It will fulfill the requirements
for a women's poetics of resistance as articulated by the anonymous
author of the El Salvador section of *Ixok Amar Go:* "our poems will
express our total range of feelings," "our poems come to the aid of
our people," "our poems will be lessons too," "our poetry will inhabit
this land forever." As this anonymous woman further notes, poetry
has been out of reach for most citizens of El Salvador, especially its
women, who, through poverty and illiteracy, have been those most
affected by "the marginality imposed by a hostile system." Like the
women poets who are their political and aesthetic precursors, the
anonymous Salvadoran writer and Mirna Martínez call for poetry
that will "engrave [women's] lives on our history, which means our
indelible memories."[12]

Jacinta Escudos's long poem *"Carta desde El Salvador"* [Letter from
El Salvador] also inscribes the power of memory from a position of
marginality, as she addresses, in frankly erotic terms, the lover she
longs for from her Salvadoran prison. Section 10 of the poem, in
particular, describes how writing poems for her beloved can create
fantasies that diminish, however temporarily, the pain and isolation
of incarceration. The poet embroiders these word fantasies, rich
cloths replete with loneliness and desire, and reveals her diasporic
consciousness:

Escucho tu voz a través de las paredes
cierro mis ojos a las distancies olvido rostros nombres

descubro cosas que no existen sombras extrañas azotan mi
    anatomia
me desconozco en plena selva quemada
y la oscuridad nunca ha sido tan negra como esta noche

[I hear your voice through the walls / close my eyes to the
distances forgetfulness faces names / discover things that don't
exist strange shadows lash my anatomy / I don't recognize
myself integral to the charred *selva* / and the darkness has never
been so black as tonight].

The exiled poet can recreate her identity and evoke her lover's pres-
ence—"*tu tranquilo cuerpo desnudo que duerme complacido / sobre mi pecho
de gacela*" [your body naked and still that sleeps with pleasant ease
/over my gazelle breasts]—only through her poetry. The future holds
little charm for Escudos; she prefers to focus, instead, on her poetic
re-memberings: "*yo no pido permiso para soñar / sólo silencio para bordarle
tu nombre a la madrugada* [and no I don't ask permission to dream /only
for quiet to embroider your name to daybreak]."

In other sections of the poem, she chronicles her struggle against
muteness, as "*se arruga toda mi memoria*" [everything remembered
shrinks]. "*Nunca*" [never], she proclaims at one point,

ha sido tan inexplicable tu ausencia
como este jueves día sin ceniza las cinco a.m.
mi cama con olor a vainilla
mujer que despierta sola
lanza al viento las sábanas de su amor

[has your absence been so inexplicable / as on this ashless
Thursday at 5 a.m. / my bed vanilla fragrant / a woman who
waits alone / throws to the wind sheets of her love].

The sheets, of course, are not only the covering on the barren bed
but also the paper on which the nocturnal poet—"*yo santa carismática*"
[I, a charismatic saint], as Escudos archly characterizes her celibate
self in one poem—inscribes her lush words. "Letter from El Salvador"
must be seen, however, in its revolutionary context as well as its
erotic one, for, as the poet concludes, a woman who sleeps alone
does not confine her resistance to language only. Instead,

mujer que duerme sola
hace un intento desesperado nefasto mortal
por salvar al hombre
encadenado prisionero altivo en las islas

[a woman who sleeps alone / makes a desperate attempt fatal
mortal / to save a man / shackled prisoner proud in the islands].[13]

One senses in reading Escudos what Díaz-Diocaretz has called a "stra-
tegic discursive consciousness" at work, that of a woman countering
a repressive political system as well as the patriarchal authority that
has traditionally rejected female expressions of erotic desire. Renam-
ing the world from a woman-oriented poetic position, Escudos reveals
her own authorial intention at several places in the poem; the result
is "the new formation of the woman's voice as collective and individ-
ual speaking subject, as discursive producer, to challenge the sover-
eignty of androcentrism."[14] Along with androcentrism and its inher-
ent objectification of women, Escudos challenges a government that
hopes to promote tourism even as it sponsors silence and repression:

No somos un pueblo
de bailes,
de mujeres hermosas,
somos un pueblo medio muerto
buscando una solución . . .

[We are not a land / of dances, / of beautiful women, / we are a
people half dead / looking for a solution . . . .][15]

If poets cannot provide this solution, Escudos suggests, they can at
least refuse cultural muteness.

The poems discussed in this conclusion are metacommentaries
on the intersection of poetry and resistance; as such, they illustrate
with particular clarity the investment many women poets have in
asserting the power and efficacy of the genre and the struggle to
which they are committed. Whether resistance poetry, finally, *does*
effectively combat oppression and contribute significantly to revolu-
tionary change remains a site of intellectual contestation. Jacques
Alvarez-Peyeyre claims that poetry has had virtually no influence on
one of its intended audiences, the architects and maintainers of apart-

heid: "One has to be frank: South African committed poetry has no more effect on the life or death of the South African government than pinpricks on a hippopotamus's hide." Poetry is tolerated by this and other repressive regimes, he argues, only when its influence is small and censorship is not worth the government's while. What resistance poetry does most reliably, he concludes, is to help struggling people discover and affirm their own spirit, thus contributing to a collective consciousness.[16] Ingrid de Kok, a South African poet of commitment, suggests otherwise; in her view, the formation of a collective resistant consciousness has threatened the Nationalist government. De Kok sees poetry of resistance—with its alternating, communal voices; its catalogs of martyrs, heroes, places of suffering and triumph—as helping "to concretize subjects that too often have been left . . . historically unspecific and safe." Rewriting history is dangerous to hegemonic power, de Kok insists, and poetry that does so can make a daily difference in the struggle for self-determination of African peoples.[17] In the words of Nelson Mandela, in his recent endorsement of a collection of poetry of witness, "poetry cannot block a bullet or still a *sjambok* [whip], but it can bear witness to brutality—thereby cultivating a flower in a graveyard." And, as Maya Angelou claims in her U.S. inaugural poem of 1993, poetry can monitor "the pulse of [a] new day . . . / Very simply / With hope."[18]

Most of the women poets examined in this book, I would suggest, concur with de Kok, Mandela, and Angelou: poems can participate in resistance by inscribing it. Where but in poems, Audre Lorde asks, is "true history" written—and written, as Claribel Alegría proclaims, with "tears, with fingernails and coal"? What we want from one another after we have told our stories, to answer another of Lorde's pressing questions, is to have these textual interventions entered into dialogically, their wisdom pondered and, ultimately, put to reconstructive use by those who would dismantle the "master's house" with tools other than his own.[19] As Barbara Harlow has eloquently asserted, "The silence imposed by the torturer is challenged by the demand for political resistance, raising again and again the urgent and critical relation between writing human rights and righting political wrongs." A women's poetics of resistance negotiates this critical terrain, dancing fearlessly through the minefields and whispering—or shouting—*nunca estuve sola, amandla,* we shall overcome.[20]

Notes

Introduction

Myriam Díaz-Diocaretz, "'I will be a scandal in your boat': Women Poets and the Tradition," in *Knives and Angels: Women Writers in Latin America*, ed. Susan Bassnett (London: Zed Books, 1990), 87; Martivón Galindo, "*Amo mi país . . . es ése un delito?*" [I Love My Country, Is This a Crime?], Galindo's translation, in *Ixok Amar Go: Central American Women's Poetry for Peace*, ed. Zoë Anglesey (Penobscot, Maine: Granite Press, 1987), 184–87; Audre Lorde, "Call," *Our Dead behind Us* (New York: W. W. Norton, 1986), 75. U.S. women who write poetry in solidarity with South Africans in struggle often honor Winnie Mandela in their work; Lorde's poem is but one example of this. For Mandela's account of her years of banishment during her husband's imprisonment, see *Part of My Soul Went with Him*, ed. Anne Benjamin (New York: W. W. Norton, 1984). For excellent interviews with Winnie Mandela and other women resisters in South Africa, see Diana E. H. Russell, *Lives of Courage: Women for a New South Africa* (New York: Basic Books, 1989). Winnie Mandela has been a source of controversy within the African National Congress (ANC) and among women's solidarity organizations since 1989, when she was accused of condoning the killing of Stompie Mokhetsi, a fourteen-year-old black boy whom members of her "football club," a group of male ANC supporters who guarded her residence before the release of Nelson Mandela from prison, allegedly tortured and murdered for being a traitor to their cause. For information on the Winnie Mandela controversy as it first broke in the United States, see Spencer Reiss, "Soweto's 'Winnie Problem,'" *Newsweek*, February 13, 1989, 35; and "Mrs. Mandela's Disgrace," *Newsweek*, February 27, 1989, 44.

1. Barbara Harlow, *Resistance Literature* (New York: Methuen, 1987), 37. I am aware of the debates, in the United States and elsewhere, regarding the terms *Third World* and *First World* and recognize that they are problematic on many levels. I use the term *Third World*, however, when referring to people of Africa, Asia, Latin America, and/or the Middle East because it foregrounds the fact that their particular experiences of colonization and militarization have radically affected their economic well-being, political realities, quality of life, and (in the case of poets) writing. I consider it politically preferable to the terms *developing* or *postcolonial* nations (which do not work to describe people anyway) and more familiar than the term *Two-thirds World*. I use *First World* to refer to people from the United States, the countries of Western Europe, and other "industrialized" nations, many of which have traditionally been colonizers, although I agree with June Jordan that surely indigenous people worldwide are more deserving of the appellation *First World*.

313

On a feminist use of the term *Third World,* see Chandra Talpede Mohanty, preface to *Third World Women and the Politics of Feminism,* ed. Chandra Talpede Mohanty, Ann Russo, and Lourdes Torres (Bloomington: Indiana University Press, 1991), ix–x. On the misappropriation of the term *First World,* see June Jordan, "Nicaragua: Why I Had to Go There," *On Call: Political Essays* (Boston: South End Press, 1985), 70–75.

2. Chandra Talpede Mohanty, "Under Western Eyes: Feminist Scholarship and Colonial Discourses," *Boundary* 2 (1984): 350–51.

3. Frank Meintjies, "Albie Sachs and the Art of Protest," in *Spring Is Rebellious: Arguments about Cultural Freedom by Albie Sachs and Respondents,* ed. Ingrid de Kok and Karen Press (Cape Town: Buchu Books, 1990), 30.

4. Chikwenye Okonjo Ogunyemi, "Womanism: The Dynamics of the Contemporary Black Female Novel in English," *Signs: Journal of Women in Culture and Society* 11, no. 1 (1985): 63–80. In undertaking an examination of women's resistance poetry from South Africa and El Salvador, I am aware of the importance of identifying the place(s) from which I speak. I speak as a white, U.S., academic feminist from a working-class background, a positionality that necessarily affects the lens through which I conduct my study. This positionality has required of me a vigilant attention to the limitations, privileges, and shiftings that have informed my "struggle for accountability" during the making of this book.

5. Harlow, *Resistance Literature,* 31–74; John Beverley and Marc Zimmerman, *Literature and Politics in the Central American Revolutions* (Austin: University of Texas Press, 1990), 81–171. Harlow's most recent book does focus admirably on women's prison writing in several countries, including South Africa and El Salvador, but does not deal primarily with poetry. See Barbara Harlow, *Barred: Women, Writing, and Political Detention* (Hanover and London: Wesleyan University Press, 1992).

6. Nadine Gordimer, *The Black Interpreters* (Johannesburg: Ravan Press, 1973); Ursula M. Barnett, *A Vision of Order: A Study of Black South African Literature in English (1914–1980)* (London: Sinclair Brown, 1983); Jacques Alvarez-Peyeyre, *The Poetry of Commitment in South Africa,* trans. Clive Wake (London: Heinemann, 1984); Piniel Viriri Shava, *A People's Voice: Black South African Writing in the Twentieth Century* (London: Zed Press, 1989).

7. Myriam Díaz-Diocaretz, "I will be a scandal," 89.

8. Ingrid de Kok, interview, *Writers from South Africa,* ed. Jane Taylor and David Bunn (Chicago: TriQuarterly Books, 1989), 59.

9. Frantz Fanon, *The Wretched of the Earth,* trans. Constance Farrington (New York: Grove Press, 1963), 148–248; Amilcar Cabral, *Return to the Source: Selected Speeches by Amilcar Cabral,* ed. Africa Information Service (New York: Monthly Review Press, 1973), 75–92; Andre GunderFrank, *Capitalism and Underdevelopment in Latin America* (New York: Monthly Review Press, 1967); Immanuel Wallerstein, *Geopolitics and Geoculture: Essays on the Changing World System* (Cambridge: Cambridge University Press, 1991), 1–15, 184–99.

10. Mohanty, "Under Western Eyes," 334. For a convincing argument that feminism has not been imposed on Third World countries by the West but has, instead, developed over the past century in many Third World countries due to changing material and historical circumstances, see Kumari Jayawardena, *Feminism and Na-*

tionalism in the Third World (London: Zed Press, 1986), 1–24; her book deals primarily with Asian countries. On the development of feminism in Latin America, see Irene Campos Carr, "Women's Voices Grow Stronger: Politics and Feminism in Latin America," *NWSA Journal* 2, no. 3 (Summer 1990): 450–63. For differing views on feminism in a South African context, see essays by Cecily Lockett, Sisi Maqagi, and Zoë Wicomb, in the "Feminism and Writing" issue of *Current Writing: Text and Reception in Southern Africa* 2 (October 1990): 1–44.

11. Zoë Wicomb, "New Nation: Race and Ethnicity—Beyond the Legacy of Victims" (paper presented at the COSAW / *New Nation* Writers Conference, Johannesburg, Dec. 1991), 1–5. I am grateful to Annie Gagiano of Stellenbosch University for providing copies of the papers from this conference.

12. For documentation of this information and these statistics, see Americas Watch, *El Salvador's Decade of Terror: Human Rights since the Assassination of Archbishop Romero* (New Haven: Yale University Press, 1991); Robert Armstrong and Janet Shenk, *El Salvador: The Face of Revolution* (Boston: South End Press, 1983); *A Dream Compels Us: Voices of Salvadoran Women*, ed. New Americas Press (Boston: South End Press, 1989), 7–20; Marilyn Thomson, *Women of El Salvador: The Price of Freedom* (Philadelphia: ISHI Publications, 1986), 1–9. The "Truth Commission" established in 1992 by the United Nations to investigate the atrocities in El Salvador issued a 1993 report verifying these figures and holding U.S.-trained Salvadoran military officers responsible for most death squad activity in the 1980s. Thus far Salvadoran president Alfredo Cristiani has not relieved these officers of their duties, despite the report's recommendation that he call for their resignations, nor has U.S. president Bill Clinton taken a public stand decrying U.S. complicity in death squad activity.

   I should note that my statement about the horrors of systematic genocide in El Salvador and South Africa was written before the practice of "ethnic cleansing" had become widespread in Bosnia-Herzegovina in 1993. Certainly, the systematic genocide of Muslims by Serbian and some Croatian forces, especially the rape and impregnation of Muslim women, should be added to any such list of atrocities.

13. For cogent assessments of U.S. and multinational policies toward South Africa during these years, see Kevin Danaher, *In Whose Interest? A Guide to U.S.–South Africa Relations* (Washington, D.C.: Institute for Policy Studies, 1984); Steven Anzovin, *South Africa: Apartheid and Divestiture* (New York: H. W. Wilson, 1987); and Christopher Coker, *The United States and South Africa, 1968–1985: Constructive Engagement and Its Critics* (Durham, N.C.: Duke University Press, 1986). For useful background into the politics of apartheid, see Ann Seidman, *The Roots of Crisis in Southern Africa* (Trenton, N.J.: Africa World Press, 1985). For recent reports on human rights abuses in South Africa, see *South Africa: A Compilation of Five Documents* (New York: Amnesty International Publications, 1991); and *South Africa: State of Fear: Security Force Complicity in Torture and Political Killings, 1990–1991* (New York: Amnesty International Publications, 1992). I should note that by the early 1990s the U.S. government and many states and municipalities had employed economic sanctions against the South African government and that by most accounts the desire to see these sanctions lifted played a major role in 1992–93 negotiations between the Nationalist government, the African National Congress, and some twenty other parties toward a new constitution and democratic elections.

These parties agreed in July 1993 that on April 27, 1994, South Africa would hold its first national election open to nonwhites; twenty-two million people are expected to vote, nineteen million of them for the first time.

14. Adrienne Rich uses this term in "Notes toward a Politics of Location," *Blood, Bread, and Poetry: Selected Prose, 1979–1985* (New York: W. W. Norton, 1986), 211.

15. Albie Sachs, "Preparing Ourselves for Freedom," *Spring Is Rebellious*, 19–29.

16. The terms *rhetoric of violence* and *violence of rhetoric* are used by Teresa de Lauretis, *Technologies of Gender* (Bloomington: Indiana University Press, 1987), 44–48. I use the term *women of color* in the sense that Sri Lankan feminist Asoka Bandarage explains and endorses it:

> Recently, *women of color* has become a popular term among Asian, African, Latin, and Native American women living in the West. It is especially popular among those who are feminists but who have fundamental disagreements with the white middle-class women's movement. For women who are oppressed by both patriarchy and white supremacy, women of color—mujeres de color—provides a unifying conceptual formula and a direction for political organizing.

Bandarage further notes that black nationalists George Padmore and Marcus Garvey were among the first to use the term *people of color* to promote mobilization and positive self-definition. See Asoka Bandarage, "Women of Color: Toward a Celebration of Power," *woman of power* 4 (Fall 1986): 8–14, 82–83.

17. Audre Lorde, "There Are No Honest Poems about Dead Women," *Our Dead behind Us*, 61.

Chapter 1

1. Harlow, *Resistance Literature*, 28–29, 33; Rosario Murillo, "Confesión," in *En las espléndidas ciudades* (Editorial Nueva Nicaragua, 1985), cited and trans. Patricia Murray, in "A Place for Eve in the Revolution: Giaconda Belli and Rosario Murillo," in Bassnett, *Knives and Angels*, 176–97, see esp. n. 7. *We Make Freedom* is the title of a collection of essays on and interviews with South African women by Beata Lipman (London: Pandora Press, 1984).

2. Harlow, *Resistance Literature*, 30.

3. For a discussion of this point, see Aída Hurtado, "Relating to Privilege: Seduction and Rejection in the Subordination of White Women and Women of Color," *Signs* 14 (Summer 1989): 849–54.

4. Chela Sandoval, "Feminism and Racism: A Report on the 1981 National Women's Studies Association Conference," in *Making Face, Making Soul / Haciendo caras: Creative and Critical Perspectives by Women of Color*, ed. Gloria Anzaldúa (San Francisco: aunt lute, 1990), 64, 70.

5. Patricia Hill Collins, *Black Feminist Thought: Knowledge, Consciousness, and the Politics of Empowerment* (Boston: Unwin Hyman, 1990), 221–38. See also Collins's essay "The Social Construction of Black Feminist Thought," *Signs* 14 (Summer 1989): 745–73.

6. Gramsci is cited in Harlow, *Resistance Literature*, 14.

7. Mphahlele is cited in Jacques Alvarez-Peyeyre, *The Poetry of Commitment in South Africa*, trans. Clive Wake (London: Heinemann, 1984), 38.

8. Díaz-Diocaretz, "I will be a scandal," 105–6.

9. For details on this part of South Africa's history, see the film *You Have Struck a Rock: Women and Struggle in South Africa* (Berkeley: South Africa Media Project, 1986).

10. *"Sin poder enamorarnos de la luna"* [We Cannot Afford to Be Enamored with the Moon], introduction to the El Salvador section of Anglesey, *Ixok*, 146–47.

11. Maria Lugones, *"Hablando cara a cara* / Speaking Face to Face: An Exploration of Ethnocentric Racism," in Anzaldúa, *Making Face, Making Soul*, 46.

12. Norma Alarcon, "The Theoretical Subject(s) of *This Bridge Called My Back* and Anglo-American Feminism," in Anzaldúa, *Making Face, Making Soul*, 363.

13. Iris M. Zavala, *"Escritura desatada"* (Santurce: Ediciones Puerto, 1973), 47; cited and trans. by Díaz-Diocaretz, "I will be a scandal," 103–8.

14. The terms *violence of rhetoric* and *rhetoric of violence* are de Lauretis's in *Technologies of Gender*, 31–50.

15. The phrase "fugitive means of expression" is Ezekial Mphahlele's; cited in Alvarez-Peyeyre, *Poetry of Commitment*, 38.

16. Harlow, *Resistance Literature*, 50.

17. Steve Biko is cited in Alvarez-Peyeyre, *Poetry of Commitment*, 185.

18. Shava, *A People's Voice*, 3–9. Nadine Gordimer is cited on p. 71.

19. Alvarez-Peyeyre, *Poetry of Commitment*, 115–16.

20. David Evans's poem is quoted by Alvarez-Peyeyre, *Poetry of Commitment*, 257.

21. Adrienne Rich, "Blood, Bread, and Poetry: The Location of a Poet," *Blood, Bread, and Poetry*, 167–68.

22. Murray, "A Place for Eve in the Revolution," in Bassnett, *Knives and Angels*, 176.

23. Anglesey, *Ixok*, 148–49.

24. Roque Dalton's poem "El Salvador" is quoted by Harlow, *Resistance Literature*, 31.

25. Carolyn Forché, "El Salvador: An Aide Memoire," *American Poetry Review* (July–August 1981): 3–8.

26. Anglesey, *Ixok*, 148–49.

27. Adrienne Rich, "Poetry III," *Your Native Land, Your Life: Poems* (New York: W. W. Norton, 1986), 68.

28. See Harlow, *Resistance Literature*, 31–74; Alvarez-Peyeyre, *Poetry of Commitment*; Shava, *A People's Voice*; and Díaz-Diocaretz, "I will be a scandal," 88 and n. 7.

29. Mohanty, "Introduction: Cartographies of Silence," in Mohanty, Russo, and Torres, *Third World Women*, 2–10.

30. Ana Guadalupe Martínez, "We Have a Commitment to Our People," in New Americas Press, *A Dream Compels Us*, 157–58.

31. For information on the Comadres, see New Americas Press, *A Dream Compels Us*, 57–63; and Sarah A. Radcliffe and Sally Westwood, eds., *Viva! Women and Popular Protest in Latin America* (New York: Routledge, 1993). On Salvadoran exilic poetry, see Claribel Alegría, "The Politics of Exile," in *You Can't Drown the Fire: Latin American Women Writing in Exile*, ed. Alicia Partnoy (Pittsburgh: Cleis Press, 1988), 172–77. Revolutionary poems by FMLN guerrillas are published in *On the Front Line: Guerrilla Poems of El Salvador*, ed. and trans. Claribel Alegría and Darwin J. Flakoll (Willimantic, Conn.: Curbstone Press, 1989); and *Pájaro y volcán* [Bird and Volcano], ed. Miguel Huezo Mixco (San Salvador: UCA Editores, 1989). The quote by Alegría is taken from her poem "Sorrow," *Flores del volcán / Flowers from the*

Volcano, trans. Carolyn Forché (Pittsburgh: University of Pittsburgh Press, 1982), 42–43.

32. See, for example, Joanna Bankier, preface to *Woman Who Has Sprouted Wings: Poems by Contemporary Latin American Women Poets,* ed. Mary Crow, 2d ed. (Pittsburgh: Latin America Literary Review Press, 1988), 11–15; Díaz-Diocaretz, "I will be a scandal," 86–90; Gloria Anzaldúa, *Borderlands / La Frontera: The New Mestiza* (San Francisco: Spinsters / aunt lute, 1987), 25–51; Norma Alarcon, "Chicana's Feminist Literature: A Re-vision through Malintzin / or Malintzin: Putting Flesh Back on the Object," in *This Bridge Called My Back: Writings by Radical Women of Color,* ed. Cherríe Moraga and Gloria Anzaldúa (Watertown, Mass.: Persephone Press, 1981), 182–90.

33. Díaz-Diocaretz, "I will be a scandal," 91.

34. For information about South African women's struggles historically, see Fatima Meer, "Organising under Apartheid," in *Third World—Second Sex II,* ed. Miranda Davies (London: Zed Press, 1987), 20–30; Christine Qunta, ed., *Women in Southern Africa* (New York and London: Allison and Busby, 1987), 76–122; *Women under Apartheid* (London: International Defense Aid Fund for South Africa, 1981); Cherryl Walker, *Women and Resistance in South Africa* (London: Onyx Press, 1982); Judy Kimble and Elaine Unterhalter, "ANC Women's Struggles, 1912–1982," *Feminist Review* 12 (1982): 11–35; and Gay W. Seidman, "'No Freedom without the Women': Mobilization and Gender in South Africa, 1970–1992," *Signs: Journal of Women in Culture and Society* 18, no. 2 (Winter 1993): 291–320. The quotes from the ANC Women's League come from their charter/constitution and their recruitment literature (1990).

35. For information on and interviews with these women, see Qunta, *Women in Southern Africa,* 112–14; *Ikon: Journal of Creativity and Change,* nos. 5–6: 15–16, 20–21; Russell, *Lives of Courage;* Lipman, *We Make Freedom,* 116–39; and Winnie Mandela, *Part of My Soul Went with Him.*

36. Poems by Kgositsile, Mandela, and Masekela are included in *Somehow We Survive: An Anthology of Southern African Writing,* ed. Sterling Plumpp (New York: Thunder's Mouth Press, 1982), but are excluded from most other anthologies of South African poetry, including anthologies of black poetry. For a list of these anthologies, see Antjie Krog's comments from the forum on "Women Writing in South Africa," *Crossing Borders: Writers Meet the ANC,* ed. Ampie Coetzee and James Polley (Pretoria: Taurus Press, 1990), 125–33. Poems by Mandela and Mhlope are included in *Breaking the Silence: A Century of South African Women's Poetry,* ed. Cecily Lockett (Johannesburg: Ad. Donker, 1990). Almost no women's work, black or white, is discussed by Alvarez-Peyeyre or Shava, with the exception of Ingrid Jonker, whom each briefly mentions.

37. Poems by Masekela and Kgositsile appear in Plumpp, *Somehow We Survive,* 17, 100–101. Mhlope's poem appears in *Sometimes When It Rains: Writing by South African Women,* ed. Ann Oosthuizen (London: Pandora, 1987), vii–viii, a collection of short stories. Zindzi Mandela has published a volume of poetry, *Black as I Am* (Durban: Sereti su Sechaba and Madiba, 1989), see esp. p. 33.

38. Bettina Aptheker, *Tapestries of Life: Women's Work, Women's Consciousness, and the*

Meaning of Daily Experience (Amherst: University of Massachusetts Press, 1989), 28–29.

39. Rich, "Notes toward a Politics of Location," *Blood, Bread, and Poetry*, 227–228.

40. Gayatri Chakravorty Spivak, "French Feminism in an International Frame," *In Other Worlds: Essays in Cultural Politics* (New York and London: Routledge, 1988), 134.

41. Irene Campos Carr, "Women's Voices Grow Stronger: Politics and Feminism in Latin America," *NWSA Journal* II, no. 3 (Summer 1990): 450–63.

42. "ANC Women Speak *Outwrite*," *Third World—Second Sex II*, 78–82.

43. Maria Lugones, "Playfulness, 'World'-travelling, and Loving Perception," in Anzaldúa, *Making Face, Making Soul*, 390–402.

44. See, for example, *Ikon* nos. 5–6, a special "Art against Apartheid" issue that contains poems by these and other U.S. poets, especially poets of color.

45. Trinh Minh-ha, "Not You / Like You: Postcolonial Women and the Interlocking Questions of Identity and Difference," in Anzaldúa, *Making Face, Making Soul*, 374.

46. Harlow, *Resistance Literature*, 73.

47. Epigraphs to this section are from Audre Lorde, "Diaspora," *Our Dead behind Us*, 32; and Janice Gould, "We Exist," in Anzaldúa, *Making Face, Making Soul*, 8–9.

48. Lorde, "Diaspora," 32.

49. Gale Jackson, "On Nites like These," *Ikon* nos. 5–6: 60–61.

50. June Jordan, "Ghazal at Full Moon," *Naming Our Destiny: New and Selected Poems* (New York: Thunder's Mouth Press, 1989), 152–53.

51. Gould, "We Exist," in Anzaldúa, *Making Face, Making Soul*, 8–9.

52. I am grateful to my colleague Andrew Ettin for pointing this out.

53. Anzaldúa, *Borderlands*, 77–78. The Spanish translates as follows:
     a soul between two worlds, three, four,
     my head buzzes with contradictions.
     I am a north wind blowing all the voices that live
     at once in me.

54. Anglesey, *Ixok*, 146–47, 228–29.

55. Adriana Rodriguez, "I Had Never Thought of Leaving My Country," in New Americas Press, *A Dream Compels Us*, 211–15.

56. Jean Franco, "Killing Priests, Nuns, Women, Children," in *Ways of Reading*, ed. D. Bartholomae and A. Petrosky (Boston: Bedford Books, 1990), 194–98.

57. Claribel Alegría, "*Eramos Tres*" [We Were Three], *Flowers from the Volcano*, 52–55; and "*Mi paraíso de Mallorca*" [My Paradise in Majorca], *La mujer del río* [Woman of the River], trans. D. J. Flakoll (Pittsburgh: University of Pittsburgh Press, 1989), 44–47.

58. Mandela, *Black as I Am*, 18, 27.

59. R. B. Kitaj, *First Diasporic Manifesto* (London: Thames and Hudson, 1989), 65–67.

60. This point is made in the preface to *Looking for Home: Women Writing about Exile*, ed. Deborah Keenan and Roseann Lloyd (Minneapolis: Milkweed Editions, 1990).

61. Ana Luisa Ortíz de Montellano, "The Space Between," in Keenan and Lloyd, *Looking for Home*, 32–33.

62. Keenan and Lloyd, *Looking for Home*, 281.

63. Anzaldúa, *Borderlands*, 79. For further discussion of the power of women's diasporic literature, see Gay Wilentz, "Toward a Diaspora Literature: Black Women Writers from Africa, the Caribbean, and the United States," *College English* 54, no. 4 (April 1992): 385–405; and Rosalyn Terborg-Penn, Sharon Harley, and Andrea Benton Rushing, eds., *Women in Africa and the African Diaspora* (Washington, D.C.: Howard University Press, 1987).

64. Lugones, "Playfulness," 390–91.

65. Claudette Williams, "Gal . . . You Come from Foreign," in *Charting the Journey: Writings by Black and Third World Women*, ed. Shabnam Grewal et al. (London: Sheba Feminist Publishers, 1988), 145.

66. New Americas Press, *A Dream Compels Us*, 199–200.

67. Alegría, "*Aún no*" [Not Yet], *Woman of the River*, 48–49.

68. Mirna Martínez, "*Porque queremos construir*" [Because We Want to Create], in Anglesey, *Ixok*, 246–48.

69. Anzaldúa, *Borderlands*, 21–23, 73.

70. Combahee River Collective, "A Black Feminist Statement," *This Bridge Called My Back*, 210–18; Gayatri Chakravorty Spivak, "A Literary Representation of the Subaltern: A Woman's Text from the Third World," *In Other Worlds*, 254.

71. Linda Alcoff, "Cultural Feminism versus Post-Structuralism: The Identity Crisis in Feminist Theory," *Signs* 13 (Summer 1988): 405–36.

72. Teresa de Lauretis, "Eccentric Subjects: Feminist Theory and Historical Consciousness," *Feminist Studies* 16, no. 1 (Spring 1990): 115.

73. Diana Fuss, *Essentially Speaking: Feminism, Nature and Difference* (New York: Routledge, 1989), 100.

74. Trinh Minh-ha, *Woman, Native, Other: Writing Postcoloniality and Feminism* (Bloomington: Indiana University Press, 1989), 6; and "Not You / Like You," 371–73.

75. Spivak, "A Literary Representation," 246–54.

76. Marjorie Agosin, "Disappeared Woman I," trans. Cora Franzen, in Keenan and Lloyd, *Looking for Home*, 102.

77. Audre Lorde, "Age, Race, Class, and Sex: Women Redefining Difference," *Sister Outsider: Essays and Speeches* (Trumansburg, N.Y.: Crossing Press, 1984), 114–16.

78. Jacinta Escudos, "San Salvador 1983," in Partnoy, *You Can't Drown the Fire*, 215–17.

79. Dora Tamana, "Dora Tamana," in *Third World—Second Sex: Women's Struggles and National Liberation*, ed. Miranda Davies (London: Zed Books, 1983), 125. See Kimble and Unterhalter, "ANC Women's Struggles," for a discussion of Dora Tamana's leadership in the Federation of South African Women during the 1950s and in the ANC, esp. pp. 32–33.

80. Trinh, "Not You / Like You," 374.

81. Rich, "Blood, Bread, and Poetry," *Blood, Bread, and Poetry*, 186.

82. Sandoval, "Feminism and Racism," in Anzaldúa, *Making Face, Making Soul*, 67; Mohanty, introduction to *Third World Women and the Politics of Feminism*, 33.

83. Trinh, "Not You / Like You," 373–75.

84. Lety, "*Cumpleaños*" [Birthday], in Alegría and Flakoll, *On the Front Line*, 70–71.

85. Spivak, "A Literary Representation," 243.

86. Masekela, "Christmas 1976," in Plumpp, *Somehow We Survive*, 65.

87. Cited in de Lauretis, "Eccentric Subjects," 123.
88. Díaz-Diocaretz, "I will be a scandal," 103.
89. Lorna Dee Cervantes, "Poem for the Young White Man Who Asked Me How I, an Intelligent, Well-Read Person, Could Believe in the War between Races," in Anzaldúa, *Making Face, Making Soul,* 4–5.
90. Díaz-Diocaretz, "I will be a scandal," 102.
91. Harlow, *Resistance Literature,* 33. In compiling these characteristics, I have drawn heavily on Harlow's book as well as on writings by Claribel Alegría; discussions with Salvadoran poets Eva Ortíz, Blanca Mirna Benevides, and Dra. Matilda Elena López; and exchanges with South African poets Boitumelo Mofokeng and Abu Solomons. I am grateful for their insights.

Chapter 2

Epigraphs are taken from Audre Lorde, "Poetry Is Not a Luxury," 37; *"Sin poder enamorarnos de la luna"* [We Cannot Afford to Be Enamored with the Moon], introduction to El Salvador section of Anglesey, *Ixok,* 149. For a different but provocative use of the quote from *Ixok,* see Harlow, *Barred,* 158–61.
1. Lorde, "Poetry Is Not a Luxury," 38.
2. The most comprehensive source for documenting these statistics is Americas Watch, *El Salvador's Decade of Terror.* See also Armstrong and Shenk, *El Salvador;* New Americas Press, *A Dream Compels Us,* esp. pp. 7–20; Thomson, *Women of El Salvador,* esp. 1–9; and Marc Zimmerman, *El Salvador at War: A Collage Epic,* Studies in Marxism 25 (Minneapolis: MEP Publications, 1988).
3. "We Cannot Afford to Be Enamored," in Anglesey, *Ixok,* 149.
4. "We Cannot Afford to Be Enamored," in Anglesey, *Ixok,* 151. Other bilingual or English-language anthologies that include Salvadoran women's poetry are Partnoy's *You Can't Drown the Fire;* Alegría and Flakoll, *On the Front Line;* Crow, *Woman Who Has Sprouted Wings;* and *Lovers and Comrades: Women's Resistance Poetry from Central America,* ed. Amanda Hopkinson (London: The Women's Press, 1989). For a valuable discussion of Central American revolutionary literature, see John Beverley and Marc Zimmerman, *Literature and Politics in the Central American Revolutions* (Austin: University of Texas Press, 1990), esp. pp. 115–43. For an overview assessment of Salvadoran women's poetry, see Mary K. DeShazer, "'From Outrage to Reconciliation': Political Poetry by Salvadoran Women," *NWSA Journal* 4, no. 2 (Summer 1992): 170–86.
5. De Lauretis, "Eccentric Subjects," 115.
6. Anzaldúa, *Borderlands.*
7. "We Cannot Afford to Be Enamored," in Anglesey, *Ixok,* 150–51; Eva Ortíz, *"En El Salvador"* (poem given to the author), trans. Serena Cosgrove; Mirna Martínez, *"Si Alguna vez Pudiera"* [If Only Someday], in Anglesey, *Ixok,* trans. Zoë Anglesey, 236–39.
8. Several poets whom I interviewed in San Salvador in June 1991 discussed women's poetry of desire as a form of resistance poetry, namely Eva Ortíz, Nora Méndez, and Celia Moran. Also helpful were discussions with Serena Cosgrove, a North American living in El Salvador who was a founder of *Taller de mujeres en la literatura,*

a workshop of which the other three are members. Other members of the *Taller* are Blanca Mirna Benevides, Ilse Margarita Escobar, Ima Guirola, Michele Herrera, and Tania Molina.

9. De Lauretis, "Eccentric Subjects"; Charlotte Bunch, "Bringing the Global Home," *Passionate Politics: Feminist Theory in Action* (New York: St. Martin's Press, 1987), 328–45.

10. Nora Méndez, *"Ana María,"* and Blanca Mirna Benevides, *"Mujer de nuevo acento"* (poems given to the author), trans. Serena Cosgrove.

11. Díaz-Diocaretz, "I will be a scandal," 89–93.

12. This term is Iris M. Zavala's, in "The Social Imaginary: The Cultural Sign of Hispanic Modernism," *Critical Studies* 1, no. 1 (1989): 23–41.

13. Méndez, *"Ana María."*

14. Benevides, *"Mujer de nuevo acento."*

15. Díaz-Diocaretz, "I will be a scandal," 91.

16. Ana del Carmen de Vásquez, *"Desaparecido,"* in Anglesey, *Ixok,* trans. Elizabeth Macklin, 202–5.

17. Matilde Elena López, *"Contra todo esperanza tu esperanza"* [Against all Hope your Hope] (poem given to the author), trans. Serena Cosgrove.

18. Joyce Hackel, "Salvador Prostitutes Hit Hard by AIDS," *San Franscisco Examiner,* March 17, 1991, 13A.

19. Celia Moran, *"A Emérita, Nena, Mercedes, y muchas trabajadoras del sexo"* [To Emérita, Nena, Mercedes, and the many other sex workers] (poem given to the author), trans. Serena Cosgrove.

20. These statistics were provided by Serena Cosgrove.

21. Benevides, *"Mujer de nuevo acento."*

22. Delfy Góchez Fernandez, "It Will be my Pleasure to Die," trans. Amanda Hopkinson, in Hopkinson, *Lovers and Comrades,* 96–97; Mirna Martínez, *"Nunca he sabido tus señas,"* in Anglesey, *Ixok,* trans. Zoë Anglesey, 244–47. Delfy Góchez Fernandez's poetry is published in Hopkinson in English only.

23. New Americas Press, *A Dream Compels Us,* 123–27.

24. Author's interview with Serena Cosgrove and Robyn Braverman, North American journalists and translators living in El Salvador, San Salvador, June 18, 1991. See also their unpublished manuscript on the lives and struggles of Salvadoran women, *Faces of Maria* (available from the authors).

25. This term is Blanca Mirna Benevides's; author's interview, June 20, 1991.

26. Reyna Hernández, *"Esta es la hora,"* in Anglesey, *Ixok,* trans. Zoë Anglesey, 222–25.

27. Reyna Hernández, *"Sexta-Avenida Sur,"* in Anglesey, *Ixok,* 224–27.

28. Mirna Martínez, *"Nunca he sabido tus señas,* in Anglesey, *Ixok,* 244–47.

29. Amada Libertad, "XIV" and *"Dentro de la voz"* (poems given to Serena Cosgrove before the poet's death), trans. Serena Cosgrove.

30. Fernandez, "It Will Be My Pleasure to Die," 96–97.

31. Jean Franco, "Killing Priests, Nuns, Women, Children," in *Ways of Reading,* ed. D. Bartholomae and A. Petrosky (Boston: Bedford Books, 1990), 194–203. Hopkinson gives this information on Góchez Fernandez in her biographical notes, *Lovers and Comrades,* 138. For a discussion of parallels between war and mothering narratives, and of the complementary metaphorization of waging war and giving birth,

see Jean Bethke Elshtain, *Women and War* (New York: Basic Books, 1987), 205–30; and Nancy Huston, "The Matrix of War: Mothers and Heroes," *Poetics Today*, 6, nos. 1–2 (1985): 153–70.

32. Ana Guadelupe Martínez, "We Have a Commitment to Our People," in New Americas Press, *A Dream Compels Us*, 157–60.

33. Lety, "*Embarazo,*" in Alegría and Flakoll, *On the Front Line*, 72–73.

34. "We Cannot Afford to Be Enamored," 148–49.

35. Carmela, "*A vos,*" in Alegría and Flakoll, *On the Front Line*, 18–19.

36. Karla, "*Alfabetizar,*" in Alegría and Flakoll, *On the Front Line*, 58–59.

37. Claribel Alegría, "*Documental,*" in Alegría, *Woman of the River*, 28–29.

38. Ilse Margarita Escobar, "*La Promesa*" (poem given to Serena Cosgrove), trans. Serena Cosgrove.

39. Nora Méndez, "*Noviembre 1989*" (poem given to the author), trans. Serena Cosgrove; Matilde Elena López, "*Lloro en la oruga por las alas del mañana,*" trans. Serena Cosgrove, in *Los sollozos oscuros* (San Salvador: Ministerio de Educacion, 1982), 27–28.

40. Mendez, "*Noviembre 1989*"; Lopez, "*Lloro en la oruga,*" 27–28.

41. Celia Moran, "*Soledad*" (poem given to the author), trans. Serena Cosgrove.

42. Blanca Mirna Benevides, "*Reflexiones*" (poem given to the author), trans. Serena Cosgrove.

43. Tania Molina, "*Prefiero morir*" (poem given to the author), trans. Serena Cosgrove.

44. Michele Herrera, "*Rompiendo el silencio*" (poem given to the author), trans. Serena Cosgrove.

45. Michele Herrera, "*Noviembre*" (poem given to the author), trans. Serena Cosgrove.

46. Roque Dalton, *Poetry and Militancy in Latin America* (Willimantic, Conn.: Curbstone Press, 1981); Harlow, *Resistance Literature*, 37.

47. Hélène Cixous, "The Laugh of the Medusa," trans. Keith Cohen and Paula Cohen, *Signs: Journal of Women in Culture and Society* 1, no. 1 (Summer 1976): 881–82; Nora Méndez, "*Nueves sensaciones,*" (poem given to the author), trans. Serena Cosgrove. For a discussion of *l'écriture féminine* and French feminist theory, see Elaine Marks and Isabelle de Courtivron, eds., *New French Feminisms* (New York: Schocken Books, 1981), 28–38.

48. Berta López Morales, "Language of the Body in Women's Texts," *Splintering Darkness: Latin American Women in Search of Themselves*, ed. Lucía Guerra Cunningham (Pittsburgh: Latin American Review Literary Press, 1990), 123–30.

49. Audre Lorde, "Uses of the Erotic: The Erotic as Power," *Sister Outsider*, 53–59.

50. Morales, "Language of the Body," 125.

51. Méndez, "*Nueves sensaciones.*"

52. Morales, "Language of the Body," 125–26.

53. Alicia Ostriker, *Stealing the Language: The Emergence of Women's Poetry in America* (Boston: Beacon Press, 1986), 164–209.

54. Eva Ortíz, "*Entrega,*" "*Pequeña Biografia,*" and "*Eva*" (poems given to the author), trans. Serena Cosgrove; author's interview, San Salvador, June 18, 1991.

55. Celia Moran, "*Paralelo de amor*" (poem given to the author), trans. Serena Cosgrove.

56. Celia Moran (untitled poem given to Serena Cosgrove), trans. Serena Cosgrove.

57. Rich, "Notes toward a Politics of Location," *Blood, Bread, and Poetry*, 212.
58. "We Cannot Afford to Be Enamored," in Anglesey, *Ixok*, 148–49.

Chapter 3

Epigraphs taken from Marta Benavides, "El Salvador: The Presence Removed," in Partnoy, *You Can't Drown the Fire*, 131; Alegría, "We Were Three".
1. Benavides, "El Salvador," 130.
2. Benavides, "El Salvador," 131.
3. For documentation of these statistics, see New Americas Press, *A Dream Compels Us*, 7–20; and Thomson, *Women of El Salvador*, 1–9.
4. Jane Marcus, "Alibis and Legends: The Ethics of Elsewhereness, Gender and Estrangement," *Women's Writing in Exile*, ed. Mary Lynn Broe and Angela Ingram (Chapel Hill: University of North Carolina Press, 1989), 270.
5. Angela Ingram, "Introduction: On the Contrary, Outside of It," in Broe and Ingram, *Women's Writing in Exile*, 6.
6. Alegría, "We Were Three," 55.
7. Claribel Alegría, "The Politics of Exile," in Partnoy, *You Can't Drown the Fire*, 173.
8. Partnoy, introduction to *You Can't Drown the Fire*, 14–15.
9. For firsthand accounts of such experiences, see New Americas Press, *A Dream Compels Us*, 117–242, and *Pajaro y volcán* 9–35, 155–80. The FMLN is the Farabundo Martí National Liberation Front, a five-party guerrilla organization that controlled approximately 30 percent of El Salvador's territory during the 1980s and had numerous urban enclaves. See *A Dream Compels Us*, 123–69, on women in the FMLN.
10. Jane Marcus, "Alibis and Legends," in Broe and Ingram, *Women's Writing in Exile*, 272; Forché, "El Salvador"; Benavides, "El Salvador," 123–33.
11. "We Cannot Afford to be Enamored with the Moon" in Anglesey, *Ixok*, 150–51.
12. Ingram, "Introduction," 12.
13. Ingram, "Introduction," 2.
14. Sara Martínez, "*Coordenadas* [Coordinates], trans. Julia Stein in Anglesey, *Ixok*, 192–93; Claribel Alegría, "*Santa Ana a oscuras*" [Santa Ana in the Dark], *Flowers from the Volcano*, 16–17.
15. Benavides, "El Salvador," 128.
16. Martínez, "Coordinates," 192–93.
17. Marcus, "Alibis and Legends," 273.
18. Reyna Hernández, "*Me sacaron de mi país*" [They Sent Me Out of My Country], trans. Zoë Anglesey, in Anglesey, *Ixok*, , 228–29.
19. Benavides, "El Salvador," 133.
20. Reyna Hernández, "San Salvador," trans. Zoë Anglesey, in Anglesey, *Ixok*, 230–31.
21. Jacinta Escudos (Rocio America), "To Come Back," in New Americas Press, *A Dream Compels Us*, 133–35. This poem is published in its English translation only.
22. Carolyn Forché, preface to Alegría, *Flowers from the Volcano*, xi.
23. Alegría, "The Politics of Exile," 175–77.

24. Forché, preface to Alegría, *Flowers from the Volcano*, xii.

25. Forché, "El Salvador," 3–8.

26. Claribel Alegría, "Sorrow," *Flowers from the Volcano*, 18–43.

27. Gloria Bonilla, "Talking," in Partnoy, *You Can't Drown the Fire*, 34–37.

28. Quoted by Partnoy, introduction, *You Can't Drown the Fire*, 14.

29. Thomson, *Women of El Salvador*, 107; Sara Martínez, "*Angustía*" [Anguish], trans. Julia Stein, in Anglesey, *Ixok*, 90–91; Ana Guadelupe Martínez, "The Secret Prisons of El Salvador," in New Americas Press, *A Dream Compels Us*, 155. For an insightful analysis of women's prison writing from El Salvador and five other nations, see Harlow, *Barred*.

30. Sara Martínez, "Anguish," in Anglesey, *Ixok*, 90–91.

31. Nora Mendéz, "*Testimonios*" [Testimonies] (poem given to the author), trans. Serena Cosgrove. Méndez told me the context of her writing the poem in an interview in San Salvador, June 19, 1991.

32. New Americas Press, *A Dream Compels Us*, 46–47; de Lauretis, *Technologies of Gender*, 42–48.

33. Ana Guadelupe Martínez, "Secret Prisons" and "We Have a Commitment to Our People," in New Americas Press, *A Dream Compels Us*, 155–57.

34. Nidia Díaz, *Nunca estuve sola* [I Was Never Alone] (San Salvador: UCA Editores, 1988), 170–72, 182–83. For further analysis of Martínez's and Díaz's prison narratives, see Harlow, *Barred*, 170–79.

35. Bernardina Guervara Corvera, "*Mi comandante Federico*" [My Commandante Federico], trans. Gina Caruso and Susan Matobo, in Anglesey, *Ixok*, 262–63; Claribel Alegría, "*La mujer del Río Sumpul*" [The Woman of the Sumpul River], *Woman of the River*, 60–61.

36. Alegría, "The Politics of Exile," 175–77.

37. Corvera, "My Commandante Federico," in Anglesey, *Ixok*, 262–63.

38. Alegría, "The Politics of Exile," 173–75.

39. Pastora, "The People's Teachers," in Partnoy, *You Can't Drown the Fire*, 181–82. Pastora's poems have been published in their English translation only.

40. Reyna Hernández, "*La Pimpa*" [Mama Bags Buys Her Clothes], trans. Zoë Anglesey, in Anglesey, *Ixok*, 222–23; Emily Dickinson, *The Poems of Emily Dickinson*, ed. Thomas Johnson, 3 vols. (Cambridge: Harvard University Press, 1955).

41. Marcus, "Alibis and Legends," 270.

42. For an account of the Sumpul River massacre, see New Americas Press, *A Dream Compels Us*, 12. Claribel Alegría describes a similar massacre at the Lempa River on the Honduran-Salvadoran border, in "The Politics of Exile," 173–74.

43. Alegría, "The Woman of the Sumpul River," *Woman of the River*, 60–69.

44. Adriana Rodriguez, "I Had Never Thought of Leaving My Country," in New Americas Press, *A Dream Compels Us*, 211–15.

45. Sharon D. Welch, *A Feminist Ethic of Risk* (Minneapolis: Fortress Press, 1990), 139.

46. Anglesey, *Ixok*, 147–51.

47. Harlow, *Resistance Literature*, 62. On this and other points regarding Latin American women's testimonial strategies, see the special issue on testimonials, *Latin American Perspectives*, issue 71, vol. 18, no. 4 (Fall 1991).

Chapter 4

This slogan has been documented in the 1986 film *You Have Struck A Rock;* Gcina Mhlope, "Say No," *Breaking the Silence: A Century of South African Women's Poetry,* ed. Cecily Lockett (Johannesburg: Ad. Donker, 1990), 351–52.

1. Gordimer is cited in Shava, *A People's Voice,* 71. See also Nadine Gordimer, *The Black Interpreters* (Johannesburg: Ravan Press, 1973).
2. Shava, *A People's Voice,* 3–9.
3. For information about South African women's struggles historically, see Meer, "Organising under Apartheid"; Qunta, *Women in Southern Africa,* 76–122; *Women under Apartheid;* Walker, *Women and Resistance;* Kimble and Unterhalter, "ANC Women's Struggles"; and Seidman, "No Freedom without the Women."
4. James Matthews and Gladys Thomas, *Cry Rage!* (Johannesburg: Spro-cas Publications, 1972).
5. Antjie Krog, forum on "Women Writing in South Africa," in Coetzee and Polley, *Crossing Borders,* 125–33. For a discussion of writing by dissident Afrikaners, see Jack Cope, *The Adversary Within: Dissident Writers in Afrikaans* (Cape Town: David Philip, 1982).
6. Krog, in Coetzee and Polley, *Crossing Borders,* 130–31.
7. These writers also presented their views on women and writing; see Coetzee and Polley, *Crossing Borders,* 119–25, 140–44. Masekela chaired this conference; her poetry is published in Plumpp, *Somehow We Survive.* Kgositsile's and Matlou's poetry is published in *Malibongwe: ANC Women: Poetry Is Also Their Weapon,* ed. Sono Molefe (Sweden: ANC, 1982). Matlou also has published, under her given name of Sankie Nkondo, a collection entitled *Flames of Fury and Other Poems* (Johannesburg: COSAW, 1990).
8. Cronin, in Coetzee and Polley, *Crossing Borders,* 144–45.
9. Barnett, *A Vision of Order;* Alvarez-Peyeyre, *Poetry of Commitment.* Some excellent critical volumes do focus on African writers who are women, but they either overlook South Africa or focus primarily on writers of fiction, ignoring women poets; see, for example, *Ngambika: Studies of Women in African Literature,* ed. Carole Boyce Davies and Anne Adams Graves (Trenton, N.J.: Africa World Press, 1986); and Lloyd W. Brown, *Women Writers in Black Africa* (Westport, Conn.: Greenwood Press, 1981).
10. What these aesthetic and political standards have been and should be, of course, is a subject of considerable cultural debate in South Africa today. See, for example, de Kok and Press, *Spring Is Rebellious;* and *Exchanges: South African Writing in Transition,* ed. Duncan Brown and Bruno van Dyk (Pietermaritzburg: University of Natal Press, 1991), for differing opinions about whether the widely held view among progressive artists in the 1970 and 1980s that culture is a weapon of the struggle continues to be aesthetically and politically appropriate in a changing South Africa of the 1990s. For purposes of this discussion, however, it seems reasonable to assume that both women's and men's resistance poetry during these decades was judged largely on its political, polemical, rhetorical, and thematic aims and strategies and only secondarily on its lyrical, formal, or stylistic attributes. Another way to say this, to recast Keats, is that the truth of resistance

poetry has been valued over its beauty. Or, as Jane Taylor and David Bunn assert, "it's hard to resist the idea in South Africa that there are only two kinds of texts: those that make a daily difference and those that don't." Cited by de Kok, *Writers from South Africa*, 53.

11. Boitumelo Mofokeng, "Where Are the Women? Ten Years of *Staffrider*," *Current Writing* 1 (1989): 41–42.
12. *Malibongwe*, 4–5, 46. All further poems from this volume will be cited in the text.
13. Harlow, *Resistance Literature*, 37.
14. Harlow, *Resistance Literature*, 34–35; de Kok, *Writers from South Africa*, 57–58.
15. Harlow, *Resistance Literature*, 45.
16. Lynda Gilfillan, "Black Women Poets in Exile: The Weapon of Words," *Tulsa Studies in Women's Literature* 11, no. 1 (Spring 1992): 79–80, 84–87.
17. For information on these ANC women leaders, see Kimble and Unterhalter, "ANC Women's Struggles," 11–35.
18. Gilfillan, "Black Women Poets," 85.
19. Mhlope, "We Are at War," in Lockett, *Breaking the Silence*, 349–50.
20. J. U. Jacobs, "In a Free State: The Exile in South African Poetry," in *Momentum: On Recent South African Writing*, ed. M. J. Daymond et al. (Pietermaritzburg: University of Natal Press, 1984), 244–45. See also *Seven South African Poets: Poems of Exile*, collected and selected by Cosmo Pieterse (London: Heinemann, 1971).
21. Baleka Kgositsile, "Exile Blues," in Molefe, *Malibongwe*, 90–91.
22. Masekela, "Demon Exile," "Uthekwane," and "Where Are They Now," in Plumpp, *Somehow We Survive*, 66–68.
23. Gertrude Fester, "This Is the Reality" (poem given to the author, June 1992); Jessie Duarte, "Toilet Paper," in *A Snake with Ice Water: Prison Writings by South African Women*, ed. Barbara Schreiner (Johannesburg: COSAW, 1992), 178.
24. Gertrude Fester, "It's Carnival Time" and "The Spirit Cannot Be Caged" (poems given to the author, June 1992). Fester has published other prison poems in *Siren Songs*, ed. Nohra Moerat (South Africa: Blac Publishing House, 1989), 94–97; and in Schreiner, *A Snake with Ice Water*, 269.
25. Barbara Schreiner, introduction to *A Snake with Ice Water*, 1–7. Further citations from this volume will be given in the text.
26. Mavis Smallberg, "June," in Lockett, *Breaking the Silence*, 343–48.
27. For a discussion of women's roles in the Soweto uprisings, see Walker, *Women and Resistance*; for a discussion of resistance by women and children in townships during the 1980s, see Fatima Meer, ed., *Resistance in the Townships* (Durban: Institute for Black Research, Madiba Publications, 1989). For an account of repression against children, see Victoria Brittain and Abdul S. Minty, eds., *Children of Resistance: Statements from the Harare Conference on Children, Repression and the Law in Apartheid South Africa* (London: Kliptown Books, 1988). For representative poetry by South African women on the Soweto uprisings, see the section of Molefe, *Malibongwe*, entitled "Spirit of Soweto: The Ghetto, Massacres, Resolve," 35–46.
28. Schreiner, introduction to *A Snake with Ice Water*, 5–6; Harlow, *Barred*, 139–40.
29. Epigraphs taken from Roseline Naapo, "Alone I Sit in My Cell," in *Buang Basadi / Khulumani Makhosikazi / Women Speak: Conference on Women and Writing* (Johannesburg: COSAW, Transvaal Region, 1989), 10–11, hereafter referred to as *Women*

Speak; and Boitumelo Mofokeng, "Domestic Workers' Plea" (poem given to the author, June 1992).

30. Culture and Working Life Project, "Albie Sachs Must Not Worry," in de Kok and Press, *Spring Is Rebellious*, 99–103.

31. Roseline Naapo, "Breaking the Silence," in *Women Speak*, 10. See also "Domestic Workers Say No to Slavery," *Speak*, no. 25 (1989): 4–7. On the painful and complex relationships between black and white women under apartheid, see also Masekela's comments in Coetzee and Polley, *Crossing Borders*, 155–56.

32. Naapo, "Alone I Sit in My Cell," 10–11.

33. Boitumelo Mofokeng, "Inside a Domestic Worker (in the 1950s)" and "Inside a Domestic Worker (in the 1980s)" (poems given to the author, June 1992).

34. Gladys Thomas, "Leave Me Alone," *Cry Rage!* 77.

35. Thula Baba Collective, "Domestic Workers," in Lockett, *Breaking the Silence*, 324; see also their book, *Thula Baba* (Johannesburg: Ravan Press, 1987), for photos and full text. I am grateful to Irena Klepfisz for providing me with a copy of *Thula Baba*.

36. Poems by Khoza and Thibedi are cited in "Freedom Means Equality and No More Lies! Progressive Arts Project Women's Group," *Speak*, no. 27 (1990): 16–21. For information about PAP Women's Group, I am grateful to Irene Stephanou (personal interview, Johannesburg, June 4, 1992); and to Thandi Khoza, Mary Thibedi, and other members of the group (personal interviews, Johannesburg, June 5, 1992).

37. "Freedom Means Equality and No More Lies!" 17–18.

38. Roshila Nair, "But Oneday Madam" (poem given to the author, June 1992).

39. Jacklyn Cock, *Maids and Madams* (Johannesburg: Ravan Press, 1984); Sisi Maqagi, "Who Theorizes?" *Current Writing* 2 (October 1990): 24.

40. M. J. Daymond, "Preface," *Current Writing* 2 (October 1990): iii.

41. Poems by MaCele of Zenzele, Silomo of the Mdlalose clan, and other Zulu women composers and performers of *izibongo* are published and translated by Elizabeth Gunner, "Songs of Innocence and Experience: Women as Composers and Performers of *Izibongo*, Zulu Praise Poetry," *Research in African Literatures* 10, no. 2 (Fall 1979): 239–67; rpt. in *Women and Writing in Southern Africa: A Critical Anthology*, ed. Cherry Clayton (London: Heinemann, 1989), 11–39; my citations are taken from the latter volume.

42. Gunner, "Songs of Innocence and Experience," 12–16. For further analysis of Zulu praise poetry, see *Izibongo: Zulu praise Poems*, ed. Trevor Cope (Oxford: Clarendon Press, 1968); and A. C. Nkabinde, *Zulu Prose and Praises: In Defence of a Living Tradition* (Kwa-Dlangezwa: University of Zululand Press, 1976).

43. Personal interviews with Lauretta Ngcobo, London, May 31, 1992; Winston-Salem, N. C., November 16–18, 1992.

44. Gunner, "Songs of Innocence and Experience," 14. Further citations from this essay will be given in the text.

45. Adrienne Rich, "Notes toward a Politics of Location," *Blood, Bread, and Poetry*, 210–31.

46. Matlou's quote comes from Coetzee and Polley, *Crossing Borders*, 132; Krog's is from p. 133.

47. Coetzee and Polley, *Crossing Borders*, 123, 133.

Chapter 5

Albie Sachs, "Preparing Ourselves for Freedom," in de Kok and Press, *Spring Is Rebellious*, 19; Frene Ginwala, "Women's Future, World's Future: Transforming the Nature of South African Society," South African Association of University Women Memorial Lecture Honouring Professor Irene Jackson, Johannesburg, May 18, 1992 (MS provided by the author); Lauretta Ngcobo, personal interview, London, May 31, 1992.

It has been difficult for me to decide when to identify a South African woman writer by race. Given the ANC's promotion of nonracialism, a philosophy adhered to by many of the writers discussed here (in part as a response to the vicious racial categorizations of apartheid), to use racial identifiers seems insensitive. On the other hand, for most U.S. readers, the race of the woman writing is likely to seem relevant to the discussion, especially given that black women writers of all countries are doubly oppressed and in need of recognition *as* black women. Therefore, I identify the race of the woman writing where I believe it will prevent confusion, reinforce a political point, or illuminate a text.

1. Frank Meintjies, "Albie Sachs and the Art of Protest," in de Kok and Press, *Spring Is Rebellious*, 30.
2. Gillian Slovo, personal interview, London, May 31, 1992; Gilfillan, "Black Women Poets," 88. This issue of *Tulsa Studies* includes an excellent forum on South African women's writing.
3. Ingrid de Kok, personal interview, Cape Town, June 15, 1992; Lisa Combrinck, personal interview, Cape Town, June 13, 1992. See also de Kok interview in Taylor and Bunn, *Writers from South Africa*, 53–61.
4. Brenda Cooper, "Underneath the Fists are Open and Vulnerable Eyes," in de Kok and Press, *Spring Is Rebellious*, 54–55.
5. Stacey Stent, "The Wrong Ripple," in de Kok and Press, *Spring Is Rebellious*, 76.
6. Culture and Working Life Project, "Albie Sachs Must Not Worry," in de Kok and Press, *Spring Is Rebellious*, 99.
7. Malange is cited in Ari Sitas, "The Sachs Debate: A Philistine's Response," in de Kok and Press, *Spring Is Rebellious*, 97.
8. Annemarie van Niekirk, "Women's Exile: Addressing the Marginalization of Women in South African Culture" (paper presented at the COSAW / New Nation conference, "Making Literature: Reconstruction in South Africa," Johannesburg, December 3, 1991), 3–9.

   I would also like to note that, although this chapter focuses on South African women writing in English in the late 1980s and 1990s, it is important to realize that women poets writing in Afrikaans won national and, indeed, international recognition throughout the 1980s. Antjie Krog, Welma Odendaal, and Welma Stockenstrom are three Afrikaner women poets who follow in the tradition of poet Ingrid Jonker. For more on Afrikaner women poets, see Antjie Krog's comments in Coetzee and Polley, *Crossing Borders*, 125–33.
9. For information on these debates, I am grateful to Fatima Meer, Frene Ginwala, and the ANC Women's League, all of whom provided me with in-house ANC documents on women, including the *Bulletin of the National Commission for the Emancipation of Women* (April 1992) and copies of speeches given at the Women's

National Coalition Workshop, April 25–26, 1992. I am also grateful to Robin Phillips and the Institute for a Democratic Alternative in South Africa (IDASA) for providing me with clippings on CODESA from Johannesburg and Pretoria newspapers during the spring and summer of 1992.

10. Daymond, "Preface," iii.

11. Nawal el-Saadawi is cited by Annie Gagiano, "The New Nation Writers Conference: A Feast of Languages," *Die Suid-Afrikaan* (February–March 1992), 33.

12. The phrase "disloyal to civilization" is Adrienne Rich's, in "Disloyal to Civilization: Feminism, Racism, Gynephobia," *On Lies, Secrets, and Silence*, 275–310; Mofokeng, "Breaking the Silence," 8. I am grateful to Junaid Ahmed and the Congress of South African Writers for providing me with a copy of these proceedings.

13. Sachs, "Preparing Ourselves for Freedom," 22; Culture and Working Life Project, "Albie Sachs Must Not Worry," 103.

14. Sachs, "Preparing Ourselves for Freedom," 21–22, 29.

15. Sitas, "The Sachs Debate," 91–92. A second volume of responses to Sachs's paper, *Exchanges: South African Writing in Transition*, ed. Duncan Brown and Bruno van Dyk (Pietermaritzburg: University of Natal Press, 1991), also provides useful information. It takes the form of interviews with prominent South African writers, black and white (many of whom are not represented in *Spring Is Rebellious*), about their view of the Sachs debates.

16. Brenda Cooper, "Underneath the Fists," 52–56; Kendell Geers, "Competition with History: Resistance and the Avant-Garde," 43–46; and Karen Press, "Surprise, Responsibility, and Power," 68–73; all in de Kok and Press, *Spring Is Rebellious*.

17. Frank Meintjies, "Albie Sachs and the Art of Protest," 30–35; Junaid Ahmed, "Culture in South Africa: The Challenge of Transformation," 121–25; Culture and Working Life Project, "Albie Sachs Must Not Worry," 99–103; all in de Kok and Press, *Spring Is Rebellious*.

18. Rushdy Siers, "Vampire Bats of Ambiguous Metaphors," 57–67, see esp. p. 58; Gavin Younge, "Running in the Sackrace," 80–84; both in de Kok and Press, *Spring Is Rebellious*.

19. Sachs, "Preparing Ourselves for Freedom," 23; Orenna Krut, "Albie Sachs' Paper: What Issues Does It Raise for COSAW?" 114–17; Sitas, "The Sachs Debate," 97–98; all in de Kok and Press, *Spring Is Rebellious*. The editors of *Exchanges* asked only one interviewee, Nise Malange, a question about gender issues in the context of the Sachs debates. The other women interviewed—Nadine Gordimer, Menan du Plessis, and Joan Hambidge, all of whom are white—were not asked about gender and writing. See *Exchanges*, 41–45.

20. Elizabeth Barad, "Albertina Sisulu on a Post-Patriarchal South Africa," *Ms.*, July–August 1992, 18.

21. Not all South Africans agree with these statistics on ANC support, and obtaining official documentation is extremely difficult. These statistics, however, were given to me repeatedly during my visit to South Africa in 1992 by ANC members and by members of unaffiliated justice organizations such as IDASA. For a critical view of the ANC and its role in eradicating apartheid in the 1990s, see the *Roca Report: A Confidential Assessment of Developments in Southern Africa*, 45 (September 1992), which alleges, for example, that the ANC's mass action campaign against the

homelands led to the slaying of twenty-nine at Bisho (correspondence should be addressed to Roca, Box 35225, Menlo Park, 0102, South Africa); and Anthea J. Jeffery, *Spotlight on Disinformation about Violence in South Africa* (South African Institute of Race Relations, no. 8, September 1992). This latter publication alleges that the ANC might well be responsible for murders it wishes to attribute to the Inkatha Freedom Party and criticizes what it considers disinformation perpetrated by such groups as Amnesty International, the International Commission of Jurists, and the South African–based Human Rights Commission.

22. Walker, *Women and Resistance,* and *Women and Gender in Southern Africa to 1945* (Cape Town: David Phillip, 1990); Fatima Meer, "South African Women—Their Subordinate Status, Their Hope for Change" (MS provided by the author); Kimble and Unterhalter, "ANC Women's Struggles," 11–35. Shope is quoted in Gilfillan, "Black Women Poets," 89; Shope made this statement at the COSAW / New Nation Writers Conference, December 1991. For further discussion by ANC members of the organization's changing policy on women's emancipation, see Coetzee and Polley, *Crossing Borders,* 119–56.

23. Machel is quoted by Cecily Lockett, "Feminism(s) and Writing in English in South Africa," *Current Writing* 2 (October 1990): 21, n. 6; see also T. Karis and G. Carter, eds., *From Protest to Challenge: A Documentary History of African Politics in South Africa 1882–1964,* vol. 3 (Stanford: Hoover Institution Press, 1972). For analyses of the legal struggles involved in the emancipation of South African women, see Susan Bazilli, ed., *Putting Women on the Agenda* (Johannesburg: Ravan Press, 1991).

24. Statement of the National Executive Committee of the African National Congress on the Emancipation of Women in South Africa, May 2, 1990; *Bulletin of the National Commission for the Emancipation of Women,* April 1992. It is worth noting that during the 1980s many ANC exiles became aware of Angolan and Zimbabwean women's feelings that their country's nationalistic, anticolonialist revolution, in which many women fully participated, had subsequently left them out. On this point, see Barbara Masekela's and Rebecca Matlou's comments in Coetzee and Polley, *Crossing Borders,* 123, 149.

25. Statement of the National Executive Committee of the ANC on the Emancipation of Women in South Africa, May 2, 1990.

26. Baleka Kgositsile, secretary-general of the ANC Women's League, personal interview, Johannesburg, June 5, 1992.

27. Frene Ginwala, Women's National Coalition coordinator and director of research, ANC, personal interview, Johannesburg, June 5, 1992; Barad, "Albertina Sisulu," 18.

28. Barad, "Albertina Sisulu," 18.

29. Frene Ginwala, "Non-Racial Democracy—Soon, Non-Sexism—How?" (speech to the Women's National Coalition National Workshop, Johannesburg, April 25–26, 1992), 1–6.

30. Frene Ginwala, personal interview, Johannesburg, June 5, 1992; Sheila Meintjies, University of the Witwatersrand, personal interview, Johannesburg, June 3, 1992.

31. Barad, "Albertina Sisulu," 18.

32. Lauretta Ngcobo, "My Life and My Writing," in *A Double Colonization: Colonial and Post-Colonial Women's Writing,* ed. Kirsten Holst Petersen and Anna Rutherford

(Australia: Dangaroo Press, 1986), 86; Zoë Wicomb, "To Hear the Variety of Discourses," *Current Writing* 2 (October 1990): 37.

33. See, for example, the "Breaking the Silence" proceedings from *Women Speak*, 6–16; and papers from the COSAW / New Nation Writers Conference by Annemarie Van Niekirk, "Women's Exile," 1–13; Lauretta Ngcobo, "Creating a Gender Sensitive Culture," 1–6; and Sankie Nkondo, "Depictions/Stereotypes of African Women in Literature," 1–9.

34. Alice Walker defines *womanist* in *In Search of Our Mothers' Gardens: Womanist Prose* (New York: Harcourt Brace Jovanovich, 1983), as "a black feminist or feminist of color" and "a woman who loves women, sexually and/or nonsexually. Appreciates and prefers women's culture, women's emotional flexibility . . . and women's strength. Sometimes loves individual men, sexually and/or nonsexually. Committed to survival and wholeness of entire people, male *and* female" (xi–xii). Chikwenye Okonjo Ogunyemi defines *womanist* in a way that she claims parallels Walker's, as "a philosophy that celebrates black roots, the ideas of black life, while giving a balanced presentation of black womandom. It concerns itself as much with the black sexual power tussle as with the world power structure that subjugates blacks." Although both privilege womanism over feminism—Walker claims that "womanist is to feminist as purple is to lavender"—Ogunyemi seems to me less inclined than does Walker to endorse alliances between womanists and feminists. See Ogunyemi, "Womanism."

   Gynocritics is a term coined by U.S. scholar Elaine Showalter to describe the sociohistorical study of women's writing; *gynesis* is U.S. scholar Alice Jardine's word for an approach to women's texts that foregrounds linguistics, deconstruction, and/or psychoanalysis. See Elaine Showalter, "Toward a Feminist Poetics," in *The New Feminist Criticism: Essays on Women, Literature, and Theory*, ed. Elaine Showalter (New York: Pantheon Books, 1985); and Alice A. Jardine, *Gynesis: Configurations of Woman and Modernity* (Ithaca, N.Y.: Cornell University Press, 1985).

35. Boitumelo Mofokeng, "Breaking the Silence," in *Women Speak*, 6–9.

36. Roseline Naapo, "Breaking the Silence," 9–11.

37. Nise Malange, "Breaking the Silence," in *Women Speak*, 11–15.

38. Wicomb, "To Hear the Variety," 40.

39. Maqagi, "Who Theorizes?" 22–25.

40. Wicomb, "To Hear the Variety," 40.

41. Gagiano, "The New Nation," 33.

42. Lauretta Ngcobo, "Creating a Gender Sensitive Culture" (paper presented at the COSAW / New Nations Writers Conference), 1–6.

43. Sankie Nkondo, "Depictions/Stereotypes of African Women in Literature" (paper presented at the COSAW / New Nation Writers Conference), 1–9.

44. Annemarie Van Niekirk, "Women's Exile" (paper presented at the COSAW / New Nation Writers Conference), 1–13.

45. Welma Odendaal, "This Is Not a Paper . . . " (paper presented at the COSAW /New Nation Writers Conference), 1–2.

46. Daymond, "Preface," i–v.

47. Lockett, "Feminism(s)," 17–19.

48. Maqagi, "Who Theorizes?" 22–23.

49. Wicomb, "To Hear the Variety," 35–40.

50. Maqagi, "Who Theorizes?" 24; Lockett, "Feminism(s), 20; Wicomb, "To Hear the Variety," 43.

51. Thokozile Chaane, "Orality and Narratives: The Art of Storytelling" (paper presented at the COSAW / New Nation Writers Conference), 1–2.

52. Ingrid de Kok, "Small Passing," *Familiar Ground* (Johannesburg: Ravan Poetry, 1988), 61–63; Gcina Mhlope, "The Dancer," in Lockett, *Breaking the Silence*, 352–53.

53. Sachs, "Preparing Ourselves for Freedom," 21.

54. Ingrid de Kok, "Our Sharpeville," *Familiar Ground*, 13–14.

55. Mhlope, "The Dancer," 352–56.

56. Karen Press, "When your child is born, mother," in *I Qabane Labantu: Poetry in the Emergency*, ed. Ampie Coetzee and Hein Willemse (Pretoria: Taurus Books, 1989), 127.

57. De Kok, "Small Passing," 61–63.

58. I discussed the reception of de Kok's poem with writer and editor Barbara Schreiner, personal interview, Cape Town, June 16, 1992.

59. De Kok, in Taylor and Bunn, *Writers from South Africa*, 53–56.

60. Cooper, "Underneath the Fists," 52–53.

61. Van Niekirk, "Women's Exile," 9–11.

62. Statement of the National Executive Committee of the ANC on the Emancipation of Women, May 2, 1990.

63. Lisa Combrinck, "Concerning the Subject Matter of This Poetry," *Unfolding Petals: Poetry 1984–1992* (MS given to the author, June 1992), 29; Heather Robertson, "Love," *Akal* 1, no. 3 (November 1989): 9.

64. Sachs, "Preparing Ourselves for Freedom," 21; Nise Malange, in *Exchanges*, 41–45, and personal interview, Durban, June 8, 1992; Lesego Rampolokeng is quoted in Lance Nawa, "Report of the COSAW Transvaal Region General Meeting, April 21, 1990," in de Kok and Press, *Spring Is Rebellious*, 111.

65. Combrinck, "To the Reader," *Unfolding Petals*, 28.

66. Robertson, "Love," 9.

67. Combrinck, "To the Reader," 28.

68. Combrinck, "Concerning the Subject Matter of This Poetry," 29.

69. Combrinck, "The Journey," *Unfolding Petals*, 30; "When at Last We Love" and "On Reading Marechera's Mindblast" (poems given to the author, June 1992).

70. Robertson, "Love," 9.

71. Sobhna Poona, "They Came at Twilight," *In Search of Rainbows* (Braamfontein: Skotaville, 1990), 48–49.

72. Deela Khan, "Cocktail Party Effect," *Facets and Scrambled Thoughts: Poems 1975–1990* (MS given to the author, June 1992), 43.

73. Deela Khan, "Love Song" (poem given to the author, June 1992).

74. Meryl Coetzee, "Institutions," in Lockett, *Breaking the Silence*, 332–33.

75. Ingrid de Kok, "To a Would-be Lover," *Familiar Ground*, 40–41.

76. Neil Miller, "Mandela Trial Stirs Up Homophobia: South African Gay and Lesbian Activists Deplore Defense Tactics," *Advocate*, no. 578 (June 4, 1991): 40–41.

77. Gertrude Fester, "Really, Woman" (poem given to the author, June 1992).

78. Audre Lorde, "Uses of the Erotic," 2–3.

79. Boikhutso Siane, "I Am a Woman," *Tribute*, May 1992; Joan Metelerkamp, "Poem," in Lockett, *Breaking the Silence*, 316–19.
80. Janet Todd, *Feminist Literary History: A Defense* (Cambridge: Polity Press, 1988), 131.
81. Wicomb, "To Hear the Variety," 36–37.
82. Siane, "I Am a Woman."
83. Boitumelo Mofokeng, "With My Baby on My Back," *Speak*, no. 27 (1990): 21.
84. Nise Malange, "Nightshift Mother," in Lockett, *Breaking the Silence*, 341–42.
85. Ingrid de Kok, "Woman in the Glass," *Familiar Ground*, 38–39.
86. Joan Metelerkamp, "Poem," in Lockett, *Breaking the Silence*, 316–19.
87. Wicomb, "To Hear the Variety," 35–36, 44.
88. Jenny de Reuck, "Writing Feminism/Theoretical Inscriptions in South Africa," *Current Writing* 2 (October 1990): 34.

Chapter 6

Audre Lorde, "On My Way Out I Passed over You and the Verrazano Bridge," *Our Dead behind Us*, 54–57 (hereafter referred to as "Verrazano Bridge.") The title "Lust for a Working Tomorrow" also comes from this poem. Maria Lugones, "*Hablando cara a cara* / Speaking Face to Face: An Exploration of Ethnocentric Racism," in Anzaldúa, *Making Face, Making Soul*, 53.
1. Harlow, *Resistance Literature*, 33–40; Rich, "Blood, Bread, and Poetry," 178.
2. See, for example, Bassnett, *Knives and Angels*; Partnoy, *You Can't Drown the Fire*; and Anglesey, *Ixok*.
3. Díaz-Diocaretz, "I will be a scandal," 86–109.
4. Harlow, *Resistance Literature*, 65.
5. Audre Lorde, "Sisters in Arms," *Our Dead behind Us*, 3–5.
6. Moraga and Anzaldúa, *This Bridge Called My Back*, 163.
7. Lugones, "*Hablando cara a cara*," in Anzaldúa, *Making Face, Making Soul*, 51–53.
8. Rich, "Notes toward a Politics of Location," 219, 223–24.
9. Sandoval, "Feminism and Racism," in Anzaldúa, *Making Face, Making Soul*, 66.
10. Rich, "Notes toward a Politics of Location," 220.
11. Michelle Cliff, "Constructive Engagement," *Ikon: Creativity and Change*, nos. 5–6 (special issue, "Art against Apartheid"): 78; hereafter cited as *Ikon*.
12. June Jordan, "Poem for Guatemala," *Naming Our Destiny*, 129–31.
13. The term *exteriorismo* is Ernesto Cardenal's; cited in Harlow, *Resistance Literature*, 73.
14. Díaz-Diocaretz, "I will be a scandal," 90.
15. Lockett, "Feminism(s)"; Wicomb, "To Hear the Variety," 35–44.
16. Audre Lorde, "Holographs," *Our Dead behind Us*, 54–57.
17. Harlow, *Resistance Literature*, 147.
18. Trinh, "Not You / Like You," 371–75.
19. Anzaldúa, introduction to *Making Face, Making Soul*, xxiv; June Jordan, "To Free Nelson Mandela," *Naming Our Destiny*, 158–60; Cliff, "Constructive Engagement," 78.
20. Sandoval, "Feminism and Racism," 62–63.

21. Alarcon, "The Theoretical Subject(s)," 364.
22. Audre Lorde, "A Litany for Survival," *The Black Unicorn: Poems* (New York: W. W. Norton, 1978), 31–32.
23. June Jordan, "War and Memory," *Naming Our Destiny*, 204–10.
24. Jordan, "To Free Nelson Mandela," 158–60.
25. Díaz-Diocaretz, "I will be a scandal," 92.
26. June Jordan, "Life after Lebanon," *On Call*, 84.
27. June Jordan, "A Song for Soweto," *Naming Our Destiny*, 122–23; and "Problems of Language in a Democratic State," *On Call*, 33.
28. Jordan, "War and Memory," 204–10.
29. Alice Walker, "The Diamonds on Liz's Bosom," and "We Alone"; both in *Ikon*, 10.
30. Díaz-Diocaretz, "I will be a scandal," 104.
31. Cliff, "Constructive Engagement," 78.
32. Sonia Sanchez, "A Letter to Ezekial Mphahlele," *Ikon*, 55–56.
33. Lorde, "Verrazano Bridge," 54–57.
34. Audre Lorde, "Apartheid U.S.A.," *Ikon*, 45–51.
35. Sara Miles, "The Name of this Flower Is the Same," *Ikon*, 74.
36. Susan Sherman, "Facts," *Ikon*, 72–73.
37. Sandra Maria Esteves, "Fighting Demons for South Africa," *Ikon*, 76–77.
38. Cited in Harlow, *Resistance Literature*, 10.
39. Harlow describes this as resistance poetry's primary function, while narratives typically analyze the past in order to point the way toward collective futures. *Resistance Literature*, 82.
40. Rich, "Notes toward a Politics of Location," 225; Carolyn Forché, "Ourselves or Nothing," *The Country between Us* (New York: Harper and Row, 1981), 55 59; Grace Paley, preface to New Americas Press, *A Dream Compels Us*, 6.
41. New Americas Press, *A Dream Compels Us*, 20.
42. For documentation of these statistics on the numbers of dead and dislocated in El Salvador, see Americas Watch, *El Salvador's Decade of Terror*; Armstrong and Shenk, *El Salvador*; New Americas Press, *A Dream Compels Us*, 7–20; and Thomson, *Women of El Salvador*, 1–9. For documentation of human rights abuses of women in more than forty countries, and women's resistance to those abuses, see Amnesty International U.S.A.'s *Women in the Front Line: Human Rights Violations against Women* (March 1991).
43. Grace Paley, "In San Salvador I and II," in New Americas Press, *A Dream Compels Us*, 4–5.
44. Forché, "El Salvador," 3–8.
45. Carolyn Forché, "The Island," *The Country between Us*, 10–12.
46. Jessica Hagedorn, "The Song of Bullets," *Ikon*, 99.
47. Forché, "El Salvador," 3–8.
48. Carolyn Forché, "San Onofre, California," *The Country between Us*, 9.
49. Forché, "The Island," 10–12.
50. Forché, "El Salvador," 3–8.
51. Carolyn Forché, "The Colonel," *The Country between Us*, 16.
52. Carolyn Forché, "Return," *The Country between Us*, 17–20.

53. Carolyn Forché, "Message," *The Country between Us*, 21–22.
54. Carolyn Forché, introduction to *Against Forgetting: Twentieth Century Poetry of Witness*, ed. C. Forché (New York and London: W. W. Norton, 1993), 46.

Chapter 7

An earlier version of this chapter was published in the *NWSA Journal* 2, no. 3 (Summer 1990): 349–73. Reprinted with permission from Ablex Publishing Corp.

1. Monique Wittig, *Les Guérillères*, trans. David LeVay (New York: Viking Press, 1969), 85; Audre Lorde, "Learning from the 60s," *Sister Outsider*, 140; Lorde, "The Master's Tools," 110–13.
2. De Lauretis, *Technologies of Gender*, 31–50.
3. Hurtado, "Relating to Privilege," 849–54.
4. Collins, "The Social Construction of Black Feminist Thought," 747. See also her book *Black Feminist Thought*.
5. Elshtain, *Women and War*, 237–41. Elshtain fails to mention that all of the feminist writers she critiques for creating "Manichean narratives" are white. My contention is that women of color are less likely to essentialize "the enemy" in such terms.
6. Mary Daly, with Jane Caputi, *Webster's First New Intergalactic Wickedary of the English Language* (Boston: Beacon Press, 1987). *Necrophilia* is defined on pp. 83–84, *biophilia* on p. 67, *crone* and *crone-ology* on pp. 114–16.
7. Elizabeth V. Spelman, *Inessential Woman: Problems of Exclusion in Feminist Thought* (Boston: Beacon Press, 1988), 123–25.
8. Anzaldúa, preface to *Borderlands*.
9. William Broyles, Jr., "Why Men Love War," *Esquire*, December 1984, 61–62. Again, it is worth noting that, when Broyles says "men," he actually describes a certain group of white men who are perhaps more likely to love war because it is more often their choice to participate in it. He does not acknowledge that men of color have not traditionally been among the military elite who declare war nor the economically secure who can buy their way out of it—that in fact, men of color have been drafted in disproportionate numbers and typically serve at lower ranks than their white counterparts. Nor does he note that many men of color identify strongly with "the enemy," most likely people of color. On these and related points, see Spelman, *Inessential Woman*, 114–15.
10. Judith Beckett, "Searching for Amazons," *woman of power* 3 (Winter–Spring 1986): 5.
11. Toni Cade Bambara, foreword to Moraga and Anzaldúa, *This Bridge Called My Back*, xvii; Cherríe Moraga, "It's the Poverty," cited in Gloria Anzaldúa, "Speaking in Tongues: A Letter to Third World Women Writers," in Moraga and Anzaldúa, *This Bridge Called My Back*, 166; June Jordan, "Poem for Nana," *Passion* (Boston: Beacon Press, 1980), 2; Nellie Wong, "How to Guard Our Dead?" *The Death of Long Steam Lady* (Los Angeles: West End Press, 1984), 44; Marjorie Agosin, "Needle and Thread Warriors: Women of Chile," *woman of power* 3 (Winter–Spring 1986): 35.
12. Claudia Tate, *Black Women Writers at Work* (New York: Continuum Press, 1983), 102.
13. Stella Dong, "Interview with Ntozake Shange," *Publishers' Weekly*, May 3, 1985, 74–75.

14. Maxine Hong Kingston, *The Woman Warrior: Memoirs of a Girlhood among Ghosts* (New York: Random House, 1975), 24.

15. Lorde, "Call," 73; Anzaldúa, *Borderlands*, 11.

16. Tate, *Black Women Writers*, 102.

17. Lorde, *The Black Unicorn*, 21, 44, 12–13; and *Chosen Poems, Old and New* (New York: W. W. Norton, 1982), 58.

18. In *Inessential Woman* Spelman discusses "somatophobia," fear and disdain of the body, as a racist as well as a misogynistic attitude. To understand oppression fully, she argues, feminists must recognize that women are differently embodied and consider the particular meanings assigned culturally to these various embodiments (126–29). For Lorde, to be a warrior is to recognize the body as a source and site of resistance and empowerment. See her essay "Uses of the Erotic," 53–54.

19. Audre Lorde, "The Women of Dan," *Black Unicorn*, 14–15.

20. Tate, *Black Women Writers*, 104.

21. Lorde, "Sisters in Arms," 3–5.

22. Audre Lorde, "Outlines," *Our Dead behind Us*, 8–13.

23. Audre Lorde, "Equal Opportunity," *Our Dead behind Us*, 16–18.

24. Collins, "Black Feminist Thought," 772.

25. The quotation is from Ray Gwyn Smith's unpublished book *Moorland in Cold Country*, cited in Anzaldúa, *Borderlands*, 54. Anzaldúa's chapter is entitled "How to Tame a Wild Tongue."

26. Anzaldúa, *Borderlands*, 21–23.

27. Barbara Smith, ed., *Home Girls: A Black Feminist Anthology* (New York: Kitchen Table / Women of Color Press, 1983).

28. Anzaldúa, preface to *Borderlands*; Rich, "Notes toward a Politics of Location," 210–31.

29. Anzaldúa, *Borderlands*, 78.

30. Anzaldúa, *Borderlands*, 194–95.

31. Gloria Anzaldúa, "Border Crossings," *Trivia: A Journal of Ideas* 14 (1989): 49–50. Anzaldúa notes here that Chicanas are not the only feminist writers of color who use hybrid language. She cites Ginny Lem, who writes in Chinese and English, and Janice Mirikitani, who writes in Japanese and English, as sisters in this regard.

32. Moraga and Anzaldúa, *This Bridge Called My Back*, 196.

33. Jordan, introduction to *On Call*, 2; Shange, Dong interview, 74–75.

34. Jordan, introduction to *On Call*, 1. Jordan now writes a regular column for the *Progressive*.

35. June Jordan, "I Must Become a Menace to My Enemies," *Things That I Do in the Dark* (Boston: Beacon Press, 1981), 145.

36. June Jordan, "South Africa: Bringing It All Back Home," *On Call*, 17–18.

37. Jordan, "I Must Become a Menace," 146.

38. June Jordan, "From *The Talking Back of Miss Valentine Jones*," *Things That I Do*, 154.

39. Shange, Dong interview, 74–75.

40. Ntozake Shange, *A Daughter's Geography* (New York: St. Martin's Press, 1983), 22–23.

41. Hurtado, "Relating to Privilege," 853–54. Lorde's statement is from *Sister Outsider*, 131–32.

42. Tate, *Black Women Writers*, 157.
43. Adrienne Rich, "Power and Danger: Works of a Common Woman," *On Lies, Secrets, and Silence*, 247.
44. Ntozake Shange, preface to *See No Evil: Prefaces, Essays and Accounts, 1976–83* (San Francisco: Momo's Press, 1984); Jordan, "Nicaragua," 70–75.
45. Kingston, *Woman Warrior*, 24; Anzaldúa, "Speaking in Tongues," 173.
46. For a discussion of men and women poets' female muses, see Mary K. DeShazer, *Inspiring Women: Reimagining the Muse* (Oxford and New York: Pergamon Press, 1987); for an analysis of women poets' "revisionist mythologies," see Ostriker, *Stealing the Language*.
47. Although Kingston's *Woman Warrior* is generally considered autobiographical fiction or memoir rather than poetry, its many lyrical passages and lush images seem to me to justify considering it as prose poetry, or, to use Anzaldúa's term, hybrid writing.
48. Lorde, "Call," 74.
49. Kingston, *Woman Warrior*. Quotes are taken from pp. 101–2, 23, 24, and 62–63, respectively.
50. On this point, see Mitsuye Yamada, "Invisibility Is an Unnatural Disaster," in Moraga and Anzaldúa, *This Bridge Called My Back*, 35–40; and Hurtado, "Relating to Privilege," 835 n. 6.
51. Nellie Wong, *Dreams in Harrison Railroad Park* (Berkeley: Kelsey Street Press, 1977), 40–41. The phrase "thinking back through our mothers" is taken from Virginia Woolf, *A Room of One's Own* (New York: Harcourt Brace and World, 1929).
52. Nellie Wong, *The Death of Long Steam Lady;* and "In Search of the Self as Hero: Confetti of Voices on a New Year's Night, A Letter to Myself," in Moraga and Anzaldúa, *This Bridge Called My Back*, 178.
53. Anzaldúa, "Speaking in Tongues," 173.
54. Jardine, *Gynesis*, 434; Cherríe Moraga, *Loving in the War Years: lo que nunca paso por sus labios* (Boston: South End Press, 1983), 29–30.
55. Alcoff, "Cultural Feminism," 405–36.
56. Fuss, *Essentially Speaking*, 99–107.
57. Cherríe Moraga, "From a Long Line of Vendidas: Chicanas and Feminism," *Feminist Studies / Critical Studies*, ed. Teresa de Lauretis (Bloomington: Indiana University Press, 1986), 180.
58. Alcoff, "Cultural Feminism," 434.
59. Moraga, *Loving in the War Years*, 117.
60. Moraga, "It's the Poverty," 166.
61. Audre Lorde, "Learning to Write," *Our Dead behind Us*, 53.
62. Adrienne Rich, "Sources XXII," *Your Native Land, Your Life: Poems* (New York: W. W. Norton, 1986), 25. See also Rich, *What is Found There: Notebooks on Poetry and Politics* (New York: W. W. Norton, 1993).

Conclusion

Mohanty, in Mohanty, Russo, and Torres, *Third World Women and the Politics of Feminism*, 34; Lorde, "Verrazano Bridge," 54–57; Maya Angelou, *On the Pulse of Morning* (New York: Random House, 1993), 8.

1. The other "socioeconomic, political, and discursive configurations" that Mohanty delineates are: (1) colonialism, class and gender; (2) the state, citizenship, and racial formation; (3) multinational production and social agency; and (4) anthropology and Third World women as "native." See Mohanty, Russo, and Torres, *Third World Women and the Politics of Feminism*, 14–15, 35.
2. Díaz-Diocaretz, "I will be a scandal," 105–6.
3. Lorde, "There Are No Honest Poems," 61.
4. Adrienne Rich, "The Spirit of Place," *A Wild Patience Has Taken Me This Far: Poems, 1978–1981* (New York: W. W. Norton, 1981), 40–45.
5. Jones, "Buckets of Music," *Ikon*, 158–60.
6. Kate Ellis, "The Secret Life of Plants," *Ikon*, 129.
7. Combrinck, "Birth of a Poem," in Moerat, *Siren Songs*, 56.
8. Frances Hunter, "In a Poem Is Life Hereafter," in Lockett, *Breaking the Silence*, 359.
9. Lorde, "Poetry Is Not a Luxury," 37–38; Rich, "Poetry III," 68.
10. Lorde, "Verrazano Bridge," 54–57.
11. Mirna Martínez, "*Si alguna vez pudiera*" [If Only Someday], in Anglesey, *Ixok*, 236–39.
12. Introduction to El Salvador section, in Anglesey, *Ixok*, 147–51.
13. Jacinta Escudos, "*Carte desde El Salvador*" [Letter from El Salvador], in Anglesey, *Ixok*, 208–11.
14. Díaz-Diocaretz, "I will be a scandal," 91–92.
15. Jacinta Escudos, "*La tarde en la nieve*" [A Snowy Afternoon], in Anglesey, *Ixok*, 210–13.
16. Alvarez-Peyeyre, *Poetry of Commitment*, 264.
17. De Kok, interview, *Writers from South Africa*, 57–59.
18. Nelson Mandela, book jacket of Forché, *Against Forgetting*; Angelou, *On the Pulse of Morning*, 10.
19. Lorde, "Verrazano Bridge," 54–57; Alegría, "Sorrow," 40–43; Lorde, "The Masters' Tools," 110–13.
20. Harlow, *Barred*, 256. *Nunca Estuve Sola* [I Was Never Alone] is the title of a Salvadoran prison narrative by FMLN commandante Nidia Díaz; *amandla*, or freedom, is a frequent cry in the black South African struggle for self-determination; "We Shall Overcome" is the title of a well-known U.S. civil rights struggle song.

Index